Here Comes the Flood

Here Comes the Flood

Perspectives of Gender, Sexuality, and Stereotype in the Korean Wave

Edited by
Marcy L. Tanter
Moisés Park

LEXINGTON BOOKS
Lanham • Boulder • New York • London

Published by Lexington Books
An imprint of The Rowman & Littlefield Publishing Group, Inc.
4501 Forbes Boulevard, Suite 200, Lanham, Maryland 20706
www.rowman.com

86-90 Paul Street, London EC2A 4NE, United Kingdom

British Library Cataloguing in Publication Information Available

Library of Congress Cataloging-in-Publication Data

Names: Tanter, Marcy L., editor. | Park, Moisés, 1982– editor.
Title: Here comes the flood : perspectives of gender, sexuality, and stereotype in the Korean wave / edited by Marcy L. Tanter, Moisés Park.
Description: Lanham : Lexington Books, [2022] | Includes bibliographical references and index. | Summary: "This book breaks down the stereotypes often expected of Korean popular culture, showing how the lines of gender, sexuality, and stereotype in Hallyu productions are often blurred to be palatable to Korean audiences or clarified to attract global audiences"—Provided by publisher.
Identifiers: LCCN 2021061353 (print) | LCCN 2021061354 (ebook) | ISBN 9781793636300 (cloth) | ISBN 9781793636324 (paperback) | ISBN 9781793636317 (epub)
Subjects: LCSH: Popular culture—Korea (South)—History—20th century. | Popular culture—Korea (South)—History—21st century. | Stereotypes (Social psychology) in mass media. | Korea (South)—Civilization—20th century. | Korea (South)—Civilization—21st century.
Classification: LCC DS916.27 .H385 2022 (print) | LCC DS916.27 (ebook) | DDC 306.09519—dc23/eng/20220208
LC record available at https://lccn.loc.gov/2021061353
LC ebook record available at https://lccn.loc.gov/2021061354

Contents

Acknowledgments

We have been working together on Korean topics for several years now; this project is the culmination of an off-hand "we should do a book together" conversation at several conferences. We are so pleased to see these chapters enter the conversation begun and populated by fine scholars before us and we are grateful to those same scholars for breaking the barriers that kept the conversation from the mainstream. We took a risk venturing into a discipline that is new for both of us, and choosing some graduate student authors because their topics were compelling and we were sure they would craft sound arguments; they did not disappoint. Our scholar-authors gave us work based on expertise of many years and we appreciate their risk in trusting their work to us. Special thanks to Michael Hurt who provided a 대박 picture for the cover of this book. We are also grateful to the models and interviewees (*gracias* Kriss!) who agreed for their images and stories to be included in the book. We are grateful for our families who did not begrudge the time we spent writing, editing, emailing, and finalizing the book. Thank you, Jessica Tepper, our editor, and Holly Buchanan, who met us in Boston, and heard about our book project days before the whole world shut down due to COVID-19.

I (Moisés) would like to thank and dedicate this book to my parents, Hae Soon Kim and Ki Chul Park. You taught me how to embrace, love, and celebrate Koreanness, and in spite of my ongoing identity crises, I will always know I am Korean, but most importantly, that I must be kind. 아빠, 엄마, 감사합니다. Special thanks to Hannah who had to wrangle our three girls, including an infant, during our work sessions. I must recognize Baylor University's Modern Languages and Cultures Department and the school's financial support for the Research Leave in the Spring of 2020 and Summer Sabbatical of 2021. Lastly, I thank the most important person in this project, co-editor Marcy Tanter. I admire your commitment to support the most vulnerable in society, be it in Korea or in the United States. This book is really yours, and I am just glad to be invited to be part of it.

Everyone who knows me (Marcy) well, knows that I have developed a deep affection and admiration for Korean history, culture, and society. It is a privilege to be able to work in a profession where I can spend time researching and talking about these things, and I feel a great responsibility to ensure Korea is represented fairly. My friend Seiichi and my son Robyn have become my best sources for discussing popular culture generally, and my daughters got me hooked on to K-dramas in the first place. I am lucky to have a friend and colleague in Moisés Park who challenges me gently and is rarely wrong. It's been so easy to work on this with him and I'm sure this won't be our last collaboration.

Lastly, thank you to the creators and fans of Korean popular culture. Their work enriches our world. May we see more creators and fans breaking barriers, and cherishing human diversity and hybridity in order to let go of prejudice and recognize ourselves in each other. 화이팅!

Introduction

Moisés Park and Marcy L. Tanter

THE "KOREAN WAVE" IS MORE THAN *HALLYU*

As *Hallyu* studies began to emerge more than a decade ago, critics focused on the cultural products from South Korea and their impact on neighboring countries. Some aspects of the phenomenon created expectations of the formulas and market ploys orchestrated by the media industry. Thus, the definition of *Hallyu* became synonymous with popularity transnationally, first, in Asia, and rapidly in "the West." This possible form of soft power confirmed that South Korea was no longer an underdeveloped or a developing country, but rather, part of a neo-hegemony or a subversive cultural exporter that defied anglo hegemony and euro-hegemony. In the second decade of the twenty-first century, however, *Hallyu* studies have expanded, and scholarship more often addresses other serious and notable topics beyond the alleged cultural neoliberal triumphalism and examining a vast body of work that no longer was relegated to K-pop and K-drama. In their most recent book, for example, Jin, Yoon, and Min (2021) trace the importance of social media and electronic mediums in the spread of *Hallyu* and how they contribute to its transformation into a transnational and transcultural phenomenon. The premise for this study included a transnational/transcultural aspect to *Hallyu*, bringing necessary discussion of reception/fandom studies, as well as *Hallyu* as an artifact. In this current book project, our authors raised questions for us that we had not expected; in mostly subtle ways, the various chapters consistently ask: What does it mean for a person or thing to be "Korean"? Is that Koreanness affected by the so-called transnational/transcultural Korean Wave? As much as Korean cultural products have been influenced by sources such as Western hip-hop, streaming platforms, fan reactions, and international branding in the creation of their domestic products, when those same cultural products reach audiences and consumers outside Korea, they can influence and predicate reaction pieces and draw in consumers because they are marked as "Korean."[1] As our contributors grapple with perspectives of gender, sexuality, and stereotype in various aspects of *Hallyu*, the notion of how to define "Koreanness" within their discussions is often an underlying theme. While Korean cultural content rides the wave that carries it around the world, transcultural adaptations and uses of that content may affect its "purity" the further it gets away from Korea.

Kim and Saeji (2020) note that

> literary theorist Lee Jin-kyung expertly articulates how 'Koreanness [has] begun to be delinked from its exclusive attachment to ethnicity.' Now that two per cent of Korea's population is foreign born, and the children of married migrants are becoming a substantial segment of the school-aged population, Korea is, of necessity, rethinking what it means to be Korean.

But it is not just a process happening inside Korea. There are Americans who pursue the dream to become K-pop idols such as Kiya Boyd who moved to Seoul to train with a K-pop agency; K-pop dance cover group B2 in Brazil who compete in international K-pop dance contests; K-pepsi became the first Chilean K-pop boy band; Korean film *Parasite* won Best Picture at the Oscars as the first non-English film to win that award; Korean variety show *King of the Masked Singer* has been rebranded as *The Masked Singer* on the U.S. Fox Network, hosted by Korean American actor Ken Jeong; K-beauty products and brands are recognized as serious contenders to the usual giants in cosmetics; K-drama and TV series can no longer be neglected as *Squid Game* (2021) becomes the most watched show in Netflix's history; restaurants around the world create dishes using gochujang and kimchi and call them "Korean fusion" food, such as American chain "Shake Shack," whose recent attempt at a Korean chicken sandwich and "kimchi fries" drew outcries as well as praise. In each of these situations, the adjective "Korean" or prefix "K-" is crucial to the identity of the activity or event. Could Boyd be a Korean pop singer if she were born and raised in the United States? Is a sandwich Korean just because it is doused with a Korean-sourced condiment? By the same token, are Korean immigrants who take on Canadian citizenship still Korean? Are non-Korean speakers Korean? Are Korean clothes worn by Vietnamese women in Vietnam but styled to their own tastes still Korean fashion? Can listening to K-pop empower those who are marginalized and result in political or social activism? Are K-pop songs in English no longer Korean? Or perhaps, "Koreanness" is a spectrum with orientalized stereotypes on one end and hegemonically trend setting on the other. Many of our authors directly or indirectly question the concept of "Koreanness" within *Hallyu*, but, of course, no one can actually capture how much of a thing is Korean or is not: "We are witnessing the very incipient stage of a process of gradual de-ethnicization of Koreanness, as Korean identity is being broadened to include plural cultures and multiple ethnicities" (Lee, 2010).

Until now, academic treatments of *Hallyu* have focused often on TV dramas and K-pop, their respective fandoms, how social media helps to spread the "wave," how the Korean tourism industry has benefited from *Hallyu*, and how Korean products have been "cool" worldwide. Whether in monographs or collected essays, these treatments seldom focus on the intersections of gender, sexuality, and stereotype. Our collection focuses on those intersections because the proliferation of Korean products creates images that consumers assume are representative of the realities of Korean culture and society. The chapters we present show how the lines of gender, sexuality, and stereotype are often blurred to be palatable to Korean audiences, and yet those lines can also be clarified to attract global curiosity and fan loyalty. Furthermore, audiences and consumers might be underestimated in their participation amplifying the (unexpected) impact that the wave has had. For instance, as the Korean entertainment industry expands its partnerships with foreign companies such as Netflix, Hulu, and other streaming platforms, secondary audiences (those outside Korea who are perhaps becoming primary audiences) are a consideration in how products are designed and marketed, whether those products are films or K-pop tours. Traditional Korean values are often reflected in entertainment products, but an awareness of those secondary audiences calls for confronting shifting attitudes from traditional to more modern values, or perhaps, the South Korean society, often considered conservative and close-minded, is in fact a lot more cosmopolitan and inclusive, especially compared to the North and other Asian societies. By the same token, global responses to *Hallyu* call for breaking stereotypes and rethinking gender/sexuality lines. The notion of portraying what is "Korean" from the domestic point of view depends on the creator of the content; understanding what is "Korean" from the cross-cultural point of view may have an impact on *Hallyu* eventually. One example of this future impact is suggested by the Netflix message boards, where K-drama fans ask for sequels to be made of popular programs such as *Run On* (2020–2021) and *Kingdom* (2019). *Run On* has no sequel planned as of this writing, but *Kingdom* was so popular domestically and internationally that its second season ran in 2020 and a third season is expected in 2022. Third seasons of Korean dramas are rare, but fan reactions via Netflix are pushing the Korean production companies to pay attention to their global audience. *Kingdom*'s director, Kim In-je, explained some of this to a reporter:

I read a lot of comments and discussions about *Kingdom* on online forums. I definitely see a lot of interest in the show. I was more surprised by how it was received globally. It was particularly interesting to see how so many were interested in the costumes when season one launched, and especially the fascination with the gat, a type of hat. So in season two, we tried to showcase a wider variety of hats, and also focused on sangbok—mourning clothes. Sangbok is a type of funeral clothing, and in the past, all Koreans had to wear sangbok for a certain amount of time when the king passed away. While people wear black in the West, Koreans traditionally wore white. I hope that more people can appreciate the beauty of hanbok in season two. (Keeley, 2020)

A WAVE VS. THE FLOOD

By now, academia is awash with the history of the spread of *Hallyu*. The term was first used in 1999 and by 2002, with the popularity of Korean dramas such as *Winter Sonata* and the visible rise of K-pop stars and fans' desires for Korean products, a pronounced "Korean Wave" swept across China, Japan, and soon after Southeast Asian countries, and eventually, to almost every other nation on earth to some extent. Some argue that this boom has allowed South Korean culture to be recognized as the "new cool," perhaps "conquering the world through pop culture" (Hong, 2014). Indeed, fans of Korean cultural products can be found on each continent and the numbers are ever-increasing. How *Hallyu* has been defined and discussed is something of a conundrum because the term was accepted as soon as it was coined without there being a clear message of what it meant exactly. *Hallyu* is not yet an item in *Webster's Dictionary* nor in the *OED*, so users can adapt it as they wish. Generally, it is accepted as the signifier for the global spread of Korean culture, but even within that understanding it can be broken down into the concepts of *Hallyu* 1.0, 2.0, and 3.0, to highlight the stages of how it has developed some claim the desire to export culture began Kim Ku's *Baekbeum Ilji* (1947), or anywhere in between then and the 1988 Olympics.

With over 100 related publications, Dal Yong Jin must be acknowledged as the most prolific scholar of *Hallyu* Studies in English. It was he who, in 2012, noted two distinct stages of how *Hallyu* developed:

Unlike *Hallyu* 1.0, emphasizing the export of local cultural goods to East Asia between the late 1990s and 2007, the growth of social media has uniquely influenced Korean creative industries, because a few media outlets, such as YouTube and SNSs, have become significant parts of the new Korean Wave (*Hallyu* 2.0). In fact, online gaming and K-pop have become the two most significant cultural genres in the Korean creative industries and have initiated the growth of *Hallyu* 2.0 since late 2007, because K-pop fans and online game users heavily access these social media to enjoy local popular culture. *Hallyu* 2.0 is the combination of social media, their practices, and the uses and affordances they provide, and this new stage has been made possible because Korea has advanced its digital technologies.

Seven years later, Sun and Liew (2019) among others added:

> The *Hallyu* narrative may differ when viewed from its reception (by the consumers) rather than from the production aspects. In this respect, we bore the specificities of China in mind and propose to frame the historical development of *Hallyu* more specifically along three categories: *Hallyu* 1.0 or the Analog Media era (1992-2004), Hallyu 2.0 or the Pre-mobile Internet era (2005–2012), and *Hallyu* 3.0 or the Mobile Internet era. (2013–present)

Lee Bae-young, president of the Academy of Korean Studies, declared in 2013 that "Now is the time of *Hallyu* 3.0, when academia could become the driving force of Korean culture promotion" (*Herald*, 2013). KOFICE (Korean Office for International Cultural Exchange, under the auspices of the Ministry of Culture, Sports, and Tourism) uses the term *Hallyu* 3.0 as the title of a committee whose mission is [when]: "The best of Korean cultural industry experts come together to research the future and development of *Hallyu*. Aside from the cultural industry, we are also looking into how our traditional culture such as *hansik* [food] and *Hangul* could be grafted onto *Hallyu*."

In 2016, CJ Group, one of South Korea's largest conglomerates whose entertainment wing CJ E&M distributes and promotes Korean cultural content in the United States regularly, noted:

> The upcoming era of *Hallyu* 4.0 is when K-lifestyles, including Korean cultural contents, make inroads into the everyday lives of people around the world and become part of mainstream culture enjoyed by the world, not just some *Hallyu* fans. According to industry experts, the era of *Hallyu* 1.0 started with dramas including Dae Jang Geum (*A Jewel in the Palace*), and *Winter Sonata* in the 1990s and early 2000s; the era of *Hallyu* 2.0 was led by K-pop; and the current era of *Hallyu* 3.0 has a broader scope that encompasses K-movies and K-beauty.

These are just a few of the disparate views of what constitutes *Hallyu*'s stages of development. Each perspective differs slightly from the others, but all are reasonable divisions. Where they intersect is in the notion that regardless of how Korean content is spread abroad, the spread is vast and continuous, but also evolving; it is not just K-pop or K-drama, but both are still spreading and also evolving. The recent phenomenal success of BTS, the Oscar wins for *Parasite*, *Squid Game*'s record breaking fandom, the growth of Korean language study across the United States, the development of Korean Studies lists among publishers in Europe and the United States, to say nothing of the explosion of Korean cosmetics and technology sales globally, all indicate that the popularity of Korean digital and tangible goods is not waning. What began as a wave in the late 1990s has surged into a global flood by the second decade of the 2000s.

Scholars have watched the *Hallyu* flood build for more than 20 years. As noted above, social media has had a significant impact on the tidal surge of the past 10 years as fans support and promote their favorite idols. Some members of active fandoms engage in social justice initiatives such as raising money to combat hunger or taking part in the Black Lives Matter movement; fans buy multiple copies of digital and physical K-pop songs and albums to push their idols up the charts; Instagram Live chats and virtual fan meetings increased during the COVID-19 pandemic. The chapters in this book reflect the flood of *Hallyu* across multiple countries, communities, and fandoms. The authors also note how the producers of cultural content keep the fans in mind when they create or how the fans drive *Hallyu* through their engagement with it, but also understand that cultural producers, artists, and fans, at time, are not tied to any monetary or political gain, but are actively immersed in experiencing the cultural products. The rolling wave did not turn into a flood on its own; it grew through the collective work of creators *and* fans. As academics, the authors of the studies presented here follow and trace the *Hallyu* current, from the peninsula to the diaspora, as it breaks against tropes of stereotype, sexuality, and gender norms, and pushes the boundaries of inclusivity.

THEORIES, PERFORMATIVITY, AND FANDOM

This volume is a needed and expected follow up to several other publications that examine gender in Korean popular culture, particularly in K-pop and K-drama. Laura Nelson's *Measured Excess: Status, Gender, and Consumer Nationalism in South Korea* (2000) and Kelly Y. Jeong's *Crisis of Gender and the Nation in Korean Literature and Cinema: Modernity Arrives Again* (2010) are among other important contributions that theorize foundational discourses of the nation, addressing questions of gender from the 1920s through 1960s modernization and more recent reformulations of South Korea's women as agents of consumption in the late 1980s. Most notably in masculinities studies, Sun Jung's *Korean Masculinities and Transcultural Consumption: Yonsama, Rain, Oldboy, K-pop Idols* (2010) has become the most cited publication that focused primarily on Korean masculinities, defying reductionist forms of emasculated masculinity. Jung's monograph was timely as the K-pop boy band craze 10 years from the book's publication has not yet peaked. Other important publications are Kyung Kyun Kim's *The Remasculinization of Korean Cinema* (2004) and Todd A. Henry's co-edited volume *Queer Korea* (2020). Nevertheless, although mainstream media might insinuate that K-pop masculinity is the most recognizable form of masculinity, the rise of several other K-pop bands (most notably Blackpink and BTS) into the mainstream and the massive success of *Parasite* in 2020 defy the stereotype that Asian men, particularly Korean (American) men, were limited to the K-pop idol flower boy, the obnoxious nerd and/or perv (*Dexter*), the hypermasculine monolingual (*Lost*), the awkward adoptee (*Arrested Development*), or the goofy clown (Psy) image. Other publications have studied womanhood, femininity, and/or female gaze, such as Jungmin Kwon's *Straight Korean Female Fans and Their Gay Fantasies* (2019), suggesting that current mainstream media, cultural productions, and female fans from South Korea have drastically changed perceptions of same-sex relationships and queer fantasies. The seminal co-edited volume by Elaine H. Kim and Chungmoo Choi's *Dangerous Women: Gender and Korean Nationalism* (1997) is an important compilation that addresses questions of womanhood through Korean nationalism and gender construction.

The inescapable study on gender and sexuality by Judith Butler should be recalled as we think of *Hallyu*. For instance, the 1988's essay "Performative Acts and Gender Constitution" initiated discussions of gender as performative. When examining cultural products from Korea, the performativity of gender is often central to addressing the hypermasculinized and militarized parades by the North or the different forms of masculinities in South Korean boy bands or romantic comedies. The 2004's *Undoing Gender* further explores notions of performativity which Butler, borrowing Freud, suggests was perpetuated through generations by normalizing processes by society through institutions and different cultural norms; "undoing gender" therefore, proposed the process of defying set norms and normalized codes that society and audiences identified as gendered. Ultimately, if gender was performative, some acts could potentially disrupt "restrictively normative conceptions of sexual and gendered life." The increasing literature on K-pop often reiterates cultural products from South Korea that defy emasculating readings of the flower boy and the reformulation of masculinity or manhood by the metrosexual aesthetics of boy bands and drama heartthrobs. We find satisfactory critical framework from Butler's contribution to theories of gender performativity and sexuality in relation to this book project, but may also include Butler's more recent *Notes Toward a Performative Theory of Assembly* (2015) where Butler examines public gatherings as forms of power and protest, in light of her previous work on performance and the body in public spaces, meditating

on the precarity of protests. Butler's publications were reflections on Black
Lives Matter protests and the increasing need to address intersections of race
and gender, as part of social constructions that became normalized, while the
protests advocated for undoing what is now commonly referred to as systemic
issues. It is vital to point out that public demonstrations have been key in
understanding South Korea's political reshaping in late 2016 and early 2017,
also known as the Candlelight Demonstrations, in a way, a follow up and
aftermath of public discontent with Park Geun-hye after her bizarre absence
immediately after the Sewol ferry disaster in 2014, which culminated in her
impeachment in March 10, 2017. Although the public demonstration might
seem unrelated, South Korean triumphalist news surrounding their seemingly successful and growing cultural soft power through K-pop, K-drama,
K-Beauty, and competitive video gaming, came to a halt as if political corruption was so heightened that not even Psy's "Gangnam Style" virality or
second- and third-wave K-pop fandom could eclipse the political turmoil.

K-pop's immense success did not weaken after the impeachment. Most
notably, *Billboard*'s Music Award for Top Social Artist, a fan-voted award
has been won by BTS consecutively for six years, tying with Justin Bieber's
six-time consecutive wins for the same award from 2011to 2016. The Korean
Wave, if we would want to extend the metaphor as maritime rather than mere
oceanic, is as much a great wave as those that surf it. In other words, the
philosophical question of "If a tree falls in a forest" is reformulated in the
maritime scenario, where the perception of the wave is certainly witnessed
and experienced to the point that the wave metaphor is becoming less suitable, as a Korean flood can better describe and explain the seemingly omni-
present soft power. In other words, the rise, popularity, and influence are no
longer marginal and generational. Korean cultural products and fandom are
no longer relegated to unnoticed subgroups and niche interested in a marginal
music genre or a novelty. Perhaps, we are facing a more permanent impact
that is transversal, affecting many cultures, generations, social classes, and
backgrounds. The performance of the consumers/fans must be acknowledged
as part of the wave transforming into a flood.

Fandom studies in Korean Studies have a growing bibliography as scholars
are determining why activism is increasingly becoming noticeable. Some
additional publications that focus on fandom studies and were instrumental
in continuing the dialogue in this book are *The Korean Wave: Evolution,
Fandom, and Transnationality* (2017), *K-pop Live: Fans, Idols, and
Multimedia Performance* (2018), *Hallyu 2.0: The Korean Wave in the Age
of Social Media* (2015), and *The Soft Power of the Korean Wave: Parasite,
BTS and Drama* (2021).

Admirers of Korean cultural products are as heterogeneous as ever. With
the overwhelming success of *Parasite* (2019), *Squid Game* (2021), and

perhaps even Kim Ki Duk's unexpected death due to COVID-19 complications in December 2020, different sectors of global cinema consumption and scholarship became increasingly interested in South Korean cultural production, which used to be limited to few cinephiles outside Korea. Data suggests that male viewers are overwhelmingly represented among South Korean cinema fans, whether they are fans of Bong Joon Ho's alternative commercial successes, Kim Ki Duk's art-house rarities, Lee Chan-dong's gripping art-house dramas, or Park Chan Wook's vengeance trilogy. All four directors had debuts outside Korea with Bong's *Snowpiercer* (2013) and *Okja* (2017) becoming the most successful of all of them so far. As of November 2021, *Parasite* has four times the reviews by males (319,008) than female users (73,731) on IMDB. His other films have even more disparate demographics, with a much larger male representation among voters, with *Memories of Murder* (2003) with eight to nine times more male reviewers (100,612) compared to female reviewers (13,246). The disparity might simply indicate that most IMDB users who rate and review are males. Yet, this imperfect and incomplete data that only represents the mostly English-speaking audience, at least evidences more interest in Korean films by male viewers. Even if it is true that the overwhelming majority of IMDB reviewers are males, consider reviews for South Korea's most successful Korean dramas: *Descendants of the Sun* (2016) has far more number of reviews by females (3,637) compared to those by males (2,317), while *Heirs* (2013) has close to three times more female reviewers (3,548) compared to male reviewers (1,291). *Moon Lovers: Scarlet Heart Ryeo* (2016) has four times more female reviewers (2,435) compared to male reviewers (726). The most reviewed K-drama on IMDB, *Guardian: The Lonely and Great God* (2016–2017) has twice as many reviews by females (4,888) compared to males (2,658). There are some exceptions with more balanced reviews such as *Mr. Sunshine* (2018), *It's OK to Not Be Okay* (2020), or *Crash Landing on You* (2019–2020), but the pattern is predictable for K-dramas to have a higher viewership among females compared to males. *Squid Game* (2021) has 4 times the number of reviews by males (120,084 versus 30,296). As expected, fandom has a wide spectrum as we consider different cultural products, be them K-pop groups, K-drama genres, or Korean films.

With a growing heterogeneity in fandom, the platforms through which cultural products are consumed, experienced, adapted, and replicated, vary as well. Though the rise of fandom dedication or devoted consumption of Korean cultural and commercial products is often attributed to access through streaming and online distribution (K-pop, K-drama, gaming, comics) and social media, ultimately, it is the audience's unrelenting loyalty as well as the heterogeneity that compels us to reconsider Koreanness with regard to the genres within *Hallyu*. We believe that perhaps the stereotypes are still lingering, and with the wake of the pandemic and a stronger activism by the Asian diaspora responding to AAPI hate, along with the multifaceted fandom that supports several aspects of Korean cultural products and the peninsula's fragile political history, those stereotypes and perceptions of Koreanness are finally becoming increasingly diverse, and aptly portray a more realistic view of the Korean peninsula, Korean diaspora, and varying versions of Koreanness. This volume is the beginning of an ongoing conversation as we hope to engage other *Hallyu* scholars and readers to explore the issues raised here.

THE CHAPTERS

When we first conceived this book, we expected the contributions to be heavily focused on issues of gender and sexuality in Korean popular culture that would showcase specific cases, most predictably the alleged emasculation of Korean boy bands and perhaps the rise in female empowerment in film and/or music. We were pleasantly surprised to find that our expectations were very different from what we received. The volume is divided into three main themes: I. Breaking the Wave: What Is Korean(ness), II. Breaking Stereotype through Korean dramas, and III. Breaking Norms: Performing and Protesting Gender.

The chapter that opens the volume, "Tracking the Korean Style: *Hallyu* in Hanoi, or Style in the Time of Corona," is a breezy narrative by Korean American sociologist/photographer Michael Hurt. Hurt focuses on "street fashion," here taking photos of Vietnamese models in street settings, dressing them in contemporary Korean youth fashion to reflect how *Hallyu* has influence in Vietnam. Peter Moody and Seung-hee Ha's "'Girl Power' DPRK Style: The Girl Group Phenomenon in North Korea and its Fans Across East Asia" explores the limits of Koreanness by examining the process of acculturation of *Hallyu* elements selected by the North Korean authorities to promote their government, along with representations and perceptions of women in North Korea that are related to the process. Moody and Ha analyze gender stereotypes by revealing the specificity of what aspects of the Korean Wave the North Korean state has accepted, noting new aspects of *Hallyu*'s transformation that have emerged in North Korea, the consumption of them by a supranational fanbase, and the significance of these changes. Kyong Yoon's "Diasporic Koreanness in *Kim's Convenience*" studies the sociocultural context and reception of the Canadian television comedy *Kim's Convenience* by situating the show within a recent stream of Asian American TV programs that question and engage with racial discourses. The chapter examines how stereotypes are negotiated in this diasporic text. Yoon offers a critical understanding of how cultural identities are represented and how the existing *Hallyu* discourse can further engage with the question of cultural diversity.

The first chapter that addresses breaking stereotypes through Korean dramas is Snigdha Gupta's "The New Country Women: Exploring Popular Representations of Korean *gwichon* and Transnational Women's Marriage-migration to the Korean Countryside." Gupta examines new spatialized relationships of power in which women from the "center" and women from Korea's new Asian "periphery" are projected into the countryside, by ana-lyzing dramatic representations of women in the Korean countryside that serve as narratives of acclimatization for women at different ends of a trans-national socioeconomic spectrum. Michael Ormsbee's "Gender, Genre and History in *Great Queen Seondeok*" considers this particular melodrama in terms of women's political legitimacy. According to Ormsbee, *Great Queen Seondeok*'s melodramatic constitution changes once we pay close attention to the gaps between the "official" history of Seondeok's actual era, what was chosen to be presented in the drama, and how the demands of melodrama influence the representation of an idealized past. Marcy Tanter's "Breaking the Stereotype of Domestic Adoption in K-dramas" addresses other taboos regarding gender roles and stereotypes. Tanter's chapter questions how Korean dramas reflect issues in contemporary South Korean society, further defying stereotypes of adoptees as troubled people who tend to grow up to become criminals or are mentally impaired. She concludes that the K-dramas discussed in her study (*Pinocchio*, *Ddanddara*, and *Madeu*) present views of domestic adoption that are deliberately positive.

Jahyon Park's "Crying Men Watching Webtoons: *Misaeng* and Korean Male Audiences" opens the third part of the volume, "Breaking norms: Performing and Protesting Gender." Park studies emotional responses to the webtoon series *Misaeng* and its K-drama adaptation, both of which were popular among office workers and attracted particularly male audi-ences' interest. Moisés Park's "*LISTEN TO K-POP, BURN THE POLICE!*: Swastikas, Feminism, and LGBTQ+ Rights in the 2019–2020 Chilean Protests" addresses the alleged links between K-pop fandom and the Chilean protests that began in October 2019 and culminated in a referendum that led to rewriting the constitution. Park examines the polemic and alleged rela-tion between fandom and protest as a correlation and/or a causation. Tiágo Canario's "Queering The Wave: Drag Queens And Drag Kings In The K-Pop Industry" looks at the representation of deviant gender expressions in con-temporary Korean music videos, examining how the mainstream connects with, gets influenced by, and transforms queer cultures in South Korea.

We close the volume with Min Suk Kim's ethnographic paper "K-pop Performance, Transcultural Negotiation of Gender Identities, and Belonging: A Case Study of a Peruvian Drag Queen Dancing to K-pop." She analyzes how theories of gender identity and performativity can be applied to the varying relationships between K-pop's gender esthetics and its queer fan population in Latin America; the influence of K-pop on a gay fan from Lima and his (gender) identity transformation throughout the process of discovering the art of dancing to K-pop girl band choreographies and ultimately performing K-pop as a drag queen. This chapter bookends the volume with Michael Hurt's opening chapter, with both questioning "Koreanness" outside of Korea through performance and art to ultimately conclude that their subjects are adapting elements of Korean popular culture on the ripples of the *Hallyu* flood, highlighting that its global reach is as personal and intimate as it is commercial and public.

NOTE

1. See Fandy Zenas Tjoe, and Kim Kyung-Tae (2016). "The Effect of Korean Wave on Consumer's Purchase Intention of Korean Cosmetic Products in Indonesia." *Distribution Science Research,* 14 (9): 65–72; Anh Le, Tuan and Mai, Nhu and Vo, Nhi and Tram, Nguyen and Nhan, Nguyen. (2020). "Factors affecting the choice of buying Korean cosmetics." *Management Science Letters.* 3097-3106; Yang, H., Jin, B. E., and Jung, M. (2020). "The influence of country image, the Korean Wave, and website characteristics on cross-border online shopping intentions for Korean cosmetics: Focusing on US and Chinese consumers." *International Journal of Costume and Fashion* 20 (2): 38–49.

BIBLIOGRAPHY

Butler, J. (1988). "Performative Acts and Gender Constitution: An Essay in Phenomenology and Feminist Theory." *Theatre Journal* 40 (4): 519–531.

Butler, J. (2015). *Notes Toward a Performative Theory of Assembly.* Cambridge, MA: Harvard University Press.

Butler, J. (2016). *Undoing Gender.* New York: Routledge, 2004.

"CJ Group Plans to Increase the Proportion of Overseas Sales in Its Culture Business by More than 50% by 2020." (2016). https://english.cj.net/cj_now/view.asp?bs_seq=13536&schBsTp=1&schTxt=

Hong, E. (2014). *The Birth of Korean Cool: How One Nation Is Conquering the World Through Pop Culture.* London: Picador.

Jung, S. (2010). *Korean Masculinities and Transcultural Consumption: Yonsama, Rain, Oldboy, K-pop Idols.* Hong Kong: Hong Kong University Press.

Keeley, P. (2020). "Writer, Director of South Korean Zombie Drama 'Kingdom' on Global Response and Coronavirus Parallels." *Hollywood Reporter,* https://www.hollywoodreporter.com/live-feed/netflixs-kingdom-creators-talk-releasing-zombie-drama-coronavirus-1290604

Kim, K. (2004). *The Remasculinization of Korea Cinema.* Durham, NC: Duke University Press.

Kim, K., and Saeji, C. (2020). "Introduction: A Short History of Afro-Korean Music and Identity." *Journal of World Popular Music* 7 (2): 115–124.

Korea Herald. (2013). Chief of Korean Studies Academy Declares "Hallyu 3.0." http://www.koreaherald.com/view.php?ud=20131126000866.

Lee, S., and Nornes, A. (2015). *Hallyu 2.0: The Korean Wave in the Age of Social Media (Perspectives on Contemporary Korea).* Ann Arbor, MI: University of Michigan Press.

Min, W., Jin, D., and Han, B. (2019). "Transcultural Fandom of the Korean Wave in Latin America: Through the Lens of Cultural Intimacy and Affinity Space." *Media, Culture & Society* 41 (5): 604–619.

Park, J. and A. Lee, eds. (2019). *The Rise of K-dramas: Essays on Korean Television and Its Global Consumption.* Jefferson, NC: McFarland.

Sun, M., and Liew, K. (2019). "Analog Hallyu: Historicizing K-pop formations in China." *Global Media and China* 4(4): 419–436.

Yong, J. (2016). *New Korean Wave: Transnational Cultural Power in the Age of Social Media.* Champaign, IL: University of Illinois Press.

Yoon, T., and Yong, D. (2017). *The Korean Wave: Evolution, Fandom, and Transnationalism.* Washington, DC: Lexington.

Chapter 1

Tracking the Korean Style

Hallyu *in Hanoi, or Style in the Time of Corona*

Michael W. Hurt

It was inexorable: The scent of lemon grass first confused me in its famil-iarity, like a long-lost friend I had forgotten I had, when I first reluctantly traveled to Saigon in 2017 for a conference to explore how far the tendrils of Korean style reached out from the Korean Peninsula. I wanted to know if they had seriously or significantly made their mark on the Vietnamese peninsula, as my then-student Thu Ha had been claiming. I had been teaching "*Hallyu* Marketing" at Yonsei University and have been arduously trying to define the Korean style I was seeing coalesce into recognizable shape since around 2007. As I did so, my student Thu Ha—who had been a stellar student in gen-eral and especially when the class and I went to Seoul Fashion Week to con-duct interviews and take pictures—began insisting that I had to visit Vietnam and see what was happening there because *no one* was more enthralled and in touch with the *Hallyu* than the Vietnamese. *No one*, she emphasized.

I confirmed my intent to go, wrote the paper feverishly and furiously fast, and soon found myself in Saigon. I quickly found out that, indeed, Korean style occupied a high place of esteem for the Vietnamese. While everyone is certainly not dressed like a cosmopolitan Korean, it is nevertheless true that most Vietnamese young people look at Korea as cosmopolitan, on top of the fact that cosmopolitanism *itself* is often seen as Korean, and vice versa.

The scope of my greater project exploring the Korean style in Asia involves using my camera to do research on the influence of a Korean style as felt in other parts of Asia, using the images my camera produces to make contacts, forge partners for projects, and to make friends and work with infor-mants. In short, the best way to study a social media–based cultural produc-tion phenomenon such as the *Hallyu* is by *being* a media practitioner engaged in social media–based cultural production. As a social scientist, the older, staid research tools and methods such as questionnaires and from-a-distance surveys are not very revealing when it comes to figuring out what is really going on, both online and offline. I am not going to find out what I want to know by going to K-pop concerts with a clipboard. I do not have the means or healthy enough knees it takes to become a K-pop performer, producer, or someone else in that field. Nor would I take seriously any data gleaned from an attempt to become a "fly on a wall" as a "participant-observer" of fashionable youth as a 49-year-old, fat, American man. In my research, I always give my informants *a reason to talk to me*, something that makes sense to both them and others.

VISIBLE AND INVISIBLE ETHNOGRAPHIES

The Style Imperative

The desire to style, be stylish, and be *recognized* in the deeply satisfying, all-legitimizing, Hegelian sense of the word as measured by follower counts—does not evaporate even in the panic of an apparent pandemic. I quote Minh-Ha T. Pham (2011) in her incisive and insightful article written just after 9/11, "The Right to Fashion in the Age of Terrorism," in which she quotes Anna Wintour, to set the stage:

> Anna Wintour, editor-in-chief of American Vogue and doyenne of American fashion, wrote in the November 2001 issue of Vogue, "Fashion is essential in these difficult times, paradoxically, to keep us in touch with our dreamy, fanciful, self-pleasing natures."

Pham takes a critical look at the narratives of consumerism against the looming dying of our freedoms, lest "they" win. It was a time in which going on to do normal things—especially in the market—was posed as a sign of resistance to terror and a furiously flagrant gesture of irrepressible *America!* in the face of *Al Qaeda*, Bin Laden, and at *the terrorists*. Despite fashion and fashionable endeavors suddenly seeming too *me* against the new need for a consolidated *we*, the pursuit of fashion became a nigh-patriotic act of resistance in a somber time in America. Even in difficult times, the idea was that *fashion keeps us human. Fashion keeps us free.* I took this notion to heart as I traveled to Hanoi from Seoul on February 18th to give a talk on Korean fashion and also do participant-practitioner-based research fashion shoots and interviews on Korean fashion as Covid-19 was beginning to hop around Asia and the Middle East (and by the end of my trip, Europe).

Fashion in the Time of Corona

Pursuing Korean style in the time of "Corona" was one of the most liberating and enlightening things I could have done. Doing this in Asia between two countries ardently struggling to not become the new Wuhan—"*it*"—was emblematic of how it should be done. Work does not disappear in a time of social panic, nor do social actions such as commerce, worship, and fashion. And neither does my research, which stands, somewhat strangely, at the overlap of fashion and work. Because for all involved, who pursued various works within the field of fashion, the specter of Covid-19 placed into sharp relief the value of what we do—whether modeling, styling, fixing, or photographing—and why it had to happen, virus be damned, and why we would simply wash our hands and carry on.

It was a bit scary going in, because the question hung still in the air—Was I simply crazy for going to a place where 99% of people had canceled their plans to go, or was I enterprising and intrepid, sticking to my research and presentation plans, going where all but angels feared to tread?

No matter how many times you run the logic and fatality rates and epidemiological history through your mind, you always wonder whether I was too biased to see it was the former that was true. By that point, the plans to give an academic talk at a local fashion and design college had started to fall apart, but the intent was still there to give it as what the Vietnamese call a "talk show" and what South Koreans call a "talk concert" (what others would call a "TED Talk-style" lecture) at a private venue and network with all the fashion students and other fashion-forward folks in the city. Also on the docket was shooting my way through Hanoi with my fashion contact and separate, hired fixer together recruiting models to shoot in either Korean *hanbok* or "Korean style" as interpreted either by the model or a Vietnamese designer known for his Korean-style looks. The plan was to get a sense of what the Korean style meant to a self-selecting group of Korean style-philes, using their pictures and poses as ethnographic data, along with formal interviews after the fact. In any case, this was the goal, and there were many ways of eliciting, sartorially, responses to what the Korean style was on an elemental level.

After arriving, acclimating, and settling into our suddenly-fire sale-cheap, US$18 per night Airbnb, and touching base with my fashion contact and fixer, I was ready to go. Korea had not become stigmatized yet, and "Covid-19" would be announced as the official name of the virus several days later. Presently, Korea was still more cool than dangerous, and my being a fashion photographer-academic from Seoul was still opening doors. As I settled in to my homestay, made final plans with my fashion industry and production fixers, while checking that my gear was all set, it was starting to become apparent that the research trip had taken on a two-pronged approach. On the obvious, pre-planned, and conscious level of the official approach of the research, the use of national dress to encourage Vietnamese models to participate in the social interaction of placing another country's national dress on their bodies to see what photographic and psychological results was perhaps a "photographic elicitation" technique that goes back decades in anthropological practice. According to visual sociologist Douglas Harper (2002), this practice is

> based on the simple idea of inserting a photograph into a research interview. The difference between interviews using images and text and interviews using words alone lies in the ways we respond to these two forms of symbolic representation. This has a physical basis: the parts of the brain that process visual information are evolutionarily older than the parts that process verbal information. Thus images evoke deeper elements of human consciousness than do words; exchanges based on words alone utilize less of the brain's capacity than do exchanges in which the brain is processing images as well as words. These may be some of the reasons the photo elicitation interview seems like not simply an interview process that elicits more information, but rather one that evokes a different kind of information.

Indeed, this kind of photo elicitation was not the typical anthropologist's go-to interaction, the taking of films of a native informant reacting to themselves on films made earlier as a way to elicit a response. This was not an old-school, Margaret Mead-in-Bali-in-1939 project (Jacknis, 1988). This was a project in which experienced models familiar with the convention of fashion photography and photo sharing on social media donned Korean clothing for the purposes of making a fashion photograph. In this way, the interactive process of making a photograph happen within this structured interaction would yield social data (what Vietnamese people thought of Korean style/fashion, and how Vietnamese models-as-influencers interpreted Koreanness in a global context in general while expressing that specifically in a single picture). Theoretically, this is what an interview does—as a structured interaction that yields social data. Both an interview and a structured editorial session are different manifestations of becoming Augusto Boal's "Spect-Actor" who is both Spectator and Actor on the social stage. Here, insightful ethnographer Quetzl Castañeda (2006) substitutes "ethnographer" for Boal's original "Spect-Actor" and "ethnographer" for "actor":

> Everything that fieldworkers do we do throughout our lives, always and everywhere, Ethnographers talk, move, dress to suit the setting, express ideas, reveal passions—just as we do in our daily lives. It also points to the quintessential fieldwork methodology of participant-observation as a form of theatre.

This point of view blurs the illusory distinction between researcher and subject and speaks to the fact that (a) both are actors in the field (and in a staged interaction that is just another version of what people do in real life, *i.e.* have conversations, talk over coffee, etc.) and (b) both researcher and the informant are equally participants in the specific social interaction that yields the social data. Casteñeda quotes Boal by adding:

> The only difference is that actors [or ethnographers] are conscious that they are using the language of theater [or ethnography], and are better able to turn it to their advantage whereas the woman and man in the street does not know they are speaking the language of theatre [or ethnography].

That is only the obvious level of how the sartorial (fashion) photo elicitation exercise can be defined within the research trip as "invisible theater." The deeper import of the research trip only became apparent as the entire fashion photo elicitation exercise and research trip around the Korean style started becoming a liability and point of concern as Korea had started to become the new "Wuhan" by the third week of February 2020. Sociologist Harold Garfinkel's infamous "breaching experiments" in which he would stage violations of social norms to test the social waters, so to speak, were the most theatrical sociological experiments, which is what the classic popular TV show *Candid Camera*, its more recent iteration *Punk'd*, or the ABC "ethical dilemma" series *What Would You Do?* with John Quiñones are: sociological "breaching experiments" on camera, which define an engrossing "invisible theater" in which the subjects of the staging are painfully unaware of the stagedness of the awkward situations in which they find themselves. This defines an "invisible research" that is informative and fun. Now, our very presence in Hanoi and ability to continue our fashion photography activities at all was becoming a "breaching experiment" unto itself that would indicate the relative power of Korea's style/fashion brand as a counterweight against the increasingly scary image that the country was quickly developing because of the newly named nemesis COVID-19. The stakes of the project had suddenly increased and were piling higher by the day.

Defining the Korean Style

All of this begs the question of the *Korean style*. Before this analysis proceeds any further, and before the research in Hanoi could hope to meaningfully progress, it is necessary to have a working definition of the Korean style to define what we were even looking to find in Hanoi.

A theoretical definition of style could easily take an entire book to even begin to explore. But to allow a concise consideration of the concept for the purposes of this brief chapter, we can take James Ackerman's classic definition as a touchstone and a point of departure for our discussion. In Ackerman's (1962) landmark essay "A Theory of Style," he defined style in art and aesthetics in terms of

> certain characteristics which are more or less stable, in the sense that they appear in other products of the same artist(s), era or locale, and flexible [. . .] . A distinguishable ensemble of such characteristics we call a style.

This definition makes a good deal of sense in art and aesthetics and has been a serviceable model for decades. Yet, for the purposes of considering the phenomenon of the Korean popular culture, it is exactly the opposite of what is needed to consider the entire warp and woof of a Korean style. In the realm of clothing, which is where "style" seems to be most frequently and consciously considered nowadays, a particular person's sartorial choices do not get added up into a calculus of how many popular items from an era or idea he or she is sporting. If this were the case, it would be easy to be "stylish" by simply being the person wearing the most number of categorically grouped items, as opposed to being well regarded for how one wore and visually linked said items.

For the Vietnamese, who are quite representative of the overall attitude toward a globalized Koreanness in Asia, the desire to embody a Korean cosmopolitan style is obvious, from the shows on television sets across the nation, to the "top Vietnamese models" I gained access to and shot for this chapter, to the individual conversations and interactions I had with many "top creators" in Vietnam's fashion and beauty industry. What the contacts and collaborators in the project valued about a Korean style was not a string of correlated aesthetic elements that were grouped together as a "distinguishable ensemble of . . . characteristics" within a given cultural text, whether a music video, film, or sartorial look displayed on a body. In clothing curated and worn on a body in a way that is understood to define a Korean style, it is surely not merely a grouping of essentially Korean elements that define the style—otherwise, pieces of traditional Korean clothing, materials, colors, or patterns would fill out the looks. Similarly, K-pop might be thought to be sonically defined by Korean traditional instruments, rhythms, lyrical patterns, or even sampled sounds from Korean life. Similarly, in the case of Korean cinema, is the filmic text defined as Korean (and hence somehow worthy of additional attention) simply because the actors are Korean? Or are they of interest because of their quintessentially Korean themes?

The answer, in all the examples mentioned here, is *of course not*. The appeal of the Korean part of the "K" is almost entirely not found explicitly in the text itself. And therein lies the rub. The Korean style lives in the interstices, in the realm of the meta-textual, the area outside or between cultural texts, in the way they define how the parts of the text are related.

This book explores the way a Korean style defines the snowballing interest in Korean popular culture that is quickly spreading across the planet. It is an avalanche, a flood—or tsunami—with varying degrees of stickiness, to be sure, but its advance is as undeniable as it is unstoppable. Yet, the problem I see with this theoretically is that scholars and other pundits tend to only pay close attention to a pop culture "wave" or other social phenomenon when clear, and by definition, exceptional cases burst forth into the popular consciousness. Examples of these cases are Psy's "Gangnam Style" video breaking the YouTube meter, BTS showing up on another numerical metric of success multiple times (*Billboard* magazine), or a Korean director winning a gaggle of Oscars, or frankly, any Korean receiving an accolade or prize in an international forum.

The problem lies in the fact that, while laudable achievements, these blips on the Top 10 or 100 or 200 *Billboard* radar screens, appearances on *Good Morning America*, or breaking the YouTube hit counter are all, by definition, exceptional. They are worth paying attention to, and being nationalistically proud of, but all the attention often masks the *why* behind the phenomenon. Much of the reporting—and academic writing, unfortunately—on the subject of Korea's pop culture success tends to focus on the fact of it having happened, with home team pride being the impetus for the coverage and treatment, followed by little else.

And when this celebratory elation only focuses on the big, obvious, and easy-to-track exceptions, the thinkers-that-be often miss the important stuff going on in the background that makes the big, obvious stuff possible. Like analyzing American football victories only by the touchdown plays, the final runs into the in-zone or summing up a basketball team's road to success over a season through slam dunk reels.

In the human body is the largely ignored "organ" known as the *interstitium*. It is the fluid that permeates all the spaces between organs and other structures and maintains a positive pressure to hold everything up and together. It also is a medium through which nutrients and chemicals are transported. It is the literal stuff that holds everything together, the watery goo through which all the various parts cohere. As I see it, there is a Korean style (beyond clothing) that allows the various parts of what people call the *Hallyu* to cohere as a singular phenomenon that acts as the interstitium.

Let us take clothing in "K-style" as the metaphor for the moment and return to the question of a Korean style as it pertains to fashions worn on the body as I pursue the issue of style considered in the general sense. With clothing, we typically talk about how someone "is put together" or how they have *styled* themselves. When we marvel at the text enough to wonder after its very construction, its place in a context, we are making a meta-textual observation. We do not do that often with books or movies unless we are in a class meant to do that exact thing as an exercise.

We are generally too caught up in the spectacle of the text itself to think about it outside of the text itself. Only certain people think, "wow, I wonder how hard it was to light that scene," and the thought "wow, this CGI is really bad" usually means that the text has failed to do its job. The viewer has been thrown out of the experience and out of the suspension of disbelief that helps foster enjoyment of it. It is usually the desire of the artist to keep the viewer from engaging the text from the outside and keep them snugly inside. This is when one starts to laugh at a film's unconvincing dialogue, acting, or special effects, or when listening to a pop star live and unplugged, when one begins to notice that one's favorite performer is singing off-key; however, the Korean style, what I argue to be the actual, unseen, and unconsidered common aesthetic denominator of all K-things, lives outside of and all around the cultural texts in question.

The true draw of the Korean style, the feeling of wondrous pleasure and fascination that Koreans call *shingi,* which unites all K-fans and makes for such promiscuous cross-pollination of interests across K-fields, lies in the interstitial spaces, in the meta-textual space of appreciation of the text. Put simply, the Korean style is a hybridically presented, meta-textually argued engagement and critique with the very media forms and conventions that constitute it, while vociferously masquerading to not be doing exactly what it is doing—being "meta" as the popular parlance now goes—often by pretending to be the simplest manifestation of what is a new and complex, state-of-the-art, new form of hypermodern expression. The style exists outside of the actual text, in the meta-zone.

In the end, whether it is as simple as breaking the fourth wall on Korean variety shows or more complexly, inviting you to consider matters outside of the immediate text the viewer finds him or herself consuming, the text invites consideration of things outside it, in a cognitive outer space in which the text can engage other things, from social critique or challenges, all the way to making interstitial connections to other K-fields. It invites semiotic pondering and meta-phenomenological consideration of other, faraway cultural texts (as Blackpink's "Kill This Love" does with both Tarantino films and the popular Instagram-friendly photo rental studios of Seoul), or even uses semiotics to thrust the viewer into other spaces, such as when CL waxes on romantically about "Dr. Pepper" but boldly refuses to explain anything about what the song's title might mean. Similarly, the Korean sartorial style I see everywhere from the streets of Seoul all the way to Saigon seems to work the same way that *haute couture* runway fashion does. It works like a hybridic and *bricolage*-like art piece that demands attention be paid to its construction, in a "look at how smartly I put this together" flexing, as opposed to merely asking to be appreciated simply and viscerally at an unconscious, unthinking level, in the same way one might appreciate a sunset on a beach and be inspired to paint it.

In sum, the Korean style is a meta-textual, winking-at-you, rhizomatically random, Marvel MCU-style "shared universe" that encompasses and gives meaning to all K-fields. K-pop is the Iron Man of the Korean Aesthetic Universe. It is the big one that started it off by putting the project on the map, but it is not everything; it is the linchpin. Korean style works in the same way that the MCU is really significant because it is a new mode of thinking, a new approach to cinema that is effortlessly, ceaselessly awesome. Like the Marvel formula for movies that is really a meta-textual re-consideration of what movies even mean, what they even are—which is why MCU movies are so weirdly, consistently excellent, since they are really only one, continuous movie—K-pop is revealing itself to be a meta-phenomenon that only formally resembles separate fields in that what we see in K-pop, K-cinema, K-drama, K-beauty, and K-fashion that are different facets of a larger KAU defined by cultural hybridity and heterogeneity (Jin and Yoon, 2016), a postcolonial mindset, coupled with a brash, semiotic bravado, and the willingness to always, always valorize Novelty as its own reward. The Korean style is this set of semiotic, artistic, and psychological actions—as well as the values that allow them to take place. It is a new form of multimedia—from screens to clothing to music—unified by a fairly definable, coherent aesthetic hybridity and semiotic brashness focused on the eagerness to smash together genres and popular conventions.

SHOOTING THE KOREAN STYLE

In the case of my then-growing predicament in Hanoi, things Korean had become quickly imbued with a sense of threat and danger, as anyone who had come from Korea was now viewed as a possible vector of infection. In a larger sense, the real test of Korea's cool would be made by watching how many of our scheduled shoots with models would end up being no-show cancelations, and whether the talk we were scheduled to give would happen. In the end, our official "talk concert" with a local fashion and textiles university fell through, as well as the rescheduled, private version of it that was briefly planned as a fallback at a local pub, because the owner did not want it known that anyone from Korea would be on the premises. In regard to general society, Korea's cool did not hold up when push came to shove.

As final preparations and confirmations happened across a flurry of Facebook and Instagram direct messages, site visits, and perhaps gallons of

Cà Phê Sữa Đá measured out in countless cups, indications started to get back to our fashion and production fixers that models were starting to get a bit nervous about my having come in from Korea. Repeated, pointed questions about "How long have they been here?" And "Exactly when did he arrive" began to take on more pointed and obvious meaning as we prepared for our first actual shoot of the trip. Yet, even as our "talk concert" plans started to crumble, the plans with the *Hallyu*-eager models were firming up. In the end, no model of nearly a dozen we had arranged to shoot ended up canceling, and everyone hit their call times and cues without a hitch.

On Day 3, we were ready to shoot our first model of the trip, Lê Vân. We had intended to shoot at the Hanoi House Cafe at the suggestion of my Hanoi-based fashion industry insider connection Hoang Minh Chau, but the place was unexpectedly closed. The walk up seemed as apropos a place to shoot a Korean hanbok as any other, full as it was of the feel, history, and grit of the city.

Here in figure 1.1, model Lê Vân stands in the doorway of the Hanoi House café; in this image, I was a little too overzealous with the MakeUp Plus app from this angle and ended up with a convergence of the present trend in Seoul of not big "ugly" sneakers, but also they have the right amount of cultivated used-aesthetic grittiness that Korean young women of my experience like, with the pattern of the modernized Korean hanbok in razor-shop relief.

It is sometimes hard to catch and to know what you are looking at, but what makes this Heo Sarang hanbok appealing and unique is the mix of Korean-alphabet Hangul with classical Chinese characters, which is how hangul was used for most of its history. What truly permeates this image is the extreme *digitality* of it, from the initial instant of recording and its related equipment to the digital editing moment made possible by a WiFi-connected camera and smartphone with its bevy of thumb-operated apps, all the way to the instant digital publishing/sharing through Instagram (which saves a high-resolution version of the uploaded images to use later (and in this book).

On Technoculture

One of the things I have observed about the Korean Style of Things—whether in K-pop (both as music and video art), K-beauty, or so-called K-fashion, is the way it refuses to apologize or cover up its extreme level of artifice. It simply embraces the Digital and the Artificial it enables and makes inevitable while baking this in as part of its aesthetic. There is a new Technoculture that allows for the advent of the many K-things. According to one of the most useful definitions that proved itself (by being written well before the advent of the social media that would reshape the modern world), Lelia Green's (2001) definition from 2001 states:

Figure 1.1   The First Shoot. *Photo courtesy of photographer Michael Hurt.*

The term has the capacity to refer specifically to technologies that facilitate communication through which culture is constructed. . . . Technocultures, as a class of technologies, involve mediated communications and they facilitate changed perceptions of space, time and place.

My Vietnamese fashion industry contact connected me with aspiring top child models to shoot while I was in Hanoi and she came up with the logically sound concept of shooting at a shop in the toy market for a background and pose appropriate to a child. The concept was also "Korean street fashion," which in Vietnam seems to connote a brash and bold female sexuality as argued through fishnet stockings and other types of "bling." Now, since the model, Phương Ngân, was twelve, the toy concept seemed like a good way to offset her somewhat inappropriately juvenile features. She photographed surprisingly well but the pictures never sat right with me. I wanted to make fashion pictures in Vietnam with Vietnamese models to convey a message about Vietnam but using "Korean style" as a *heuristic*—something that becomes a means of learning something or a tool to generate social data—and remember, I was in Hanoi doing fashion shooting as a way of learning how Vietnamese people think about Korean style and make sense of it by having them *do* it, act it out.

In this exposure (figure 1.2), the lighting was spot on—something made possible by the cheap, high-quality portable studio strobes coming out of

Figure 1.2 Lighting a Korean-Styled Model. *Photo courtesy of photographer Michael Hurt.*

China—and even though I had a portable, foldable beauty dish firing from around 2 meters outside the shot, the shadow falls just right, that is not on the toys, but right behind the model; on the floor almost directly behind her buttock is cut off by zooming to crop out the extraneous floor and larger store while making the subject larger, along with the toys.

In the end, the model's image is much more stylized and feels *playful* in how it blurs the image in a vignette pattern that gets increasingly blurrier outside the central area of the image, as the filter's algorithm seems to choose the highlight points (where the image blows out to white) and place white starbursts atop them. I reduced the strength and number of the threshold with a slider I took down to near zero to make the starbursts as small as possible but noticeable enough that they caused a "bling" effect into the visual mix. It is unnatural but not really noticeable. I was able to place the child model into a fantasy, play space visually along with the toys, to make for a *mise en scene* that steers the image away from an adult, sexualizing, Jodie Foster-in-*Taxi Driver* kind of creepiness that is not what I wanted in shooting a child model.

Finding "Korea" in Vietnam

Hoang Minh Chau—the Hanoi fashion connector, industry influencer, and stylist—had already found a new, cool place to shoot, before it became too popular, but already possessed of a bit of buzz by those in the know, a place called the Viet Gangz Brotherhood. It is a brand mall complex with coffee shops, brand stores, barbershops, and even jail cells that all combine into a highly Instagrammable, Korean-style place that nothing in Seoul could even dream of touching.

Gang culture as the main prism for hip-hop, African-American, and urban culture is a mode of global understanding of American *cool*. As problematic as globalized notions of American culture as a narrow understanding of a black, urban, gangster experience mostly gleaned from a singular, southern California-based subset of the African-American experience, I was quite happy to see these familiar faces in Hanoi. The model and I decided to shoot in front of the Tupac mural because there was less stuff to clear out from in front of it, despite not being my favorite rapper of the group on the wall.

I tried to make the shot in figure 1.3 look like it was outside and set up my smaller flash unit to simulate car headlights and cast a hard and clear shadow on the wall behind her. I also added in some heavy grain hoping to gritty up the scene; our common association of film grain, especially in B&W, has to do with the fact that police surveillance/social documentary photography tended

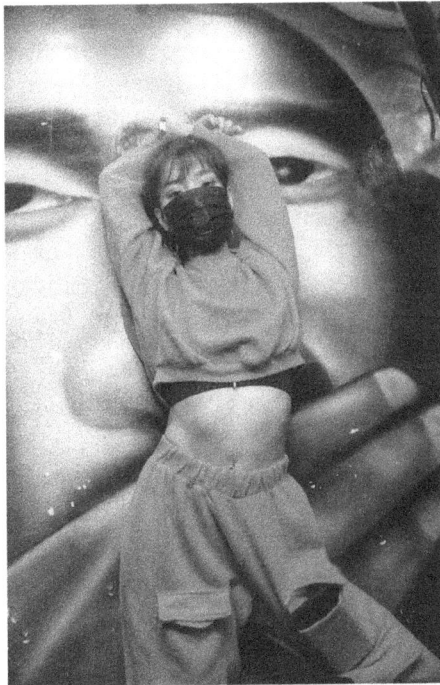

Figure 1.3   Model Yen Takes on the Korean Style as Hip-Hop. *Photo courtesy of photographer Michael Hurt.*

to use Kodak films pushed to ISO 3200, 6400, or even 10,000, which made for
heavy and harsh, noticeable grain, which caused the association of grain with
cinema verité or "reality." Unfortunately, it all did not gel, as it felt staged and
stiff, all too editorial. This is where the shoot and the model Yến started to gain
some creative traction. We had extra black masks in tow from Korea, and the
Coronavirus was in the air (albeit, we hoped, not literally), so we decided to
work a mask into the concept. The model went in different directions with this,
especially as she noticed me zooming in tighter for face shots.

Next, we moved from the idea of Korean national dress argued through a
Vietnamese idea of a "Korean style," to using the traditional Korean dress,
the hanbok, to be the point of photo-sartorial riffing, with the Vietnamese
model taking the social norms and cues as contained in the hanbok and the
idea of Koreanness it conveys and allowing them to embody a preset, iron
cage of Koreanness, which they would interpret by fitting it into their notions
of what a Korean girl is supposed to do as influenced by the hanbok dress.
They would also interact with me, though I would try to adjust to their cues
and ideas; also, the hanbok dresses we had in tow would be a bit easier
to digest and interpret because they were modern takes on the hanbok as
opposed the stiff, bulky ones from 100 years ago and often found at ceremo-
nies and state dinners—those would be a bit much for young, Vietnamese
models to interpret into meaning on the modern streets of Hanoi. The modernized *hanboks* from designer Heo Hye-yeong of Heo Sarang Hanbok in
Seoul are still unmistakably *hanboks*, with the high, peculiar, Korean cut of
the *jeogeori* blouse, along with the telltale style of the modernized skirt bot-
tom, the *chima*, which is quite updated and hip in the modernized versions we
had in tow. The models had no problem making modern Vietnamese sense
of them. I, as photographer and researcher, simply made sure the settings
and mise en scéne were as clear as possible to work within for the models.
Now, the posings and setting of the Korean element in the picture were more
directly imposed from above, leaving the Vietnamese side less a burden of
planning and allowing the individual model to simply interpret.

As the shooting in Hanoi settled into more serious tones, we tightened up
on the Korean style as a critical heuristic, a lens through which to recognize,
track, and even focus on Koreanness as it might be defined in Vietnam. High
schooler Trang was a Vietnamese Instagram model who was young and fresh
to the game, but entrepreneurial and professional in her pursuit of climbing
higher up the ladder of the modeling and fashion worlds. Trang was already
self-consciously a wrangler of Koreanness, as she reported noticing that she
received more attention in her Instagram feed and getting more work the
more she channeled a Korean look and image.

You never know with people—this is a young woman whose Instagram
conveyed her to be someone very into a "Korean style" of makeup, clothing,

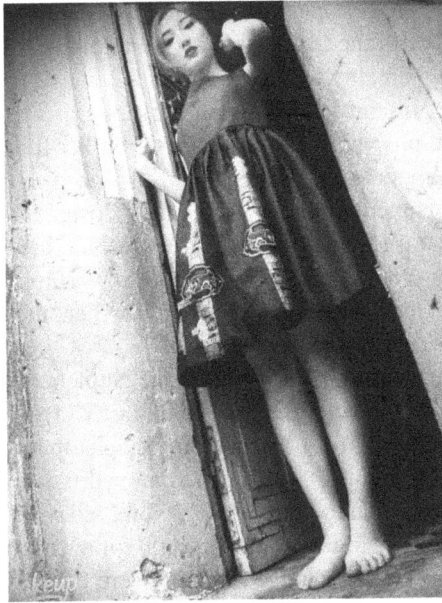

Figure 1.4 Model Trang Simply Embodies Koreanness, for Both Fun and Profit. *Photo courtesy of photographer Michael Hurt.*

and general comportment. Trang simply LOOKS like a Korean. That is not a mere accident of expressed genes, a phenotypical coincidence, but is something that required WORK, as in aesthetic/stylistic labor. Trang has a Korean LOOK that serves her well in GETTING PAID WORK. In the Vietnamese modeling/beauty market, the more Korean one looks, the more positive response one gets, resulting in more Instagram likes, as well as concrete work if one is modeling.

In this shot figure 1.4 in an A-line hanbok dress by Heo Sarang, Trang assumed both a Korean-influenced position and positionality, both a pose and a posture, a holding of her body in space in a Korean fashion, as well as a mode of BEING Korean. From my read of Trang's feed and from working with her and the resultant pictures, I do think part of Trang's quick ascendance and popularity as a model lies in her ability to aesthetically perform and project Koreanness.

Autoethnographically speaking—from my own experience shooting and working with many Korean models up and down the pecking order of Korean modeling Instagram—I felt like I was working with a Korean model, especially after Trang embodied the hanbok dress. Since the designer had indicated that she was going in a "softer" direction for her new looks and brand image, I decided to take cues from dominant photo trends in Korea and go in that direction. For me, this was taking a natural light portrait at the Hanoi House Cafe, with the idea of her standing on the balcony to welcome the light, with a soft, dreamy feel to her look. I captured this by telling her to walk out into the light and look down at the camera. The model assumed a demure, naturalistic pose with a quizzical look on her face.

With this many models in, it was getting to be time for the big model event, which was planned around a Vietnamese designer who partially operates within the general idea of "Korean street fashion" and the concept for a mega-shoot with his clothes and styling by HOANG Minh Chau was "Korean style." It would be a nice capstone on the trip. By then, the novel Coronavirus had already exploded in Korea.

As I think is common knowledge now, the Shincheonji Church of Jesus cult and Patient 31 had infected seemingly half of Korea. Korea had become the new "Wuhan." Flights from Korea were being stopped, though it was not policy yet. My return flight to Incheon was moved twice already by Korean Air, so I kept a close eye on my emails. What I feared would happen was happening, as running empty flights back and forth for a week was not something any airline could continue for long, and they were consolidating flights. The announcement had been made that KAL would cease flights from March 4th, my flight was now on March 3rd. It would be the last flight out. The last shoot took on new meaning. And it was about to fall apart.

Minh Chau sent me a message saying the models were getting cold feet, so I stepped in with a measure to raise confidence in the project. While I cannot quite say this saved the shoot, it certainly did not hurt that I sent a "temperature selfie," to show the models that I was healthy and was not bringing the virus to them. Korea has connoted "cool" and "cosmopolitan" for a while in Vietnam now, but now, it suddenly connoted "Corona."

The shoot was on, with a group of four models on the docket for the big "Korean street fashion" shoot that included an "alien stuck on earth doing social research," with Model Nhung, who offered her first look of her take on "Korean style" in front of the stunning façade of the Ngon Villa Restaurant.

Our movable feast was on its way to the famous Hanoi Train Street, which I thought would be a tricky place to shoot inside, which it was. After making our way over to the Train Street cafes, the woman owner of the cafe we scouted the night before had snagged us already, but we were grateful. An older woman elbowed us past the grumpy guard and set us up at her place. We dutifully ordered a whole bevy of drinks and I set up my studio strobe across the street at another cafe, from where I directed the models to act like they would in a cafe as friends.

The Korean-styled photo is populated by the Vietnamese designer Huu Anh Zoner of brand ZONER, with Vietnam's Next Top Model contestants who sported authentically intense glares and stares (see figure 1.5). It was tough

Figure 1.5 Vietnamese Fashion Models (@nguyenchinh199, @trainee_nim, and @tran-nungochanh from left to right) Embodying the Korean Style. *Photo courtesy of photographer Michael Hurt.*

shooting on the Train Cafe street. The railway company employee kept trying to stop us from shooting, even though the entire area exists in a quasi-legal commerce zone in which the old houses by the tracks had turned themselves into either coffee shops or extra seating for houses that had turned into coffee shops. So everyone ignored him while humoring him for politeness' sake. We had to shoot not knowing if we had be stopped or stymied in the next minute, so there were a lot of compromises (along with pictures of bystanders I had have otherwise re-shot). Once the shoot was over, we returned to the wonderful Chu Min La8 Lounge/cafe for a breather and to change clothes, exchange information, and have a drink. After Hanh had changed, I noticed her wearing loose, black slacks, so I thought of the black *hanbok* blouse top/*jeogeori* I had in tow as I made a fashion culture connection in my head. I also had a traditional Vietnamese *nhon la* farmer's hat at hand for another shoot, so a flash of realization made me ask her to put on the hanbok top and the hat, which with her dark, heavy makeup look, should add up to something pretty serious.

Now that the concept I had been toying with had had a test run in reality, and the other models and my Vietnamese fixers seemed to like it, it was time for the final, powerful *pièce de résistance* shoot, for which we would have to call in our dark Raven. She was our final model, recruited from an open call by Hoang Minh Chau, and would be coming back from a long trip in the evening of the final night of the shoot. She was not put off by any coronas, Korean origins, or any of that. She was a determined beginning-stage model out to build her portfolio/ comp card with strong, professional, editorial looks, and she was down for whatever was thrown her way.

So, to make what was looking to be a portrait of a Viet Cong soldier that would look realistic and respectful without looking like hokey cosplay, I asked Minh Chau where there might be what Americans call an "army surplus store" as I did not even know if Vietnam would have such a thing. But it did, as Minh Chau quickly replied on Messenger, without skipping a beat, exactly where to go to buy things the Viet Cong wore in the "American War."

We met the dark-featured Raven in the Hanoi Botanical Garden and moved directly into the shoot next to a huge tree with dramatic lighting from my smaller strobe with a honeycomb on it to point the beam tighter. We let flow her knee-length, stick-straight, black hair into this all-black look with hanbok jeogeori and simple black pants and heels. Against this tree, we barely even needed the military accessories. Between the tree, the *hanbok*, the hair, and the look, it seemed almost a shame to go down the rabbit hole of literality. Using all the tricks up my sleeve, it comes out in a nostalgic way that almost gels, but not quite. The thing that bothers me most is the *nhon la* itself, which looks too much like a touristy, farmer's version with the red brim and checkered chinstrap.

Bringing it down to black and white and losing more detail made this digestible, making the concept of a possible "Female VC portrait," in figure 1.6 along the lines of the unsung, dedicated Vietnamese photographers who did make

Figure 1.6 Model Raven Models a Korean Hanbok That Is Eerily Reminiscent of American War–Era Viet Cong Fatigues. *Photo courtesy of photographer Michael Hurt.*

Figure 1.7 Model Raven Models a Korean Hanbok That Is Eerily Reminiscent of American War–Era Viet Cong Fatigues. *Photo courtesy of photographer Michael Hurt.*

such portraits and pictures on the front lines of the War and whose inspired photography I am trying to honor in figure 1.7. My hope and intent were to do that work justice, inspired as I was by North Vietnamese photographers such as Le Minh Truong, but it was the talented model Raven who *got* the concept as channeled by the clothing and accessories around a fairly unusual conceptual synthesis. The VC concept was a bit tricky and stressful to do, given the histori-cal and ideological sensitivities surrounding the American War.

After the initial concept was done, it was only downhill from there, and I was seriously impressed with Raven's intensity and her ability to handle interpreting pretty open-ended concepts, so we kept the look, lost the gear, and shot mini-concepts that she would riff within. It was the last shoot of Hanoi, so we wanted to see where half a hanbok could and would go in a freestyle, final session.

CONCLUSION

In the end, what enabled my ongoing fashion research into Vietnamese con-ceptions of a Korean style was the fact that so many models, makeup artists, and other fashion-affiliated professionals were able to stick with the project, even after Korea had been named the "IT" country for epidemiological escapades. This itself was a testament to how influential South Korea is to Vietnamese youth, many of whom are quite interested in Korea as not only a style leader but as an example of the style in which to engage in leading the rest of the world as we all careen and career our ways through "Societies of Spectacle" in this new, hypermodern moment.

Korean youth strive to carve out new identities in a hypermodern world in which every option is a worthy choice. In Korea, the difference between reality and its alternatives is flattened, leaving a lot of pressure on individuals to figure out their own paths instead of having it assigned to them. This is why Korea is having an existential debate about queerness and LGBTQIA+ identity with big political stakes. For Vietnamese young people, on the global stage, it seems like every Instagram post, every attempt to make it as an influencer, a model, or stylist, is a pointed attempt to transgress against the old ways of being Vietnamese, of being in the "Vietnam" metaphor of someone else's lost war, a signifier of some former colonizer's moment of existential angst. It is a chance to move forward as developing-to-developed, modern-to-hypermodern. It seems like the appeal of the Korean, hypermodern mode of existence itself defines the luxurious possibility of leaving the sandbags of pre-modernity and (developmental) modernity behind. The Korean style may be an indicator of a means to carve out a way of being maximally, globally Vietnamese in new, unforeseen, and unimagined ways—in a way that worked—as it did for South Korea. For many Vietnamese, Korea and Koreanness define that extra-textual, interstitial, critical space in which one has both the freedom and the privilege to dare to be different.

After returning to Korea, I continued to make beauty in this time of Corona. Looking back again at technocultural practices and processes, people in Korea tend to wear masks and wash their hands a lot, but doing fashion-related shoots requires distancing. Even for a test shoot in which we physically met for the first time to do a get-to-know-you shoot, after coffee at a large coffee shop which had a temperature sensor gun-equipped hostess and free hand gel at the door, we could converse at a safe distance, which is about the same distance as normal in a coffee shop as large as the one in the Dongdaemun Design Plaza main building.

All of the above is how and why one "does" fashion in the time of the Coronavirus. Actually, it is not too different than during a time of no Coronavirus. I went to Vietnam as things were calming down there, and then shortly thereafter, South Korea deteriorated quickly while I was away, even as Vietnam officially declared itself Corona-free. As I came back to Seoul, things had calmed down, and then Vietnam re-exploded because of a Vietnamese socialite and European travelers re-introducing the virus to Vietnam. Along the way, it was interesting to focus inward and do beautiful things—those essential human things—even when circumstances seemed to dictate that non-essential things need to stop. But they do not.

We were careful and conscientious. We did fashion, but with concern for one another. We maintained physical distance while closing distance with the lens. We were and are living proof that handwashing and ample sanitizer are good weapons against not germs but are a salve against social panic itself. Initially, Vietnam successfully mitigated the spread of the virus. Eventually, the country suffered similar shortages and traumas that other neighboring countries experienced. Korea also experienced waves of shutdowns and paralysis, and the virus seemed to be teetering like a drunk looking for a place to sit and catch his breath for *just* a minute. Second and third waves came and went, with the question of having to shut down the economy in Korea forcing a response, even as the vaccine is poised to act as the knockout punch as of this writing in mid-2021.

Indeed, the need for social contact does not suddenly stop, even in an epidemic. Young people in Seoul, especially, are going on dates and meeting friends, having chats over coffee, even watching movies theaters. But now, these things are done with care and proper preparation. Because places like Vietnam or Korea have learned how to fight back against the fear, have gone past the initial attacks of panic, and learned to carry on with life using a combination of measures such as social distancing, ubiquitous masking, and socially responsible self-monitoring and free testing that allows life to not only go on, but for that to happen while beating the virus. The reason I have room to travel and continue on with my visual sociology research while models, stylists, and other aesthetic creators have the ability to continue on doing style, art, and other non-survival pursuits is because these places were *prepared* and free of hubris. We had *room* for thinking about style in the time of Corona. The ability to have a range of personal choices came from structural choices made far before any moment of agency was presented to me.

After working with and interviewing Vietnamese fashion insiders, their top modeling talent, and myriad other subjects, it was easy to reach the conclusion that there was a consensus as to what Korean sartorial style represented to the subjects and models embodying and conveying it in Vietnam. In the end, the very reason I was able to travel even as the pandemic was digging its claws into global plans, not to mention pursue seemingly ephemeral activities such as ethnographic research into the question of *Hallyu* and Korean style, is because of the very structural factors that allowed South Korea to build up *Hallyu* in the first place—the Hanoi trip was merely a testament to the global strength of Korean style and the much broader structural undergirding that made the Korean style a possible, probable, and in the end, powerful force of a transnational, Korean-shaped cosmopolitanism.

BIBLIOGRAPHY

Ackerman, J. S. (1962). A Theory of Style. *The Journal of Aesthetics and Art Criticism* 20 (3): 227–237.

Castañeda, Q. E. (2006). The Invisible Theatre of Ethnography: Performative Principles of Fieldwork. *Social Thought & Commentary* 79 (1): 75–104. http://www.jstor.org/stable/4150909.

Green, L. (2001). Technoculture: Another Term That Means Nothing and Gets Us Nowhere? *Media International Australia* 98 (1): 11–25.

Harper, D. (2002). Talking about Pictures: A Case for Photo Elicitation. *Visual Studies* 17 (1): 13–26.

Jacknis, I. (1988). Margaret Mead and Gregory Bateson in Bali: Their Use of Photography and Film. *Cultural Anthropology* 3 (2): 160–177.

Jin, D. and Yoon, K. (2016). The Social Mediascape of Transnational Korean Pop Culture: Hallyu 2.0 as Spreadable Media Practice. *New Media and Society* 18 (7): 1277–1292.

Pham, M. T. (2011). The Right to Fashion in the Age of Terrorism. *Signs* 36 (Winter): 86.

Yoon, T. (2017). Postcolonial Production and Consumption of Global K-pop. In *The Korean Wave: Evolution, Fandom, and Transnationality*, edited by Yoon, T. and Jin, D., Lexington: Lexington Press.

Chapter 2

"Girl Power" DPRK Style

The Girl Group Phenomenon in North Korea and Its Fans across East Asia

Peter Moody and Seunghee Ha

INTRODUCTION[1]

During the 2018 Pyeongchang Winter Olympics in the Republic of Korea, the Democratic People's Republic of Korea sent its Samjiyon Orchestra to the south for a special performance. As part of this performance, the Orchestra singers took the stage for the song "Dash to the Future" dressed in black hot pants and red tank-tops, which invited comparisons between them and K-pop girl groups.[2] Since 2012, the Kim Jong Un regime has gradually appropriated and incorporated stylistic elements of global pop music (not limited to K-pop) while making sure the lyrics reflected the state's priorities. Sending Samjiyon Orchestra to the Olympics was Kim's attempt to show the world his progressive and modern culture.

Starting in 2012, the emergence of "girl groups" in North Korea as a propaganda tool has spurred something of a phenomenon, especially focused on the Moranbong Band, which originally performed "Dash to the Future," but was not selected to attend the Olympics. The group developed in the wake of the international rise of K-pop, serving to divert a certain degree of attention away from the South Korean cultural industry which had piqued the interest of some North Koreans. Even with its propaganda function, the novel stylistic features of the Moranbong Band have resulted in a fandom that can be considered parallel to the *Hallyu* phenomenon, even if on a much smaller scale. Within North Korea, the excitement triggered by the band's electronic strings section and simultaneous singing and dancing routines has at times resembled fandom practices in capitalist states, but the cultural sector made adjustments to both sustain people's interest in them and to prevent an "arts for the sake of arts" reception that could easily diverge away from their propaganda function. However, outside North Korea, spontaneous pockets of fandom have emerged, especially in China and Japan, beginning with mere curiosity and involving interest that has nothing to do with the political objectives of the North Korean state. What has fueled this international interest in the Moranbong Band has been the novelty of the girl group element as well as the consideration of them alongside their South Korean K-pop counterparts.

In order to understand these trends, it is worth moving away from the 2000s for a moment to examine what distinguishes the recent girl group phenomenon from North Korean music ensembles of the past. The first of these ensembles was the women's instrumental section of the Mansudae Art Troupe that was established in 1969. Later popular music groups that appeared in North Korea were the Wangjaesan Light Music Band (1983) and the Pochonbo Electronic Ensemble (1985). In the DPRK, cheerful and optimistic music played by relatively small-scale bands with popular musical instruments is defined as "light music." This explains the "Light Music Band" component of Wangjaesan Light Music Band, but in fact, this group was an "Art Troupe" that included instrumental music, dance routines, and singers together.[3] As for the Pochonbo Electronic Ensemble, this group was based on disco-style electronic music, which was popular around the world at that time, and consisted of male instrumentalists, male conductors, and female singers. The first five singers of the group each performed as solo singers with their own special auras and their own signature songs.

It was not until the 2010s that a girl group consisting of only female instrumentalists and singers emerged in the North with the debut of the Moranbong Band. Now known as the Moranbong Electronic Ensemble, the music group is a fusion of sorts when considered alongside other forms of global popular music. The singing ensemble is the part that resembles a K-pop-style girl group, for they are all young women who sing and perform dance moves simultaneously. As for the instrumentalists of the Moranbong Band, the string section of the band is perhaps most similar in music and in concept to the British electronic string quartet female group Bond that attained worldwide popularity in the 2000s (Ha, 2019). Additionally, as musicologist Keith Howard (2020) points out, the mix of foreign and local music as well as the Western training and mannerisms of the soloists makes them comparable to the Chinese folk orchestra, "12 Girls Band" who, from the time of their 2003 debut, has played a variety of genres on traditional Chinese instruments.

So far, researchers of the Moranbong Band and the music of the Kim Jong Un period have looked largely at the cultural production side with only brief exploration into how they have resonated with audiences (Korhonen and Cathcart, 2017; Lim, 2017: Kang, 2018; Howard, 2020). One scholar who has addressed the consumption side is Zeglin (2016) who attributes the impetus for forming the Moranbong Band to a strategy to redirect libinal pleasures away from outside global culture like K-pop (that younger people along the border and in Pyongyang were increasingly coming in contact with) and back toward the familial embrace of a celebrity dictator. Lu (2019) has highlighted how the DPRK regime is making use of information technology to this effect, revealing that North Koreans cannot download the music of state-administered music groups from the country's intranet but instead have to go to a shop called the Information Exchange Center to select songs to save on their phones.[4] Jeon and Han, authors of the aptly titled *NK-Pop* (2018), interpret the process of the DPRK cultural sector adopting foreign music trends to respond to changing popular tastes as having continuity with the earlier development of an indigenous electronic and popular music style as a means to counter the worldwide disco craze in the 1980s. They point to Pochonbo Electronic Ensemble concerts on Mansudae TV, a channel that featured art performances, movies, and sports, and was primarily for residents of Pyongyang. Ha (2019) has also looked at how changes in people's tastes have expanded the parameters for popular music in North Korea, noting specifically how cultural administrators have sought to induce audience participation in live performances.

This chapter aims to draw more attention to the consumption side of North Korea's indigenous girl group phenomenon both inside and outside the country, as well as the Moranbong Band's various changes in style and repertoire. Because of the difficulty in acquiring a sufficient amount of reliable information on topics related to North Korea, it is important and perhaps even essential to adopt a hybrid methodological approach. In addition to synthesizing the secondary research material on the topic, this chapter brings together the approaches of "Pyongyangology" performance analysis and interviews with people who have lived in North Korea. Pyongyangology, outlined by Korhonen and Mori (2020), is derived from Cold War-era Kremlinology, an interpretive analytical approach of zeroing in on key details in films, photographs, and other official sources and then making inferences about society, culture, and politics based on them.[5] We have opted to supplement our interpretive analyses of performances by conducting interviews with Chinese individuals who studied abroad in North Korea during the period of the Moranbong Band's popularity and an ethnic Korean resident of Japan who has trained with musicians in the North and has knowledge about Moranbong Band fandom in Japan. A small number of accounts from North Korean defectors are also included to provide illustrations of findings learned from other sources.

In isolation, both of these aforementioned methodological approaches are incomplete and have the potential to be unreliable; however, when integrated, findings from one approach can support those of another to the point where researchers can draw firmer conclusions. As Korhonen and Mori (2020) remind us, historians often have to engage in interpretive analysis when dealing with a limited number of data points. The impossibility of stepping into the past is after all somewhat analogous to the near non-existent opportunities of stepping into North Korea to conduct social research for a present and ongoing phenomenon.

With the exception of Jinyu Lu, a Chinese national who is a researcher of Moranbong Band and Ri Unha, an ethnic Korean resident of Japan who asked to be identified by her pen name, we have decided to not reference our interview subjects by names but instead by their designation (Defector, Chinese, or Japanese), followed by the word Respondent, followed by a letter of the alphabet. We made this consideration to protect people's identities, which is not only important for defectors who still may have family members in the North but also for interview subjects from China and Japan who might face scrutiny for their perspectives about a North Korean music group.[6]

INFLOW: *HALLYU* IN NORTH KOREA
BEHIND CLOSED DOORS

As a phenomenon that has spread globally, *Hallyu* has reached North Korea. Its path of inflow has been the so-called *jangmadang* where unofficial private economic activity takes place. In the midst of the North Korean famine of the 1990s, the *jangmadang* sprung up as local private markets that were created spontaneously through the initiative of the North Korean people when the government's public distribution system collapsed (Kim and Yoon, 2019).[7] Various goods are distributed and traded in the *jangmadang*, and amid this process of exchange has been a phenomenon of *Hallyu* inflow (Ahn and Hyeon, 2017). The government tacitly tolerated the *jangmadang* as they expanded through the country, and in some regions, secret trade among residents began. At that time, due to the extreme economic difficulties and the relaxation of border control, smuggled trade with China became widespread, and a considerable amount of media footage from the outside world flowed in. At the same time, as North Korean defectors started to settle in South Korea, contact with their families in North Korea through Chinese brokers became an important information channel. While it can be costly, it has now become commonplace for North Korean defectors to make contact with their family members in this way and even to send money to them (Kang and Park, 2012).

Hallyu content has circulated in North Korea mainly through storage media, which has changed according to updates in technology. As Kretchun and Kim (2012) have found, it was not until 1997 when radio devices became commonly available, and availability of other media devices followed in the next decade with televisions (2000), DVD players (2004), laptops (2008), and USB drives (2001). South Korean dramas and songs have entered North Korea mainly through USB drives, CDs, and DVDs. Moreover, in 2003, China developed its own electronic device, the EVD Player (Enhanced Versatile Disc), capable of playing DVD, CD, and USB. This device, also called the "Notel," became a major medium contributing to the mass distribution and spread of *Hallyu* cultural content as it entered North Korea in the mid-2000s. USB storage devices can be easily hidden, and with the Notel device, they can be removed at a moment's notice to make it look as if the user was listening to or watching something permissible from the CD/DVD drive. Eventually, in an accommodation to grassroots changes, the DPRK government legalized Notels in 2014 (Seo, 2013; Pearson, 2015). In addition, as antennas and TV transmission technologies have been developed, South Korean TV programs and videos can be watched in some areas despite interference with the electrical wave signals by the North Korean government (Ahn and Hyeon, 2017).

The North Korean authorities have sought to restrict the consumption of South Korean media, and if one is caught in the possession of such media, they can face punishment such as imprisonment; there are cases in which those subject to punishment can get out of it by paying bribes. This has become a tacit practice, and in some cases, those responsible for the crackdowns on illicit media consumption have straight up demanded payment (Kang and Park, 2012). Additionally, consumers of South Korean music in the North minimize the risks by obtaining media from trusted connections and only viewing them with close friends and family members (Fahy, 2019). Recently, in December 2020 at the 12th Plenary Meeting of the 14th Standing Committee of the Supreme People's Assembly, the North Korean authorities enacted the "Reactionary Thought and Culture Exclusion Act." With this law, the maximum sentence for distributors of video materials in South Korea was elevated to the death penalty. As such, it can be presumed that the Korean Wave has had a great influence in North Korea since the North Korean authorities have made punishments more severe to prevent the inflow of foreign cultures (KCNA, 2020).

Among the *Hallyu* products introduced through the *jangmadang*, K-pop music has reached the ears of a certain segment of the population and has even been introduced through the official route of inter-Korean exchange events. This includes the 2003 performance of the girl group Baby V.O.X. at a unification concert in Pyongyang, leading one recent North Korean defector to grow interested in K-pop to the point of wearing the same colorful pants as members of the Girls Generation in the video for the 2009 song "Gee" (Denyer and Kim, 2019). Defector Respondent A shared with us his memory of first listening to K-pop music and feeling as if he were experiencing a completely new world.

External information about the world gleaned through *jangmadang* trade along with the influence of *Hallyu* has brought about many changes in the values and lifestyle of the people. As the influx of *Hallyu* media within North Korea continues to flow in through official or informal channels, North Korean society and the people's perceptions have changed in the process. To respond to these changes, the North Korean authorities have sought to appropriate certain elements of the Korean Wave and thus adopt global trends in cultural production for political purposes. At the same time and to some degree similar to the case of K-pop, we can see a tendency to acculturate (in the sense of "going with the flow") in order to partake in the changing trends of world popular music. The most representative case where this dialectic between appropriation and acculturation is present is the Moranbong Band.[8]

ACCULTURATION VS. APPROPRIATION: PROPAGANDA POP MUSIC IN THE KIM JONG UN ERA

On July 7, 2012, a little over half a year after Kim Jong Un became leader of North Korea, the [North] Korean Central Television network made an announcement that the new leader had formed the Moranbong Band for the purpose of igniting the arts sector and meeting the needs of the new generation (KCTV, 2012a). Following this announcement was a so-called "demonstration performance" of 10 instrumentalists (an electric guitarist, bassist, electronic drummer on an electric drum set, two keyboardists, a pianist, and an electric string quartet) and five singers in luxurious dresses with sparkling jewelry. Starting with an upbeat and peppy arrangement of the beloved Korean song *Arirang*, the members of this new ensemble had, by the second half of the event, performed music from across the globe including European classical, the Chinese propaganda song "Red Flag Flying," the theme from the Hollywood film *Rocky*, and a medley of "world famous children's songs" that included mostly Disney songs. During this Disney portion of the concert, the women were joined by jesters in full Disney character costumes looking as if they were teleported from the Magic Kingdom. Conveniently timed to mark 100 years after the birth of Kim Il Sung (year 101 according to the *Juche* calendar that the DPRK uses in addition to the global standard one), this concert excited the audience and created anticipation for what the new leader would do for the country.

Despite the unconventional format and repertoire of the performance, the concert was heralded in the North Korean media for its continuity, namely that Kim Jong Un was inheriting his father Kim Jong Il's legacy of Music

Politics. While North Korea has long utilized music to reinforce social solidarity and for other propaganda purposes, in 2000 the term "Music Politics" was formalized as a Kim Jong Il innovation of utilizing music to "overcome adversity and embrace hope about the future"[9] in the aftermath of a famine and economic crisis that had killed up to one million people, roughly 5% of the population according to estimates (Haggard and Noland, 2007). As Jeon (2007) has pointed out, Music Politics was a way for the state to demonstrate that it was not out of touch with the people's desires for updated and diversified forms of entertainment while at the same time providing itself with a mechanism to determine the parameters for the expansion of musical forms and what precisely the content would be. In a similar vein as his father and grandfather, Kim Jong Un's frequent appearances at performances and pictures with performers have demonstrated his involvement in the music production process.

In assessing the Music Politics of the Kim Jong Un era, it is helpful to think in terms of four periods: an initial phase of liberalization (2012–2013) followed by localization (2014–2015), standardization (2016–2017), and the ongoing era or normalization (2018–present). If we consider the cultural and political developments in music during these different periods, we can begin to properly understand the strategy behind contemporary music production in the DPRK as well as its characteristics.

Liberalization

The liberalization period involved experimenting with a fusion of elements of the global soundscape as well as features of the concert experience that capitalist countries have exhibited. As mentioned above, the demonstration concert in the summer of 2012 was arranged for an electronic string ensemble as well as a synth-pop rock band. Several outside observers have speculated the reason for the incorporation of so many foreign songs into the repertoire, particularly the medley of Disney tunes, and their explanations have ranged from the DPRK sending a message to the outside world that it was opening up to foreign culture to simply reflecting Kim Jong Un's own preferences from his experience living abroad in Switzerland (Oh, 2014). Considering that the audience members were as young as 10 and old as 60 (Oh, 2014), the decision to borrow from a wide range of foreign styles was likely a way to attract attention from a broad segment of the population. The cameo appearances of the Disney characters (who were not unfamiliar to North Koreans) was a way to stimulate the interest of young children and thus ensure the longevity of the Moranbong Band's appeal over the long term.

A second notable concert exemplifying this liberalization phase was the 2013 New Year's Concert at the Ryukyeong Jeong Ju-yeong Gymnasium—the same location where South Korean pop music acts played in 2003 as part of the cultural exchange ventures of the South Korean government's Sunshine Policy with the North. The atmosphere for the 2013 concert was celebratory not only of the New Year's holiday but also in recognition of developments in science and technology as North Korea's first successful satellite launch had occurred a few weeks earlier. The gymnasium venue of the concert with its large seating capacity, a stage that could be surrounded by three sides of audience members, and the relative ease in setting up a runaway (Oh, 2014) was somewhat new to North Korea at the time and allowed for intimate and dynamic interactions to take place between performers and audience members, creating a concert atmosphere that, as Cathcart and Korhonen (2017) aptly point out, looked as if it were "simultaneously staged and real." For instance, for the song "Let the New Year's Snow Fall" (Mokran Video DPRK, 2013a), the laser lighting and techno dance beat that overlaid rock and jazz solos from each of the instrumentalists elicited a steady stream of clapping in the middle of the song. The singers stepped into the audience shortly after arriving on stage, and by this time, the level of excitement reached a peak as some audience members waved their hands in the air as if they were in Seoul rather than Pyongyang.[10]

Later in the set list was the song "Tansume" ("charge forward" or "without a break" depending on how it is translated) to specifically commemorate the satellite launch (Mokran Video DPRK, 2013b). As an instrumental arrangement of a previous song, it featured riveting alternating electric guitar and electric violin solos. With the videos and sounds of the launch in the background as well as flame pillars lighting up at certain times, much of the audience was brought to their feet for a good portion of the song. Young women in colorful hanboks took the lead of coming out into the aisles and dancing in front of the stage. A group of men quickly followed them, hopping to the other side of the stage with their hands flailing. From the televised performance, it is hard to see the full extent of the excitement, but during the encore when the camera scanned the audience, one could notice entire patches of empty seats from where audience members had leapt from their seats.

Localization

The opening liberalization round of Music Politics in the Kim Jong Un era triggered mass adrenaline and generated enthusiasm among audiences, but what is less clear is whether the novelty of the medium was supporting or overshadowing the political aim of legitimizing Kim Jong Un's authority. The cultural administrators in the DPRK Propaganda and Agitation department made a number of changes to Moranbong performances that, as Oh (2014) points out, were apparent by a September 3, 2014, concert called

"The Concert of New Works" (Mokran Video DPRK, 2014). In this concert, there was a slight scaling back of the prominent position of the instrumentalists, three songs of the *minyo* (folk song) style, more lyrics about Kim Jong Un's leadership, and percussion parts more characteristic of military marches than electronic dance music. Additionally, the elaborate wardrobe of the Moranbong members narrowed to its signature design which was a white military-style uniform with a relatively short skirt but not as revealing as the previous outfits (Oh, 2014).

All of these changes suggested a new localization phase of the Moranbong Band's evolution and in North Korean propaganda pop music in general. While localization has been defined as the modification of streams of global culture to suit local tastes and circumstances (Roudometof, 2018), in this case, North Korean cultural administrators were adjusting their own cultural product to restrain the global features of the music and performance from taking too firm a hold. They sought to secure more advantage locally, to align the cultural product with political objectives in a way that was easier to control. There is some speculation (Lim 2017, 603–604) that the sudden absence and subsequent reappearance of certain Moranbong Band members from 2013 to 2015 as well as the emergence in 2015 of a rival girl group (the Chongbong Band) was related to this impulse of the regime to keep the performers in line and loyal to the leadership.

At the same time the regime sought to restrain divergence from party leadership, it was also trying to expand the appeal of this "authorized pop" form of music.[11] On May 29, 2014, the Moranbong Orchestra was designated as a model for performing arts in the 9th National Artists Contest. From that point on, various musical forms have been tried out, such as using modern rhythms or singing the national anthem with an R&B singing style. The image of the band, however, moved in a conservative direction as it acquired military status and was designated as an army band on October 25, 2015 (Ha, 2019).

Standardization

As mentioned above, in 2015, another women's propaganda pop group, the Chongbong Band appeared. The members of this band wore evening dresses and gave off a feminine and elegant atmosphere. By 2016, the Chongbong Band had changed, reflecting the girl group concept of the Moranbong Band. In 2016, a joint concert performance titled "Follow Our Party Forever" was held to celebrate the 7th Korean Workers' Party Congress, and it featured the Chongbong Band, the Moranbong Band, and the State Merited Chorus (KCTV, 2016). The early choreography of the Chongbong Band was mainly simple arm, shoulder, and hip movements and some walking across the stage, but after the reorganization, they performed completely different dance patterns involving more dynamism and sophisticated synchronization. And as part of the joint concert performance, there was a medley in which Moranbong Band and Chongbong Band performed together. In what resembled a "battle" or "dance off" that is characteristic of global music genres like K-pop, the two groups interacted, taking turns and looking as if they were competing with each other in their singing and dancing (Ha, 2019).

To extend the reach of the new bands' appeal, the Moranbong band toured across the provincial areas from September to December 2017 in a repeat of the joint concert format with the Chongbong Band and the State Merited Chorus. In addition to this concert tour bringing Music Politics to more groups of people through live entertainment (sometimes with three performances a day in different localities), the KCTV network broadcasts of the performances gave behind-the-scenes glimpses of the backstage and tour bus areas, including interviews with both performers and fans and at least one shot of an interaction between the two (Lu, 2019). It is rare for these groups to perform outside Pyongyang, and in earlier decades people in provincial areas were not even exposed to propaganda pop bands because the TV channel they were featured on could only be viewed in Pyongyang (Defector Respondent B). Defector Respondent C revealed that in the pre-Moranbong Band era, even a tape of the state-administered group the Wangjaesan Light Music Band that she came into contact with was a bootlegged product made in China.

Normalization

There were signs that the localized and increasingly standardized strategy for political hegemony amounted to a neglect of the long-standing North Korean practice of utilizing music groups for soft power internationally. In December 2015, the Moranbong Band arrived in Beijing to perform a concert which was abruptly canceled. The reasons for the cancellation are ambiguous. While rumors flew that the Chinese government was uncomfortable with a repertoire of so many songs praising Kim Jong Un (Lim, 2017), another plausible explanation (considering the timing) is that it was the result of the two countries having a feud over diplomatic protocol. As Chinese scholars indicated shortly after the event (Perlez, 2015), there was a question of whether or not Chinese president Xi Jinping or Premier Li Keqiang would be in attendance for the concert; however, after Kim Jong Un declared that his country possessed a hydrogen bomb, the Chinese side decided to send lower ranking officials instead, which may have been interpreted as an insult to the North Korean side, presumably leading them to recall the Moranbong Band.

The normalization of Music Politics in the Kim Jong Un period can be thought of as the blending of North Korean music groups together for performative purposes and the routine use of them for both international and domestic purposes.[12] A watershed moment in this respect was the dispatch of the Samjiyon Orchestra to South Korea for two performances during the 2018 Pyeongchang Olympic Games emceed by the Moranbong Band director Hyon Song-wol and featuring the Moranbong Band song "Dash to the Future" with choreography. "Dash to the Future" was also part of a music performance of North Korean musical artists in Beijing the following year as part of a strengthening of bands between the two countries in the midst of a period of North Korean diplomacy with South Korea and the United States. Starting in 2019, the annual New Year's concert moved outdoors with a countdown similar to those held in New York and other cities around the world. The Moranbong Band changed its name to the Moranbong Electronic Ensemble, and there were no visual signs of the instrumentalists in the newly arranged songs with updated synthesizer parts (KCTV, 2019). The outdoor format was repeated in 2020 with light sticks and group dances in the audience.

DISSEMINATION AND DIFFUSION: FEATURES OF FANDOM IN THE RECEPTION OF DPRK MUSIC

Whether or not this official music, highly derived from commercial forms of music in other countries, has resulted in the emergence of fandoms is important to understand, as the cultural ramifications of this official sponsorship could affect North Korean entertainment more generally. We define fandom in terms of people spontaneously (i.e., without the mandate of the state) making choices to purchase and/or exchange knowledge and sentiments about a given cultural product for the purpose of appreciating it and as part of some form of a social grouping. This interpretation, rather than involving a strict wall of separation between official culture and popular culture, acknowledges, as Fiske points out, that official culture "can be readily converted into career opportunities and earning power" (1992) for the private benefit of individuals. Moreover, as Mazierska (2016) argues, ideology imposed from the top can be "rework[ed] at the grassroots level" to the point where "(ordinary) people . . . affect ideologies" just as it affects them. North Korean music, as an embodiment of state ideology—"state telegraph" as Howard (2020) puts it—can be reworked at the grassroots level in a process that shapes music styles, musical formats, and ultimately, content at the official level. Two factors that have allowed this relationship between the official culture and popular culture to flourish have been the gendered novelty of girl groups like Moranbong Band as well as the ongoing consideration of these acts alongside their South Korean K-pop counterparts.

Within North Korea: The Emergence and Development of a "Conduit Fandom"

Jinyu Lu, an international student from China who lived in North Korea from 2011 to 2015, witnessed the transformation of the North Korean soundscape following the emergence of Moranbong Band. After Moranbong Band held their first concert in 2012, it was not long, she said, before they became popular with young people as they were associated with youth more than any other music act. Across from her dormitory was a factory that regularly blared the band's music from loudspeakers, so it was impossible not to come in contact with their music. Another Chinese international student, Chinese Respondent B who was in North Korea in 2014, said that a common place to come in contact with the Moranbong Band was on the streets of Pyongyang where propaganda cars with speakers regularly traveled. Even with these settings outside, Jinyu believes that the most common way that people learned about them was inside the home through their TV sets considering that nearly all of their concerts were broadcast live.

While the Moranbong Band was a top-down initiative, there are signs they have indeed resonated with the population. Jinyu Lu mentioned how in the initial years of their formation, a number of young women started to dress like them, wear their style of make-up, and cut their hair in the same way as them. Oh (2014) visited Pyongyang in August 2013 and heard that there were a number of young people that spent a *sabi* (a premium) to get a front seat spot for the concert. As he assessed the phenomenon, "we can't stretch the meaning of this to commercialism but can confirm the intention of [a certain segment of the North Korean population] to readily pay a price to go to a fun concert" (Oh, 2014). In a concert Jinyu attended in 2015, she noticed that the men in the audience, by and large, were sitting calmly, and it was the women who were reacting in a more excited fashion, clapping to the beat and singing the lyrics out loud. Like the case of the 2013 New Year's performance of the song "Tansume" discussed in the previous section, there were audience members coming out into the aisles for the last song, which reinforces the claim in the previous section that the Moranbong Band concert atmosphere provided the space for less restrained behavior than one can witness in pre-Moranbong concert performance settings.

During 2017, the year of the Moranbong Band's concert tour with Chongbong Band and the State Meritorious Choir, more people in the provinces could attend the concerts than had been possible before, and there were signs of a craving for this kind of entertainment. One female attendee said after a concert performance, "The audience fever is unprecedented . . . people not able to come wouldn't be able to understand," and a man said "I couldn't control my tears. I don't think I will be able to fall asleep even when I go home tonight."[13] The KCTV program covering the concert tour featured a scene of audience members going to the front of the stage and getting autographs from the Moranbong Band members (Channel A, 2017). Incidentally (or perhaps not), this was the year of North Korea's ICBM tests and, similar to the case of the 2013 New Year's concert, the regime wanted to get people enthusiastic about the launches; the excitement the music generated could be harnessed to fulfill that purpose. One woman remarked after a performance "I am most happy when I see the rockets [on the concert video screen] launch up to the sky. We won! This is the greatest joy!"[14] While such statements could have been encouraged or even elicited, it is worth keeping in mind how rare it was for people outside Pyongyang to attend this kind of music performance.

As Moranbong Band and others gained popularity and audiences were allowed to react as fans much like their South Korean peers, the heavy role of the government affected the development of something like a fandom, especially as it spent decades investing in propaganda and agitation for collective activities. The fandom might best be described as a "conduit fandom," collective acts of adoration and/or obsession that are prompted from the top and act as a means to inspire awe and reverence for the North Korean leaders and the system they have control over through the music acts.

At the same time, there is a tension between this "conduit fandom" of the "propaganda pop music" created by the state and people's individual interests in it. One Chinese source Jinyu Lu interviewed said that when you ask young people about Music Politics, they give a textbook-style response with an official-style speech demeanor; however, when you ask them about Moranbong Band in particular, they switch to a conversational style and tell you what they really believe (Lu, 2019). This suggests that the fervor for the music groups may not be so integrated with the party agenda as much as the state might like them to be. When it came to the North Korean sources with whom Lu spoke, the reasons they gave for liking the Moranbong Band were not so related to the political content as much as the virtuoso talent exhibited by the musicians and the stylistic elements of the music (Lu, 2019). It is therefore no surprise that the state has gradually scaled back the showcasing of the Moranbong Band instrumentalists who were not even on the stage for the 2018 and 2019 New Years' concerts. Instead, the Moranbong singers were part of an integrated performance with more traditional forms of propaganda music (like the military-style choirs). At the same time, there were new sophisticated EDM (electronic dance music) interludes in some of their songs to fuel their continued appeal.

THE NORTH KOREA THAT IS NOT LIKE NORTH KOREA: CHINESE FASCINATION WITH MORANBONG BAND FROM CULTURAL IMMERSION TO FAN SITES

North Korean universities have language programs for international students and Chinese nationals that make up a significant share of the population.[15] The Chinese students have various reasons for studying abroad in North Korea: some are part of official exchange programs between the two governments, and others, especially from Dandong city on the Chinese side of the border, are there to help their families' businesses with Sino-North Korean trade. Jinyu Lu studied abroad at the urging of her father who wanted her to learn Korean and believed that experiencing the North Korean variety of Korean would be a good way to acquire the language in its pure form. Naturally, her language-learning experience included cultural immersion, and a part of that cultural immersion experience was learning songs.

The three Chinese exchange students we talked to all did language study in Pyongyang in the 2010s and did not have much knowledge of or interest in North Korean music before going to the DPRK. Owing to the popularity of *Hallyu* in China during much of the 2000s–2010s, they were much more familiar with South Korean music.[16] Their experience learning songs involved social gatherings after dinner when North Korean students taught them while playing guitar and/or accordion. There was also a practice of singing songs on school field trips to various spots in North Korea. Chinese Respondent B emphasized that she did not internalize the lyrics when she learned and sang the songs but instead considered it a purely cultural experience during which she "just focused on the melody, forgetting the words coming out of [her] mouth."

To describe Moranbong's performance at the 2015 70th Workers Party anniversary concert that she attended with other international students on a field trip, Jinyu Lu used the expression "North Korea that is unlike North Korea" to describe her reaction to the song "With Pride," which alternates from showcasing singers to musicians. She elaborated as follows:

> The dancing in this song left a deep impression on me. The dance line was somewhat glamorous, and the dance moves were big and energetic. It felt like they were following South Korean girl groups.

After the song, she and her friends agreed an appropriate description of what they had just seen was "the Girls' Generation of North Korea," comparing them to one of the most popular K-pop groups. Before leaving North Korea the following year, she made sure to purchase a DVD of the performance as a souvenir to remember her experience.

The characterization of Moranbong Band as "the Girls' Generation of North Korea" has been echoed in the comment section of at least one video uploaded to the Chinese video sharing site BiriBiri, one of many online forums where Chinese people with an interest in Moranbong Band express their positive impressions. One person who is part of an emerging community of fans (if not an outright fandom) is Chinese Respondent C who had studied Korean in North Korea for only six months before returning home and did not know about the Moranbong Band while she was there. After her return to China, however, she did an online search of some of the songs she learned in the language program and discovered a whole online community of fans who uploaded songs on Chinese music apps and translated the lyrics into Chinese. She confirmed that Han Chinese (as opposed to only ethnic Korean Chinese) made up a big part of this fandom because of how precise the translations of the songs were in certain dialects. She ended up starting her own blog on the Chinese social media application We Chat, where she posts information about the band's songs, and as of the writing of this work, has amassed 1,800 followers.

Whether or not the online circulation of media and comments qualifies as a fandom is up for debate. Chinese Respondent B acknowledged a large number of people who have engaged in online forums, sharing experiences about visiting North Korea and/or having genuine interest in the Moranbong Band, but she does not spontaneously encounter fans outside of those forums. There is also little opportunity to purchase band merchandise in China such as concert DVDs although the 798 Art Zone in Beijing is one notable place where these kinds of items might be available. When we asked Chinese Respondent C if she was a Moranbong Band fan since she started her band blog, she demurred: "I'm certainly not a '*gwangpan*'" (Korean for "crazy" or "die-hard" fan) as she denoted some of the people who visited her blog. According to her, what separates these *gwangpan* from a casual fan who may simply watch the videos or listen to the songs online are practices such as making edited videos with Chinese subtitles of the lyrics or even making their own memorabilia items like postcards. She also said that more members of the online communities are male than female, and are drawn to the music for various reasons including getting addicted to the passionate sounds and cheerful rhythm, feeling impressed by the confidence that the band members exhibit, and believing that North Korean girl group members have comparatively more natural beauty and less plastic surgery modification than their South Korean counterparts.

Characteristics representative of fandom, such as the purchasing of products and collective appreciation mechanisms, certainly exist in China for the Moranbong Band. What is missing of course is the concert experience, for very few Chinese people have seen their concerts live. "Latent fandom" or "invisible fandom" may then be the best way to describe the digital presence of Moranbong Band followers as it does not include more interactive social elements or economic impact. What would likely make the Chinese fandom more active would be a Moranbong Band concert tour in China, but so far, it has not happened.

Imitation is the Most Sincere Form of Excluding Politics: A Visible Yet "Curtailed Fandom" of the Moranbong Band in Japan

Like the case of China, there is evidence of a Moranbong Band fandom in Japan. For instance, a Twitter user created the account "The Moranbong Band Fan Club, Japan Branch" in September 2014, and it is still active with over 950 followers and over 65,000 tweets (Yabe, 2014). Most of the tweets are song postings and music scores for the Moranbong Band, or posts related to North Korea. Japan has also witnessed the emergence of a Japanese girl group that dresses up like Moranbong members and appreciates North Korean culture. This fan group made up of Japanese women who adore Moranbong Band, is called "The Military First Girls." The members of the group publicly perform Moranbong Band choreography and songs while wearing similar costumes as the Moranbong Band members (Reuters Staff, 2017).

Ri Unha (pen name), the only member of the "Military First Girls" group who is Zainichi (ethnic Korean in Japan), believes that the Otaku (i.e., nerd) culture in Japan helps explain the North Korean music fandom phenomenon in Japan.[17] "The fans are either Otaku or people who like all kinds of music in Asia including Chinese and South Korean music," she told us in an interview. Unha has experience with North Korean music herself, having grown up attending Chosun schools run by the Chongryon (The General Association of Korean Residents in Japan) community who have maintained ties with the North Korean government since the mid-1950s. As a student, she learned about contemporary DPRK music acts from her textbook and exercised to their songs during gym class. She also remembers attending a Pochonbo Electronic Ensemble concert when they toured Japan. Upon entering high school, she was selected to learn the *So haegeum*, a North Korean fiddle,[18] directly from North Korean masters in Pyongyang during the summer breaks from school. Although she no longer considers herself a part of the North Korean aligned organization, her experiences with music at the Chongryon schools stayed with her long after she left, and whenever she heard a North Korean song, she felt a sense of excitement and nostalgia, thinking back to how easy it was to memorize the tune and the lyrics, and how friendly and intimate the songs felt.

In 2012, Unha came across the Moranbong Band demonstration performance described earlier in this chapter by way of *Youtube*, and reminisced about how even with the electronic strings and Japanese company instruments, their music was at its core the sound of North Korea that she was very familiar with. That same year, she joined Twitter and discovered a number of Japanese people who, like her, had recently become interested in the Moranbong Band. The male fans of the band outnumbered the female fans by far, so the few women who found each other felt a special connection and ended up meeting each other in person and on social media. It was these settings that sparked the idea to make costumes and learn the choreography.

The leader of Military First Girls is a Japanese woman in her 20s who, as a university student majoring in painting, came across North Korean propaganda art and grew interested in North Korean culture. She started the Military First Girls after gathering with women who had the same interests and ideas as her. In interviews they gave with reporters, they said they would talk about North Korea and practice dancing together. They held concerts, were featured in several domestic and international news outlets, and secured many fans of their own (Reuters Staff, 2017). With this case, we can get a sense of the image and perception of North Korea that some Japanese young people have even if it is a relatively small subculture. Lured by their initial curiosity, these fans have participated in such a fandom through identification with the band members as they engage in acts of imitation. The political perspective is excluded in the process, and the fandom that has emerged focuses on the music and choreography of a largely unknown culture.

The attention the band received also brought scrutiny and condemnation particularly from right-wing organizations in Japan, who have criticized this fandom phenomenon. As the members have communicated to the press, "Unfortunately, we often get asked questions like 'Isn't this anti-social behavior?' and 'Are you North Korean spies or defectors?'" (Reuters Staff, 2017). In response to such questions, the members of the Military First Girls said they were only interested in the cultural parts and did not support the North Korean system. They pointed out how they are similar to those who like K-Pop and the Korean Wave, saying, "You know how there are people who like K-pop and South Korea culture or who like Taylor Swift and copy her make-up. It's just like that but with North Korean culture" (Reuters Staff, 2017).

Ri Unha (2021) told us about the backlash she and the other members personally experienced:

> The situation got serious after we did our first interview with Chunichi News, and then the criticism got even worse after the Reuters article on us. One member ended up losing her job. The people who criticized us were deluded into

thinking we were propagandists for the Kim Jong Un regime even though it clearly said in the articles that we did not politically support the government.

In the time since the Military First Girls appeared in the press, their Twitter account has been deleted. Because of controversies like North Korean missile launches and Kim Jong Il's 2002 admission that North Korean agents had abducted Japanese nationals decades earlier, negative perceptions of North Korea have been widespread in Japan for quite some time; there may be limits to how far a fandom for a North Korean music group can spread as a result of the political circumstances. We can say then that the practice of imitating or following North Korean culture to the point of fandom can become a burdensome act and is thus a "curtailed fandom." This indicates how the scope of fandom of a North Korean music group cannot help but be bound to the political circumstances of each country.

Still, the Japanese fandom of North Korean music (not just of Moranbong Band but earlier acts like Pochonbo Electronic Ensemble too) has not been stamped out. In an informal survey conducted in early 2021 with DPRK music aficionados whom Unha reached out to, a number of the respondents said they found the music to be an alternative to commercialized J-pop; some also found it preferable to K-pop. There was some interest in the group members' physical appearance and in their fashion expressed by male and female fans, respectively, but a more prevalent reason expressed for liking DPRK music was that it had modern music arrangements with electronic sounds while at the same time managed to retain some familiar music idioms of past forms of music such as *enka*, *trot*, or even Japanese military music. One female respondent used the term "newtro," a term she said was South Korean, to describe the mix of new and retro elements in the music that she found appealing.

North Korean music has played a role in reducing social distance between Japanese fans of North Korean music and members of the Chongryon community through joint meetings and events. Ri Unha (2021) told us that although some Japanese people have attended Chongryon music events for quite some time, it is only recently that members of this community have been a part of the karaoke parties and other music appreciation events that Japanese fans have organized. In these settings (of around 30–40 people), the Japanese fans have asked the North Korean residents about their life circumstances, their culture, and fashion trends. Although there are still just a small number of Japanese people that are part of these cross-cultural interactions, Unha believes this emerging phenomenon is a promising development that can counter Japanese stereotypes of Zainichi Koreans as spies or criminals and also help Chongryon members expand their social connections outside of their exclusive, tight-knit communities.

CONCLUSION

As a result of the economic crisis caused by the North Korean famine, the spontaneous emergence of the unofficial market known as the *jangmadang* served as a major channel for external information, and various media including *Hallyu* content began to flow into the DPRK. To adapt to the changing tastes of the population resulting from this inflow, North Korean music groups administered by the state took on features of global music such as simultaneous dancing and singing, which is confirmation that the state intended to incorporate a number of trends of global popular music into its cultural production.

This intentional change in North Korean music witnessed since Kim Jong Un became leader has taken place at the same time as the explosive international popularity of K-pop; in some ways, the public response to it has run parallel to K-pop's international reception even if on a much smaller scale. In the process of the spread, patterns of consumption of the Moranbong Band in North Korea, China, and Japan can be detected. The consumption patterns in North Korea have not been free from the political nature of the state's role in administering cultural production and dissemination; however, the fandoms that emerged in China and Japan started as fan appreciation, and the political aspects of the music have been superseded by the simple enjoyment of the cultural experience.

The exposure to and perceptions of North Korean culture are different depending on the political circumstances of each country. In Japan, much of the public opinion regarding the Moranbong Band fandom has been negative with criticism that fans are political supporters of the North Korean regime. In South Korea as well, the practice of following North Korean culture to the point of fandom can be considered taboo and has become a burdensome act due to ROK censorship measures like the National Security Act.[19] Nevertheless, as the case of Japan demonstrates, the pattern of cultural consumption through imitation demonstrates that North Korean music can be excluded from politics and accepted purely as culture. Moreover, while men outnumber women in the online fandom communities outside North Korea (according to the respondents we spoke with), women have taken important roles in stimulating interest in them including being interviewed for this work. In North Korea, too, women are among the most avid consumers of Moranbong Band music (as evidenced by their audience participation and following the fashion trends of the members), suggesting an appeal of the music that is not merely driven by the sexualization of the band members and their exotic nature. As for the male fans, we were not able to conduct any first-hand interviews with them, so more research should be conducted to learn more about what may be driving their interest.

Hallyu is currently in a paradigm shift, which, as the Korea Creative Content Agency (2019) calls for, involves a transformation from its conventional purpose of entering and dominating overseas markets into a cultural phenomenon aimed at promoting mutual interests and shared economic growth. One way to do that may be to harness the worldwide curiosity people have about North Korea and engage in cultural exchange and joint recording ventures with North Korean performance artists. While a negotiation process with North Korean authorities about appropriate songs to promote and other matters would undoubtedly be challenging, extending an invitation to the North for this kind of initiative would set an example for openness to and acceptance of foreign music. It could be too late to do this with the Moranbong Band, for they may have become a thing of the past. At the 2020 New Year's Concert, they were not the headliner act, and at the 2021 New Year's Concert, they did not even appear. However, there may be international interest in more recently formed singing ensembles such as a male Popera-style trio that performed at the 8th Party Congress in early 2021 (KCTV, 2021).

The fundamental debate on whether or not North Korean culture tied to politics can be considered art is bound to continue. Along with this, there are still many discussions about whether the flow of change in North Korea can act as part of a global culture, and whether the new cultural flow unique to North Korea, newly transformed partially in response to the Korean Wave, can coexist with and be consumed in the international community as part of a New Korean Wave. Through these discussions, we can grasp how North Korea will come into contact with other waves of culture through an inflow, acculturation/appropriation, and dissemination/diffusion process. This is why we should keep paying attention to future developments in North Korean music.

NOTES

1. This research was supported by the 2020 Academic Exchange Support Program for North Korean and Unification Studies at the Institute for Far Eastern Studies, Kyungnam University.

2. See for instance: No and Mok (2018)

3. In its early days, the Wangjaesan Light Music Band included dance routines, but with the light music band label, they showcased their light music aspects more than their dance routines. However, in 2011, they were reorganized as the Wangjaesan Art Troupe and became exclusively a dance performance group. See: Ha (2019, 18)

4. This way of listening to music has been particularly popular with university age students who prefer it to the passive form of consuming music on the television, which as Lu learned, has recently been associated with old people.

5. Korhonen (2019) in particular, has been a pioneer of this Pyongyangology analytical approach having started a website "Moranbong Band Discography," where he keeps track of Moranbong Band performances and gleans as much information about the performers as possible based on the videos of the performances and photographic data from other sources.

6. While we have permission from all the named and unnamed interviewees to document their responses, we believe it is best to only identify the locations and dates of the interviews with the named sources.

7. As of February 2018, there were reportedly 482 of these official *jangmadang* markets (Jo 2019).

8. While North Korean music has exhibited features of global forms of pop music in terms of composition and performance since the 1980s, its primary purpose continues to be for propaganda as it is administered by the propaganda and agitation department of the Central Committee of the Workers' Party of Korea. The term "propaganda pop" captures both its stylistic features and its function.

9. KCNA (2000).

10. While the concert atmosphere in Pyongyang prior to this point was not exactly stoic (thunderous applause and clapping to the beat were common before and still are), seemingly unrestrained acts like waving one's hands in the air, cheering at the performers midway through the song, and spontaneously getting out of one's seat to dance in the aisles are all acts that the researchers of this chapter have not encountered in videos of concerts prior to this one. For comparative reference, see: KCTV (2012a).

11. See Howard (2020, 241–244) for more on this notion of "authorized pop."

12. Lim (2017, 605) also uses the term "normalization" to refer to the use of the music groups for the 7th Workers' Party Congress in May 2016. He makes this determination not only on the fact that the two presumably rival acts of Moranbong and Chongbong were playing together but also a picture was taken of Moranbong Band members watching the Chongbong Band performance with Kim Jong Un and his wife (thus portraying a lack of tension between the two bands). In looking at not only Moranbong Band but also Music Politics in the Kim Jong Un era, we believe that the resumption of sending North Korean musicians abroad was a more critical signal of a stabilization in how North Korean propaganda pop bands would be deployed (particularly when following a phases of localization and standardization). While the Moranbong's absorption into joint performances with the more traditional State Merited Chorus was certainly a feature of the normalization process, there is the possibility that the rivalry between Moranbong Band and Chongbong Band has been overstated.

13. The interview responses start at 6:29 of a KBS program video (KBS News, 2018).

14. The interview response starts at 6:54 of a KBS program video (KBS News, 2018).

15. For instance, one of the Chinese respondents reported that the year she was in North Korea, the number of students the Chinese government sent was more than both the number the Russian government sent that year and the handful of students from other places like Laos, Canada, and France who were all self-funded.

16. *Hallyu* was introduced to China in the late 1990s. In the 2000s, the Chinese media started to use the term *Hallyu*, and from then on, Chinese interest in Korean pop culture intensified. See: Sohn (2009).

17. The term "Otaku" has been used in Japan since around the 1980s to refer to people who have deep obsessions or knowledge about particular things but lack social skills or social connections in certain respects. While its connotation is typically negative, the designation has been normalized to some extent to refer to those with niche interests such as particular Manga (comics) or Anime (animations). See: Galbraith (2019).

18. The *so haegeum* is a four-stringed soprano version of a number of updated versions of the Korean traditional fiddle, the two-stringed *haegeum*. Both the modified *so haegeum* and the original *haegeum* are played while sitting down. For more, see: Howard (2020, 78-87).

19. Chapter 2, Article 7 of the National Security Act of South Korea, states "Any person who praises, incites or propagates the activities of an anti-government organization, a member thereof or of the person who has received an order from it, or who acts in concert with it, or propagates or instigated a rebellion against the State, with the knowledge of the fact that it may endanger the existence and security of the State or democratic fundamental order, shall be punished by imprisonment for not more than seven years." North Korea is officially considered an anti-government organization in the South Korean legal code. Accordingly, access to North Korean websites in the Republic of Korea is blocked as illegal and harmful information sites, and the act of delivering information such as North Korean songs, movies, and broadcasts is prohibited (Korean Ministry of Government Legislation, 2020).

BIBLIOGRAPHY

Ahn, J. and Ju, H. (2017). 자본주의 미디어가 사회주의 국가의 주민들에게 미친 영향에 관한 연구 : 동독과 북한비교를 중심으로 [The Influence of Capitalist Media on Socialist Residents: A Comparative Focus on East Germany and North Korea]. 한독사회과학논총, 27 (2), 55–86.

Channel A (2017). 벤츠 버스 타고 공연 다니는 모란봉악단, 무대 뒷모습 공개 [A Backstage Look at the Moranbong Band Who Rides a Mercedes-Benz Bus and Attends a Performance]. *YouTube Video*,10:53, November 28, https://www.youtube.com/watch?v=5JJL6Chj2r0

Denyer, S. and Kim, M. (2019). How K-pop Is Luring Young North Koreans to Cross the Line. *Washington Post*, August 23, http://www.washingtonpost.com/world /asia_pacific/how-k-pop-is-tempting-young-north-koreans-to-cross-the-line/2019 /08/19/0f984654-839f-11e9-b585-e36b16a531aa_story.html

Fahy, S. (2019). *Dying for Rights: Putting North Korea's Human Rights Abuses on the Record*. New York: Columbia University Press.

Fiske, J. (1992). The Cultural Economy of Fandom. In *The Adoring Audience: Fan Culture and Popular Media*, edited by Lisa A. Lewis, 30–49. London: Routledge.

Galbraith, P. (2019). *Otaku and the Struggle for Imagination in Japan*. Durham, NC: Duke University Press.

Ha, S. (2019). North Korean musical groups: History and development (1945~2018). PhD diss. (in Korean), University of North Korean Studies.

Haggard, S. and Noland, M. (2007). *Famine in North Korea: Markets, Aid, and Reform*. New York: Columbia University Press.

Howard, K. (2020). *Songs for "Great Leaders": Ideology and Creativity in North Korean Music and Dance*. New York: Oxford University Press.

Jeon, Y. (2007). 김정일 시대 통치스타일로서 '음악정치' ["Music Politics" as a Ruling Style of the Kim Jong Il Era]. 현대북한연구, 10 (1), 51–85.

Jeon, Y. and Han, S. 2018. NK POP: 북한의 전자음악과 대중음악 *[NK Pop: North Korean Electronic Music and Popular Music]*. Seoul: 글누림.

Jo, S. (2019). '김정은 시대' 북한, 성장과 붕괴가 동시 진행 ["Kim Jong Un's Era" North Korea is Growing and Collapsing at the Same Time]. *Inews*, February 13, http://www.inews24.com/view/1157453.

Kang, D. (2018). 김정은의 음악정치: 모란봉악단 김정은을 말하다. *[Kim Jong Un's Music Politics: The Moranbong Band Says Kim Jong Un]*. Busan: 나드리.

Kang, D. and Park J. (2012). 한류 통일의 바람 *[The Wind of Korean Wave Unification]*. Seoul: 명인문화사.

KBS News. (2018). [클로즈업 북한] 다양해진 北 음악 공연…그 의미는? [Close-up North Korea: What Is the Meaning of North Korean Music Performances that Have Become More Diverse]. 남북의 창 *[Window into Inter-Korea]*, November 24, https://news.kbs.co.kr/news/view.do?ncd=4080835

KCNA (2000). 영도자의 노래정치 [The Leader's Song Politics], May 29.

KCNA (2020). 조선민주주의인민공화국 최고인민회의 상임위원회 제13기 제12차 전원회의 진행. [The First and Second Plenary Meeting of the 14th Standing Committee of the Supreme People's Assembly of the Democratic People's Republic of Korea]. December 5.

KCTV (2012a). [Concert] Unhasu Orchestra Concert on KCU Anniversary (June 6, 2012) {DPRK Music}, *YouTube Video*, 1:24:43, from a performance televised on June 9, posted by "dprkconcert," June 9, https://www.youtube.com/watch?v=XhEdDoecKNo

KCTV (2012b). 경애하는 김정은동지를 모시고 진행한 모란봉악단 시범공연 [The Moranbong Band Demonstration Concert That Has Proceeded with the Esteemed Comrade Kim Jong-un], *YouTube Video*, 1:40:10, from a performance televised on July 6, posted by "Samhero," July 12, https://www.youtube.com/watch?v=DaB8tZT591s

KCTV (2016). We Love- Moranbong Band & Chongbong Band (2016-05). *YouTube Video*, 9:39, from a performance televised on May 11, posted by "Kenny Kim," May 17, https://www.youtube.com/watch?v=-Fm-QATrYWg

KCTV (2019). Moranbong Band - New Year Performance Medley. *YouTube Video*, 5:02, from a performance on January 1, posted by "Moranbong Band," January 1, https://www.youtube.com/watch?v=Jlv5vQwVBg8

KCTV (2021). 北朝鮮「党に捧げる頌歌 (당에 드리는 송가)」KCTV 2021/01/25 日本語字幕付き. [North Korea's "Hymn to the Party" KCTV January 25, 2021 Japanese subtitles], *YouTube Video*, 6:17, from a performance on January 25, posted by "dprknow," January 27, https://www.youtube.com/watch?v=lcNf1zr4bAA

Kim, J. and Yoon, S. (2019). 북한 '장마당'의 변화과정에 대한 진화론적 분석 [An Evolution Analysis of the Process of Changing the "Jangmadang" in North Korea] 사회과학연구, 45 (3), 83–105.

Korea Creative Content Agency. (2019). 한류의 패러다임 전환을 위한 신한류 확산 전략 연구 *[A Paradigm Shift in the Korean Wave: Focusing on Cultural Diffusion Strategies of the "New Korean Wave"]*. Naju: Korea Creative Content Agency.

Korea Ministry of Government Legislation (2020). Accessed December 5, https://www.law.go.kr/LSW/lsInfoP.do?efYd=20170707&lsiSeq=179033#0000

Korhonen, P. (2019). Moranbong Band Discography. *Wordpress*, Last Updated January 1, https://morandisco.wordpress.com

Korhonen, P. and Cathcart, A. Tradition and Legitimation in North Korea: The role of the Moranbong Band. *The Review of Korean Studies*, 20 (2), 7–32.

Korhonen, P. and Mori, T. (2020). The Samjiyon Orchestra as a North Korean Means for Gender Based Cultural Diplomacy. *European Journal of Korean Studies*, 19 (2), 57–82.

Kretchun, N. and Kim, J. (2012). *A Quiet Opening: North Koreans in a Changing Media Environment*. Washington, DC: Intermedia. https://www.gwern.net/docs/technology/2012-kretchun.pdf

Lim, T. (2017). State-Endorsed Popular Culture: A case study of the North Korean girl band Moranbong. *Asia & the Pacific Policy Studies*, 4 (3), 602–612.

Lu, J. (2019). Music Policy During Kim Jong Un's North Korea Administration: Focusing on Moranbong Band, MA Thesis (in Korean), Hongik University.

Lu, J. (2020). Interview by Peter Moody. Personal interview with email follow-up. Seoul, June 7.

Mazierska, E. (2016). Introduction. In *Popular Music in Eastern Europe: Breaking the Cold War Paradigm*, edited by Mazierska, E., 1–27. London: Palgrave Macmillan.

MediaVOP (2018). 북한 댄스가요 '달려가자 미래로' 서울공연 고화질. [North Korea dance song "Dash to the Future" Seoul Performance High Definition], *YouTube Video*, 3:02, from a performance on February 8, posted by "MediaVOP," February 16, https://www.youtube.com/watch?v=M3wQM_ypPpQ

Mokran Video DPRK (2013a). Moranbong Band - Let New Year's Snow Fall. *YouTube Video*, 4:54, from a performance on January 1, posted by "Moranbong Band HD," December 29, 2018, https://www.youtube.com/watch?v=rVsaOYZl3E0

Mokran Video DPRK (2013b). Moranbong Band – Tansume. YouTube Video, 6:37, January 1, posted by "Morangbong Band HD," April 21, 2018, https://www.youtube.com/watch?v=FUjqYfyvynQ

Mokran Video DPRK (2014). A Moranbong Band Concert with New Works. *YouTube Video*, 48:27, from a performance on September 4, posted by "Moranbong Band HD," September 15, 2019, https://www.youtube.com/watch?v=mcKbfRqjtU8

No, J. and Mok, Y. (2018). [평창에서] 북 예술단, 북한정권 선전곡 '달려가자 미래로' 공연 [In Pyeongchang, a North Korean art troupe, the North Korean regime's propaganda song "Dash to the Future" performance]. *Radio Free Asia*,

February 2, https://www.rfa.org/korean/in_focus/nkperform-02082018092445 .html

Oh, G. (2014). 평양 걸그룹 모란봉 악단 *[The Pyongyang Girl Group Moranbong Band]*. Goyang: 지식공감.

Pearson, J. (2015). Portable media players give North Koreans an illicit window on the world". *The Guardian*, March 28, https://www.theguardian.com/world/2015/ mar/28/north-korea-internet-notel

Perlez, J. (2015). "Mystery cloaks North Korean pop band's canceled Beijing dates. *The Orange County Register*, December 22, https://www.ocregister.com/2015/12 /22/mystery-cloaks-north-korean-pop-bands-canceled-beijing-dates/

Reuters staff. (2017). 日本の北朝鮮ファンクラブ、「先軍女子」がダンス披露 [Japan's North Korean Fanclub the Military First Girls perform a dance]. *Reuters*, November 6, https://jp.reuters.com/article/idJPKBN1D60XQ

Ri, Uni (2021). Interview by Peter Moody. WeChat email with email follow-up, February 5.

Roudometof, V. (2018). "Recovering the local: From glocalization to localization". *Current Sociology*, 67 (6), 801–807.

Seo, M. 중국산 '노트텔' [The Chinese Product, the Notel]. *Yonhap News*, October 22, https://news.naver.com/main/read.nhn?mode=LSD&mid=sec&sid1=102&oid =001&aid=0006551829

Sohn, Seunghye. 학술 논문의 메타분석을 통해본 한류 10년 : 연구 경향과 그 정책적 함의에 대한 탐색적 연구 [Ten years of Hallyu, the 'Korean Wave' - What we have learned about it]. 사단법인 언론과 사회, 17 (4), 122–153.

Yabe, A. (2021). [@arthuryabe_mrb]. 모란봉악단 애호회 일본지부 [Moranbong Band Fan Club, Japan Branch]. *Twitter*, September 24, 2014, https://twitter.com/ arthuryabe_mrb, Accessed February 16.

Chapter 3

Diasporic Koreanness in *Kim's Convenience*

Kyong Yoon

INTRODUCTION

"Representation matters." Paul Sun-Hyung Lee, star of the popular Canadian Broadcasting Corporation (CBC) TV sitcom *Kim's Convenience* (2016–2021), made this statement in his acceptance speech at the 2018 Canadian Screen Awards, where he won Best Lead Actor in a Comedy. Upon winning the award for the second time, following the previous year's surprise, Lee stated, "I need to say that representation matters. I think a show like *Kim's Convenience* has proved that representation matters." He then added, "When communities and people see themselves reflected up on the screens, it is an inspiring and very powerful moment for them. Because it means they've moved from the margins into the forefront." Wearing a black pin in solidarity with the #AfterMeToo campaign, Lee noted how representation can empower marginalized people: "It gives them a voice. It gives them hope. Hope is a very empowering thing because it inspires people. When you give people a voice, other people start listening. When people start listening, things start to change. And we need change."

Lee's statement matters. The short yet powerful speech seemed to reveal what had been missing in Canadian media. Indeed, as can be inferred from Lee's urge for change, mainstream Canadian media has until recently paid minimal attention to Asian Canadians' lives. *Kim's Convenience* is the first-ever Canadian sitcom led by an Asian cast (Hunt, 2016). The show quickly became popular and critically acclaimed, and in 2018, the second season won the award for the Best Comedy Series at the Canadian Screen Awards. This prime time sitcom reminded audiences that Asian Canadian voices have long been absent from the Canadian mediascape and how deep-rooted stereotypical representations of Asians in the Western media can be reappropriated and negotiated.

Both audiences and critics consider the success of *Kim's Convenience* to be a meaningful moment of the cultural recognition of Asians in Western media (e.g., Hsu, 2019). But how is the show relevant to the ongoing discussion about the global waves of South Korean (Korean, hereafter) popular culture overseas—*Hallyu*—and its reproduction and negotiation of stereotypes? Given the definition of *Hallyu* as waves of *Korean* popular culture, *Kim's Convenience*—a made-in-Canada cultural product—may not strictly seem to belong to the category. However, while this show is a Canadian product by nationality, it is still a cultural text that addresses an important, yet often neglected, aspect of Koreanness—the Korean diaspora. In this regard, this chapter suggests that the diasporic cultural identity represented in *Kim's Convenience* offers momentum that diversifies the Koreanness narrowly defined in the dominant discourse of *Hallyu*.[1]

As several scholars argue, studies of *Hallyu* should move beyond their nationalist discourse, in which the research focus is primarily on the transnational flows of made-in-Korea cultural products (Fuhr, 2016; Joo, 2011; Jin, Yoon, and Min, 2021; Won, 2017). Drawing on cultural nationalism, the dominant discourse of *Hallyu* has tended to reduce the cultural waves to the overseas penetration of Korean products that contributes to the country's national branding or promotion. In this regard, *Kim's Convenience* constitutes an alternative mode of *Hallyu* that includes heterogeneous voices, such as those of diasporic Koreans. The show's storytelling about and by diasporic Koreans may be different from that of the conventional *Hallyu* texts, such as K-pop, Korean TV dramas (K-dramas), and webtoons. Moreover, *Kim's Convenience* is produced in the context of Canadian media industry (CBC), while being circulated globally through the U.S.-based mega-platform Netflix.[2]

This globally circulated Canadian show has not been detached from *Hallyu*; it can be situated in the discourse of the *Hallyu* diaspora, in which diasporic flows of popular culture are produced and consumed among Koreans overseas (Yoon, 2020). The diasporic imagination of Koreanness may in turn affect the directions and diversity of the global flows of *Hallyu* by dismantling the celebratory discourse of the global expansion of the once-peripheral Korean cultural industries.

STORIES OF KOREAN DIASPORAS

Kim's Convenience is based on the highly acclaimed play of the same title written by Korean Canadian Ins Choi. Raised in Toronto, Choi developed this play based on his experiences as a child whose immigrant Korean family lived above a convenience store run by his uncle (Hunt, 2016). After acclaimed performances, the play was developed by Vancouver-based Thunderbird Films and CBC and was co-created by Ins Choi and Canadian writer/producer Kevin White as a 13-episode prime time sitcom for CBC that aired at 9:00 p.m. every Tuesday (except for the finale, which aired at 8:00 p.m.). The show tells the story of the Kims, a Korean immigrant family that runs a convenience store in downtown Toronto. Each episode revolves around family members Mr. and Mrs. Kim (played by Paul Sun-Hyung Lee and Jean Yoon), who immigrated in the 1980s; their grown-up children Jung and Janet who were born and raised in Canada (played by Simu Liu and Andrea Bang);[3] and their neighbors and colleagues.

The show engages with the identity and history of first-generation Korean Canadians and their children. According to Kim, Noh, and Noh (2012), the first groups of permanent Korean migrants settled in Canada in the 1960s, after the Canadian government established diplomatic relations with South Korea (1963). It was not until 1973 that Canada began to receive a sizable number of Korean migrants; since the 1970s, the Korean Canadian community has slowly grown (Kim, Noh, and Noh, 2012). According to the latest census data (Statistics Canada, 2016), 198,210 people identified their ethnic origin as Korean, while 153,425 people identified Korean as their mother tongue.

The story of the Kims is not different from that of many Korean immigrant families in the United States and Canada. The show depicts the parents' dedication to their small business 365 days a year, as well as their close relationship to their ethnic community. Mr. and Mrs. Kim sometimes reveal a traditional perspective on the family and the children's career, which might be derived from the 1980s' Korean society from which they emigrated. For example, Mrs. Kim seems to maintain a narrow definition of the ideal career and marriage for their children, as shown in her dissatisfaction about Jung's job (an employee at a car rental office) and her call for candidates to be Janet's boyfriend among those who are Korean and Christian. Meanwhile, Mr. Kim sometimes reveals his Confucian mindset. When arguing with Janet who has asked him to appreciate her art works, Mr. Kim exclaims vehemently, "You is my work. Me and Umma [i.e. Mr. and Mrs. Kim] is struggle to make whole life for you" (Season 1, Episode 2: "Janet's Photos").

The parents' lifestyle and attitudes are contrasted with their children's pursuit of engagement with the general, non-ethnic economy and communities. Raised in Canada, Janet and Jung appear to be uninterested in taking over the convenience store business at least until the last season of the show; instead, they seek professional occupations. Twenty-year-old Janet, an art school student, wants to be a professional photographer while helping to run her parents' business in her free time. She lives in the parental home, which is located above the convenience store, but by the end of Season 1, she is seeking to leave it and live in her own rented apartment with her friends. On several occasions, Mr. Kim attempts to teach Janet how to run the store, assuming that it might be taken over by his children after his retirement, but neither child seems interested in pursuing this path. For example, Janet complains about her unpaid domestic labor and seeks independence from her parents, while stating, "running the store isn't exactly my dream" (Season 1, Episode 2: "Janet's Photos"). In response, Mr. Kim clarifies his interest in handing the store over to his children, saying, "If you work very hard, one day I sell to you store" (Season 4, Episode 11: "Birds of Feathers").

Just like Janet, Jung too is not interested in the continuation of the convenience store as a family business—at least until the show's finale. Janet's older brother Jung does not get along with the family's patriarch Mr. Kim as he ran away from home, dropped out of school, and got into petty street crime, which ended with his short-term stay in juvenile detention. While putting his past behind him, Jung (now in his mid-20s) works hard as an employee at a car rental office. Despite his hard work and enthusiasm, Jung struggles with advancing his career because of his past record. In the show's finale (Season 5, Episode 13: "Friends and Family"), having just completed business courses and seeking better job opportunities, Jung laments, "Now I'm back wiping windshields at Handyland (i.e. referring to his car rental company Handy)." To encourage him, his sister Janet suggests that Mr. and Mrs. Kim invite him to give a presentation on future development plans for the Kim's convenience store. Following the presentation, Mr. Kim, whose tension with Jung has significantly lessened throughout the progress of the show, offers Jung the opportunity to take over the store—an offer that Jung appears to be willing to consider. As shown in this finale, taking over and furthering the development of the family's small business is presented as a gesture of generational reconciliation. While the children of first-generation Korean immigrants tend to prefer to participate in mainstream economy over inheriting a business from their parents (Min and Noh, 2014), continuation of parental businesses can be an option for second-generation Korean Canadians and a way to understand the first generation's legacies.[4]

Due to several factors, such as language and cultural barriers, Korean immigrants have tended to open their own small businesses, such as groceries, convenience stores, dry cleaners, and restaurants, rather than pursuing the occupations they used to have in Korea (Chan and Fong, 2012). Despite being relatively highly educated (compared with the overall Canadian population), the average income of Korean Canadians is far lower than that of the average Canadian (Park, 2012). This decades-long trend of occupational adjustment, which is often accompanied by underemployment, can be summarized in the phrase "from white-collar occupations to small business" (Min, 1984). Self-employment is almost exclusive to first-generation Korean immigrants who were born in Korea and immigrated after their childhood, while Canadian-born Koreans are mostly wage and salary earners (Chan and Fong, 2012).

Kim's Convenience captures the lives of Korean immigrant families by comically engaging with the settings of a downtown convenience store and an ethnic Korean church, both of which are often considered landmark components of Korean Canadian communities—especially first-generation immigrants. Until recently, of all forms of small businesses, the convenience store was a popular entrepreneurial choice for Korean immigrants (Ju, 2018). In the show, Mr. Kim, who used to be a teacher in Korea, could not continue his career in Canada, and seems to lament his underemployment after immigration. In one episode, to show customers his former professional career as a teacher in Korea, Mr. Kim displays his teacher certificate behind the checkout desk in the convenience store. He complains that people only see him as a shopkeeper (Season 4, Episode 3: "The Help"). In addition to the convenience store as a symbolic location of immigrants' underemployment and struggles, ethnic churches have played a significant role in Korean Canadian community development. Thus, a Korean Canadian church appears as the main (if not the only) site of Mr. and Mrs. Kim's social lives in *Kim's Convenience*. The diasporic Koreans' involvement in Korean churches is "a way to assert a distinctive Korean religious and therefore cultural identity, not a way to assimilate into" the host society (Baker, 2008).

The show introduces Korean Canadians and other Asian Canadians (e.g., the two Asian characters Mr. Chin and Mr. Mehta, who are Mr. and Mrs. Kim's close neighbors) into the mainstream popular culture. The presence and recognition of Asians in the show is significant, as Asian Canadians are positioned as storytellers and as "us" rather than as the "others" of white storytellers and audiences. The success of *Kim's Convenience* also reminds us that the incorporation of diasporic Koreans' stories into the recent *Hallyu* discourse has been limited. Among the various cultural forces and voices associated with *Hallyu*, the involvement of diasporic Korean or non-Korean talents in cultural production requires further discussion. As shown in the K-pop industry, diasporic Koreans and Asians play an increasingly important role as content creators and consumers, but their stories are not being integrated to a significant extent into mainstream *Hallyu* content.[5] Diasporic talents, such as second-generation Korean musicians, are consumed in the context of the dominant discourse of Koreanness in the *Hallyu* industry (Fuhr, 2016). In this regard, the diasporic storytelling in *Kim's Convenience* may offer insights into how the dominant Koreanness can be questioned through diversified storytellers who are not Korean-born Koreans.

THE RECEPTION OF DIASPORIC COMEDY

Kim's Convenience emerged as a popular primetime TV series in Canada
and then attracted global attention. With an average audience of 933,000 in
Canada, the show was the third most-watched CBC program in 2016, just
behind the two long-run hit shows *Murdoch Mysteries* and *Heartland* (Reid,
2016) and has thus continued with successive seasons. Most reviewers have
acclaimed the show and highly evaluated its refreshing, heartwarming, come-
dic family subject, and ensemble performance.

Kim's Convenience's nationwide success has brought it to overseas audiences, including South Korea, through Netflix since 2018, and rave reviews
have followed. For example, *The New York Times* stated succinctly, "The
show is single-camera comedy, but it has the gentle warmth and slower
pace of a multicamera show. If you miss when *Modern Family* was good,
try this" (Lyons, 2018). In this way, *Kim's Convenience* was compared with
the relatively original early seasons of the praised American sitcom *Modern
Family*, which depicted American families from various backgrounds. In the
Canadian TV industry, in which original content has been lacking due to the
dominance of American content (Mirrlees, 2019), the emerging global popularity of *Kim's Convenience* is noteworthy.

The global success of *Kim's Convenience*, which might be coincidental
with the rise of Korean popular culture in overseas markets, has sometimes
caused the show to be associated with the discourse of *Hallyu*, especially
by Korean-based or ethnic Korean media. The Korean media, as well as the
Korean Canadian media, paid considerable attention to the show, especially
in 2019 when it began to air in Korea and the lead cast was invited to the
Seoul Drama Awards. Broadcast television and several national newspapers
reported the main cast's press conference in Seoul, while a TV entertainment
news program (*Section TV* by Munhwa Broadcasting Corporation) aired a
separate special interview with the three lead actors—Paul Sun-Hyung Lee,
Jean Yoon, and Andrea Bang. The Korean news media introduced *Kim's
Convenience* as a successful TV show that was contributing to the global
recognition of Korean culture. In fact, due to the show's success and the
need to inform the audiences about South Korea (the host country of the
PyeongChang Winter Olympic Games in 2018), the CBC produced an information program in which *Kim's Convenience* star Andrea Bang traveled to
Korea to experience the country in 2018. The Canadian national newspaper
The Star invited the two leads, Lee and Yoon, to demonstrate how to cook
the Korean foods *kimchi bokkeumbap* (kimchi fried rice) and *kongnamul
muchim* (seasoned soybean sprouts) in the newspaper's food section and on
its YouTube channel (Liu, 2020).

While the majority of Korean media reports briefly introduced the show as a global hit, giving it favorable reviews, some analyses indicated that it was an unexpected *Hallyu* item or a cultural item that could promote Korean culture overseas. For example, a Korean government agency's report included *Kim's Convenience* as an example of *Hallyu* in Canada, stating that "The Canadian public broadcaster's popular sitcom *Kim's Convenience* has effects to promote Korean foods and culture in Canada" (Korea Foundation, 2020). Moreover, referring to the show's success, another report published by a Korean government-funded agency suggested that Korean cultural content should be more customized to different local audiences while also considering diasporic Korean audiences (Bang, 2018). Similarly, an article published by another government-funded agency noted that the show offered insights into how Korean media industries should produce more culturally diverse content (Lee, 2018). These reports defined *Kim's Convenience* as an example of *Hallyu* or at least an item that facilitates the *Hallyu* phenomenon.

As *Kim's Convenience* portrays immigrant Korean families, various forms of Korean cultural customs, foods, and brands are naturally incorporated into the show's narratives. Interestingly, despite the show's frequent references to Korean culture in general, recent forms of Korean popular culture, such as K-pop, drama, and films, do not explicitly appear, except for a few passing occasions. In particular, there are few references to indicate that the younger Korean characters (Janet, Jung, and Kimchee) in the show are immersed in Korean pop culture, especially compared to their parents who are portrayed as regular Korean TV viewers.

In the show, references to Korean pop culture, albeit limited, emerge primarily in relation to Mr. and Mrs. Kim—the first-generation immigrants. For instance, in one episode (Season 2, Episode 9: "New TV"), Mr. Kim brings home a newly purchased high-definition TV set, saying to his wife who is disappointed that she was not consulted: "Think about Korean drama in HDR! [i.e. High Dynamic Range TV, which is an advanced version of high density TV]." In another episode (Season 3, Episode 4: "Thy Neighbor's Wifi"), Korean Canadian women's viewing of Korean dramas is portrayed in detail. In the episode, when the Kims' Wi-Fi is temporarily out of operation, Mrs. Kim is worried about the probable interruption of her viewing a cliffhanger type Korean drama. Later in the episode, when the Wi-Fi is repaired, Mrs. Kim, along with two other Korean women and Latin Canadian pastor Nina, view the drama in the Kims' living room without subtitles. Pastor Nina, whom Mrs. Kim invited only "to be polite," apparently does not understand the drama's Korean-written conversations yet seems very excited about the drama. This sequence comically portrays how appealing Korean drama could be to diasporic Koreans and non-Korean viewers of color as well.

Kim's Convenience implies generational differences in the diasporic consumption of Korean popular culture. That is, the parents who are first-generation immigrants may routinely access and consume the media of their left-behind home country in a relatively traditional format (TV drama) rather than newer genres, such as K-pop. In comparison, the children (i.e., the second generation) may not particularly be interested in Korean popular culture. The generational differences may resonate with Yoon's (2017, 2019) findings. According to the studies, in their leisure time and even during their work hours at their small businesses, first-generation Korean immigrants habitually and often exclusively consume a vast amount of Korean content. Small business–running Korean immigrants frequently access Korean TV via the Internet, but sometimes during their small business work hours they have Canadian TV and radio programs turned on as a kind of "white noise" (Yoon, 2017). Prior to the introduction of Internet streaming video services, groceries, and supermarkets in Korean neighborhoods offered rental services of VHS recorded Korean TV shows (Yoon, 2019). In comparison, younger Korean Canadians' consumption of Korean popular cultural items is selective rather than inherited or habitual (Yoon, 2019).

It should be noted that *Kim's Convenience* is written and performed by second-generation Koreans and thus their perspective rather than the first generation's might be incorporated more explicitly into the show. In particular, creator and co-writer Ins Choi's experiences are more similar to those of the children (Jung and Janet) in the show. In addition, the actors cast as Mr. and Mrs. Kim (Paul Sun-Hyung Lee and Jean Yoon) and their children (Andrea Bang and Simu Liu) grew up in Canada as the second generation with limited exposure to the contemporary popular culture of their ancestral homeland. In several interviews, Paul Sun-Hyung Lee notes that he tried to keep away from Korean culture to "fit in" when he was young: "When you're a kid and you're really trying to fit in, you push away everything that reminds you of your family because your family is different" (Lee, 2016). This tendency of avoiding the culture of their ancestral homeland is commonly observed among some second-generation young people (Kibria, 2003). For example, in Yoon's (2019) study of Korean Canadian youth, a second-generation college student who grew up in white-dominant neighborhoods notes: "I wanted to fit in, so I had no choice but to avoid the whole K-pop [phenomenon] and listen to what my other friends were listening to, which was like just Western pop instead of K-pop."

Recent Korean pop culture is even critically (if not stereotypically) depicted through the eyes of younger characters in a few episodes. For example, in one episode (Season 1, Episode 4: "Frank and Nayoung"), Janet meets with her cousin Nayoung, a young Korean woman visiting Toronto. Janet seems embarrassed by Nayoung's behaviors, which are depicted somewhat stereotypically in the show. Nayoung is depicted as a grown-up who is wearing excessively cute dress and makeup, and makes certain gestures observed in Korean pop culture (e.g., forming the finger–heart symbol, which is a cliché in K-dramas, and taking selfies frequently, which is a common stereotype of Asian tourists). While the depiction of Nayoung as an otaku-like (a pop and consumer culture obsessed person) figure is problematic for some viewers, the occasional, yet exaggerated, characterization of Koreans from Korea (e.g., Korean travelers) in the show—Nayoung in particular—may serve to implicitly critique the commodification of Korean youth culture, which is increasingly distant from the culture of diasporic Korean youth (as shown in the distant between Nayoung and Janet).

BEFORE AND AFTER THE "ASIAN AUGUST"

Asian characters are seldom portrayed by the mainstream Canadian and U.S. media. In addition to their portrayal being rather sporadic, Asians in North American mainstream media have been depicted stereotypically, whether negatively or positively. While the negative "yellow peril" stereotype was more extensive, another somewhat positive stereotype—the "model minority"—has increasingly emerged (Ono and Pham, 2009; Park, Gabbadon, and Chernin, 2006).[6] Furthermore, these two stereotypes are not necessarily separable, as they are interchanged dialectically (Kawai, 2005). The media industry has constructed race through stereotypical representation (Saha, 2018).

It is only within the past few years that the North American media industry has witnessed noticeable changes in the representations of Asians. These changes have been facilitated by the social atmosphere, in which further representation and the rights of women and people of color are increasingly being demanded due to various campaigns, including the Black Lives Matter movement and the #OscarsSoWhite campaign. In the mid-2010s, media audiences participated in an anti-whitewashing campaign after witnessing Hollywood blockbusters casting white stars in Asian roles in several films, such as *Ghost in the Shell*, *Aloha*, and *21*. In response, a meme with the hashtag #StarringJohnCho circulated online, urging people to imagine having Asian American actor John Cho in major roles in Hollywood films.

Since the mid-2010s, Asian leads have appeared more than before in North American media, especially in August 2018, when several films and TV shows with Asian characters and producers—for example, *Crazy Rich Asians*, *Searching*, and *To All the Boys I've Loved Before*— had tremendous success in the market. This "Asian August"—a term coined by the Coalition of Asian Pacifics in Entertainment to recognize the major success of Asian American content in the mainstream media market—might be the symbolic moment in which the presence of Asians in the North American media increased (Rubin, 2018). The increasing number of Asian roles in the mainstream media landscape is encouraging for Asian American cultural industries and audiences, as well as for the industry as a whole. There are existing dilemmas regarding how Asian Americans should be represented without reproducing racial stereotypes as exotic others, and how Asian American content can be disseminated to larger audiences.

As Saha (2018) argued, ethnicized cultural content tends to be marketed either to appeal to the bigger general audience or to target niches comprising ethnic audiences. The recent Asian American TV shows target not only ethnic but also wider audiences. For those mainstream shows with Asian casts, writers, and/or directors/producers, the nuanced and fair representation of Asians is an ongoing task. For example, the production team may have to question how "authentically" and "specifically" ethnic cultures should appear in these shows while simultaneously including "universal" themes to appeal to both ethnic and non-ethnic audiences (Feng, 2017). As shown in the case of *Kim's Convenience*, the creators seek a balance between specificity (of an ethnic group) and universality (that can be shared across ethnic groups). As Feng (2017) aptly defines in his study of recent Asian American TV series, mainstream TV shows involving minority viewpoints and characters have negotiated the "contradiction between originality and comprehensibility" (126). In other words, recent mainstream shows with Asian leads may have to address primetime audiences (not limited to Asian Americans) and thus have to be "specific enough that racial minorities will find them authentic, but they are relatable enough that they are universal" (Feng, 2017).

Recent Asian American TV shows primarily take the form of the (romantic) comedy genre; for example, several TV sitcoms with Asian leads, including *Selfie* (ABC, 2014), *Fresh off the Boat* (ABC, 2015–2020), *Dr. Ken* (ABC, 2015–2017), *Master of None* (Netflix, 2015–2017), and the *Mindy Project* (Fox and Hulu, 2012–2017). In the comedy genre, archetypes and stereotypes tend to be used as an instrument to establish quickly recognizable character types and become a central source of humor (Bowes, 1990; Macey, 2012). Topics and characters in TV comedy shows are often depicted "in a comically exaggerated or satirically distorted manner" (Kamm and Neumann, 2015). In other words, stereotypes are deployed in TV comedy to achieve humorous and satirical effects. The use of stereotypes does not necessarily involve the simple repetition of cliché. The use of stereotypes can be intended to challenge the status quo (Kamm and Neumann, 2015). In particular, the post-network TV era has witnessed the emergence of "transgressive comedy" that involves intentional offensiveness as a source of humor (Tueth, 2005). Like many other narrative genres, comedy has been oscillating between the reproduction of conventions and their transgression. In this regard, TV comedy, including Asian American comedy, may involve stereotypical and alternative representations.

Of course, stereotypes are often troublesome and have detrimental effects on audiences, the stereotyped groups, and the general public (Kawai, 2005). In particular, stereotypes reproduce a particular imaginary of marginalized groups of people as the other of the dominant social order (Dyer, 1993; Hall, 1997). The reproduction of stereotypes involves power relations between those who stereotype others and those stereotyped. As Hong (2019) observes, Asian Americans were primarily the objects of comedy (i.e., those who were made fun of) but are increasingly emerging as the subjects of comedy. Thus, Asian characters are no longer simply stereotyped by others but, rather, engage with the process of creatively playing with and challenging stereotypes. Indeed, Asian American TV sitcoms revolve around existing stereotypes of Asians, while reworking, challenging, and/or negotiating them (Feng, 2017). As the first Asian-led Canadian TV sitcom of its kind, *Kim's Convenience*, written and performed primarily by Asian Canadians, reveals the racialization of Korean Canadians. However, this does not mean that the Korean Canadian leads are racialized simply to be stereotyped; rather, they are racialized as a way of doing their identity politics (Feng 2017).

THE NEGOTIATION OF STEREOTYPES
IN *KIM'S CONVENIENCE*

(In)convenient Stereotyping

In its portrayal of Asian characters, *Kim's Convenience* seems to move beyond the binary opposition of Asians as either the "yellow peril" or the "model minority." However, like many other TV sitcoms, this show is not entirely free of stereotypical representations. The show involves archetypical and/or stereotypical portrayal of characters. As the creator and cast suggested, the show's portrayal of the Kims may be archetypical rather than stereotypical (Westerman, 2019). Archetypes as "the broad blueprint of recombinant characters" (Macey, 2012) are often used in narrative media genres for time-efficient character building and storytelling. Yet, if placed in a dominant system, archetypes can become stereotypes that associate certain groups of people with specific, fixed, often negative, attributes (Macey, 2012).

Kim's Convenience creatively presents its archetypical character study as being in tension with (rather than simply giving in to) the dominant cultural forces that reproduce the stereotypes of minorities. In so doing, the show reveals the pervasiveness of the stereotypical understanding of others in our daily contexts and dominant systems. Its comic episodes implicitly (and explicitly in some cases) address the ways in which the stereotypes are negotiated and critiqued. The show engages with ethnic tropes, especially when portraying some of the main characters (particularly Mr. and Mrs. Kim). For example, audiences may consider Mr. and Mrs. Kim's communication patterns—including their gestures and accents—to be stereotypical. As first-generation immigrants, Mr. and Mrs. Kim use Koreanized English. By using Koreanized English, cast members Paul Sun-Hyung Lee and Jean Yoon, who are, in reality, native English speakers, play authentic yet legible Korean characters (Feng, 2018). The modified accent of the visible minority characters—especially Mr. and Mrs. Kim and their neighbors, including Mr. Chin (John Ng) and Mr. Mehta (Sugith Varughese)—accommodates a general audience (Jang and Yang, 2018; Lee, 2016) and, more importantly, is an essential component of the narrative of shows that tell the stories of immigrants (Davé, 2017).

Mr. and Mrs. Kim's racialized accents can be seen as an example of the stereotypical representation of the Korean Canadian characters in the show. Their Koreanized English accents distinctively highlight their characters' identities as first-generation immigrants. Their accents are especially contrasted with the English that their children speak. Mr. and Mrs. Kim's racialized accents contribute to the authentication of their characters (Davé, 2017; Jang and Yang, 2018). The accent and language barrier also effectively show the struggles of immigrants in their everyday lives. On several occasions, Mr. Kim, a convenience store owner who interacts with many people on a daily basis, encounters challenges due to his accent. For example, in one episode (Season 1, Episode 3: "Ddong Chim"), Mr. Kim is frustrated after he has difficulty ordering eggs over the phone. In the same episode, he wants to call the police to report a parking violation outside his store, but he asks Janet to do so, complaining that "Police hear accent, they don't take serious!"

As observed in Mr. and Mrs. Kim's racialized accents, first-generation immigrants and Korean travelers are stereotypically portrayed in several episodes of the show. In Season 2, Episode 7 ("Sneak Attack"), Mr. and Mrs. Kim meet a group of Korean travelers at a restaurant near the airport. The Kims are there to buy a large amount of Korean face cream without going through customs so that they can resell it in their store at a higher price. In this episode, the Korean travelers stick together and speak very loudly without considering the other customers, including police officers.

It may be undeniable that *Kim's Convenience*, like other Asian American TV shows, involves stereotypical portrayals (Feng, 2017). However, this may not necessarily mean that the show reproduces pervasive stereotypes and thus serves the dominant social order; rather, *Kim's Convenience* appropriates and makes fun of the stereotypes, and, in so doing, it comically questions the dominant discourse that often implies and reproduces various power hierarchies. By frequently exhibiting the lead characters' doing and undoing of stereotypes, the show questions pervasive stereotypes and racism. Most stereotypes presented in the show are not implicitly hidden to generate pleasure by sacrificing the voice of minorities but, rather, reflexively reveal how the stereotypes operate and are negotiated. The Asian Canadians and other recurring characters in the show are not depicted as simply the objects of pervasive stereotyping (i.e., being stereotyped by others); they are also depicted as its subjects (i.e., doing the stereotyping of others). The Kims often encounter the racialization of Asian Canadians while also conveniently stereotyping others—typically members of other minority groups.

By boldly addressing the issue of stereotyping, the show consistently questions and challenges the ongoing discrimination and prejudice that affect both dominant groups and various visible minorities. In so doing, the complexity of identity and the need to further understand cultural diversity and inclusion are implied. This implied message is evident from the very first episode of the show (Season 1, Episode 1: "Gay Discount"), which opens with a scene in which a gay customer accuses Mr. Kim of being homophobic. When two gay men ask Mr. Kim if they can put up their Pride parade poster in window of the convenience store, he says, "I have no problem with the gay. But I have a problem with the parade. Traffic, garbage, noise. If you are the gay, why can't you be quiet, respectful gay?" In response, one of the gay men accuses Mr. Kim of being homophobic. Wanting to prove that he is not homophobic, Mr. Kim begins offering a gay discount at the store. Later in the episode, in his conversation with his neighbor Mr. Chin, Mr. Kim claims he can tell who is gay. This implies that he has stereotypes of gay people. As his conversation continues, Mr. Kim realizes there are various types of genders and sexualities. He speaks with Mr. Chin about potential types of intersectional/ trans identities that he might not have thought about in depth before. Mr. Chin says to Mr. Kim, "For example, if a gay man discover he is transsexual . . . then if he has sex change and becomes a woman . . . then discover she is actually transgender." In response, Mr. Kim asks, "What's the difference between transgender and transsexual?" As evident in this conversation, *Kim's Convenience* challenges the essentialized notion of identities by emphasizing the fluidity of gender and sexual identities. The show engages with the questions of stereotypes and identities, rather than conveniently repeating and reproducing existing stereotypes.

Being Stereotyped

As members of a visible minority group, the Kims are often exposed to white people's racialization of Asians. For example, in one episode (Season 1, Episode 6: "Rude Kid"), Janet's professor assumes that Janet's personal

background is dismal. While commenting on Janet's photography assign-
ments, the professor asks, "Where was your family's journey to Canada?
Where was the refugee experience?" Janet responds, "My parents aren't
refugees." However, the professor keeps assuming: "Well . . . boat people."
Janet says, "My parents flew here," but the professor corrects her: "You mean
fled." The white female professor stereotypes Janet as the daughter of a struggling immigrant family and abusive parents. Afterward, the professor visits
Kim's convenience store with her child. In response to the professor's child
making a mess in his store, Mr. Kim flicks the child's head. Gasping, she
raises her voice to Mr. Kim, "Negative! Negative! You must apologize immediately!" When meeting with Janet in person at her university office later on,
the professor says sympathetically, "I realize how difficult it must be for you
to create art with a father like that." Janet attempts to brush the professor's
comment off by saying, "No, my dad's fine, he's just Korean. It's how he was
raised." However, the professor insists, frowning, "See, this is a classic case
of the victim rationalizing the behavior of the aggressor." The white, middle-
class, art professor reveals racial stereotypes of Asian immigrant parents as
an unintelligent and potentially violent group of people, while assuming their
children as "victims."

In another episode (Season 2, Episode 2: "Date Night"), Jung, accompanied by his white boss and love interest, Shannon, attempts to buy a pre-
owned collector-item sneakers. He meets with a white middle-aged man
who listed online the type of shoes that Jung is looking for. The man's first
words to Jung are "Um . . . *Konichiwa*. I am sorry. It's the only Oriental I
know." Later, the white man also says, "I know *you people* like bargain."
When Shannon is perplexed and asks, "You people?", he replies, "Chinese.
You like pinching your pennies." In this manner, the show often, albeit comically, explores how Asians are exposed to everyday racism and ignorance;
however, the Asian characters in the show only comically challenge others'
stereotyping of themselves, and sometimes they even appropriate the same
logic toward others. Interestingly, the main characters also use pervasive
stereotypes of Asians for their short-term gain. For example, in one episode
(Season 2, Episode 7: "Sneak Attack"), Janet uses a Korean accent and pretends to be a North Korean refugee to enable her to get into a film festival
that is already at capacity. In another episode (Season 1, Episode 6: "Rude
Kid"), she intentionally takes advantage of her professor's stereotype of her
as a struggling immigrant child to get a better grade. In several comic tropes
of "acting stereotyped Asians," the Asian characters in the show reveal how
people of color learn to live with pervasive stereotypes.

In a later episode (Season 4, Episode 3: "The Help"), a rich patron Mrs.
Taylor mistakes Mrs. Kim for a server at Janet's university exhibition.
Afterward, while chatting with Janet and Mr. Kim in the convenience, Mrs.

Kim speaks about the situation, which she considers "funny." Hearing about this incident, Janet seems deeply offended by this white person's assumption of her mother as a server, calling the misrecognition "racist," while Mrs. Kim states, "I was standing beside food. Lots of waitress is Asian people. Innocent mistake. (. . .) I was wearing same clothes as waitress." However, Janet exclaims, "NO! It's typical white, unconscious bias." Listening to their conversation, Mr. Kim adds, "Hmm, happen to me all time." Later, when complaining to her professor about the incident, Janet finds out that the rich patron's family adjudicates a prestigious university art award for which she is one of finalists. When the patron along with the professor drops by Kim's convenience to apologize, Mrs. Kim pressures her to give Janet the award, which later actually happens as "a done deal."

In this manner, the show addresses the ways in which people of color are exposed to the dominant white gaze that associates them with particular stereotypes. Through comical situations, the show often reveals that the Asian characters negotiate stereotyping forces. In some episodes, the systematic racial hierarchies are not necessarily addressed structurally but rather dealt with at an interpersonal or individual level. Given the nature of this show as situation comedy, it is not surprising that solutions to racial stereotyping are not systematically proposed in the show. However, it is important that through the examples of Asian characters stereotyped by white people, the show reveals that racial stereotyping can be a mundane and pervasive practice. Moreover, the show invites the viewer to think about power relations behind media stereotyping by raising the question of who represents whom and how.

The Stereotyped Who Stereotype Others

While the Kims are stereotyped by others, they do stereotype others too. Indeed, the show often depicts how the Korean Canadian characters make assumptions about other visible minorities and marginalized groups, and in so doing, it reveals that the main characters with whom audiences may identify are not free of the dominant representational system. By showing occasions when characters are both the objects and the subjects of stereotyping, *Kim's Convenience* critically engages with the ongoing stereotyping of minority groups in Canadian society, offering audiences self-reflexive moments.

Mr. Kim habitually stereotypes his customers and others. For example, in one episode (Season 1, Episode 7: "Hapkido"), a black man enters the store, and Mr. Kim asks Janet, "What do you think? Steal or no steal?" He then says, "He's a no steal, because he's a black guy, brown shoes." He asserts, "That's no steal. That's a cancel-out combo." Speechless, Janet responds provocatively to Mr. Kim, "A fat Asian gay man with long, straight hair,

and a black lesbian with a ponytail and cowboy boots—steal or no steal?"
Mr. Kim is confused by these combinations, which extend far beyond his
stereotyping scheme. Thus, he claims that "Gay Asian is never fat" and adds,
"Only skinny Asian is the gay. That's rule. That's how they doing like that."
This episode succinctly captures how Mr. Kim, a middle-aged heterosexual
man of color, may also be likely to stereotype others—especially other racial
groups—and how easily his stereotypes can be dismantled. First-generation
Korean immigrants' patriarchal culture is critically portrayed in the show. In
one episode (Season 3, Episode 12: "Hit 'n' Fun"), pastor Nina pointed to a
misogynous Korean man (Jimmy)'s sexist jokes, while Mrs. Kim is upset at
Mr. Kim who is silent about Jimmy's misogynous talks. As the episode pro-
gresses, Mr. Kim becomes critically aware of Jimmy's patriarchal attitudes,
and thus, argues against him.

The Kims' stereotyping is often toward other marginalized people, such as
people of color and LGBTQ (lesbian, gay, bisexual, transgender, or queer).
As shown in the above episode, Mr. Kim's stereotypical understanding of his
customers is evident when he encounters black characters. His stereotyping
of black people seems more evident in the play version than in the TV sitcom
version of the show. In the analysis of the theater play, Daniher (2018) argues
that *Kim's Convenience* is not exclusively a drama about Korean Canadians
but is also about the racialization of Korean Canadians interrelated with Black
and White racialization. Daniher refers to Claire Jean Kim's (1999) discussion of "racial triangulation" through which "a dominant racial-social grouping [whites] valorizes one minority racial–social grouping [Asians] in order
to subordinate another [blacks]" (Daniher, 2018: 17). Daniher (2018) notes
that *Kim's Convenience* effectively reveals "how Black and Korean Canadian
lives become entwined through the intersections of global immigration, urban
commerce, housing policy, and racial minoritization" and how this makes
Kim's Convenience "such a remarkable teaching text on contemporary race
and racism in Canada." However, Daniher (2018) laments that critics often
categorize the show as Korean Canadian or Asian Canadian without paying
due attention to its interracial conjunctions.

By showing Mr. Kim's stereotyping of others, *Kim's Convenience* offers
viewers a moment to critically reflect on the process through which prejudice
operates and becomes pervasive in society. The main character's stereotyping of others reveals vividly and comically how *we* are tempted to stereotype
others and how the process should be questioned.

How Representation Matters

The stereotyping by and of minorities in this show does not simply reproduce one-dimensional depictions of others, but offers moments of reflection.

Critical engagement with stereotyping serves as the basis for narrative development in several episodes. The Kims negotiate different occasions of stereotyping in which they are discriminated against or realize their own prejudice against others. The main characters are multidimensional in that they show diverse, sometimes even contradictory, patterns of behavior and reflect on their mistakes. Minorities in the show are not essentialized but rather (at least eventually) humanized. In this regard, the characters in the show do not remain stereotypical as they consistently challenge the dominant system's reproduction of stereotypes.

Janet questions stereotypes while negotiating her identity between Canadian and Korean. Often questioning Mr. Kim's rigid notion of Koreanness, as exemplified in his anti-Japanese sentiment, Janet is not comfortable with being considered to be either "too Korean" or "not enough Korean" (Carras, 2019). Moreover, she attempts to challenge the dominant social order that racializes her and thus restricts her agency. As an art student, not only does she cope with others' stereotyping of her as a woman of color, but also seeks to explore her own identity. In one episode (Season 2, Episode 9: "New TV"), Janet criticizes her male photography lecturer, whose work seems to draw on a conventional beauty standard that idealizes tall, slim white women. However when she is surprisingly asked by the lecturer to assist him, she attempts to tan her skin so that she can look more stereotypically Asian to increase her value as an "authentic Asian" model. It turns out that the lecturer did intend to hire Janet as a technical assistant, not as a model. In this way, it is revealed that Janet is not free of the stereotyped Asianness that is imposed by the white-dominant racial order, and in this regard, she is not substantially different from her male lecturer of color who reproduces the dominant white male gaze. Janet's irony echoes previous studies' finding that people of color in cultural industries may gradually internalize the white mainstream understanding of race (Saha, 2018).[7]

While addressing various everyday situations in which racial and other stereotyping operates, *Kim's Convenience* questions the media's pervasive and convenient stereotyping of others. Interestingly, by engaging with a somewhat clichéd portrayal of visible minorities, the show offers moments of reflection on the Canadian society's (myth of) multiculturalism. It is probable that the clichés and stereotypes in the show, as well as their twists, may be differently received by different groups of audiences. As the first Asian Canadian-led sitcom, *Kim's Convenience* explores how Asians can speak for themselves in the mainstream media. Given that Canada's settler colonialism has continued through the dominant groups' power to narrate and restrict other groups' narratives (Said, 1994), the momentum that enables minorities to speak for themselves is invaluable. In a recent interview, award-winning Korean American screen writer Diana Son expressed her excitement about watching Korean characters on TV. After lamenting about the difficulties in creating Asian characters in the white-dominant U.S. media industry, Son referred to *Kim's Convenience* (Miller, 2020: 230):

> My family and I have been watching this Korean Canadian show called *Kim's Convenience*, which is about a convenience store, and there's a dad and a mom, and an adult son and daughter. And people ask me, "Is it good?" And I say, "I actually have no idea." I have no idea because it's like when you're drunk without drinking, seeing Korean people on TV that aren't doing K-dramas, but are speaking English and working in a store. I had to work in my parents' store. So I can tell you that I love it, and my family really enjoys it, but I don't know if it's any good. But I'm just so flush. [The characters] speak English ninety-nine-point-nine percent of the time, but every once in a while, a Korean word, like a pet name or a curse, will slip out, and the recognition of hearing that is just shocking. I do think that playwrights of color are going to TV, and saying, "Oh, I can tell my story here."

This account resonates with Paul Sun-Hyung Lee's award acceptance speech cited at the beginning of this chapter and reaffirms why representation matters. For many Korean Canadians and Korean Americans, the archetypical Kims are probably some of the rare media characters with whom they can identify. This archetypical yet lively characterization of Korean Canadians as storytellers questions the dominant system that has reproduced stereotypical storytelling about minorities. As observed in *Kim's Convenience*, diasporic Koreans and Asians have just begun to openly tell their stories and write their histories, moving beyond the dominant token representation of visible minorities. The show contributed to facilitating discussions about whose stories should be further included and how the stories should be told in the mainstream media industries. Moreover, the show's storytelling of diasporic lives may facilitate a critical understanding of the somewhat monolithic, dominant discourse of *Hallyu*, while adding other voices.

CONCLUSION

Kim's Convenience has been one of the most successful Canadian TV programs in recent years. The show's storytelling of people of color and immigrants may contribute to the diversification of and questions about what actually constitutes "Canadian content."[8] However, the discontinuation of the show after the remarkably successful five seasons reveals that Canadian media industries' infrastructure is still too limited to sustainably embrace the stories of Asians. The praise for *Kim's Convenience* may be largely derived from audiences' desires for cultural diversity and inclusion, which the North American media has severely lacked. Meanwhile, the show may serve to question what the discourse of the *Hallyu* is missing—that is, the voices of diasporic Koreans and Asians. Regarding the increasing importance of the diasporic flows of Korean popular culture, Yoon (2020) has proposed further studies, which he tentatively called "*Hallyu* diaspora studies." This approach addresses "how the Korean diaspora affects *Hallyu*'s production and circulation and/or how the phenomenon affects Korean diasporic identity" (Yoon, 2020). Diasporic Koreans are not only consumers of recent Korean pop cultural content but also producers and mediators of *Hallyu*. In this regard, it is important to explore how diasporic storytelling of *Kim's Convenience* is integrated into the recent global waves of Korean pop culture.

By examining the ways in which the cultural stereotypes are identified, questioned, and negotiated in the popular TV show, created and performed by Asian Canadians, this chapter has questioned how colorblindness of Western mainstream media industries can be questioned. Moreover, the chapter has suggested that *Kim's Convenience* offers a potential antidote to clichés and stereotypes observed in mainstream Korean pop culture and its global flows. K-pop videos and romantic K-dramas have been criticized for their recurring clichés and stereotypes, such as traditional gender roles and Confucian age-based hierarchies (Epstein and Turnbull, 2014; Unger, 2015). Indeed, the stereotypes that are often observed in mainstream *Hallyu* texts as a method of marketing particular forms of body images and identities are problematic. The diasporic narratives in *Kim's Convenience* confront the pervasive stereotypes and thus ask questions of identity in transcultural contexts. The show provides an interesting case study of how diasporic Korean storytelling and representations contribute to expanding the narrowly defined and imagined Koreanness in contemporary Korean popular culture. The diasporic negotiation of stereotypes in *Kim's Convenience* serves to expand the boundaries not only of Canadian media but also of *Hallyu*. The diversification of representation matters.

CODA

On March 8, 2021, in the midst of running of the fifth season of *Kim's Convenience*, the CBC abruptly announced the discontinuation of the show. It was an unexpected cancellation as the CBC had already ordered a sixth season. In response to the news, fans expressed their disappointment and attempted to revive the show by spreading the hashtag #SaveKimsConvenience. The

cast of the show also individually shared their frustrations in several interviews and social media postings. The CBC's decision was reportedly due to
the creator Ins Choi's uncertainty about the next season. As the show was
rooted in his autobiographical stories and characterization, the executives did
not want to continue production without Choi's involvement (Houpt, 2021);
however, as Choi did not make public comments on the show's cancellation,
there emerged speculation about the specific reasons for discontinuation and
debates about the probable revival of the show by other showrunners.

This unexpected closure revealed the structural restrictions of Canadian
media industries, in which few creators of color have played an active role.
For example, Ins Choi was often the only writer of Asian heritage on the
production team, and thus he may have had significant responsibilities during the five seasons of *Kim's Convenience* (Houpt, 2021; Weaver, 2021).
The difficulty in recruiting writers to continue the show indicates that even
the globally successful *Kim's Convenience* was not free from the white-
dominant production culture in which most mainstream TV shows are run
by white creators (Weaver, 2021). The near absence of creators of color in
Canadian media industries is shocking given that the Canadian TV industry
has recently been enjoying success in both domestic and global markets
(Weaver, 2021). Given the structural problems in the industry, the legacy
of *Kim's Convenience* is invaluable. It opened doors for culturally diverse
storytelling in Canada and facilitated public debates about what type of storytelling should be facilitated to better engage with the question of cultural
diversity (Weaver, 2021).

After the cancellation announcement, CBC revealed its plan to run two
new comedies starring two cast members of *Kim's Convenience*. As a spi-
noff scheduled for the 2021–2022 season, *Strays* stars Nicole Power, who
played Jung's white love interest Shannon in *Kim's Convenience*. This
new show revolves around Shannon who begins a new career in another
Canadian city. *Strays*, produced by *Kim's Convenience* co-creator Kevin
White, however, does not involve Ins Choi. Meanwhile, Andrew Phung,
who played Jung's Korean roommate Kimchee in *Kim's Convenience*, stars
in a new CBC comedy show *Run the Burbs* that he created. Reportedly,
these two shows were already planned before the cancellation of *Kim's
Convenience* (Houpt, 2021).

The fans, the cast, and Asian Canadian communities could not save the
show as its finale aired on April 13, 2021. Despite its unexpected early departure, the show has undeniably left legacies and tasks for the representation
of Asians in the Canadian media landscape. Indeed, the show's contribution
to expanding the diasporic scope of "Korean" popular culture (or popular
culture by diasporic Koreans) suggests how the diasporic dimension of the
Korean Wave can engage with the narratives of cultural diversity.

NOTES

1. *Kim's Convenience* is not the only case that demonstrates the diversified waves of Korean popular culture that include cultural texts not only made-in-Korea but also made-*about*-Korea. Several other important cultural texts have contributed to the re-orientation of *Hallyu* toward further transnationally diverse and complex cultural waves. The acclaimed American independent film *Minari* (2020) by Isaac Lee Chung heartwarmingly portrays an immigrant Korean family's struggle in 1980s Arkansas. While it is an American film by nationality, its director, cast, and themes are diasporic—both Korean and American. *Minari* reveals how Korean popular culture elements (e.g., the roles played by Korean actors Yuh-jung Youn and Yeri Han) and the diasporic Korean themes and talent are incorporated into American independent filmmaking. Similar to *Kim's Convenience*, *Minari* indicates how diasporic cultural practices can enrich the content and form of diversity in cultural industries.

While *Minari* shows how diasporic Korean cultural practices can impact the evolution and diversification of *Hallyu*, the multi-award-winning Korean film *Parasite* (2019) by Bong Joon-ho illustrates how *Hallyu* can be transnationalized through local storytelling that resonates with global audiences. Set in contemporary Seoul, *Parasite* offers a satirical social critique of class division in Korea, which is rarely attempted in mainstream *Hallyu* content, such as kaleidoscopic K-pop videos and urban trendy K-dramas. In an early press conference in Seoul, the director Bong described the film as "being full of Korean-specific nuances (. . .) that only Korean audiences can fully appreciate" (Yim, 2019). It turned out that the film's Korean-specific references were translatable and were understood by global audiences because the theme of class division was timely and appealing to other local contexts.

Furthermore, it is worth mentioning that Psy's *Gangnam Style* (2012) can be considered an example of variation in the dominant discourse of *Hallyu* (rather than an example of the dominant *Hallyu* trend). Although overshadowed by its global megahit and comical dance moves, *Gangnam Style* is a harsh satire of middle-class Seoulites' materialism. Moreover, Psy is not categorically a conventional K-pop idol systematically "manufactured" for local and global audiences. *Gangnam Style* might be an early example of an alternative direction of *Hallyu*—not only made-in-Korea but also made-*about*-Korea. This new direction involves cultural content that strongly draws on local themes and references rather than intentionally targeting global markets.

2. Netflix typically does not release specific viewer counts of its shows. Thus, the international reception of *Kim's Convenience* can only be estimated. According to Parrot Analytics' (tv.parrotanalytics.com) data as of January 2021, outside Canada, the show is particularly popular in the United States and Australia—in those two countries, the show ratings are far higher than the average of other comedy programs on Netflix. According to the data, the show's popularity lags in South Korea.

3. Interestingly, the Kims' eldest child Jung has a Korean name, while Jung's younger sister Janet has an English name only. In one episode (Season 3, Episode 1: "New Appa-liance") in which Janet wants to have a unique Korean name instead of her English name, Mr. Kim reveals a history behind the children's names: Janet was

given an English name because her older brother Jung was teased by his peers for his Korean name. Mr. Kim says to Janet, "(It was) Just to be safe for we not give you a name people make fun of. 'Dumb Dumb Jung,' 'Ping Pong Jung,' 'Donkey Kong Jung.'"

4. The theme of generational reconciliation is not rare in Korean Canadian or Korean American media narratives. For example, the father-son reconciliation through the continuation of a family business in the ethnic economy portrayed in *Kim's Convenience* resonates with some second-generation Koreans' stories (e.g., Historica Canada, 2015).

5. It is no longer the exception that K-pop idol groups include diasporic Korean or non-Korean members. For example, the globally popular K-pop group Blackpink comprises one Korean, one Thai, and two diasporic Koreans. The Netflix original documentary *Light Up the Sky* (2020) reveals the four members' journey to global stardom. As three members out of the four were raised overseas, the documentary portrays those members' transnational experiences to a large extent. However, as portrayed in *Light Up the Sky*, young multinational trainees are disciplined according to the uniquely Korean in-house training system through which all elements of production, management, and marketing of idols are assembled under the control of major Korean entertainment companies (Shin, 2009). In addition to the strict idol manufacturing system, existing cultural nationalism in Korea has restricted how diasporic or non-Korean talents are represented and represent themselves (Fuhr, 2016).

6. As historian Henry Yu (2010) noted, Asians in North America have resisted the label "model minorities," as it comes with high costs: "One cost was the destruction of anti-racism coalitions with Jewish-Americans and African-Americans that had helped overcome white supremacy during the Civil Rights era. Another cost was the revival of the racist image that Asians were a threat to 'normal' white Americans" (para 7).

7. The internalization of racial order has also been echoed by Korean Canadian actor Sandra Oh. In an interview on her role as the main character Eve in the award-winning TV show *Killing Eve* (2018–present), Oh admitted that she did not expect she would be offered the main role because she had been told to limit herself as a person of color in the white-dominant media industries for decades. Critically reflecting on how she had internalized the white mainstreaming understanding of race, she stated, "Oh my god! They brainwashed me!" (Jung, 2018)

8. In keeping with the stipulations of the Broadcasting Act of Canada, Canadian radio and television broadcasters must provide a certain percentage of content that is produced by Canadians. While this Canadian content quota is maintained to protect the Canadian media industry and Canadian cultural identities, there are ongoing debates regarding the nature of Canadian content (e.g., whose Canadian content?) (Mirrlees, 2019).

BIBLIOGRAPHY

Baker, D. (2008). Koreans in Vancouver: A Short History. *The Journal of the Canadian Historical Association* 19 (2): 155–80.

Bang, J. (2018). The Korean Wave in Canada Seen Through Kim's Convenience. https://news.kotra.or.kr/user/globalAllBbs/kotranews/album/781/globalBbsDa taAllView.do?dataIdx=164696&column=&search=&searchAreaCd=&searchNa-tionCd=&searchTradeCd=&searchStartDate=&searchEndDate=&searchCategory-Idxs=&searchIndustryCateIdx=&page=36&row=100.

Bowes, M. (1990). Only When I Laugh. In *Understanding Television*, edited by Goodwin, A. and G. Whannel, 128–40. London: Routledge.

Carra, M. (2019). Kim's Convenience's Millennial Cast Explains How the Canadian Sitcom Subverts Stereotypes in a Real Way. *Bustle*, May 28, 2019, https://www .bustle.com/p/kims-conveniences-millennial-cast-explains-how-the-canadian-sit-com-subverts-stereotypes-in-a-real-way-17898589.

Chan, E. and E. Fong. (2012). Social, Economic, and Democratic Characteristics of Korean Self-Employment in Canada. In *Korean Immigrants in Canada: Perspectives on Migration, Integration, and the Family*, edited by Noh, S., A. H. Kim, and M. S. Noh, 115–32. Toronto: University of Toronto Press.

Daniher, C. (2019). On Teaching Kim's Convenience: Asian American Studies, Asian Canadian Studies, and the Politics of Race in Asian Canadian Theatre and Performance Studies. *Theatre Research in Canada* 39 (1): 8–27.

Davé, S. (2017). Racial Accents, Hollywood Casting, and Asian American Studies. *Cinema Journal* 56 (3): 142–47.

Dyer, R. (1993). *The Matter of Images: Essays on Representations*. London: Routledge.

Epstein, S. and J. Turnbull. (2014). Girls' Generation? Gender, (Dis) empowerment, and K-pop. *The Korean Popular Culture Reader*, edited by Kim, K. and Y. Choe, 314–36. Durham, NC: Duke University Press.

Feng, P. (2017). Asian American Media Studies and the Problem of Legibility. *Cinema Journal* 56 (3): 125–30.

Fuhr, M. (2016). *Globalization and Popular Music in South Korea: Sounding out K-pop*. London: Routledge.

Hall, S. (1997). The Spectacle of the 'Other'. In *Representation: Cultural Representations and Signifying Practices*, edited by Hall, S., 223–90. Milton Keynes: Open University Press.

Historica Canada. (2015). Jason's story: Embracing the Hyphen in Korean-Canadian. https://www.youtube.com/watch?v=IBaWoeXE5Uc

Hong, C. (2019). Comedy, Humor, and Asian American Representation. In *Oxford Research Encyclopedia of Literature*. doi.org/10.1093/acrefore/9780190201098.0 13.809.

Houpt, S. (2021). The Abrupt End of Kim's Convenience: Why did CBC Let its Beloved Sitcom Close Up Shop? *The Globe and Mail*, March 26, 2021.

Hsu, H. (2019). 'Kim's Convenience,' the Genial Canadian Sitcom That Feels Like Watching Another Time Line. *The New Yorker,* August 28, 2019, https://www .newyorker.com/recommends/watch/kims-convenience-the-genial-canadian-sit-com-that-feels-like-watching-another-time-line.

Hunt, N. (2016). Breaking New Ground: Kim's Convenience to be Canada's 1st Sitcom Led by Asians. https://www.cbc.ca/news/entertainment/kims-convenience -diversity-1.3783998.

Jang, I. and I. Yang. (2018). Linguistic Representations of Korean Immigrant English in North American Media Space: An Analysis of Appa's English in Kim's Convenience. *Sahoeeoneohak (Sociolingustics)* 26 (2): 1–36.

Jin, D., K. Yoon, and W. Min (2021). *Transnational Hallyu: The Globalization of Korean Digital and Popular Culture*. Lanham, MD: Rowman & Littlefield.

Joo, J. (2011). Transnationalization of Korean Popular Culture and the Rise of "Pop Nationalism" in Korea. *The Journal of Popular Culture* 44 (3): 489–504.

Ju, H. (2018). Sushi Restaurants Instead of Conveniences Become Popular among Korean Immigrants in Canada. https://news.joins.com/article/22601942.

Jung, E. (2018). It Took Sandra Oh 30 Years to Get to Killing Eve. *Vulture*, April 9, 2018, https://www.vulture.com/2018/04/sandra-oh-killing-eve.html.

Kamm, J. and B. Neumann. (2015). Introduction: The Aesthetics and Politics of British TV Comedy. In *British TV Comedies: Cultural Concepts, Contexts and Controversies*, edited by Kamm, J. and B. Neumann, 1–20. New York: Palgrave.

Kawai, Y. (2005). Stereotyping Asian Americans: The Dialectic of the Model Minority and the Yellow Peril. *The Howard Journal of Communications* 16 (2): 109–30.

Kibria, N. (2003). *Becoming Asian American: Second Generation Chinese and Korean American Identities*. Baltimore, MD: Johns Hopkins University Press.

Kim, A. H., M. S. Noh, and S. Noh. (2012). Introduction: Historical Context and Cotemporary Research. In *Korean Immigrants in Canada: Perspectives on Migration, Integration, and the Family*, edited by Noh, S., A. H. Kim, and M. S. Noh, 1–18. Toronto: University of Toronto Press.

Kim, C. J. (1999). The Racial Triangulation of Asian Americans. *Politics & Society* 27 (1): 105–38.

Korea Foundation (2020). *2019 Hallyu in the World: Americas*. Seoul: Korea Foundation.

Lee, A. (2016). How to Do an on-Screen Accent—and Why It Can Be Okay: The Man Who Plays 'Appa' in *Kim's Convenience* Launches into a Passionate Argument about Accents on TV. *Maclean's,* October 11, 2016, https://www.macleans.ca/culture/arts/how-to-do-an-on-screen-accent-and-why-it-can-be-okay.

Lee, Y. (2018). Can We Have a Program like Kim's Convenience in South Korea? *Bangsong Teurendeu & Insaiteu (Broadcasting Trend & Insight)* 4, http://www.kocca.kr/trend/vol17/sub/s41.html.

Liu, K. (2020). Easy Korean Dishes from the Stars of Kim's Convenience. *The Star*, January 29, 2020, https://www.thestar.com/life/food_wine/2020/01/29/easy-korean-dishes-from-the-stars-of-kims-convenience.html.

Lyons, M. (2018). How Much Watching Time Do You Have This Weekend? *New York Times*, July 13, 2018, https://www.nytimes.com/2018/07/13/arts/television/world-cup-what-to-watch-this-weekend.html.

Macey, D. (2012). Ancient Archetypes in Modern Media. In *Media Depictions of Brides, Wives, and Mothers*, edited by Ruggerio, A. A., 49–62. Lanham, MD: Lexington Books.

Miller, H. (2020). *Playwrights on Television Conversations with Dramatists*. London: Routledge.

Min, P. (1984). From White-collar Occupations to Small Business: Korean Immigrants' Occupational Adjustment. *The Sociological Quarterly* 25 (3): 333–52.

Min, P., and S. Noh. (2014). Introduction. In *Second-Generation Korean Experiences in the United States and Canada*, edited by Min, P. and S., Noh, 1–14. Lanham, MD: Lexington Books.

Mirrlees, T. (2019). Canadian TV Goes Global: Within and Beyond Cultural Imperialism. In *World Entertainment Media: Global, Regional and Local Perspectives*, edited by Sigismondi, P., 11–8. New York: Routledge.

Ono, K., and V. Pham. (2009). *Asian Americans and the Media*. Oxford: Polity.

Park, J. (2012). A Demographic Profile of Koreans in Canada. In *Korean Immigrants in Canada: Perspectives on Migration, Integration, and the Family*, edited by Noh, S., A. H. Kim, and M. S. Noh, 19–34. Toronto: University of Toronto Press.

Park, J., N. Gabbadon, and A. Chernin. (2006). Naturalizing Racial Differences through Comedy: Asian, Black, and White Views on Racial Stereotypes in *Rush Hour 2*. *Journal of Communication* 56 (1): 157–17.

Reid, R. (2016). CBC Orders More Kim's Convenience. https://playbackonline.ca/2016/12/20/cbc-orders-more-kims-convenience/

Rubin, R. (2018). What Can Hollywood Learn from #AsianAugust? *Variety*, September 10, 2018, https://variety.com/2018/film/news/crazy-rich-asians-black-panther-hollywood-diversity-1202926661.

Saha, A. (2018). *Race and the Cultural Industries*. Oxford: Polity.

Said, E. (1994). *Culture and Imperialism*. London: Vintage.

Shin, H. (2009). Have You Ever Seen the Rain? And Who'll Stop the Rain?: The Globalizing Project of Korean Pop (K-pop). *Inter-Asia Cultural Studies* 10 (4): 507–23.

Statistics Canada. (2016). Census Profile, 2016 Census. https://www12.statcan.gc.ca/census-recensement/2016/dp-pd/prof/index.cfm?Lang=E.

Tueth, M. (2005). Breaking and Entering: Transgressive Comedy on Television. *The Sitcom Reader: America Viewed and Skewed*, edited by Dalton, M. and L. Linder, 25–34. Albany, NY: State University of New York Press.

Unger, M. (2015). The Aporia of Presentation: Deconstructing the Genre of K-pop Girl Group Music Videos in South Korea. *Journal of Popular Music Studies* 27 (1): 25–47.

Weaver, J. (2021). How Kim's Convenience Showcases the Difficulties Faced by Diverse Creators. *CBC News*, April 15, 2021, https://www.cbc.ca/news/entertainment/kim-s-convenience-end-diverse-1.5988267.

Westerman, A. (2019). Kim's Convenience' Is a Sitcom about Asian Immigrants–With Depth. *NPR*, January 9, 2019, https://www.npr.org/2019/01/09/682888290/kim-s-convenience-is-a-sitcom-about-asian-immigrants-with-depth.

Won, Y. (2017). Numerous Discourses, One Perspective. In *The Korean Wave: Evolution, Fandom, and Transnationality*, edited by Jin, D. Y. and T. J. Yoon, 23–42. Lanham, MD: Lexington Books.

Yim, H. (2019). Bong of Parasite Says, "Unlikely to Win at Cannes". *The Korea Economic Daily Hankyung*, April 22, 2019, https://www.hankyung.com/entertainment/article/201904229822k.

Yoon, K. (2017). Korean Migrants' Use of the Internet in Canada. *Journal of International Migration and Integration* 18 (2): 547–62.

Yoon, K. (2019). Diasporic Youth Culture of K-pop. *Journal of Youth Studies* 22 (1): 138–52.

Yoon, K. (2020). Diasporic Korean Audiences of Hallyu in Vancouver, Canada. *Korea Journal* 60 (1): 152–78.

Yu, H. (2010). Maclean's Must Answer for Racial Profiling; Asian-Canadians Aren't Just Being Too Sensitive. There's a History Behind their Reaction to the Magazine's 'Too Asian?' Article. *The Vancouver Sun*, November 27, 2010. C.4.

Chapter 4

The New Country Women

Exploring Popular Representations of Korean Gwichon *and Transnational Women's Marriage-Migration to the Korean Countryside*

Snigdha Gupta

INTRODUCTION

In the debate on the "Agrarian Question,"[1] the teleological argument for the inevitable dissolution of the peasantry has been the most influential thesis of all; its simple, progressionist rationality of tracing the transfer of society from *gemeinschaft* (simple, undifferentiated, and rural) to *gesellschaft* (differentiated, complex, and industrial) has become an integral component of many modern theories of social change (Araghi, 1995). Early scholars of this teleological school of thought, including Marx, saw peasantry and the countryside as "a class with no future," a "barbaric" people fated to disappear (Araghi, 1995). In spite of the far-reaching popularity of this idea, the image of an unadulterated countryside has been a constant in the imagination of the urban population in Europe. In his canonical work of literary theory, *The Country and the City* (1973), Raymond Williams analyzes popular representations of the countryside in English literature and finds that the imagery embedded in this writing depicts the country to be a pristine haven of a simple bucolic life, absent any of the harsh realities in the wake of its many social upheavals. The city, on the other hand, has been depicted as a symbol of capitalist production, a center of rationality and modernity, but also an exploitative and oppressive place—a "dark mirror" of the country. He dismisses this as an ahistoricized, romantic ideal of the country, "a myth functioning as a memory" that distorts people's understanding of the past and prevents them from dealing genuinely with the problems of the present.

These imagined, mythical ideals of the countryside are also present in societies which underwent forces of modernization much later than Britain. South Korea (hereafter "Korea"), setting out on its path of industrialization in the second half of the 20th century, also started developing its own share of nostalgic imagery of the countryside. Jiseung Roh's study on the representation of the countryside in the films of the 1960s notes how the novels of 1920s and 1930s were reproduced for their images of the rural and then conferred with additional ideas of trauma and nostalgia arising from the new realities of rapid urbanization and development in the 1960s (Roh, 2014). These images, on one hand reified the countryside as unchanging and simple, a place where traditional values were still preserved, but on the other hand, also mourned for, as being the next target of the forces of modernization. Roh found these representations to have been constructed solely from the perspective of the urban population of the time. He calls it "the nostalgia and fantasy of anti-modernity" that had begun during the Japanese colonial rule which he argues "bore itself deep into the minds of many more people through its popular depiction in films in the 1960s" (Roh, 2014). Further, Roh finds many of the existing stereotypes and myths about the countryside to have emerged from this very period.

Through each stage of Korea's accelerated modernization, the rural has been imagined and reimagined in popular media to suit the urban population's fantasies and nostalgia toward the countryside. Beginning from the 1980s, a new genre of *Jeonwondeurama* (countryside drama) became a mainstay on Korean primetime television. This genre focused primarily on the lives and relationships of the people in the countryside (Chang, 2004). The most well-known example of the genre is *Country Diary (Jeonwonilgi)*, which ran for more than 22 years on MBC, from 1980 to 2002. The show proved to be so popular that the founder of Hyundai, Chung Ju-yung, expressed a desire to appear on it, as it was said to remind him of his village and his father back home (Son, 2009). While the show endeavored to present the lives of the rural populace in a changing era, it mainly served up a slice of nostalgia for those like Chung, an urban viewer who longed for the countryside, having left it in his own lifetime, but whose new life had led him far away from its hardships. Despite the popularity of countryside dramas, by the early 2000s, the genre had all but disappeared from television (Chung, 2009).

The downfall of countryside dramas did not translate into a disappearance of the countryside itself from popular media. The fantasy and nostalgia of the urban population toward the rural had simply been transformed as the accelerated modernization of Korea progressed. The urban viewers who felt nostalgia watching the films of the 1960s and the countryside dramas of the 1980s and 1990s had direct connections to the countryside, as many of them had left their rural homes and made their way to the city in their own lifetimes, owing to the rapid urbanization of the period.[2] However, in the 2000s, many of the younger viewers in the urban centers had been born in the cities and had lived through the (post-1997 IMF crisis) peak of Korea's neoliberalization. As noted in Roh's study, the concerns of urban viewers (in creating the imagery of the countryside) were different in the 1960s than in the Japanese colonial era due to new realities of modernization. Similarly, the motivations of contemporary younger viewers are different than that of the previous generation. In the 2000s, the countryside has been reinvented as a space for convalescence, or escape from the stresses of the city. The rural no longer just appears in long drama form on television, but also in the short and snappy "variety show" format and short-form documentaries. The shows feature young celebrities who, on outdoor variety shows like tvN's *Three Meals a Day*, rear cattle, plough fields, build fires, and cook with what is available in the country, capturing the fascination of their urban audiences looking for respite from their highly pressurized work-lives.[3] This new nostalgia for the countryside does not emanate from any lived experiences of the rural, but rather from, what Appadurai calls, "a loss which never took place" (Appadurai, 1996). Appadurai sees this as a manufactured nostalgia that is particular to modern consumer culture: "Rather than expecting the consumer to supply memories while the merchandiser supplies the lubricant of nostalgia, now the viewer need only bring the faculty of nostalgia to an image that will supply the memory of a loss he or she has never suffered" (Appadurai, 1996).

This imagined nostalgia forms the basis of the modern-day imagery of the countryside. Television programs such as SBS's *Modern Farmer*, JTBC's *Hyori's Homestay* (*Hyori's Bed and Breakfast*), MBN's *Naturally*, TvN's *Food Diary*, and many such others, project a vision of the countryside as an idealized space—a freeing, timeless order, untainted by the forces of capital and hence, attracting not only young Koreans in the city but also *Hallyu* fans who are also made to feel a similar sense of nostalgia and fantasy toward a country/countryside not their own. Korean cinema on the other hand has offered somewhat more diverse depictions of the countryside. The establishment of the Gochang Rural Film Festival in 2018 and the relative success of independent films such as *Old Partner* (2009) and *Earth's Women* (2009) have shown a different side of the rural than that which appears on television. Nonetheless, a romanticized image of the countryside is still fairly common in popular cinema. While films such as *My Father* (2009), *Little Forest* (2018), *Farming Boys* (2016), and *The Way Home* (2002) all paint a picture of an idealized countryside, other mainstream films such as *The Wailing* (2016), *Moss* (2010), *Mother* (2009), *Memories of a Murder* (2003), *Running*

Turtle (2009), and *Chaw* (2009) depict the countryside as a primitive place, a mysterious backdrop for heinous crimes and supernatural activity.

In the 2000s, the countryside was not merely being depicted as a place for imaginative escape but for the first time, transformed into a destination for actual escape. While most of the second half of the 20th century was marked by the depopulation of the countryside and rapid urbanization, since the 2000s the opposite has been happening on a major scale, with new groups of people entering the countryside—namely, the *gwichonin* and marriage-migrants. The latter refers to mostly female marriage-migrants from Korea's new Asian "periphery"—young women from developing countries who are marrying older South Korean bachelors in rural areas. The first group, the *gwichonin*, refers to Korean people who choose to undertake *gwichon*—a return to the countryside from the city. Although the Hanja "歸"(*Gwi*) literally translates to "return," the term *gwichonin* also applies to those who migrate to the countryside, despite never having actually lived there in their own lifetimes. These people choose to return to the countryside for a myriad of reasons; however, the most common ones are work-related stress and burn-out.[4] Although young people are seen to be "returning" in similar numbers, young women's *gwichon* is particularly interesting because of the massive exodus of young women from the countryside that had ensued in the previous generations.[5] The ensuing depopulation from this had resulted in the rapid aging and simultaneous feminization of the countryside.[6]

In 2018, most of the population in the countryside was above the age of 60, and 52.7% of all farm laborers were women (Seo, 2019). While older women have become the backbone of Korean agriculture and the countryside, population control measures introduced in the 1960s has left the countryside unable to regenerate, recording extremely low levels of fertility.[7] These declining demographics are being tackled by the government with the intro-duction of incentives for marriage and childbirth, especially in rural areas where there is an acute lack of young women of marriageable age. However, with the increase in female education, more and more Korean women are pursuing their own careers and marrying late, which has not only resulted in a deficit of women in the marriage market, but also has decreased the chances of marriage with rural men who are typically neither highly educated nor high income. This has caused rural men to search for brides outside the country to replace Korean women, leading to increased marriage-based migration of foreign women into Korea (Seo, 2018). Recently, however, young Korean women have also "returned" to many rural areas— yet, not through marriage, and not assuming the social positions their predecessors left, but instead look-ing for autonomy and agency in the space of the countryside.

This chapter studies how dramatic representations of women in the Korean countryside act as narratives of acclimatization for two sets of women at different ends of the transnational socioeconomic spectrum, namely mar-riage-migrants and *gwichonin*. Both of these groups are seen as the natural inheritors of the Korean countryside; hence it is rational to query how they are placed in the hierarchy of gender, class, and race, and how it affects their relationships. To answer this question, this chapter analyzes four cin-ematic and televisual representations of these two sets of new entrants in the countryside. It explores what the space of the countryside means to these two groups of women, and how cinematic and televisual depictions of them coincide with societal and state aspirations from them. It outlines a cyclical trajectory in how the positions of these two groups of women have changed and overlapped in the countryside. In analyzing the cinematic and televisual representations of these women, the chapter also historicizes the gendered nature of the inward and outward migrations of the countryside.

THE NEW COUNTRYWOMEN: GWICHON WOMEN IN FILM AND TELEVISION

Researchers find work-related issues to be one of the main reasons why peo-ple choose *gwichon*, or the move "back" to the countryside (Statistics, 2019). While men and women are seen to be returning in somewhat equal numbers, it is the women's *gwichon* that is the most interesting for two reasons. The first one is delineated in the last section, regarding the mass exodus of women from the countryside in the previous decades. The second is the work-based inequality that women face which makes them likely to choose the move away from the city. Throughout the 1970s, women worked in factories for longer hours than men (Park, 1993), yet they were also expected to take on the full burden of housework and child care at home. Such an expectation was not just a societal one, but fully backed by the state, which used the narrative of "familialism" and tradition to replace actual welfare policies for the labor-ing classes (Kim, 2016). In contemporary Korea however, women no longer populate the ranks of the manufacturing sector as in the 1970s. There has been an influx of migrant workers, while many jobs have been outsourced to third world countries (Shin, 2010; Mundy, 2013).

Although it is beyond doubt that the standard of women's lives has gen-erally improved, women are still far from achieving workplace equality in Korea. South Korea ranks worst out of all OECD countries in terms of the gender pay gap, rampant workplace harassment, (as was made clear by the recent #MeToo movement), and rising digital crimes against women. In the wake of the IMF crisis (and after 2003 and 2009 recessions), while most Korean people suffered immense difficulty, women's employment rate saw the sharpest decline (Geum, 2011). Women are forced to take up contract-based, freelance, or other temp jobs that men are far less likely to be employed in (Geum, 2011). While such jobs, on one hand, promise flexibility to women who have to perform housework and childrearing duties, on the other hand, new forms of employment have created a gendered intensification of work-life, leading to stress and burnout. In this regard, it is also important to note that during the COVID-19 pandemic in 2020, the group that saw the largest jump in the rate of suicide are women in their 20s, a demographic whose opportunities in the workplace seem to foreclose before any other group in society during a recession (Lim, 2020).

As noted previously, after leaving in the 1970s and 1980s, it is only now that younger Korean women have started making a return. In 2019, of the 444,464 people who made a return to the countryside, 46.8% were women. Interestingly 49.7% of the total figure were in their 20s and 30s, while 16.4% were in their 40s (Statistics, 2019). This contemporary phenomenon of *gwichon* has been accompanied by the development of a newly rehashed ideal of the countryside presented in newer forms of media too. Recently, Korean television has been awash with variety shows, short-form documentaries, and dramas depicting villages and small towns as spaces of escape, rest, and spiritual or physical convalescence. Shows such as MBN's *Into the Wilderness*, JTBC's *Camping Club*, and tvN's *Laborhood on Hire* regularly referred to as "healing" (or *hilling* shows in Konglish), follow celebrities into the countryside, where they take on the slow-life, "finding themselves" as they farm and cook their meals.

Hyori's Bed and Breakfast (JTBC, 2017–2018)

In the recent history of variety shows, perhaps the most popular "healing" program has been *Hyori's Homestay* (*Hyorine Minbak;* 효리네민박, *Hyori's Bed and Breakfast*), which revolves around the first-generation female K-Pop idol, Lee Hyori, and her musician husband, Lee Sang-soon. Together, they form the most representative *gwichon* couple in the entertainment industry, who got married and made the big move to Jeju in 2013, where they continue to live (neither of their hometowns are Jeju, as Lee Hyori belongs to small town of Cheongwon whereas her husband hails from Seoul). After a hiatus of four years, in 2017, Lee Hyori made a reappearance on national television with this TV show, where she and her husband invited guests to live with them in their own home-turned-B&B in Jeju Island. The guests in Lee's B&B were ordinary people who applied to be on the show, where they were given a complete "healing" package, including being shown around Jeju, fed meals full of local produce, taught yoga, and even given life advice, all by Lee Hyori herself in the intimate space of her home.

Many *gwichon* women like Lee Hyori run pensions, B&Bs, or various village "experience centers" in the countryside rather than partake in agricultural labor. An interview-based survey in Jeollabuk-do found that almost none of the women who have moved back to the countryside are employed as agricultural laborers, but instead do freelance jobs, work in welfare, teach at hagwons, run pensions and agriculture experience centers, or even lead women's farming cooperatives (Park, 2016). In this way, Lee Hyori's makeshift B&B too appears to be one such experience center combined with a bed and breakfast. The image of Lee Hyori running her B&B in this program serves as an example of how the young women who have made a belated "return" to the countryside no longer need to hold the positions women did in the countryside of the past, namely one of agricultural, reproductive, and domestic labor, but can endeavor to find a new life for themselves based on a more idyllic and liberating alternative livelihood.

When Lee Hyori, an extremely popular "bold-concept" K-Pop and variety television star, decided to have a "small wedding," take a break from the entertainment industry and move to the countryside, not only did she start the minimalism movement in the wedding industry, but also inspired many a young couple, and especially young women like herself, to move to the countryside.[8] In the show, Lee Hyori is assisted by popular *Hallyu* female stars, such as Yoona and IU, who are also seen to be taking respite from their busy schedules, escaping their stressful city lives. A notable aspect of the show is the bubbling tension between Lee Hyori and her husband with regard to her remaining desires toward her K-Pop career and life in Seoul, which Lee Hyori regularly brings up to her husband, who in turn appears more than content with his life in rural Jeju. Although it was treated in the show with humor, Lee Hyori's remaining aspirations in the fast-moving world of K-Pop can be seen as a microcosm of the halted mobility many Korean women face in their careers. In the same year the first season of the show aired on TV, Lee Hyori released a new song titled "Seoul," the lyrics of which also heavily suggest her longing toward the city: "I turned my back and came far away/ But when I close my eyes, I remember it/ I look back when I'm awash with longing/ But it's too late to go back/ Seoul/Seoul/ . . . Will I look for you again? / Or should I forget? Or should I long for it?"—"Seoul," Lee Hyori (translated by the author).

Interestingly enough, this show catapulted Lee Hyori to the center of attention once again. After two hit seasons of *Hyori's Bed and Breakfast*, Lee Hyori not only began appearing in other *gwichon* variety shows like *Camping Club* (2019) but also debuted again as a member of the star-studded musical trio "SSAK3" and a girl group named "Refund Sisters" in 2020 (Seung, 2020). Lee Hyori's return to the countryside (and its subsequent aestheticization through television), led her to find a new path in her halted career, but because the average returnee is not a famous celebrity, Lee Hyori's experience can be seen to be non-representative of ordinary women making the move. Nevertheless, her portrayal as a jet-setting *gwichonin*, going from Seoul to Jeju, and the romanticization of the notion of *gwichon* while simultaneously depicting the countryside as a locus of opportunity create the illusion of an idealized existence and greater mobility for those looking to move to the countryside. This show elicits a number of themes that can be traced in many recent K-Dramas as well. A string of shows released on Netflix just before and during the pandemic in 2020 are a case in point— *When the Camellia Blooms* (September–November 2019), *It's Okay to Not be Okay* (June–August 2020), and *Do Do Sol Sol La La Sol* (October–November 2020), all portray young female protagonists who, facing troubles related to their careers and money in the city, choose to impulsively "return" to small seaside towns to pursue a new life. There, they embark upon a new enterprise (opening a bar, a piano *hagwon*, or writing a new book) and find independence, love, and a new path for life.

As a study on young people's urban to rural migration in Korea notes, more than the mere "push" factor of the city, the notion of "imagined mobility" is central in the decision-making process of *gwichon* for younger Koreans (Kim, 2019). The interviewees in the study expressed their inability to sustain their lives in urban areas and the impossibility of envisaging their futures in the city, the place where they experienced immense stress and instability. For these young people, the countryside was a space where they could imagine a future for themselves. Once there, the interviewees found autonomy and agency, finding self-satisfaction in the fruits of their labor and a sense of ownership over their own lives (Kim, 2019). In Benedict Anderson's seminal study about the notion of "imagined community," the nation is seen as a socially constructed entity, solidified only by the imagination of the people who perceive themselves to be a part of it (Anderson, 2006). The media's (or "print capitalism") role in the creation of this imagined community is seen to be crucial, as the vernacular and the images used by the media serve to construct the idea of the nation in people's minds. "Imagined mobility" is also a related concept. It is the desire for change and mobility in the face of social conditions of stagnation, strengthened only through the power of imagination. In Kim Ban-seok's study, young people stuck in exhausting lives in the city imagined for themselves a future through moving to the country. As Appadurai notes in his anthropological study on globalization, *The Future as a Cultural Fact*, it is the act of imagining that subverts and inverts the order of things and translates into actual agency and mobility toward the future (2013). It was not the just the stresses of the city that "pushed" out these youths, but the promise of the countryside that attracted them. Hence the act of imagination, and the tools which help the construction of this imagined ideal/promise of the countryside, become crucial.

While the notion of "Imagined Mobility" is applied to all of the young people in Kim's study, it can be said that such aspirations are especially evident in young women who, as mentioned before, are more likely to face low-paid and unstable work, unemployment, and interruptions in their career (경력 단절) in the city. The depictions of women undertaking *gwichon* discussed in this chapter are not only depictions of imagined mobilities of the women themselves but can also be seen to create the very images that formulate imagination and agency. Hence, the image of Lee Hyori, a first-generation K-pop idol with her career long behind her, restarting her life in the country and "finding herself" once again in the midst of nature, leading a simple, unadulterated existence, becomes an approachable, tangible "dream" of the countryside. This notion of imagined mobility can be traced throughout the various depictions of *gwichon* discussed in this chapter.

Little Forest (Yim Soon-rye, 2018)

The aspirations of city women toward the countryside are depicted most evidently in Yim Soon-rye's 2018 film *Little Forest* (리틀 포레스트), which portrays the life of a young woman who returns to her childhood home in a remote village. Yim Soon-rye, perhaps the most prolific female filmmaker in Korea, is associated with the Korean New Wave and is known for her examination of gendered social norms and the relationship between humanity and nature, hence, her films are often set in natural and the countryside locations, as is the case with *Sorry, Thank You* (2011), *Rolling Home with a Bull* (2010), and *Romance Joe* (2011). However, her latest work is not only set, but propelled by its rural locale. In the film, Han Hye-won, a 20-something unemployed teaching aspirant, returns to the small village of Miseongri, where she grew up, after failing the national teaching qualification exam. When Hye-won's boyfriend in the city passes the same exam, her mixed emotions prompt her to leave the city without telling him, eventually resulting in their break up. While in the city, Hye-won works multiple part-time jobs to support herself and has to rely on instant meals or expired convenience store food for sustenance.

Food plays a central role in the film. This is made especially evident in the scene where Hye-won's friend, Eun-sook, asks Hye-won why she has come back, to which Hye-won responds by simply stating "Because I'm hungry." This dialogue between the two establishes the ideal image of the country, as an ever-welcoming plentiful utopia, a place to escape the hunger and the rotten food (and life) of the city. The parts of the story are organized by the seasons, sandwiched between seasonal recipes that Hye-won attempts from her mother's cookbook. The artfully rustic kitchen in Hye-won's house, added to perfect *yoribangs*—food recipe shots—complete with *mukbangs* of her friends slurping down the food noisily, has a dreamlike quality, a stark-green contrast to the greyed tones of the city. Romanticized shots of flowers placed delicately on pasta, verdant rice fields, and the fashionably antiquated interiors of Hye-won's traditional *hanok* house combined with ASMR-level vegetable chopping, bird singing, and the crunching of flower fritters create a "healing" paradise for stressed young viewers in the city who are hungry for vicarious satisfaction (*daerimanjok*). The city, in comparison, is depicted as a cold, joyless space, where Hye-won feels like she is "always starving"; the most representative shot being the deep focus of Hye-won's fridge, containing a dried apple, a banana, and a rotten onion in her tiny Seoul "one-room" apartment. Chin Eun-Kyung in a comparative study of the Japanese and Korean versions of *Little Forest*, makes the important observation that while both the Japanese and Korean versions view the space of the village from an urban perspective, as perfectly balancing humanity and nature, the Korean version highlights the human aspect further as having a meal with her friends and the rituals around the food itself are seen to provide the protagonist with a safe space of community and human relationships (Chin, 2020). Growing and cooking her own food, Hye-won is seen to come closer not only to nature but also to those around her, including her estranged mother.

Hye-won's mother, while absent throughout the film, is a central character. In Hye-won's flashbacks about her, she is seen to have followed her sick husband back to his village from the city, and after his death raised Hye-won there. When Hye-won turns into a young adult and decides to leave for the city, her mother suddenly disappears. Throughout the film, Hye-won grapples with her remaining resentment and anger toward her mother but with each passing season and each seasonal recipe of her mother's that she attempts, a memory of her mother preparing that dish, along with her life lessons, emerges, bolstering Hye-won's resolve to stay in the village and understand her mother's decision. In the film, both Hye-won and her mother are portrayed as finding the countryside to be a safe space, full of opportunities, where they can perform their suppressed dreams and desires. Hye-won's mother—who wanted to make a fresh start after her life as a woman and an individual had halted since her marriage, subsequent widowhood and single motherhood—finds her strength from her personal "little forest"—the rural village and her daughter. Hye-won, dejected in her urban dreams of passing the national qualification exam and becoming a teacher, returns, and is able realize her full potential in the countryside where she grows her own food, cooks, and works the field, finding community and agency. Both of their tales are that of a renewed mobility, and further, of empowerment.

Hye-won's "little forest," her community, is completed by her two child-hood friends Eun-sook and Jae-ha. Jae-ha, a *gwichonin* like Hye-won, is shown to return to the village after being verbally abused by his boss in the city. Hye-won and Jae-ha develop romantic feelings for each other, and the countryside, becomes a space not only for empowerment, or community but also romantic love. Hye-won breaks up with her boyfriend in the city because of feelings of failure which arose from competition, yet with Jae-ha, she feels a sense of community and is able to have a relationship based on equality, especially evident in shots showing the two of them working shoulder-to-shoulder in the fields. It remains vague whether Jae-ha and Hye-won actually date by the end, letting Hye-won remain as a self-sufficient, independent single woman, yet backed with a strong support network in her little community. In other words, the love she finds in the countryside does not undercut her new-found freedom. Near the end of the film, Hye-won is seen going to Seoul, after preparing for the relocation of saplings (*aju simgi-* the first step toward permanent farming), which informs Jae-ha and the viewer of the fact that she will return. After earning enough money through part-time jobs in Seoul, Hye-won returns to Miseongri, only to find the door to her house open—suggesting that Mother is back—and runs happily toward it. In this way, the process of reconnecting with her mother—extending her community or her "little forest"—concludes in parallel to her decisive reconnection with the countryside.

The film presents a rare image of the rural in a country which has undergone accelerated modernization of the cities, and in that regard, is an important feat, as it is reflective of the desires of the urban population (Kim and Bang, 2019), especially women like Hye-won who are exhausted and overworked. The release of *Hyori's Bed and Breakfast* and this film, in 2017 and 2018 respectively, were simultaneous with the height of *gwichon* in Korea. This was not regarded to be coincidental by news media and scholars such as Kim Jee Hee and Bang Jai Suk who saw the desire for *gwichon* to be "derived" from TV programs and films like *Little Forest*.[9] However, some felt this film to be uncomfortable to watch (Lee, 2018; Bae, 2018). Film critic Lee Soo-hyang places this feeling in the utter arti-ficiality of Hye-won's country life (Lee, 2018). To others, like the actual residents of the countryside, it was more than just a vague discomfort—the film had created a false ideal which couldn't be any further from the real-ity of their lives. Kim Hu-ju, a female farmer from Asan and a journalist for *Hanguk Nongjeong*, told all her friends who were hastily making plans of moving to the countryside that the film was nothing but a fantasy (Kim, 2019). She speaks about the character of Hye-won in her criticism of the film:

The fact that the film sets up a protagonist who is "in her 20s+unmarried+woman" is because this is the group most desirous of *gwichon,* yet the least able to access it. . . agricultural policy is always male-centered. Women can never be the principal agent in the countryside, at best they are homemakers or agricultural laborers, at worst just birthing machines. Just by looking at how the local governments are running 'foreign bride agencies' one can see how appalling their views about women are.

Hye-won is a character full of contradictions. On the one hand, she is reflective of urban desires of mobility but on the other hand, to those in the countryside, she can be a bitter reminder of the real status of young women of the country who are being whitewashed by the film. Organic Punk, an archivist of female farmworkers and the women of the countryside, discovered that most women who watched the film found it "annoying" to say the least (Organic Punk, 2020). Especially scenes like Hye-won fixing her house after a typhoon, with ease and without a hair out of place, was taken to not only be unrealistic, but strengthening ideas of *Kkumimnodong,* which refers to makeup as labor, as well as women having to do work while maintaining a made-up exterior—a term synonymous with the Anticorset/Anticosmetic feminist movement (*Talko Undong*) in Korea. She calls the film another example of the city telling the country, through images it's made up (or "imagined") of the country, that the countryside is livable after all (*salmanhada*). "And that is exactly where their privilege lies"—she states (Organic Punk, 2020).

Heaven's Garden (Channel A, 2011–2012)

As the name suggests, the serialized drama, *Heaven's Garden* (천상의 화원 곰배령) is another tale that weaves a paradise in the countryside, albeit not completely without trouble. The drama is unique in depicting both a *gwichon* woman and a marriage-migrant woman (though the protagonist is still the *gwichon* woman). *Heaven's Garden* centers upon a family of four: mother Jung Jae-in, daughters Eun-soo and Hyun-soo, and Grandpa Jung Boo-sik. The story begins when Jae-in, who has been estranged from her father ever since her marriage to a divorced man, returns to her countryside home in the picturesque hamlet of Gombaeryong in Gangwon-do, impoverished and on the verge of a divorce. Jae-in, who has not seen her father in more than a decade, and resents him deeply, is left with no other option after her cheating husband's business fails, he is jailed, and she is harassed by his creditors.

Jae-in, like Hye-won, comes back to the countryside from the city full of disappointment and pain. She had left Gombaeryeong along with her mother and brother for Seoul when she was a child, but their father had decided to stay back. Grandpa Boo-sik is presented sympathetically despite being an old man of very few words—we learn that he had remained in the village because he was waiting for his older brother, from whom he was separated during the Korean War. Jae-in is initially ignorant of her father's difficult past, but after living with him, she slowly comes to understand his decision. Much like Hye-won's relationship with her mother, Jae-in too, reconnects with her father, as well as the countryside in tandem. A marked similarity with *Little Forest* is the role of community in the female protagonist's development and mobility. Jae-in, like Hye-won, develops intimate human relationships in the country which helps her to build a new life for herself and her children.

In contrast to Hye-won, for whom a community, in the shape of her child-hood friends, was readily available in Miseongri, Jae-in had a tough begin-ning in Gombaeryeong. Due to an old familial feud with the village head's family over the Jungs' ancestral land, topped off by the fact that Jae-in is divorced and from the city, the village women dislike Jae-in at first, creating rumors and harassing her on every occasion. Jae-in also does not understand the traditional ways of the countryside, and on one occasion, is shown to pro-voke the ire of the village head by peeking into a traditionally male prayer-ceremony for good harvest. These events in the first few episodes of the drama add a realism effect to Jae-in's story of rural return. In a survey done in Jinan, the greatest problem that the *gwichon* women were seen to face was the inability to have developed relationships with the local village residents who are more traditional and generally older (Jin and Park, 2012). This dose of realism does not last very long; Grandpa Boo-sik is able to reclaim his land and divide it, graciously so, among the very same villagers who cheated him, creating peace in the village. With this, Jae-in is seen to be readily accepted back into the fold by the village women and soon becomes a strong part of the community. One may argue that such an depiction of harmonious assimila-tion into the countryside for *gwichon* women is overly idealized owing to the fact that many of the women in the survey stated that they found themselves to be at odds with the older villagers often in their daily lives, and in light of the sentiments of the women Organic Punk archives who also stated their dis-comfort with seeing such representations of *gwichon*, in that far from dream-ing about making friends around the village, most of these single women just hope that their neighborhoods are not unsafe (Organic Punk, 2020).

Jae-in, who is depicted as bogged down by worry and exhaustion when she arrives in the village with her children, is shown to become happier and healthier the longer she lives in the countryside and away from the city (and her cheating husband), strengthening her familial relationships—reconcil-ing with her father, developing stronger bonds with her step-daughter, but also, crucially, finding employment in the countryside. Jae-in becomes the deputy in-charge of Gombaeryeong's large agricultural cooperative, nego-tiating with big hotels and striking deals, all while serving the local people.

The community does not only aid her psychological development but also becomes the network which propels the livelihood of the protagonist. After years of temporary work in the city, Jae-in is able to secure stable, meaningful employment once she becomes a member of the village community. In one scene, the village head questions the decision to send her and another *gwichonin* café owner as representatives to a business pitch instead of him. Jae-in and the café owner have no experience of farming but they are seen to be more educated and "suitable" for the role by the other villagers.

In the research on *gwichon* women in Jinan, the local governments often expected *gwichon* women to take up roles in the countryside that the local people were seen to not be able to do (Jin and Park, 2012). Recent women entrants to the countryside were mostly working on contract-basis in educational, cultural, and administrative fields rather than directly in agriculture (Jin and Park, 2012). Hence, Jae-in's high position within the cooperative reflects the desires of the government from women moving to the countryside, where depopulation and aging have resulted in brain drain (Bae, 2009; Bae, Ha, and Jo, 2010).

Jae-in not only finds economic mobility in the countryside, but like Hye-won, she also finds love in the form of a fellow *gwichonin* man. Living in the countryside, Jae-in finally gathers the courage to divorce her cheating absentee husband, distancing herself from all that he stands for: capitalistic greed and the unending anxieties of the city. In contrast, the owner of the only café in the village, Shin Woo-gyun, is depicted as a supportive friend and romantic interest for Jae-in, uninterested in material wealth, having left his well-paying job as a policeman in the city in order to run a laidback café in the mountains. Married to Kang Tae-sub in Seoul, Jae-in was isolated, tied down taking care of his child from a previous marriage as well as her own daughter, working part-time jobs, all while being constantly lied to by her husband. Her relationship with Woo-gyun in contrast, is based on equality— they are both single parents, working as partner deputies at the cooperative and, like Hye-won and Jae-ha, best friends. In spite of this, Jae-in does not marry Woo-gyun and their relationship remains vague, preserving her single status and her new-found autonomy.

Hye-won and Jae-in, after finding mobility and growth through the space of the countryside, are depicted as continuing their self-sustained existence, without tying themselves down to any promises of marriage. In *Heaven's Garden*, as in *Little Forest*, the countryside for the *gwichon* woman is presented as a space to escape the atomized and toxic relationships of the city and build supportive, community-based relationships—whether it is her romance with Woo-gyun, the camaraderie between the village women in the idealized space of the agricultural cooperative, or her friendship with the foreign bride, Kim Myeong-ok (who will be discussed in the next section).

Jae-in's daughters, Eun-soo and Hyun-soo, and their friends are often the eyes through which the viewer witnesses the beauty of Gombaeryeong, a little village nestled among mountains on all sides. Romanticized time-lapse shots of streams, squirrels and birds, trembling flowers, and changing seasons in the village all make Gombaeryeong a haven of untouched nature. It is often mentioned in the show that, since moving to the village, both Eun-soo and Hyun-soo have become healthier and happier. The well-being of children is an important reason why *gwichon* women make the decision to move to the countryside in the first place. According to a *gwichon* government survey in 2019, the biggest concerns for *gwichon* women under 40 are childcare services and education (Statistics, 2019). As discussed earlier, images such as this arguably play an important role in the construction of the imagination of mobility, in this case the depiction of Jae-in, a young mother who comes to the countryside and raises her children in an alternative, stress- and pollutant-free environment, escaping her stalled mobility in the city.

THE NEW COUNTRYWOMEN: RURAL FEMALE MARRIAGE-MIGRANTS IN FILM AND TELEVISION

In recent depictions of the countryside in film and television, the rural environs are envisioned as a place for escape from the city, of healing, and finding oneself. In this idealized space, the acute difficulties of the countryside hardly appear. In the rare cases that they do, like in *Heaven's Garden*, these difficulties find a neat solution, ensuring that the pristine image of the countryside is preserved. This newly imagined countryside has no space for the depiction of women marriage-migrants either—the other major group of young female entrants in the village. According to the latest numbers, a total of 132,391 foreign female spouses reside in Korea, which is 82% of all marriage-migrants (Statistics, 2019). The sender countries are diverse, with women hailing from Asian countries such as China, Vietnam, Cambodia, Mongolia, Philippines, and Thailand, among others (Statistics, 2019). The Korean men regularly belong to either rural areas or the lower economic strata in urban areas (Kim, 2012). At its peak in 2004, more than one in four rural marriages involved a female marriage-migrant (Statistics, 2004).

Korea's development has created a wealth inequality that has left certain groups of men, especially in the countryside, with little to no option of marriage within the country. Yet the traditional imperatives toward marriage remain. On the other hand, Korea's developed status and propagation of its wealthy image through *Hallyu*, corporate outsourcing, and ODA to the developing world has created a "pull" factor for citizens of these developing countries, especially in Korea's Asian "periphery" to find a better life for themselves and their families in Korea, driving the marriage-migration of women (and the migration of labor, mostly consisting of men) to Korea. The gap between these two phenomena, of rural unmarried older men, having "fallen back" in a wealthy country, and poorer young women from the third world, looking to "move ahead" onto a better life in South Korea, gave rise to international marriage brokers in the late 1990s who, in exchange for a hefty fee, matched rural men with women from poorer countries (Cheng, 2011). Many of these agencies are known to be corrupt, openly advertising sexualized photographs of marriage candidates, even promising a partial refund if the wife runs away (Ock, 2019). Until 2008, the international marriage market was more or less unregulated, allowing for fraud, with multiple cases of domestic and sexual abuse emerging, and in some extreme cases even deaths, owing to the fact that many women were not informed of their husbands' criminal background or history of mental instability or violence (Jin, 2005).[10] To tackle this, the government adopted the *Act on the Regulations of International Marriage Brokerage* and the *Act for the Support of Multicultural Families* in 2008 (Cheng, 2011). Since then, "multiculturalism" (*Damunhwa*) has become a catch-all term under which the government has promoted initiatives to assist marriage-migrants and their families on both central and local levels.

It is noteworthy that hardly any Korean dramas or films include representations of female marriage-migrants. As Joo-yeon Rhee points out in her analysis of migrant workers and foreign brides in popular films, in spite of the immense government focus on *Damunhwa*, widespread popular discourse about the future of multicultural society (*Damunhwa Sahoe*), and the critical changes in the fabric of Korean society in the last few decades (depopulation, rapid aging, jump in marriage-migration—questioning of ideas of racial homogeneity or *danilminjok*), there have been no major feature films that represent the lives of the many multicultural families that now exist in Korea, except for *Wandugi* (2011, dir. Yi Han) which depicts a poor urban multicultural family (Rhee, 2016). Marriage-migrants in the countryside can only be found in variety shows and short-form documentaries, and sometimes, albeit rarely, in dramas too. It is here that one can observe how society at large views them and desires from them, and how the women's own desires are interpreted.

HEAVEN'S GARDEN: KIM MYEONG-OK

In *Heaven's Garden*, Kim Myeong-ok is a foreign bride who plays an important supporting role. *Heaven's Garden* was the top viewed drama at the time of its airing (Kang, 2011); as one of the very few television programs that not only depicted *gwichon* but also marriage-migration of foreign women, it offered a peek inside the world of the new countryside to its urban viewers. Representation of the countryside and its people, who are already on the margins of television (and the society), and minority figures, such as female marriage-migrants, is crucial in the shaping of mainstream views regarding them.

Myeong-ok's story begins when she is discovered by *gwichonin* protagonist Jae-in while attempting suicide by walking into a stream. Jae-in runs into the water after Myeong-ok, saving her life. She brings Myeong-ok to her own home where she finds out that Myeong-ok tried killing herself because the man who promised to marry her ran away with her money; the two bond over their mutual pain and resentment toward the absentee men in their lives. Myeong-ok is depicted as pretty and very young, speaking with a heavy North Korean accent—yet at this stage it is not clear whether she is North Korean or Korean-Chinese (*Joseonjeok*). When Myeong-ok leaves the house, Jae-in spots an envelope full of money, stolen from the house, poking out of Myeong-ok's coat but keeps quiet and lets her go. This initial meeting between the *gwichon* woman and the foreign woman is important for two reasons: on the one hand, this meeting establishes their sisterhood through common gender-based experiences and, on the other hand, the incident with the envelope sets the class hierarchy that remains throughout the story. Although Myeong-ok comes clean in the same episode, she is promptly forgiven by Jae-in and is thus doubly indebted to Jae-in from the very beginning of their relationship, which skews the balance of power. From this point, Jae-in can be seen to help Myeong-ok in different ways, the most important being introducing Myeong-ok to the middle-aged neighborhood bachelor, Nam-gil.

Nam-gil is a farmer who lives with his feisty mother in Gombaeryeong and, to his mother's disdain, is seen to have some interest in the divorced city returnee, Jae-in; however, when he sees Myeong-ok working at a *naengmyeon* restaurant, he instantly falls for her stubborn charm and her knowledge of *naengmyeon*. Jae-in sets them up and then Nam-gil falls head over heels for Myeong-ok. Myeong-ok is revealed to be a North Korean refugee but hides her country of origin from Nam-gil, telling him that she is from Yanbian, China.

Unlike Jae-in and Woo-gyun, who spend the entire show getting to know each other and do not get married, Myeong-ok decides to marry Nam-gil immediately. Nam-gil charms her with his masculine protectiveness, forcefully entering her residence and leaving his shoes by her door, reducing Myeong-ok's character to that of a weak woman needing protection. This trope runs throughout the show, as Nam-gil protects her from his mother, too, after marriage. Nam-gil's mother is against their marriage at first, citing Myeong-ok's young age which will keep her from being able to taking care of her mother-in-law, her beauty which will make her arrogant, and most of all, the fact that she is from Yanbian, because according to her, all *Joseonjeok* are criminal-minded: stealing people's money through voice-phishing or running away with their in-laws' money after marriage. She only agrees to the marriage after eating the food Myeong-ok prepares, finally believing in her abilities as a daughter-in-law. This is not only telling of the patriarchal nature of the countryside, but of the prejudices people have against marriage-migrants (like the many billboards advertising "She won't run away! We guarantee you") and especially for those from a *Joseonjok* background who are regularly stereotyped as being petty criminals.

Jae-in plans the ceremony, but just a few days before the wedding, Myeong-ok breaks down and hides, feeling guilty about not telling Nam-gil where she is really from. When Nam-gil does find out, he nobly forgives her subterfuge and they swiftly get married. However, when Nam-gil's mother discovers the truth a few months later, she throws Myeong-ok out of the house in anger, only to accept her back upon finding out that Myeong-ok is pregnant. Myeong-ok delivers a baby boy who becomes the pride and joy of her mother-in-law, firmly securing Myeong-ok's place in the family. At this point, Myeong-ok's story retreats to the background, motherhood becoming her sole occupation. Myeong-ok, hereafter, is sometimes spotted as Jae-in's trusted companion, helping Boo-sik look for his estranged brother in the North and giving life advice to Eun-soo, and is depicted as a vessel for the "healing" or catharsis of those around her. In the case of Myeong-ok, unlike *gwichonin* women, the countryside is not a space of autonomy or agency, but one of domesticity and adjustment. It is not a place for new employment opportunities, or love, but rather tradition and childcare. It is noteworthy that this drama happens to present the countryside and traditional motherhood as a solution for the poor foreign female migrant. No government agency is mentioned in the drama, but her desires appear to cleanly dovetail with the well-known reality of the drive of the state to regenerate the countryside through the introduction of marriage-migrants, at this very time. This drama was broadcast on television at a time when marriage-migration was booming, presenting a marriage-migrant content with her traditional duties of mother-hood. Both the depictions of the *gwichon* woman and the marriage-migrant woman in *Heaven's Garden* are absent of any real complexity that women face in the countryside, which provides swift solutions to all their problems.

NAMCHON OVER THE MOUNTAIN (KBS 1; 2007–2014)

Another television drama that features a female marriage-migrant char-acter in the countryside is the first season of *Namchon over the Mountain*

(전원드라마: 산 너머 남촌에는 1기), a "new-age" *Jeonwondeurama* that began after the end of *Country Diary* and KBS's *Love on a Jujube Tree*, and was the last program of its genre to air on any major channel (Chung, 2009; Jeong, 2016). It promised to be different from its predecessors by representing the changes occurring in the countryside through the inclusion of a *gwichon* family and a foreign marriage-migrant into the story, while keeping the old-world charm and nostalgia alive for viewers in the city. The story focuses on three families: the main family run by a matriarch, a *gwichon* family, and the village head's family.

The village head has a Vietnamese daughter-in-law, Haiyen. In the fifth episode "Fairy and the Woodcutter," the village head's middle-aged son, Bong Soon-ho, goes to pick up his new wife from the airport. Soon-ho waits for her at the airport, but she does not appear. Far from being worried about her safety, people around Soon-ho (neighbors and even the airport staff) conjecture that she only got married for the visa and has already taken off because, according to them, women getting married to reside illegally in Korea is a common occurrence; however, Haiyen does appear, albeit late because she lost her bag. A man appears to be helping Haiyen and when Soon-ho spots her, and he is quick to pull her away from him, telling her "Every man apart from me is a robber." This is similar to Nam-gil's overprotectiveness of Myeong-ok after their very first meeting as well. This initial meeting at the airport sets the tone for how Haiyen is treated throughout this show—pulled and dragged around with ease.

A month previous to this day, Soon-ho had met Haiyen, a woman 14 years his junior, through a marriage agency in Vietnam and gotten married, all within three days' time. Haiyen's character is a sexual and racial Other, at the odd crossroads of constant infantilization and sexualization. On the way back from the airport, she is shown to develop car sickness as apparently "Vietnamese people are not used to riding cars." Despite this crude attitude, Soon-ho's father, upon detecting her sickness, is suspicious and takes Haiyen to get a pregnancy test done at the local clinic. Such surveillance of her and her body, from the very beginning, introduces the unequal power relations of the story which undercut Haiyen's bodily autonomy and places her in the hands of her Korean in-laws.

Haiyen is also the subject of great attention by the village community. Everyone, from the little nephew to Soon-ho's friends, cannot stop talking about her youth and beauty. Soon-ho is warned repeatedly by his friends and neighbors of the fact that she can run away at any time. The community fails to be a "little forest" for Haiyen, in the way it was for Hye-won or Jae-in. It does not become a space for mobility, but instead becomes a place where she is tied down and her movements are controlled. She is treated like a child by Soon-ho; in episode 39, Soon-ho finds out that Haiyen has made a Vietnamese

friend at the village "multicultural center" who is also helping Haiyen to get
a job, so, he hides her passport away and questions why she needs money.
This friend, unlike Haiyen, is an unmarried working woman, with no proper
Korean manners (like getting up while an elder is speaking) and always
expressing herself freely. Soon-ho wants Haiyen to have no Vietnamese
friends and warns Huong multiple times to stay away from Haiyen. The
contrast in the representation of these two minority women reveals deep-
rooted ideas of gender and racial prejudices. If Haiyen is depicted as a figure
of an innocent and unknowing foreign woman who can be groomed, Huong
is the figure of an uncivilized foreign woman led astray, who can only be a
"negative influence" by encouraging Haiyen to run away. It can be seen as a
racialized version of the chaste and the fallen woman dichotomy, resulting in
a masculinized and polarized conception of women from developing countries. This friend is the first semblance of an intimate human relationship for
Haiyen who offers her a job, or economic mobility. The village community
and her immediate family, in contrast, are only concerned with making sure
she doesn't run away, keeping her sexuality in check.

Soon-ho's controlling (and at times illegal) behavior like hiding Haiyen's
passport, confining her at home, and not letting her work are accepted as a
normal part of being married to a foreign bride by those around him. In spite
of this mistrust of her, Haiyen is always forgiving and understanding of her
husband. Haiyen is an archetypical image of a perfect bride, a child-like
figure, always willing to learn and assimilate, and falling in line with the
patriarchal order. Chandra Talpade Mohanty, in her critical work of postcolonial feminist research, *Under Western Eyes*, argues that "assumptions
of privilege, ethnocentric universality, and inadequate self-consciousness"
have led to the construction of the image of third world women as "a singular
monolithic subject" that is passive and powerless (Mohanty, 1988). While
Mohanty is primarily referring to the West, those like Parameswaran apply
her idea to the representation of third world women in news and media in the
West (Parameswaran, 1996). Mohanty opens up her critique to non-Western
centers of power that employ identical strategies too (Mohanty, 1988). To use
Mohanty's argument, the characters of Haiyen and Myeong-ok can both be
read as falling under the same frame of "passive and powerless" women who
need to be saved by their Korean husbands. While both the dramas are rare
portrayals marriage-migrant women, they fail to construct characters which
are more than just two-dimensional approximations of perfect brides.

The focus put on Haiyen's passport and Soon-ho's ability to take it away
from her inadvertently normalizes how marriage-migrant women often find
themselves precariously dependent on their husbands. Marriage-migrants
are dependent on their husbands not only because of their visa, but also for
simple, yet important tasks like making a personal bank account, taking

loans, or accessing government welfare services. In addition, these women can only become beneficiaries of the Natural Basic Livelihood Security Law as mothers of children with Korean fathers, which leads to welfare services being conditional on the woman's reproductive role (Cheng, 2011). In many cases, this lack of a support network and resultant high dependency leads to alienation and depression (Jang, 2014).

Along with Haiyen's beauty, what is constantly pointed out under the guise of a compliment is the similarity of her looks to a Korean woman's. In the same vein, it is also mentioned to the couple that they are lucky their soon-to-be-born child will look Korean. While Soon-ho treats Haiyen like a child in the first season, by season 2, six years have passed; Haiyen has had her child and Soo-ho has become much more critical of her behavior. When Bang Bo-bae, their daughter, does not learn Korean fast enough, Soo-ho blames Haiyen. In spite of this, when Bo-bae starts to go to school, she faces discrimination, and in episode 162, she is called "too dark" by other children to play the role of Snow White in a school play. The child ends up blaming her mother; after Haiyen gives a special workshop about multiculturalism and Vietnam to the children at the school on the behalf of the government multicultural center, the bullying stops. According to a survey in 2012 (at the time this drama was broadcast on TV), 37% of all children from multicultural families faced racial discrimination and bullying at school, not only from their peers but also from their teachers (Kim and Yang, 2012). The government center sending Haiyen to give a workshop to the children is a key scene, alluding to the achievement of a political goal, one of sensitizing people in the countryside to multiculturalism while also alleviating the fears of marriage-migrant women who are often afraid that their children will face discrimination in school.

The façade of Haiyen having a "fulfilling" family life comes at the cost of her being constantly pushed to fit into the existing patriarchal norms of the Korean countryside, while the countryside keeps its traditions without any change. Korean language and food are regularly emphasized in the household, with Vietnamese food dismissed as tasting rotten or strange; the entirety of the village comes together in the spying and controlling of Haiyen's behavior. The countryside for Haiyen is an orthodox and oppressive place, which does not allow for friendship or economic independence, but only marriage and motherhood. Rare portrayals of minority figures such as Haiyen and Myeong-ok are opportunities for more than just the circumscribed depiction offered to them, one entirely correlative with South Korean policy efforts toward marriage-migrant women, which is based purely on the reproductive level, as has been pointed out constantly by scholars (Kim and Kilkey, 2017). Korean language classes, cooking classes, cultural education (childrearing and homemaking), and even counseling for domestic issues are provided at

multicultural centers (like the one Haiyen attends in *Namchon*) to the women
by the government. As Cheng points out, however, these services may use
the language of "multiculturalism," but in fact, they are the state's attempt to
"Koreanize" marriage-migrants and ensure the propagation of Korean families, and by extension, ensure the longevity of the countryside too (Cheng,
2011). Haiyen, like Myeong-ok, is another mother-to-be-assimilated into the
folds of the rural. It is important to see characters on-screen that are above
and beyond the "passive and powerless" figures that Mohanty refers to. To
borrow Williams's argument, the construction of a romanticized space of the
countryside, where perfect brides such as these two characters reside, is detrimental to the pursuit of any genuine social change because of how warped
our ideas of the present are.

CONCLUSION: THE CYCLICAL
TRAJECTORY OF THE COUNTRYSIDE

The extent to which dramatic representations of women in the Korean countryside act as narratives of acclimatization for women at different ends of
the transnational socioeconomic spectrum are a key but understudied aspect
of Korean film and television. The new spatialized relationships of power,
in which women from the "center" and women from Korea's new Asian
"periphery" are projected into the countryside, can be seen in the dramas and
films discussed above.

The imagined mobility of young women from the city can be observed
in the representation of the *gwichon* characters analyzed in this chapter.
Gwichon women such as Hye-won and Jae-in in *Little Forest* and *Heaven's*
Garden, respectively, are depicted as seeking in the countryside a locus of
new opportunity, a place where they find community, love, and autonomy,
whether in the form of a new self-sufficient life or a job that gives them satisfaction. However, this love is not one that ties them down and gets in the way
of their new-found agency, but is a supportive and empathetic love, exemplified by the characters of Jae-ha and Woo-gyun. Through aestheticized
depictions, the countryside is promised as a space of healing, rediscovery of
the self and of a healthier, happier life, not only for the women, but for their
children too. It is a place for meaningful employment and fruitful subsistence
farming. These are narratives of acclimatization in a countryside that not only
provide a push to overcome women's halted mobility, but also empowerment.

Furthermore, these portrayals delineate how the reproductive role in the
countryside is not delegated to *gwichonins,* but to marriage-migrants. As
seen in Myeong-ok in *Heaven's Garden* and Haiyen in *Namchon Across the
Mountain,* motherhood is the most important role that they can undertake,

their stories revolving around the process of adjustment into a new society, pregnancy, and childcare. Both the characters are described as innocent and honest, as ideal mothers and wives, and their in-laws are economically stable, undercutting any need for them to work outdoors. Unlike the *gwichonins*, love for them does indeed come in the way of their personal agency and autonomy, as they regularly have to deal with jealousy and protectiveness of their husbands. The community is not a space for mobility, but for control. In the case of Haiyen, the entire countryside was seen to participate in the monitoring of her behavior. While these two dramas included the aspirations of the Korean society for the marriage-migrant women (one related to their reproductive role), their own aspirations got sidelined or absorbed by what is expected from them. In reality, the countryside is often found to be far from the image that is expected by the women, the one propagated by *Hallyu* (Yoon, 2004). This gap between their aspirations and the reality is what is made clear in a variety show like *Gobuyeoljeon* (EBS), which focuses on the conflict in multicultural families. Although the rendering is frequently biased, and portrays the marriage-migrant women as a cultural and racial "other,"[11] it makes the fact of their discomfort from being placed in traditional roles that they did not expect to find themselves in, crystal clear. These shows are narratives of acclimatization in a countryside that is familial and controlling. *Gwichon* women are not expected to be dutiful mothers for the state like women were expected to be during the developmental era. Instead, this role has passed on to the young marriage-migrant women from poorer countries for whom the countryside can never be depicted as a space for autonomy or agency. This is the cyclical trajectory of rural women—while both of these groups of women are shown as the natural inheritors of the Korean countryside, they occupy different levels in the hierarchy of race and class.

Illustrations of the countryside as a space of healing for *gwichon* women is often a fantasy, as many are forced to leave the countryside again because of a lack of proper economic opportunities or support, a problem many see the government to not have provided solutions for as yet (Jin and Park, 2012). There exist state aims toward the rejuvenation of countryside through both these groups of women, and there also exists accompanying gender discrimination toward both groups, albeit a layered one. On the one hand, *gwichon* women are sold the dream of the countryside but are not able to access the necessary welfare policies that would enable them to have sustainable lives once there. On the other, the reproductive role of the migrant women and their assimilation into the Korean society are the only two things taken into consideration under the guise of policies for "Multiculturalism." To return to Williams and the beginning of this chapter, romanticized depictions of the countryside and its new entrants only serve to distort the understanding of the society toward the needs of the present, and hamper efforts for change.

Instead, a more honest representation of the new realities of the contemporary Korean countryside, not just from an urban perspective but from the people of the countryside themselves, is the need of the hour.

NOTES

1. "Agrarian question" refers to the classic debate on the fate of the countryside at the time of capitalist expansion in the late-nineteenth-century Europe (Araghi, 1995).

2. "The popularity of the countryside dramas of the 1980s is related to the fact that 'rural to urban migration' was underway at the very same time. The young and the middle-aged at this time experienced life both in the country and in the city. They felt nostalgia towards the countryside of their youth, and got vicarious satisfaction through watching countryside dramas. The viewership ratings of these shows had to go up. . . . By 2010 however, the migration of population to the cities was coming to a close. 'Countryside is just full of old people' became an oft-heard sentiment. The advertisers at broadcasting companies made those in their twenties and thirties their primary focus. Because this was the age range most likely to buy products after watching ads on television. However, most of these young people were born and have lived only in the cities. Feelings of nostalgia, longing and interest towards the countryside appear less marked. Broadcasting companies have to reflect the desires of their viewers. The fact that countryside is missing from dramas is not unrelated to this situation" (Jeong, 2016, translated by the author).

3. This news article in the Donga Ilbo is a case in point: "From 'hometown' to 'tourist attraction" (Jeong, 2016).

4. The main reason for people moving back to the countryside was seen to be work— 34.1%, followed by housing—26.9% and family—24.8% (Statistics Korea, 2019).

5. Accelerated development in the second half of the 20th century fundamentally transformed women's economic role in society. In 1960, 70.5% of all working Korean women were engaged in economic activity within agriculture or fisheries, but by the year 2000, this number had reduced to just 17%. As Korea began industrializing at record pace, young unmarried women from the country started migrating to the cities in search of jobs in far greater numbers than men. These young women, sometimes called gong-suni (factory girls), were often in their teens or early 20s, worked long hours in difficult conditions, and were paid less than half the wage of their male counterparts (Kim, 2006; Park, 1993).

6. As most young men and women of working age left the countryside, farming was left to older people—mostly older women. Married women accounted for 99% of the female workforce in 1990 whereas single women constituted only 1% (Park, 1993).

7. As of 2018, 78% of countryside "eub/myun" districts have been confirmed as "population extinction risk zones" (Lee, 2018).

8. Lee Hyori has become synonymous with the idea of *gwichon* in popular discourse. Many who chose gwichon refer to this show as their source of inspiration. For example, this is an interview in a popular gwichon magazine *Hello Farmer*: "These

days Little Forest is very popular but when I made the move, it was Lee Hyori. When I saw pictures on her blog I'd think, 'Ah this is it! This is how my country-side life will look like" (Song, 2019). These articles are a case in point: Song, 2018; Newsjelly, 2018.

9. "People dream of moving to the space of the countryside. The success of shows like Three Meals a Day, Hyori's Bed and Breakfast, and the need to 'return' derived from these shows, are not phenomenon that can be put aside as trends but instead there is a need to study the particularities of this space that forms the background of these shows" Kim and Bang, 2019, 301; (Translated by the author) Also see Lim, 2020.

10. Also see: "Marriage migrants often at mercy of Korean husbands" (Ock, 2019), "Korean Convicted of Raping Filipino Wife" (*Korea Times*, 2009).

11. See Shin and Yoo 2015 for an analysis of the racial politics in *Damunhwa Gobuyeoljeon.*

BIBLIOGRAPHY

Anderson, B. (2006). *Imagined Communities: Reflections on the Origin and Spread of Nationalism.* London: Verso.

Appadurai, A. (1996). *Modernity At Large: Cultural Dimensions of Globalization.* Minneapolis, MN: University of Minnesota Press.

Appadurai, A. (2013). *The Future as Cultural Fact. Essays on the Global Condition.* London: Verso.

Araghi, F. (1995). Global Depeasantization, 1945-1990. *The Sociological Quarterly* 36 (2): 337–368.

Bae, D. (2002). 22년 최장수 드라마 '전원일기' 막내린다: so-chae ko-kal tŭng i-yu yŏn-mal-kke chong-pang. *Busan Il-bo*, October 17, http://www.busan.com/view/busan/view.php?code=20021017000281

Bae, G. (2009). 우리 시군경제력은. *President's Website Records*, (Regional Development Association), December 3, http://17region.pa.go.kr/pds/development _read.php?board_id=31&page=3&id=41924

Bae, G., Ha, J., Jo, Y., and Park, Y. (2010). 지역발전위원회 공동 기획: 한국의 지역 경쟁력 조사 - 귀농자 은퇴자 가릴 것 없다, 인재를 찾자. *Donga Ilbo Business Review* 49 (2). December 30, https://dbr.donga.com/article/view/1202/article_no/2679/ac/magazine

Bae, S. (2018). 시골생활이라는 정적판타지- 리틀 포레스트. [The Silent Fantasy of the Country-life - Little Forest] *News 4000*, March 8, https://www.news4000 .com/news/articleView.html?idxno=28291

Chang, Y. (2004). 텔레비전 프로그램 장르 분류기준에 관한 연구. [Studying the Categorization of Genres on Television]. *Journal of Broadcasting Research* 59 (2): 105–136.

Cheng, S. (2011). Sexual Protection, Citizenship and Nationhood: Prostituted Women and Migrant Wives in South Korea. *Journal of Ethnic and Migration Studies.* 37 (10): 1627–1648.

Chin, E. (2020). 일상성으로 본 농촌영화 비교 한국과 일본의 리틀 포레스트를 중심으로. [Comparison of Rural Films from Quotodiennete Focusing on Little Forest in Korea and Japan]. *Association for Study of Literature and Environment Journal* 19 (1): 101–127.

Cho, S. (2018). A Bride Deficit and Marriage Migration in South Korea. *International Migration* 56 (6): 100–119.

Chung, Y. (2009). Contemporary topology and historicity of Korean TV dramas. *Korea Society for Journal and Com*munication Studies 53 (1): 84–108.

Geum, J. (2011). 외환위기 이후 여성 노동시장의 변화. *Korea Labour Institute Wŏlgannodongnibyu* 79 (December Issue): 47–69.

Jang, J. (2014). 결혼이주여성 10명 중 3명은 우울증..일반인의 4배. *E-Daily News,* January 13, https://www.edaily.co.kr/news/read?newsId=01308726602677720&mediaCodeNo=257

Jeong, H. (2016). 드라마에서 농촌이 실종됐다– 고향에서 여행지로. *Dong-a Il-bo*, March 23, https://shindonga.donga.com/3/all/13/528314/1

Jin, K. and Kim, H., Ministry of Health and Welfare (2005), 여성 결혼이민자 생활 실태 조사결과 및 보건복지부 대책방안, July 15, https://eiec.kdi.re.kr/policy/materialView.do?num=75053.

Jin, M. and Park, S. (2012). 귀농 귀촌여성의 농촌생활 경험 분석 : 진안지역 사례. *The Women's Studies* 83 (2): 275–297.

Kang, E. (2011). 착한 드라마'도 힘이 세다. *Donga Ilbo,* December 23, https://www.donga.com/news/Vote2016/article/all/20111213/42562518/1

Kim, B. (2019). 모빌리티의 상상과 새로운 삶의 실험: 농촌 이주 청년들의 서사를 중심으로. [*"Imagined Mobility" and Experiment for New Way of Life: A Study of Young People's Urban-to-rural Migration in Korea*]. (Masters Thesis). Seoul National University.

Kim G. and Kilkey, M. (2017). Marriage Migration Policy in South Korea: Social Investment beyond the Nation State. *International Migration* 56 (1): 23–38.

Kim, H. (2012). Marriage Migration between South Korea and Vietnam: A Gender Perspective. *Asian Perspective* 36 (3): 531–563.

Kim, H. (2016). 동원된 가족주의`의 시대에서 `가족 위험`의 사회로. *Korean Society* 17 (2): 3–44.

Kim, H. (2019). Nongmin Column: 멀고 먼 '리틀 포레스트' 혜원이의 꿈. *Hanguk Nongjeong*, July 23, http://www.ikpnews.net/news/articleView.html?idxno=37923.

Kim, J. and Bang, J. (2019). 영화 〈리틀 포레스트〉 속 공간적 특성과 의미에 대한 고찰. (Contemplation on the Spatial Characteristics and Meaning of Hometown in the Movie Little Forest: Focusing on the Returning to Rural Communities). *Wonkwang Journal of Humanities* 20 (3): 299–324.

Kim, L., Park S., Choi J., Dong J., Park, D., Ahn, S., and Kim, N. (2018). 농촌 다문화가족의 사회통합 실태. *Korea Rural Economic Institute Research Report*, December, http://library.krei.re.kr/pyxis-api/1/digital-files/13a3e42f-859e-4f2a-86f5-2492bff072ed

Kim, M. (2006). 한국 여성노동력의 성격변화와 노동정책: 1960-2000. (A Critical Review on the Profiles of Korean Female Labor Force: 1960-2000). *Korea Journal of Population Studies* 29 (1): 133–156.

Kim, Y., Yang, M. (2012). 다문화 가정 자녀 37%가 왕따… '엄마, 학교엔 제발 오지마' [37% of All Multicultural Children Face Bullying… 'Mom, Please Don't Come to School'] *News Chosun*, 10th January, https://www.chosun.com/site/data/html_dir/2012/01/10/2012011000131.html

Korea Times Reporter. (2009). Korean Convicted of Raping Filipino Wife. *Korea Times*, January 16, https://www.koreatimes.co.kr/www/news/nation/2009/01/113_37965.html

Korean Rural Economy Institute (KREI). (2009). *Gwichon-Gwinong Survey*, February 26, https://www.korea.kr/news/pressReleaseView.do?newsId=156377448

Lee, S. (2018). 이수향의 시네마 크리티크] 20대의 귀거래사歸去來辭 - 영화 <리틀 포레스트. [Lee Soo-Hyang's Cinema Critique: The Great Deal of Your 20s: Little Forest]. *Le Monde Diplomatique*, March 5, http://www.ilemonde.com/news/articleView.html?idxno=8405

Lee, Y. (2018). 저출산·고령화로 시군구 약 40% '소멸위험'…대도시로도 확산. *Yonhap News*, August 13, https://www.yna.co.kr/view/AKR20180813040200004

Lim, J. (2020). Why are increasing numbers of young Korean women taking their lives? *Hankyoreh News*, 22 November, http://english.hani.co.kr/arti/english_edition/e_national/970975.html

Mohanty, C. (1988). Under Western Eyes: Feminist Scholarship and Colonial Discourses. *Feminist Review* 30: 61–88.

Mundy, S. (2013). South Korean companies: Needed on the home front. *Financial Times*, November 19, https://www.ft.com/content/c63ed192-4bac-11e3-a02f-00144feabdc0

NewsJelly Reporter. (2018). 이효리처럼 살기? 적어도 3억 필요하다 [Living like Lee Hyori? Almost 3 million]. *OhmyNews*, September 14, http://www.ohmynews.com/NWS_Web/View/at_pg.aspx?CNTN_CD=A0002033463

Ock, H. (2019). Marriage migrants often at mercy of Korean husbands. July 24, http://www.koreaherald.com/view.php?ud=20190724000709

Organic Punk. (2020). 농촌이 살만하다'는 말의 특권. [The Privilege in the Words 'The Countryside is Livable]. *Organic Punk Archive*, January 15.

Parameswaran, R. (1996). Media representations of third world women. *Peace Review* 8 (1): 127–133.

Park, J. (2017). '무작정 상경' — 서울 이주자에 관한 담론과 젠더 [Migrating to Seoul Recklessly: Gendering Discourse on Migrants from Rural Areas to Seoul]. *Sahoewa yŏksa* 113: 311–344.

Park, K. (1993). Women and Development: The Case of South Korea. *Comparative Politics* 25 (2): 127–145.

Park, S. (2016). 귀농 귀촌과 젠더 이슈: 귀농귀촌 여성의 지역정착 방안 in 김정섭 , 오정훈 편, 귀농·귀촌에서 젠더 이슈와 귀농인의 지역사회 참여 귀농·귀촌 정책 연구 포럼 제3차 토론회 자료집, edited by Kim, J., and Oh, J., 4–28. Korean Rural Economy Institute, Naju-si, Republic of Korea.

Roh, J. (2014). 반(反) 모더니티의 모더니티 1960년대 문예영화에서의 농촌 표상. [The Modernity of Anti-Modernity: The Representations of Rural Areas in Literary Films of the 1960s]. *Study of Humanities* 21 (June Issue): 39–67.

Seo, Y. (2019). 여성 농업인이 52.7%인데 지위낮아⋯농식품부 여성농업인 전담팀 올해 상반기내 구성. *Choongang* Daily, April 16.

Seung. (2020). 이효리, '섹시 퀸'은 건재했다. News Chosun, December 9, https://www.chosun.com/entertainments/entertain_photo/2020/12/09/JLKP2OSBNSK D2F7H2D2PF24G6E/

Shin, K. (2010). Globalisation and the Working Class in South Korea: Contestation, Fragmentation and Renewal. *Journal of Contemporary Asia* 40 (2): 211–229.

Shin, Y. (2015). Koreanizing Marriage Migrant Women: A Critical Review of Damunhwa Gobuyeoljeon. *Trans-Humanities Journal* 8: 169–193.

Son, P. (2009). 최불암고 정주영 회장, 전원일기 출연할 뻔. *Kyŏnghyangshinmun,* December 8, http://news.khan.co.kr/kh_news/khan_art_view.html?art_id =200912081834081.

Song, B. (2018). 파라다이스 꿈꾸는 귀촌은 실패한다. [Paradise Dreaming of Hometown Fails]. *NewsAsian*, August 17, http://www.newsian.co.kr/news/articleView.html?idxno=32176

Song, J. (2019). 내일내일을 기대하는 농부, 송주희 을 기대하는 농부, 송주희. [A Farmer Looking Forward to Tomorrow, Song Joo Hee.] *Hello Farmer*, April 25, https://post.naver.com/viewer/postView.nhn?volumeNo=19492595&memberNo =38593788&vType=VERTICAL

Statistics Korea. (2019). http://kostat.go.kr

Williams, R. (1973). *The Country and the City.* Oxford: Oxford University Press.

Yoon, H. (2004). 국제결혼 배우자의 갈등과 적응. 최협┌김성국┌정근식┌유형기 편. 한국의 소수자, 실패와 전망, edited by Choi, H. et al. Paju-si, Republic of Korea: Hanwool Academy Press.

Chapter 5

Gender, Genre, and History in *Great Queen Seondeok*

Michael Ormsbee

INTRODUCTION

During the early decades of *Hallyu,* Korean television dramas enjoyed a pride of place among the South Korean cultural exports gaining international recognition and widespread popularity. Especially popular with international audiences was the Korean historical drama (often referred to as "fusion *sageuk*"), a fact which may seem surprising given that these shows dealt with events that were often unknown to viewers not yet familiar with Korean culture or history. Although the major drivers of *Hallyu* have shifted in recent years away from broadcast television toward K-pop supergroups and social media, historical dramas continue to play a significant role. Considering the central importance of historical dramas to the early decades of the Korean Wave, as well as their ongoing popularity, it is worthwhile to revisit the Korean historical drama and describe it more carefully in terms of its generic features and conventions. One thing that most popular historical dramas from the early years of the Korean Wave have in common is the intermingling of historical material with elements of other genres including folklore and fairy tales, the "trendy" drama, and above all, melodrama.

After considering how theories of melodrama of Western origin[1] change once we examine them in a specifically Korean context, I trace the ways in which Korean literary critics have described both melodrama and the evolution of popular narrative genres (*daejungseosa*) from the Japanese colonial period to the present day. With this critical conversation as a background, I turn to the wildly popular 2009 historical drama *Great Queen Seondeok,* which presents a heavily fictionalized account of the rise to power of Queen Seondeok (r. 632–647 CE), the first female ruler of Silla. Paying particular attention to the drama's charismatic villain, Mishil, I argue that *Great Queen*

Seondeok constructs its own version of the "moral occult" of melodrama (Brooks, 1976), not along traditionally gendered lines—in which Virtue is aligned with the suffering heroine and Villainy with male oppression—but explicitly in terms of political legitimacy. Finally, I attempt to show how our understanding of what I call *Great Queen Seondeok*'s "melodramatic constitution" changes once we pay close attention to the gaps between "official" history and what is represented in the drama. Examining *Great Queen Seondeok* alongside its main historical sources—the canonical Goryeo-era history *Samguk sagi* (History of the Three Kingdoms) and the more controversial *Hwarang segi* (Generations of the Hwarang)—shows how the demands of melodrama influence the re-representation of an already idealized past.

SITUATING GENRE THEORY WITHIN THE CONTEXT OF KOREAN MODERNITY

Any attempt to approach popular narratives of different literary traditions by means of generic modes or conventions has to be wary of the extent to which genres, and even the ways in which we *perceive* genre, are historically conditioned. In addition to the danger of losing sight of the importance of historical context for genre formation, genre-oriented approaches must also acknowledge the risk of allowing a particularly influential theory to affect which texts we choose to analyze—in the worst case, this means restricting our focus solely to those texts which confirm the elements of a particular theory. Pak Yu-hee discusses how this process has worked historically in the context of Korean melodrama studies, describing the two most common methods through which critics have attempted to define the scope of Korean melodrama: "Either they borrow [*chayong*] from Western theory [*seogu iron*], or else they try to extract the defining characteristics of 'Korean melodrama' from actual texts" (Pak, 2009).[2] The latter method seems more promising, yet it too faces the danger of circularity, as Pak points out: "Even if they turn to actual texts in order to determine the identity of Korean melodrama, researchers could only begin having already selected texts according to their pre-existing notions of melodrama."

Of the "pre-existing" theories of melodrama that have influenced Korean critics in their investigations into "the identity of Korean melodrama," perhaps none have been more influential than the work of Peter Brooks in *The Melodramatic Imagination*. His account of melodrama's "moral occult," and of the particular affinity melodrama has for evoking and resonating with the experience of modernity, has proved useful for many Korean critics analyzing what most agree to be the privileged status of melodrama (however one defines it) in Korean popular narrative genres, even as they variously adapt, challenge, and move beyond Brooks's work. While Brooks in *The Melodramatic Imagination* looks back to French stage drama of the early 1800s in order to investigate the melodramatic elements in later realist novels, students of distinctively Korean forms of the melodramatic imagination usually look back to *sinpa-geuk,* the "new theater" that developed during the period of Japanese colonial rule. Lee Seung-hee's 2002 article, "The Modern Imagination of Melodrama: Focusing on *sinpa-geuk* in 1910s Korea," provides a thorough treatment of *sinpa* theater's origins and influence on later Korean film and television. While sharing Brooks's (1976) recognition of "the melodramatic mode as a central fact of the modern sensibility," Lee points out the importance of historical context when approaching different genres: "*Sinpa* theater developed out of conditions that had nothing to do with the class ideology of the emerging bourgeoisie, the spirit of the French Revolution, or the flow of Romanticism." At the same time, the historical shift that Brooks traces from *melodrama* (as noun and theatrical genre) to *melodramatic* (as adjective and expressive mode) finds a close analog in the development from *sinpa* (a theatrical genre) to *sinpa-seong* ("*sinpa*-ness"), an expressive mode that operates across many different Korean popular narrative genres in the twentieth and twenty-first centuries. European melodrama in the wake of the French Revolution and *sinpa* theater, while by no means the same, share deep structural affinities and are further alike in having both developed into generic modes that have spread far beyond their origins on the stage. Over the course of South Korea's "postcolonial modernization," *sinpa-seong* and the melodramatic imagination have both "spread to other media," from film in the Golden Age of Korean cinema to television in the 1970s (Yi, 2018).

A common thread that appears in most accounts of Korean melodrama, whether they build on Brooks's "melodramatic imagination" or not, is the idea that something about melodrama's affective excess resonates with a uniquely Korean experience of modernity. In her 2018 article "Melodramatic Tactics for Survival in the Neoliberal Era," for example, We Jung Yi powerfully extends existing work on melodrama[3] in order to argue that the melodramatic mode has been for Korean audiences a "popular mechanism for making sense of the unprecedented changes brought by modernity":

From the serial newspaper novel to sinp'a stage drama . . . and early cinema, the visceral collision of modern and traditional under colonial rule was reenacted with excessive pathos and moral rectitude—in other words, melodramatically. Translational and combinative from the beginning, the melodramatic mode has since been embraced by the Korean masses, who have enthusiastically responded to and participated in the development of melodrama. They found the "melodramatic imagination" engaging not simply because the exaggerated representation of violent modernization was revelatory of their everyday suffering but also because its "moral occult" promised, in the realm of fantasy, the ultimate victory of the hitherto persecuted.

Adapting Brooks's "melodramatic imagination" and Elaine Hadley's "melodramatic tactics" to the specific context of democratic, neoliberal South Korea, Yi argues that recent Korean dramas including *Heirs* (2013) and *You Who Came from the Stars* (2014) use melodrama in order to project the "fantasy that the survivalist ideology of our time can be countered by *reformed* heirs from the higher social orders." My approach differs from Yi's in analyzing melodrama solely in connection with Korean *historical* dramas; melodrama—inveterately associated with modernity—operates in a unique way within narratives that take pre-modern societies and historical events as their subject matter.

If the evolution of melodrama follows a unique course through Korea's postcolonial development, so too does the evolution of the historical drama. Historical dramas have been a staple of Korean broadcast television for close to 60 years, and in that time they have changed noticeably. Ju Chang Yun argues in "Generic History of Historical Dramas in Korea: 1964-2005" for four distinct periods in the evolution of the Korean historical drama until 2005: From 1964 to 1972, the historical drama was concerned primarily with "old legends and education" (*yaet iyagi wa kyoyang*); from 1973 to 1980, the historical drama became a means of expressing a "national ideology"; from 1981 to 1994, dramas tended to tell the stories of "great and virtuous men" (*jeongsa*); and from 1995 to 2005, dramas grew larger in scale and acquired popular appeal (Ju, 2007). Although it would be valuable to examine each of these periods in more detail, the fourth period—when historical dramas began to enjoy greater popularity, both in South Korea and abroad—coincides with the development of what came to be known as *Hallyu* and is most relevant for a discussion of *Great Queen Seondeok* (which aired in 2009). Ju emphasizes the importance of imagination or fancy in the historical dramas produced after 1995, along with a "melodramatic structure," the "representation of historical spaces," the intensification of spectacle, and stories unfolding out of the private sphere. As this "melodramatic structure" permeates more extensively through historical dramas, favoring certain narrative structures and tropes while intensifying emotional spectacle, fidelity to historical record becomes less important. We might say, tentatively, that Korean historical dramas became more popular in the 1990s and 2000s as they became more melodramatic. But this generalized formula cannot explain how specific conventions of melodrama interact with fictionalized representations of historical events in the context of a specific work. To develop a more concrete understanding of how melodrama operates in historical drama during the early years of *Hallyu*, we can turn to the historical drama *Great Queen Seondeok*.

GREAT QUEEN SEONDEOK'S "MELODRAMATIC CONSTITUTION"

Both Brooks's "melodramatic imagination" and Hadley's "melodramatic tactics" enact a shift from genre to mode of expression, picturing melodrama as something that could conceivably enter any other genre (infiltrating it from the inside, as it were, while changing it in the process) at any time. Neither "imagination" nor "tactics," however, contains a sense of *structure*; melodrama, even when it operates as a mode of expression based on excess, is often inextricable from narrative structure. When Ju identifies "melodramatic structure" as one of the key changes in historical dramas after 1995, he is referring to a wide-ranging and much-studied collection of narrative elements including "predetermined outcomes," a focus on inter- and intra-family conflicts, and a Manichean struggle between Good and Evil (Pak, 2009; Brooks, 1976). Ideally, the terms with which we discuss melodrama ought to encompass not only its status as a mode of expression, but also its influence on the structure of the narratives we perceive to be "melodramatic." For this reason, I propose the term "melodramatic constitution," which follows the examples of Brooks and Hadley by conceiving broadly of melodrama as a mode of expression characterized by excess, yet goes beyond their terminology by alluding to melodrama's affinity for particular narrative configurations and specific political ideologies. In the sense of constitution as "structure," the "melodramatic constitution" is associated with the audience's anticipation of predetermined narrative outcomes. In *Great Queen Seondeok*, this takes the peculiar form of doubled or redundant foreshadowing. Next, we can interpret "constitution" as the peculiar *disposition* of melodrama, a mode of excess that induces physical and emotional reactions from the audience through the alternation of action (accompanied by music) with frozen pictorial moments (tableaux) that arrest the narrative momentum. Finally, there is the political sense of constitution as the set of fundamental principles guiding the governing of a nation, state, or body politic. Here the phrase "melodramatic constitution" stands in metonymically for a kind of "democratic imagination"[4] that permeates *Queen Seondeok*, casting its moral Manichaeism explicitly in terms of political legitimacy (where Evil corresponds to rule through fear and superstition, while Virtue corresponds to rule through the informed and freely given consent of the governed). All three aspects of the show's "melodramatic constitution" emerge clearly in the first two episodes, which narrate events leading up to the birth of the protagonist (born Princess Deokman, later she becomes Queen Seondeok) and establish the rise to power of the show's antagonist (Mishil).

The first episode opens with King Jinheung (r. 540–576 CE) surveying the borders of his nation when he is attacked by assassins from Baekje.[5] An armored figure intervenes and saves the king; the figure takes off their helmet, revealing herself to be a woman. This is Mishil, portrayed as a leader of the *hwarang* ("flower boys"), the famous scholar-warriors of Silla who followed the "three teachings" of Buddhism, Confucianism, and Taoism. It would be hard to overstate the appeal the *hwarang* have had for historians of pre-modern Korea, though opinions vary greatly on the history, structure, and practices of their order. As the author of the *Hwarang segi* (a document of contested authenticity, and one of the key sources for *Great Queen Seondeok*) puts it, "It is impossible to be ignorant of the history of the flower boys" (McBride, 2008). In the section of the *Samguk sagi* detailing King Jinheung's reign, Kim Pusik, a Goryeo aristocrat and the author of the *Samguk sagi*, cites a record written by a Tang envoy describing the *hwarang*: "They selected the handsome boys of the nobility and adorned them, powdering their faces and calling them Hwarang. The people of the country all respected and supported them" (Kim, 2012). I will return to the nature of the *hwarang* and how Mishil is said to be connected to them. For now, it suffices to point out the deliberate reframing of male-centric historical "grand narratives" enabled by the choice to open the first episode with a woman—who may or may not be entirely fictional—saving a king whose name comes to us through history and legend (Yang, 2018). At the same time, this opening signals that the traditionally gendered dynamics of melodrama,[6] in which innocence and virtue are inherently feminine while the villain is associated with patriarchal power and masculinity, may not be of much use to us in determining which aspects of melodrama (if any) operate in *Great Queen Seondeok*.

The drama establishes the terms of its "moral Manichaeism" (Brooks also refers to this as the "moral occult") immediately following the opening scene, in a conversation between King Jinheung and Mishil about the true source of political authority. Significantly, Jinheung and Mishil are traveling in a *gama*, a Korean palanquin held up by anywhere from 4 to 20 men bearing poles on their shoulders ("'Gama': A Comprehensive Art," 2015). At one point the *gama* jolts and progress halts; one of men holding up the *gama* has stumbled. Mishil looks outside in order to grasp the situation; she gives a look to a warrior on horseback who cuts down the unfortunate servant without mercy. The irony of this act becomes clear a second later when King Jinheung tells Mishil that a monarch's right to rule derives ultimately from the people. Citing his miraculous defeat of a tiger when he was young, an incident which established his reputation and convinced many talented people to follow him into battle and put their talents at his disposal, Jinheung offhandedly

rejects the notion that the "will of heaven" is enough to establish an effective
ruler. While any king could be said to be blessed by heaven's will merely by
occupying his position in the first place, the true leader must win over the
minds and hearts of people. In contrast to King Jinheung as he is described
in the *Samguk sagi*, "[supporting] Buddhism singlemindedly" and wearing
a monk's robes near the end of his life (Kim, 2012), this Jinheung espouses
what amounts to a proto-democratic ideology. This ideology (Jinheung's
"democratic imagination," despite the apparent anachronism) finds its conceptual opposite in Mishil's casual murder of the *gama* bearer, one of the
common people literally and symbolically carrying the ruling class on their
shoulders. The contrast established in this scene becomes a common refrain
throughout the drama; here, it casts the moral Manichaeism of melodrama
explicitly in terms of political legitimacy. Deokman, our as-yet-unborn protagonist, will be doubly legitimate—she will be of Jinheung's lineage, and
(more importantly) she will share his democratic imagination, viewing herself as a servant of the people and governing by virtue of their freely given
support. The association of melodrama with a specifically democratic ethos is
not unique to Korean forms of melodrama; in fact, it is one of Brooks's core
arguments about melodrama, which, he says, "represents a democratization
of morality and its signs" (Brooks, 1976). This "democratization of morality"
is just as important, perhaps even more so, for the "melodramatic constitution" of Korean historical dramas, even as the gendered division of morality
(Good as the innocent feminine and Evil as the predatory masculine) becomes
less starkly apparent.

The affinity between melodrama and various democratic imaginations is
perhaps less familiar than another of melodrama's distinguishing features: its
mode of emotional excess. The emotional and affective audience responses
associated with melodrama are usually invoked by the alternating of action
(accompanied by music) with the staging of charged, frozen moments *tableaux* (Williams, 2012); in terms of its penchant for dramatic music and
tableaux, *Great Queen Seondeok* has much in common with earlier theatrical
genres including *sinpa-geuk* and post-French Revolution popular theater in
Britain and France. The tableau has been a part of stage melodrama since its
early nineteenth-century beginnings: an individual actor strikes an extended
pose, or "attitude." Carolyn Williams explains: "In its most literal definition,
melodrama consists of a combination of music and drama in which passages of music either alternate with passages of dramatic speech or subtend
them almost continuously and in which speech and action are interrupted by
moments of static pictorial composition, the tableaux." Brooks draws heavily
on Denis Diderot's account of the tableau in his discussion of the figure of
the mute in *The Melodramatic Imagination*. The character without a voice,
who must make every gesture replete with meaning, becomes the ideal figure

for melodrama itself, which strives to become what Brooks calls the "text of muteness"—in such a text, *everything* that is witnessed becomes "meaningful though unspeakable" (Brooks, 1976). The tableau is the moment in which everything and everyone on stage or in the frame attains the purely signifying—though speechless—status of gesture.

In *Great Queen Seondeok*, tableaux almost always incorporate an observer-figure, someone witnessing villainy even as they participate in it or are victimized by it. Every episode features numerous examples of these tableaux, most often during moments of recognition or discovery. A particularly illustrative example serves as the climax of Mishil's palace coup halfway through episode 1. As Mishil strides over the dead bodies of palace guards, bearing a goblet with poison intended for the king, the camera cuts to King Jinheung. He is already dying, but with his last words he reveals the "impossible dream" that he has for Silla. He hopes that Silla will unify the Three Kingdoms (Silla, Baekje, and Goguryeo) and become the unquestioned ruling power of the Korean peninsula. When Mishil arrives in the throne room, King Jinheung is already dead. Mishil's co-conspirators arrive a moment later, led by her husband (Sejong), her lover (Seolwon), and her brother (Misaeng);[7] naturally, they believe that Mishil has killed the king. Mishil turns to the throne and addresses the deceased king directly, mirroring his earlier words about power ultimately deriving from people: "Your Majesty, you said the one who gains people gains the whole world. You said the one who gains people will become the ruler of an era. People? Look, your Majesty! They are *my* people! Not yours—they are Mishil's people! And now it is Mishil's era." The tableau crystallizes as Mishil falls silent. She stands at the foot of the throne, flanked by her three strongest supporters, with Jinheung's corpse on the throne itself and young Prince Baekjeong (Jinheung's grandson) hiding behind the throne. The tableau, with Baekjeong in the role of innocent witness, stages a "public recognition of where virtue and evil reside" (Brooks, 1976). Mishil's betrayal—and more importantly, the perversion of Jinheung's democratic imagination that allows her to affect a violent transfer of power—invites the audience to witness Baekjeong recognizing Mishil as "simply the conveyor of evil."

All of the action of the first episode, which condenses a great deal of historical and invented material, builds up to a final tableau in which Mishil's character is fixed irrevocably as a kind of avatar of political illegitimacy. After King Jinji (the old king's nephew, who colludes with Mishil in her original coup) refuses to make Mishil a legitimate queen,[8] Mishil abandons the child she had with him and lays new plans. Using her status as *weonhwa* (leader of the *hwarang*), Mishil leads a contingent of *hwarang* to disrupt a ceremony the king is attending. At her command the soldiers begin to commit suicide, one row after another, at which point Mishil's conspirators reveal the last words of the previous king—which Mishil and Jinji had conspired to suppress—that name Prince Baekjeong as the rightful successor. This time the tableau crystallizes with Mishil standing in front of the rows of dead *hwarang* confronting the king, with horrified nobles arranged in a circle. Once again Baekjeong functions in the tableau as a terrified witness, except that now he realizes his purpose in Mishil's game—he is to be the next puppet-king, dancing while she pulls the strings.

The most striking part of this tableau is unquestionably the *hwarang* warriors; young men all, they have donned elaborate face makeup along with full battle armor, supposedly to signal their willingness to fight to the death. An explanatory Korean subtitle appears on the screen (as part of the original broadcast, not the external subtitles meant for international audiences) when two characters first discuss this curious practice, leaving viewers unsure whether the so-called "*Nangjang* Resolution" is fictional or based on historical record. The ritual itself is fictional; although sources like the *Samguk sagi* mention that the *hwarang* wore makeup, the specific practice of applying makeup before battle so as to be beautiful even in death was a product of the writers' imaginations.[9] This tableau, with Mishil at the head of ranks of *hwarang* both living and dead, is one of the defining moments of the drama. Its purpose is clear—it confronts us with the spectacle of an audience witnessing pure evil.

If *Great Queen Seondeok*'s "melodramatic constitution" has so far exaggerated the political and de-emphasized the traditional gendered associations of melodrama, it operates within the narrative structure as well by incorporating multiple forms of foreshadowing. Melodrama is often described as highly teleological in its narrative structure—portents and prophecies are only some of the time-honored techniques, familiar in nineteenth-century stage productions and modern televisual melodrama alike, for inviting an audience to anticipate certain preordained outcomes. A version of this foreshadowing, of a kind only possible for narratives incorporating historical events, occurs in the form of King Jinheung's "impossible dream": the belief, stated shortly before the king's death, that Silla must conquer the nearby nations of Baekje and Goguryeo and become the sole ruling power on the Korean peninsula. Even a very basic familiarity with the history of the Three Kingdoms era allows us to recognize this "impossible dream" as historical allusion—Silla conquered Baekje in 660 and Goguryeo in 668, while resisting the efforts of Tang China to subjugate the peninsula (Kim, 2012). Although the Unified Silla dynasty did not control *all* of the northern territory originally held by Goguryeo (some of Goguryeo's former territory was held in later years by the smaller kingdom of Parhae), historians still point to the almost complete control that Silla gained over the peninsula when making the case that Silla is the main source of a uniquely Korean national identity and culture. The classic form of this argument comes from Lee Ki-baik's *A New History of Korea* (1984), when he asserts the historical significance of United Silla defeating the forces of Tang China:

> Clearly, Korean society would not have been able to develop unhindered under T'ang political domination. Fortunately, however, Silla was fully able to resist T'ang aggression and maintain its national independence. This constituted the foundation on which the development of the society and culture of Unified Silla rested and what is more it laid the groundwork for the independent historical development of the Korean people.[10]

In light of this argument, we see how the *telos* of Jinheung's "impossible dream" gestures not merely to Silla's future safety and security, but to nothing less than the future "development of the Korean people."

The dream of a unified Korean peninsula resonates even more deeply with a modern audience after the Korean Armistice Agreement in 1953, which established the Demilitarized Zone (DMZ) that still divides North and South Korea. For an audience familiar with these watershed events in ancient and modern Korean history, King Jinheung's "impossible dream" implicitly foreshadows a future moment in the narrative that the audience knows has both already happened (when Silla became Unified Silla) and is yet to come (through the long-anticipated unification with North Korea). King Jinheung's "impossible dream" only makes sense in the context of a legitimately democratic ethos when we recognize it as prefiguring the modern yearning (from the standpoint of a democratic South Korea) for unification with North Korea—that is, as the reforging of a lost but recoverable unity, rather than as the imperialistic conquering of neighboring nations. It is in this spirit that a historical drama like *Great Queen Seondeok*, combining a turn toward an idealized past with the *telos* and emotional excess of melodrama, seems particularly well suited to express and respond to the historical trauma embedded within the Korean experience of modernity.

An audience who knows nothing of the history of the Korean peninsula cannot recognize Jinheung's "impossible dream" as foreshadowing—for this audience another type of foreshadowing would be necessary. This second form of foreshadowing appears, in fact, in the strange guise of a supernatural message from the dead King Jinheung to his loyal follower Munno who has been officiating over a Buddhist ceremony on a mountaintop. The posthumous prophecy states that the person who can oppose Mishil will appear "when the seven stars of the Big Dipper become eight." It might seem as though the sudden appearance of a prophecy from beyond the grave would signal the intrusion of the fantastic or the supernatural into what was before merely the imaginative retelling of historical events, but it is not quite that simple; seemingly fantastic elements are already woven into pre-modern Korean history. In the introduction to the English translation of *The Silla Annals to the Samguk Sagi*, for example, we learn that some criticize Kim Pusik (a Goryeo-era historian and author of the *Samguk sagi*) for the "depiction of marvels—such as stories related to the foundation of Silla and miraculous events surrounding the life of the Silla general Kim Yusin" (Kim, 2012). Yet "Kim Pusik himself recognizes in his historical commentaries that such stories are 'too fantastic to be believed,'" while some have even taken the opposite position, "[criticizing] the *Samguk sagi* for its limited recording of marvels—namely the foundation myth of Goguryeo." But even after we acknowledge that the presence of a "marvel" like Jinheung's post-humous prophecy is consistent with the blend of myth and verifiable history in the *Samguk sagi* (to say nothing of the even more fantastic Goryeo-era *Samguk yusa*), we can still recognize from the way the prophecy is phrased that it operates entirely within the melodramatic mode. The audience, like Munno, is directed to anticipate the "person who can oppose Mishil." The significance of the person yet to come lies first and foremost in her ability to oppose Mishil—and by now the audience recognizes that Mishil exists to be opposed. Her defeat is necessary to signify, as Yi puts it, the "ultimate victory of the hitherto oppressed" (Yi, 2018). Thus, the prophecy becomes a vehicle for two common elements of melodrama: the moral Manichaeism that pits Evil against Innocence (in this case, political illegitimacy against political legitimacy); and the use of foreshadowing to "establish predeter-mined outcomes" (Pak, 2009). King Jinheung's "impossible dream" and his posthumous prophecy both serve the same purpose—directing the audience to anticipate a predetermined outcome—but they serve that purpose for dis-tinct audiences: those with enough knowledge of history to recognize in the "dream" of a unified Korean peninsula the mingling of historical fact and hope for the future; and those without. The doubled forms of melodramatic foreshadowing, serving a similar purpose to that of redundancy in communi-cation, show how shrewdly *Great Queen Seondeok* addresses itself simulta-neously to both domestic and international audiences.

Of the generic modes operating within the Korean historical drama, melo-drama comes closest to occupying the position of the "dominant" (Jakobson, 1971), while interacting in important ways with aspects of other genres including the fairy tale, the "trendy" drama—which generally depicted Cinderella-esque love stories between working-class women and "diasporic or cosmopolitan male personae with tragic pasts" (Yi, 2018), and even the Bildungsroman. When the protagonist Deokman is born, for example, the prophecy that she will one day defeat Mishil leads to circumstances that resemble nothing so much as the story of Snow White: a loyal maid flees into the wilderness with baby Deokman, while Mishil sends out a huntsman figure (her most loyal *hwarang*, Chilsook) to kill them. Deokman grows up in a trading outpost in the Mongolian desert, and with the cosmopolitan education she receives there (which includes foreign languages and familiarity with recent advances in astronomy) she begins to look astonishingly like the (male) protagonists of "trendy" dramas of the 2000s with their traumatic pasts, formative years spent abroad, and tumultuous returns to their home country. And in the choice to make Queen Seondeok a young woman,[11] centering the narrative around Deokman's journey from birth through childhood to early adulthood, *Great Queen Seondeok* also adopts a structural logic similar to that of the *Bildungsroman*, or novel of formation. In fact, one can divide the series into four periods (after the initial episodes leading up to Deokman's birth) that correspond to four discrete stages of Deokman's journey of self-formation: her initial education abroad as a child; her military apprenticeship as a *Nangdo* (follower of the *hwarang*) while dressing as a man; her political apprenticeship when she enters the palace and reclaims her royal status; and her final role as Queen. Each of these genres, fairy tale, "trendy" drama, and Bildungsroman, have their own history and function in Korean popular narratives in the twentieth century, distinct from though often related to the evolution of Korean melodrama.

AT THE CROSSROADS OF FICTION AND HISTORY

In order to understand how *Great Queen Seondeok*'s status as an explicitly historical drama relates to the "melodramatic constitution," we must look at the critical controversy surrounding the *Hwarang segi* (Generations of the *Hwarang*), a text of dubious historical authenticity and one of the major sources for the plot of *Great Queen Seondeok*.

The original *Hwarang segi* was supposedly written by Kim Taemun, a Silla nobleman. In the *Silla Annals of the Samguk Sagi*, Kim Pusik quotes Kim Taemun on the benefit to the nation of the practices of the *hwarang* order: "Wise advisors and loyal subjects excelled out of this. Outstanding generals and brave soldiers were produced from this" (Kim, 2012). The original *Hwarang segi* was long reputed to have been lost, but in 1989 scholars discovered "two related manuscripts in the calligraphy of Pak Ch'anghwa" that some thought were a copy of the original text. Scholarly interest in the *hwarang*, which had always been strong, flared into a heated debate concerning the authenticity of the manuscripts. The stakes were high; as historian Richard McBride II puts it, "If the manuscripts of the *Hwarang segi* were genuine, our understanding and appreciation of the *hwarang* and the dynamics of early Silla's history and socially stratified culture would be altered" (McBride, 2008). McBride himself believes that "Pak composed the

Hwarang segi as historical fiction" and that, when viewed in light of Pak's other writings (which included the "creative rewriting of the annals of Silla kings"), the *Hwarang segi* manuscripts constitute the "culmination of Pak's imaginative re-creation of the 'way of the *hwarang*' (*hwarangdo* 花郎道) and its rise and fall in Silla history." Korean historians are divided on the issue, although some, particularly Lee Jong-Wook, believe in the manuscripts' authenticity, others "cast serious doubt" (Kim, 2012). McBride characterizes the split as one between "empiricist" and "nationalist" schools of historiography, and also between older and younger groups of historians:

> Although most of Korea's established positivist (empirical) historians range from skepticism to criticism of the manuscripts (e.g. Lee Ki-Baik [Yi Kibaik], Lee Kidong [Yi Kidong], Noh Tae Don [No T'aedon], Kwŏn Tŏgyŏng), younger and less eminent nationalist historians have accepted them almost without question (e.g. Lee Jong-Wook [Yi Chong-uk], Yi Chaeho [Yi Chaeho], Choe Kwang Sik [Ch'oe Kwangsik]).[12]

In addition to offering "one coherent narrative on the origin and formation of the *hwarang*" (McBride, 2008), Pak's *Hwarang segi* manuscripts differ from other historical records in terms of the importance they attribute to matrilineal descent in Silla society. Essentially, the *Hwarang segi* describes a state of affairs in which one's status within the upper ranks of Silla's caste system (the "true bone" caste in particular) depends a great deal on one's mother: "Most of Silla's kings belong to this true-bone tradition of legitimate succession, not because of their fathers, but because of their mothers." The state of affairs in the *Hwarang segi* represents a fairly radical challenge to the ways in which historians have traditionally understood Silla society, as McBride points out: "This is fundamentally different from the mainstream academic interpretation of true-bone and holy-bone status in Silla, which recognizes the importance of matrilineal social status only in its capacity to confirm or preserve status originally provided by the paternal line." Much of the conflict described in the *Hwarang segi* involves the struggle between competing matrilineal lines (the true bone lineage and the "divine succession of the great prime").

Mishil is undoubtedly the most fascinating character in the *Hwarang segi* manuscripts, all the more so for being potentially fictional—no one named "Mishil" appears anywhere in the *Samguk sagi*, our main historical source with information about this era. In the *Hwarang segi*, Misil leads the "ritual-oriented group" known as the *Misil-pa*, which competes with other factions within the *hwarang*. Reputedly "highly skilled in the arts of the bedroom" (she is said to have had children with three generations of Silla kings, from Jinheung to Jinji), she was also revered by the *hwarang* as the *weonhwa* (a word that can refer either to the leader of the *hwarang* or to the values and practices of their order) and exerted tremendous political influence at court. She and her followers were mostly of the "divine succession of the great prime," whereas the kings of Silla were mostly of true bone status—this detail is important for understanding the palace intrigue in *Great Queen Seondeok*, which attributes some of Mishil's insatiable greed for power to being of supposedly lesser status than the royal family.

Mishil's character soon drew both scholarly and popular attention. Lee Jong-Wook (one of the staunchest advocates of the authenticity of the *Hwarang segi* manuscripts) published a monograph about her in 2005; 2005 also saw the publication of Kim Byul-Ah's *Mishil*, an award-winning novel inspired by the *Hwarang segi* and narrated from Mishil's perspective (Lee, 2005; Kim, 2005). And of course there is *Great Queen Seondeok* itself, which models much of its plot on the palace intrigue and the infighting between *hwarang* factions described in the *Hwarang segi*, even as it restores protagonicity to a young and heavily fictionalized version of Queen Seondeok.

In rewriting Mishil first and foremost as the quintessential villain of melodrama, the writers of *Great Queen Seondeok* took great license in interpreting Mishil's relationships with her lovers; nowhere is this more evident than in the case of Sadaham, a Silla noble depicted in the drama as Mishil's first and greatest love. The *Silla Annals of the Samguk Sagi* describe Sadaham as an accomplished warrior who led 5,000 soldiers as part of the military effort to quell the people of Kaya when they rose in rebellion. Sadaham won great merit in battle, but apparently held sympathy for the conquered people as well: "The King rewarded him with fine-quality land and two hundred prisoners of war but Sadaham declined this three times. When the King forced him, he received the people and freed them to be commoners and divided the fields among his solders. The people of the country admired him" (Kim, 2012). In the *Hwarang segi*, Mishil and Sadaham are said to have been lovers; Mishil composes a *hyangga* ("native song" or "country song"; a form of pre-modern poetry with very few extant examples) for him when he leaves to fight in the war against Kaya. This poem, which addresses the wind and the waves while hoping for her love's swift return, has sparked a heated debate among literature scholars that is related to but distinct from the debates about the *Hwarang segi's* authenticity (Lee, 1997). While McBride sees this *hyangga* as the crowning achievement of Pak Changhwa's imaginative foray into historical fiction, "most literature scholars are reluctant to label it a forgery or modern composition," and believe that "this *hyangga* must be the product of several authors and that it must have been passed down over several centuries, perhaps in Pak Ch'anghwa's own family, before taking its current written form" (McBride, 2008). Authentic or not, the poems Mishil and Sadaham supposedly composed for each other depict a loving relationship that coexisted alongside Mishil's many other liaisons with generations of Silla rulers.

The writers of *Great Queen Seondeok* refashion the relationship between Mishil and Sadaham so as to avoid the risk of the audience seeing Mishil in too sympathetic a light. In *Great Queen Seondeok*, what distinguishes Sadaham from the rest of the men in Mishil's life is his willingness to give up *everything* for her—to sacrifice without hope of return. Mishil waxes eloquent on Sadaham's selflessness in a discussion with one of her followers in episode 13: "All other men tried to gain something from me. As much as they gave me, they wanted to receive in return. Lord Sadaham, though, was a person who only gave." In abandoning any notion of reciprocity, Sadaham becomes the image of the bad democratic subject—and that is precisely what Mishil loves about him. There is no notion of reciprocity for Mishil, whether romantically or politically—her asymmetric relationship to Sadaham finds its political parallel in her preferred style of governance, which relies on the hoarding of scientific knowledge in order to cow a superstitious populace. The power struggle between Mishil and Deokman (who was introduced to us in King Jinheung's posthumous prophecy as the one destined "to oppose Mishil") becomes a near-allegory for the struggle between political ideologies based respectively on the exploitation of popular superstition and rule by the rational consent of an informed public. The eventual triumph of Good over Evil (an outcome necessary for most forms of melodrama, however otherwise differentiated) is heralded in the drama by the construction of *Cheomseongdae* ("star gazing platform"), an astronomical observatory that still stands in modern-day Gyeongju. In *Great Queen Seondeok*'s "melodramatic constitution," what distinguishes virtue from villainy has little to do with one's gender, and much more to do with one's adherence to democratic principles and the idea of knowledge as a public good.

MELODRAMA, HISTORY, AND THE
REPRESSION OF FEMALE DESIRE

Although Mishil of the *Hwarang Segi* and Mishil of *Great Queen Seondeok* are both the most fascinating characters in their respective narratives, they do not have much else in common beyond their names. As a melodramatic villain[13] who, while charismatic and undeniably compelling, is ultimately beyond sympathy or redemption, the latter Mishil loses much of what fascinates about the earlier Mishil. In particular, she loses the ability of Mishil's character in the *Hwarang segi* to unsettle our relationship to history by prompting us to imagine a past in which sexual liberation and political power were alike within a woman's reach. Just as the *Hwarang segi* suggests (or

imagines) that matrilineal descent could have played a greater role than
previously believed in the distribution of power within Silla society, a character like Mishil invites readers to imagine a Silla radically different from
its descriptions in traditional histories in terms of the political power and
personal agency that a woman could achieve.

What stands out most in *Great Queen Seondeok*'s rewriting of Mishil—and
in its representation of female characters more generally—is the repression or
effacement of female desire. This represents a decisive break, within the context of Korean historical dramas, from melodrama's relationship to repression
as theorized by Peter Brooks; specifically, it complicates his "hypothesis that
melodramatic rhetoric, and the whole expressive enterprise of the genre, represents a victory over repression. . . . Desire cries aloud its language in identification with full states of being" (Brooks, 1976). According to Brooks's
view of melodrama, virtue (always associated with victimized femininity)
must be able to cry out, with Emilia in *Othello*, "'Twill out, 'twill out. —I
peace? / No, I will speak liberal as the north. / Let heaven and men and dev-
ils, let them all, / All, all cry shame against me, yet I'll speak" (Shakespeare,
2017). Yet when we re-evaluate the "melodramatic constitution" in *Great
Queen Seondeok* in light of its overwriting of the *Hwarang segi*, what strikes
us, somewhat paradoxically, is precisely the *repression* of (female) desire.
This is true with regard to the protagonist Deokman who never once acts
on her love for her general, Kim Yusin—but it is also true, in a subtle but
profound way, in the construction of Mishil as a melodramatic villain. We
begin to perceive behind her the outline of another Mishil, one who seems to
defy any traditional category that would seek to contain her. Although many
of the elements of melodrama in *Great Queen Seondeok*—predetermined
outcomes gestured to by dramatic foreshadowing; the use of music and
tableaux to imbue the narrative with unambiguous meaning; and above all,
moral Manichaeism—are familiar to us from previous texts and traditions,
paying equal attention to history and to the authenticity debates surrounding
the show's sources gives us a more nuanced sense of how melodrama actually
interacts with historical "content" in a narrative that takes it upon itself to represent the past. Specifically, we can see the potential for loss that arises when
melodrama projects its Manichaeistic structure onto pre-existing individuals,
relationships, and events.

By ignoring the radical potential of Mishil's character in the *Hwarang segi*
while rewriting her as the unambiguously evil villain of traditional melodrama, *Great Queen Seondeok* brings a peculiarly conservative tinge to its
democratic imagination. And in its effacement of a potentially radical female
figure, *Great Queen Seondeok* shows a surprising affinity with the predilec-
tion of "official" history to record only the "public" deeds of men, ignoring
the voices of women by relegating them to the private sphere. As Yang

Geun-Ae (2018) puts it, "In historical records like the *Joseon Wangjo Sillok* [Veritable Records of the Joseon Dynasty] and the *Samguk sagi*, female characters rarely appear. Even when they do, in more cases than not women play a supplementary role by assisting men, or else they occupy a marginal position in a narrative centered around men." In the rare cases that a woman both wields power *and* has her story recorded in history (or, even rarer, manages to write it herself), there is often a backlash. In the historical case of Queen Seondeok, for example, the *Samguk sagi* emphasizes the prejudices against female rulers that played a role in what is known as Pidam's Rebellion: "Pidam and Yŏmjong, believing a Queen is not fit to govern well, plotted a rebellion and raised troops, but could not succeed" (Kim, 2012).[14] Even Kim Pusik himself takes time in his commentary at the end of this section in the *Silla Annals* to reflect on what seems to him the great danger of allowing a woman to rule:

> According to the laws of heaven, *yang* is firm and *yin* is gentle and according to the laws of man, man is honorable and woman is demeaning. How can one permit an old woman to leave the woman's quarters and determine the governmental affairs of the state? Silla, helping a woman to rise to occupy the royal throne, is a product of an age of unrest. It is fortunate that the state did not collapse.

With historical commentary like this, one can see how refreshing it is to watch Queen Seondeok's story retold as a clash between two powerful women, with most of the men in the narrative appearing in supplemental roles. Yet what initially seems like a reversal or inversion of traditional gender roles is more of a deliberate shift in emphasis *away* from explicit attention paid to gender. That is to say, what matters in *Great Queen Seondeok* is rarely one's gender, but rather where one falls in the overarching "moral occult" that aligns Virtue with Seondeok's political legitimacy and Villainy with Mishil's political illegitimacy. This de-emphasizing of gender *qua* gender (what Yang Geun-Ae refers to as "gender unconsciousness" [*jaendeo mu-euishik*]) breaks away not only from the male-centric narratives of history, but also from the representation of women in earlier historical dramas, who, while gaining more agency, were still "constrained by the shadow of traditional femininity" (Yang, 2018).

The "melodramatic constitution" of *Great Queen Seondeok* jettisons the traditional gendered dynamics of melodrama in order to focus almost exclusively on political legitimacy, but in doing so it also changes Mishil from the *Hwarang segi* almost beyond recognition. Whereas Mishil of the *Hwarang segi* resonates with modern calls for female empowerment along with greater political and sexual agency, Mishil of *Great Queen Seondeok* serves mainly to align political illegitimacy with Evil through the symbolic logic of melodrama's moral occult. Kim Byul-ah says it best in a 2009 interview with

Weekly Donga about the differences between her version of Mishil (from her 2005 novel based largely on the *Hwarang segi*) and Mishil from the television show. Kim characterizes Mishil as a "'wicked woman' [*ang-nyeo*] overflowing with charisma and greed for power," but expresses her disappointment with the drama's narrow focus: "Whether or not it was a result of the show's generic attributes—the need to emphasize the Manichaeistic structure [*seonak kudo*; 'structure of good and evil'] in order to grab viewers' attention—I thought it was a shame that they overemphasized Mishil's greed for power [*kweollyeong-yok*] only" (Lee, 2009). Women in literature, Kim argues, have historically been divided into "female saints" (*seongnyeo*) and "prostitutes" (*changnyeo*). Mishil's character reveals—or ought to reveal— the inadequacy of those categories.

NOTES

1. Here I refer to major theories of melodrama developed by Western critics. In particular, see Peter Brooks, *The Melodramatic Imagination: Balzac, Henry James, and the Mode of Excess*, and Elaine Hadley, *Melodramatic Tactics: Theatricalized Dissent in the English Marketplace*. Among earlier attempts to theorize stage melodrama, the most influential would probably be the work of Denis Diderot.

2. All translations of quotations from this and other Korean language sources are my own.

3. Although she addresses Brooks's account of the "melodramatic imagination," Yi responds most directly to the work of Elaine Hadley, particularly the idea of politically charged "melodramatic tactics" at work in the sphere of public discourse. See *Melodramatic Tactics*, 1-13.

4. Here I adapt Isobel Armstrong's terminology from *Novel Politics*. Armstrong argues for a "democratic imaginary" in many Victorian novels that runs counter to the prevailing understanding of the Victorian novel's "default position" as "conservative and hegemonic." See Armstrong, 2016. In spite of the apparent anachronism, I can think of no phrase that better captures the ideology expressed by King Jinheung, and later by Queen Seondeok and her supporters.

5. Baekje was Silla's neighbor and perennial enemy. Baekje, Silla, and the northern kingdom of Goguryeo are the "three kingdoms" whose history is recorded in the *Samguk sagi* (History of the Three Kingdoms), compiled by Goryeo-era historian Kim Pusik. For an introduction to the history of pre-modern Korea, see Lee 1984, especially chapters 3–5.

6. For an introduction to the intersection of gender and melodrama in a nineteenth-century context, see Newey, 2018: "The invention of the melodramatic heroine, as individuated feeling person, is one of the enduring legacies of melodrama's cultural work." Yet it would be a mistake to assume in advance that the gender dynamics familiar from nineteenth-century Western melodrama apply to the melodrama we see operating in recent Korean historical dramas.

7. Genealogical charts of Mishil's relationships can be found in the *Hwarang segi kwallyeon mungeon*, which predates the *Hwarang segi* itself. For a discussion of the significance of these charts, see McBride, 2008.

8. Ancient Silla society operated according to a strict hierarchical caste system called the "bone-rank system" (*geolpeumjae*). For more on this system, see Lee 1984. Mishil is not of the "true bone" line of descent, while most rulers, including King Jinji, are.

9. After the episode aired in 2009, *"Nangjang* Resolution" briefly became the most-searched term across Korean Internet portals, testifying to the impact this scene had on viewers at the time. See "What Is the 'Nanjang Resolution'?"

10. Lee acknowledges that "Silla's unification did not include the entire Korean peninsula," but maintains that this "does not diminish the importance of the Silla unification, the significance of which above all lies in the creation of an environment wherein the process of the formation of the Korean people might take an independent course."

11. According to the *Samguk sagi*, Queen Seondeok ascends to the throne as an older woman—she even received a title that translates to "hallowed royal grand-mother." See Kim, 2012.

12. For a summary of both sides of the debate written roughly a decade after the discovery of the manuscripts, see Kwon, 2000.

13. Of the archetypes and tropes most often associated with melodrama, the villain is probably the most recognizable. See Brooks, 1976, for a discussion of why the villain, though "highly characterized," is rarely "psychologically complex": "Indeed, evil must be fully personalized, the villain highly characterized, in the post-sacred universe [. . .] This does not mean that the villain is complex or nuanced as a psychological character. On the contrary, he is reduced to a few summary traits that signal his position, just as, physically, do his swarthy complexion, moustache, cape, and concealed dagger. But he is strongly characterized, a forceful representation of villainy." For Mishil, the "forcefulness" of her characterization—her overwhelming greed for power, her signature chilling smile—does not lessen our sense of the "reduction" that has to take place before the Mishil described in the *Hwarang segi* becomes recognizable as the melodramatic villain.

14. The editors of *The Silla Annals* point out in a footnote that "This revolt witnessed a clash between the power of the central aristocrats in the Hwabaek Council who sided with Pidam and the supporters of stronger royal authority who sided with the monarch." This complicates but by no means weakens our sense of the influence of Queen Seondeok's gender on Pidam's decision to rebel.

BIBLIOGRAPHY

Armstrong, I. (2016). *Novel Politics: Democratic Imaginations in Nineteenth-Century Fiction.* Oxford: Oxford University Press.

Brooks, P. (1976). *The Melodramatic Imagination: Balzac, Henry James, and the Mode of Excess.* New Haven, CT: Yale University Press.

'Gama': A Comprehensive Art. February 25, 2015, https://m.koreatimes.co.kr/pages /article.asp?newsIdx=174091.

Hadley, E. (1995). *Melodramatic Tactics: Theatricalized Dissent in the English Marketplace, 1800-1885*. Stanford, CA: Stanford University Press.

Jakobson, R. (1971). The Dominant. In *Readings in Russian Poetics: Formalist and Structuralist Views*, edited by Matejka, L., and Pomorska, K., 82–91. Cambridge, MA: MIT Press.

Ju, C. (2007). Yeoksadeurama Eui Jangleusajeok Byeonhwakwajeong [Generic History of Historical Dramas in Korea: 1964-2005]. *Hanguk Geuk Yaesul Yeongu* 25 (4): 369–98.

Kim, B. (2005). *Mishil*. Munidang. Seoul

Kim, P. (2012). *The Silla Annals of the Samguk Sagi*. Translated by Edward J. Shultz and Hugh H.W. Kang, with Daniel C. Kane. Seongnam: The Academy of Korean Studies Press.

Kim, Y., and Park, S. (2009). 선덕여왕 [Great Queen Seondeok]. Seoul: Munhwa Broadcasting Company. https://www.viki.com/tv/281c-the-great-queen-seondeok.

Lee, J. (2009). Na eui Mishil-eun modeun haengbok-eul Ggumggweot-deon yeoja ["My Mishil is a woman who dreamed of every kind of happiness"]. *Weekly Donga*, July 8, 2009, https://weekly.donga.com/List/3/all/11/87935/1

Lee, K. (1984). *A New History of Korea*. Translated by Edward W. Wagner with Edward J. Shultz. Seoul: Ilchokak.

Lee, S. (2002). Mellodeurama Eui Keundaejeok Sangsangryeok: 1910 Nyeondae Sinpageuk Eul Chungshimeuro [The Modern Imagination of Melodrama: Sinpa Drama in the 1910s]. *Hanguk Geuk Yaesul Yeongu* 15: 93–129.

McBride II, R. (2008). Pak Ch'anghwa and the Hwarang Segi Manuscripts. *The Journal of Korean Studies* 13: 57–88.

Newey, K. (2018). Melodrama and Gender. In *The Cambridge Companion to English Melodrama*, edited by Williams, C., 149–62. Cambridge: Cambridge University Press.

Pak, Y. (2009). Hanguk Mellodeurama Eui Hyeongseong Kwajeong Yeongu: Jeoneollijeum e Natanan 'mellodeurama' Jangleu Kaenyeomeul Chungshimeuro [A Study of the Formation of the Concept of the Korean Melodrama Genre]. *Hyeondae Munhak Iron Yeongu* 38: 181–212.

Shakespeare, W. (2017). *Othello*, edited by Pechter, E. New York: W.W. Norton and Company.

Shultz, E. (2004). An Introduction to the 'Samguk Sagi.' *Korean Studies* 28: 1–13.

"What Is the 'Nanjang Resolution'?" *New Daily*, Accessed December 12, 2020, http://www.newdaily.co.kr/site/data/html/2009/08/17/2009081700030.html.

Williams, C. (2012). Melodrama. In *The Cambridge History of Victorian Literature*. Cambridge: Cambridge University Press.

Williams, C. (2019). Tableaux and Melodramatic Realism. *English Literature* 6: 101–24.

Yang, G. (2018). Yeoksadeurama Eui Jaendeo Wa Jeongchiseong [Gender and Politics of Historical Drama]. *Hanguk Geuk Yaesul Yeongu* 62: 229–58.

Yi, W. (2018). Melodramatic Tactics for Survival in the Neoliberal Era: Excess and Justice in The Heirs and My Love from the Star. *Journal of Korean Studies* 23 (1): 153–73.

Chapter 6

Breaking the Stereotype of Domestic Adoption in K-dramas

Marcy L. Tanter

As international appetites for cultural products from South Korea increase, the popularity of Korean dramas seems unbounded. Drama chat groups on social media add new members daily and production companies post their global ratings. In Korea, ratings are strong for K-dramas, especially as writers are experimenting with non-traditional topics in their plots. With topics such as adoption, support for homosexuals, the benefits of mental healthcare, and women choosing career over marriage, some dramas reflect these issues in contemporary South Korean society. For a long time, adoptees have been stereotyped in dramas as troubled people who tend to either grow up to become criminals or are mentally impaired. More generally, "in the past several decades, popular media representations that focus on adoption rather than relegating it to backstories or subplots have increased, bringing new visibility to the experiences of birth mothers and adoptive mothers" (Shoos, 2020). Global interest in adoption and adoptees means that these stories resonate and attract audiences, regardless of their country of origin. Subtitling is so widespread that even viewers in countries such as Romania and Nigeria can access K-dramas.

Since 2015 some K-drama productions have addressed the adoption issue head-on, in what seems to be an effort to combat this negativity. If the productions are reflecting changes in Korean society, then the K-drama industry can be seen as a mirror that is pulling plots from quotidian life its audience will recognize; if the productions are seeking to influence Korean society, then the industry is setting itself up to be more than an entertainment portal. The K-dramas discussed in this study (*Pinocchio, Entertainer*, and *Mother*)[1] all present views of domestic adoption that are deliberately positive. I have not found any scholarship that assesses the impact of these dramas on viewers, so the purpose of this study is to acknowledge the increasingly positive messages about domestic adoption in K-dramas and to make the case that the positive messages signify changing attitudes in Korean society. Given the impact the Korean celebrity endorsement and product placement in dramas has on the Korean economy, it is logical to assume that the positive portrayals of domestic adoption will have some impact on audiences. According to Anna Cheang (2015), Korean dramas often depict Korean society accurately, despite exaggerations; a dearth of scholarship on this topic complicates research, but one can assume that changing attitudes toward domestic adoption in recent dramas mirror changes in societal attitudes.

DOMESTIC ADOPTION IN MODERN KOREAN SOCIETY

The birthrate in South Korea is declining as women of childbearing age opt to enter careers instead of marrying or having children. The total fertility rate dropped to 0.84 during the second quarter of 2020 (Hankyoreh, 2020). Despite this decline, there are still many children being raised in Korean orphanages because women are often ostracized if they become pregnant and have no male partner (Evans, 2015, 2017). Of the children waiting to be adopted, the majority of those raised to adulthood in the orphanages are boys. According to Lee (2014), there are several reasons why Korean adoptive parents prefer girls, including the perception that a daughter is more likely to take care of the parents when they are elderly; approximately 90% of Korean domestic adoptees are girls. The Korean government, the Korean entertainment industry, and Korean media are working to destigmatize adoption to encourage more families to adopt children of both sexes. The Mission to Promote Adoption of Kids (MPAK) has been "actively engaged in adoption promotion activities in Korea. They [have] appeared in a lot of TV programs to inculcate the public with the image of happy adoptive families and [work as][2] instructors of anti-prejudice programs in [schools]" (Ahn, 2020).

The number of children adopted in Korea has declined every year over the past five years. In 2019, the number of South Korean children adopted within the country was 387, whereas 317 children were adopted abroad (Statista, 2020). The government and media have joined together on multiple occasions to release announcements and promote initiatives to encourage domestic adoption; the entertainment industry moves cautiously and slowly to include adoption in different genres, but it is most prevalent in Korean dramas. How the industry impacts adoption numbers is yet to be studied, but the prevalence of adoption in dramas has increased over the past decade.

In order to consider the adoption theme in K-dramas, one must come to terms with the awkward place adoption has in Korean society. Thousands of orphaned children were adopted internationally after the end of the Korean War because neither the South Korean people nor their government felt they had the means to care for those children. Many South Korean birth mothers viewed transnational adoption as the best option for their children, who bore the stamp of illegitimacy. While the biological children of South Korean men were able to obtain citizenship regardless of their natal mothers' nationality, "children born to Korean women and foreign men could not" (McKee, 2016). This law severely impacted children born to Korean women and American men. Not only did these children not receive South Korean citizenship, they also could not obtain American citizenship due to constraints concerning paternity. Only when the law was revised nearly 50 years later in September 1997 did children of Korean women obtain South Korean citizenship rights (McKee, 2016).

In hindsight, many Koreans feel shame for sending those children abroad, as one government official noted in 1988: "If we had abided by our cultural traditions, it would never have happened" (Chira, 1988). The 1988 Olympics increased the embarrassment felt by the government because of foreign backlash against the number of children being adopted internationally. After the Olympics, the Korean government began efforts to slow the rate at which children were being sent overseas. Consul Baek-Sang Cho of the South Korean Embassy said that "the Olympics coverage 'forced my Government and the Korean people to sit down and think about what direction Korean international adoptive policies were heading'" (Lewin, 1990). Loeb (1991) noted that "to this day South Koreans say they were shamed and embarrassed by the accusation of 'baby selling' and the foreign perception that they were too callous to care for their own. Koreans are intensely proud of their country and highly sensitive to what is being written and said about it overseas."

Foreign criticism was not the only reason for the government's push to increase domestic adoption and to slow international adoption. A decline in the birth rate and social stability helped to increase domestic adoptions in the early 1990s. Korean Adoption Services [KAS] (n.d.) records show "the government also provided adoptive families with housing loans, medical expenses, educational costs, and living expenses. However, with the tradition of valuing blood ties and the reality of keeping adoption secret, the financial support for adoptive families did not act to vitalize domestic adoption." The push-pull inefficiency of adoption policy brought the plight of adoptees into the press and then into popular culture. By 2004, international adoptees were featured in some Korean films and television dramas, paving the way for the topic to become a basis for discussion in Korean society as it had not been before (Park, 2005).

ATTITUDES TOWARD ADOPTION

Because of the Confucian principle that the family is more important than its individual members (Park and Cho, 1995) and due to the importance of bloodlines in Korean culture, adoption of non-blood-related children has long been a difficult and secret practice in Korea. The main reason for adoption has been, traditionally, to provide a male heir where there was none. Since the Korean War left many orphaned children, foundations were established to find homes for many of them overseas and led to thousands of Korean children being raised abroad with no sense of their "Koreanness" and little to no contact with Korean culture. Recently, laws were established to make overseas adoption more difficult as many transnational adoptees have formed organizations to find their birth families, and many also want to return to Korea (Jones, 2015).

For adoptees in Korea, there is a stigma that has been attached to them as they usually have no proof of family lineage or no other way to prove who they "are." According to Lee (2006) and Burwell (2018), most abandoned children are still placed in residential facilities rather than with families, although there have been slight increases in domestic adoptions since 2006. Many domestic adoptions are done secretly to avoid embarrassment for the family. Tu (1996) notes that Confucian family affairs are often seen as public affairs, so secret adoptions are a way to avoid public notice and humiliation.

While aspects of Korean life are deeply rooted in Confucianism, Hong (2015) points out that "throughout Korean history, it is important to note that Confucianism is not a fixed value, having changed and altered its form according to growing modernity," yet she claims that attitudes toward motherhood and adoption have remained more static than most other values. As domestic adoptees are included as characters in contemporary K-dramas, some conflict arises between the positive images the producers and writers want to exhibit and the realities of Korean attitudes toward adoption in a society that still adheres somewhat to the notion that family lineage is paramount to one's strength of character. Indeed, Tu (1996) states that "the East Asian form of modernity is in a substantial way 'Western,'" yet is still challenged by some Confucian ideals of the family structure. As a cultural group, Korean dramas highlight well the challenges of presenting adoptees as society expects to see them and still connecting with target audiences that are diverse and multinational. Korean audiences may be the primary target of K-dramas, but international viewers in other parts of Asia and the United States have had some impact on how dramas are produced. "South Korean television dramas have over 1.5 billion fans worldwide of whom the Chinese audience makes up one third," according to Han Jiyuan, director of South Korea's Investment Promotion Bureau (Qizi, 2014). So, with that in mind, the television companies must be cautious that their audiences are wide and varied, which can impact the success and even the direction of the dramas. Since domestic adoption continues to be a feature of K-dramas, it can be assumed that the public is receptive of the topic, both at home and abroad. If it is true that "audience members in Korea agree that broadcasting performs a public function for people and television has the power as social force to change society" (Kim, 1998), then it is reasonable to expect those broadcasting networks to take on the responsibility of producing shows with social messages.

THE STIGMA OF SINGLE MOTHERHOOD

When adoption and adoptees are part of the plot in early Korean dramas, the audience does not learn why the child was given up; sometimes we learn that a child was found without any background story, a mother became pregnant out of wedlock and could not keep the baby, or she was forced to give the baby up by the father's relatives. Although negative stigma is attached to adoption, single motherhood is considered a far worse situation. Choe (2009) quotes a transnational adoptee in the *New York Times*: "what we see in South Korea today is discrimination against natural mothers and favoring of adoption at the government level." Adopted characters often live in poverty or constantly experience misfortune; even if the adopted character is generally happy, his/her life can be fraught with difficulties and tragedies, suggesting that the adopted person is somehow cursed because they are an adoptee.

Korean attitudes toward adoption are complicated at the best of times and the dramas reflect varying degrees of positivity and negativity. In a 2015 segment, *Arirang Issue*, a division of the Korean English television service Arirang, noted that positive slogans promoting domestic adoption are not enough to encourage potential parents to consider adopting. The segment highlights strong family bonds created through domestic adoption and concludes that "adoption is a blessing and a gift but more than slogans, we need a change in systems and public awareness." Perhaps it is not coincidence that recent Korean dramas are increasingly depicting domestic adoption as a normal, ordinary family arrangement.

THE STIGMA OF BEING AN "ADOPTED KID"

Hollee McGinnis (2017) shows that growing up in Korean orphanages can have an adverse effect on the social and scholastic development of children, but she also points out that "child welfare facilities in Korea are well maintained, and adequately meet the basic health care, nutrition, and environmental stimulation necessary to prevent global developmental failure." Schoenmaker et al. (2014) conclude that children do better in a family situation than if they grow up in an institution. Entering the family at a younger age is best for their development, but joining a family after some time in an orphanage is better for the child than no time at all in a family:

"In family care, the positive influence of parenting is expected to be larger than in an institutional setting with limited or lacking individualized and stable childcare, and therefore the child's transition from institutional care to family care is presented as one step further on the continuum of positive parenting influence."

Pinocchio

In 2014, Seoul Broadcasting Service (SBS) produced *Pinocchio*, a hard-hitting drama in which the female protagonist, In-ha, has been raised by her father and grandfather after her parents' divorce. Her mother is career-focused and has not seen her daughter in 13 years. The male protagonist, Ha-myeong, was orphaned after his fire-chief father died in a blaze and his mother committed suicide. She leapt off a cliff with Ha-myeong, but he survived and was found in the sea by In-ha's grandfather, Choi Gong-pil, who brought him home and adopted him. In this way, In-ha and Ha-myeong were raised together as niece and uncle but they are age-mates (the family consists of the three of them and In-ha's father, Dal-pyeong). Until 2007, adoptive parents in South Korea could be no more than 50 years older than the child being adopted. The audience does not know Gong-pil's age, but their age difference is probably more than 50 years but less than the 60 years now allowed (Hong, 2015). Ha-myeong knows who he really is; he remembers his older brother, yet he pretends he has amnesia and cannot recall who he is. His new family embraces him and they bond well, but Gong-pil's mild Alzheimer's disease sometimes has him thinking Ha-myeong is truly his dead son whose name was Dal-po; hence, Ha-myeong is now known as Dal-po.

When Ha-myeong/Dal-po was found in the sea, he was about 10 years old. Given that he was basically a foundling and has no family to claim him, it is remarkable that there is no stigma attached to him within the family or among the community. In fact, he is insistent on pretending to be Dal-po because Gong-pil suffers from a condition that causes him to black out when he thinks about his natural son's death. The current Dal-po has heard that his predecessor had lived with mental illness so he pretends that he is intellectually disabled himself and has the worst grades in his school when, in fact, he is highly intelligent. He pulls off this ruse for the sake of Gong-pil's health, so as not to make his impersonation obvious. While the plot of this drama is quite complicated, at its core is the message that having a strong family, regardless of its composition, is the key to a successful life; within that structure, someone who is adopted is as capable of being loved as someone with blood ties. The message underscores the idea that it does not matter that Ha-myeong/Dal-po is not really Gong-pil's son, Dal-pyeong's brother, nor In-ha's uncle; what matters is that they are a family and care for one another deeply.

Park Hye-ryun was a seasoned K-drama writer (*Dream High*, 2011; *I Can Hear Your Voice*, 2013, among others) when she wrote the script for *Pinocchio*. It is unclear if she meant to make the adoption message of the drama a central focus for the audience, but two scenes in particular highlight the positive relationships that can come out of adoption. In episode 12, Dal-po has found his brother Jae-myeong and intends to investigate their father's death (Dal-po is now a television journalist), so he decides to move out of Gong-pil's house and into his brother's apartment. He comes to Gong-pil to say goodbye and the following exchange ensues:

GP: House, you have found one?
DP: Yes. I am thinking of living in my hyung's house.
GP [with a pained look on his face]: How about continuing to live here? Can't you? I . . . whatever your story is, it doesn't matter. Just, you are my son. Choi Dal-po.

(Park and Won, 2014)

What is significant here is the emotional bond between the two men.[3] Gong-pil does not care what Dal-po's story is; he has come to love him and considers him family as much as his natural son and In-ha. Dal-po loves Gong-pil just as much but feels he must leave to avenge his real father and save his brother. Gong-pil loves Dal-po as he is, for who he is. For the audience, seeing these two men sitting on a floor facing each other and crying while saying words of parting melts away any doubt that regardless of his name, Ha-myeong/Dal-po has become Gong-pil's son and the love that has grown between them breaks the stereotype that adoptive families are harsh and cruel. Even though we know the origin of this relationship, it just does not matter—people can become family without sharing blood ties. When Dal-po asks Gong-pil to dissolve his adoption so he can reclaim his birth name, Gong-pil looks at Dal-po as if he had been slapped hard. The scene ends without the request resolved, but we find out the result later. Dal-po's emotions become jumbled and he is confused now that he has found his biological brother and must clear his father's name: his affection for the family that took him in and raised him to be a man of principle never wanes, and he also feels a strong sense of loyalty to his birth family. The bonds of family can be forged through birth, marriage, or adoption; how a person comes into the family is nothing compared to one's worth within it.

Choi Gong-pil does not dissolve the adoption when Dal-po asks for it. Letting go of Dal-po in this way would force him to face losing his natural son Dal-po twice and this adopted son at the same time, which would be more than he could bear. For Dal-po, dissolving the adoption is not meant as a sign of disrespect, but it is a means of claiming his own identity as a man. In the short term, reclaiming "Gi Ha-myeong" ties him to his natural brother and father; in the long term, reclaiming the name returns him to who he was before he was "Choi Dal-po," not to dismiss the importance of being Dal-po in Gong-pil's life but to allow Gong-pil to have his natural son back. At the moment Ha-myeong asked to have the adoption dissolved, he believed himself to be unworthy of Gong-pil. By episode 20, however, the world of this drama has shifted greatly and the relationship between these two men is much stronger.

Episode 20 is the series finale. At this point, Dal-po has resolved his issues, save for one. He and In-ha want permission from Gong-pil to marry—permission from his father and her grandfather. They go to Gong-pil together and kneel before him, as they should, calmly and respectfully. Gong-pil's face lights up when he sees them and Dal-po says they have something to tell him. The scene fades and then opens a year later, on the actual last day of the show: January 15, 2015. The audience realizes that Gong-pil did not give the couple permission to date, but their affection has only grown stronger and they want to be together. How they are going to convince him is the problem. At one point, Gong-pil and Dal-pyeong come across Dal-po's wallet. Gong-pil looks inside and sees a photo of Dal-po and In-ha with their friend's baby. At that moment, Gong-pil realizes that Dal-po and In-ha make a good couple and we see him start to consider the possibility of giving them his permission. A short time later, Gong-pil visits Dal-po, who is broadcasting from the municipal court, and they share another poignant conversation after Dal-po asks why his father is there:

GP [with happiness on his face]: Your adoption. I came to submit the papers to invalidate it. That's why I came.
DP [looking confused and then with understanding, kneels]: Father.
GP: Now, I want to stop telling lies and I want you to find your true name. I'm sorry. You see, I cherished you so much that I was unnecessarily stubborn for too long.
DP [his voice full of emotion as he realizes what is happening]: Father.
GP: Now you can live with your name. The name Choi Dal-po, you can throw that away now, you get that?

(Park and Won, 2014)

The scene slowly cuts away with them sharing a long embrace. Gong-pil understood always that this Dal-po was not his real Dal-po, but he needed to come to terms with his loss. For 30 years he grieved and could not face having lost his son. Now, he can let go of both Dal-pos and live happily with his family. Ha-myeong will always be a son to him, but as In-ha's husband. Screenwriter Park shows that the adopted child can assimilate into the family and play an important role within it. What matters is how the family treats him and how comfortable he is made to feel, so that he never feels as though being adopted makes any difference. How he entered the family is irrelevant; now he is part of it forever.

Pinocchio confronts the stereotypes and prejudices of adoption that previous dramas about adoption did not address. This production shows the positivity that comes from adoption and tells the audience without equivocation that an adopted member has the same right to a place in the family as those born into it. Putting this message in front of the audience where it cannot be avoided is a powerful support for domestic adoption. With popular actors Park Shin-hye and Lee Jong-suk in the lead roles, the drama's ratings were consistently high during its run in Korea, with some episodes earning more than 10% of national and Seoul viewership, which is a strong rating. Unpopular plots can hurt a drama, even if the lead roles are played by actors the audience wants to see. For example, Lee Min-ho's much anticipated return to acting after his military service ended was not highly successful. The drama, *King: The Eternal Monarch*, achieved low ratings because the plot was not appealing to the domestic audience, but it did well internationally via Netflix (Valley, 2020).

Although they are writing about Korean workers, Yeo, Wildman, and Choi (2017) show that some Confucian values still affect Korean society. Their findings can be applied to the strong adoptive father–adoptee son relationship in *Pinocchio* to explain the bond that develops between Ha-myeong and Gong-pil. In their article, the authors posit,

> Based on a loving heart for human beings, Ryu and Lee (2010) argued that a leader with high levels of Confucian values should first treat his or her supervisors in the way that he or she hopes to be treated by subordinates, and should treat his or her subordinates in the way that he or she wishes to be treated by supervisors.

From the start, Gong-pil accepted Ha-myeong as a member of the family, demonstrating his "loving heart," treating Ha-myeong as Dal-po, expecting him to reciprocate the affection. In a short time, the "new" Dal-po reflects Gong-pil's trust, applying the Confucian values Yeo et al. see in supervisor/ subordinate relations at work. Considering this notion of Confucian trust/ heart with respect to the drama as a whole, writer Park kickstarts Confucian values for a twenty-first-century audience. Park puts a modern spin on the old values by showing Ha-myeong/Dal-po treating Gong-pil with the highest level of respect while not losing sight of his loyalty to his birth family and to himself. Traditional Confucian values require a person to suppress their own needs or goals for the good of the family, but Park rewrites the rule just enough so that Ha-myeong can satisfy the traditional family values and push for his own desire: to marry In-ha. Even within his own brand of selfishness, he is a symbol for the present-day audience who can literally "marry" old and new values and still maintain balance in the world.

Entertainer

New values and attitudes toward domestic adoption are cropping up in Korean dramas more frequently than ever before. It is somewhat puzzling and yet heartening that some dramas reflect very open, positive attitudes toward adoption at the end of this century's second decade. While there is no indication of an agreement among the writers or a particular government action that has brought this on, audiences are being introduced to adopted characters who are surrounded by friends and loved ones who do not regard the adoptions as unusual or shameful. In Entertainer (*Ddandara*), adoption is embraced without shame or stigma by the adopted character's friends and colleagues. The unfolding of their attitudes is a realistic portrayal of insecurity and unconditional acceptance.

Entertainer is an SBS production from spring, 2016, about a boy band. In true K-drama fashion, each of the four band members has an embarrassing situation: Ha-neul was wrongly accused of sexual assault; Yeon-soo is a single father whose wife abandoned him and their son; Jae-hoon has an overbearing mother who does not support his dream of playing drums in a band; and then there is Kyle, a talented guitarist who attended Julliard but is now back home in Korea trying to make a living. For most of the 18 episodes, Kyle is a source of mild comedy, making jokes and keeping the others laughing. The band's manager, Suk-ho, is planning to move the band to a new management company and during a business meeting with the band members, the tone becomes serious.

In episode 17 the band members do not want to change to the new company, and they protest the move. Suddenly Kyle, who has had few serious moments until this point, speaks up. He tells the others he has something to tell them and says he understands that President Shin (Suk-ho) wants to "send them off" to a better place, but that doing so feels more like they are being abandoned, "thrown away." Suk-ho tells him to stop "saying nonsense," but Kyle continues:

K: "I don't think I can raise you well." "Meet better parents, get adopted and grow up in a better environment." To that child, it's being thrown away, not sent away.

SH: Why would you bring up adoption? Pull yourself together.

K: You can't confirm if adoptive parents are better or not. I have never met my biological parents. How could I know if they are better or worse than my adoptive parents? [Camera pans the others, who look surprised]

The conversation here is very clever; Suk-ho wants to help the band members because he thinks he cannot give them what they need. His notion of "sending them off" is, in his mind, doing the right thing for them. But for Kyle, the feeling of abandonment is overwhelming in that moment and his part of the conversation is a strong statement of how it feels for an adoptee to grow up not knowing why he was given up or who his real parents are. Kyle addresses his friends, with a tone that is serious and yet comforting, as he makes it clear that his adoptive parents have been good and raised him well. He does not resent being raised by them, but not knowing who his birth parents are or why they gave him up bothers him. This situation gives Kyle the agency to confidently tell Suk-ho that what he is doing is like throwing away a child without good reason. Suk-ho is stunned by this revelation; it is a perspective he never considered.

Kyle's success was encouraged by his adoptive parents. Only top students are admitted to Julliard, so their support was not just monetary but also educative. He is confident and caring, which shows that he was raised with a sense of security within the family structure. The work of Feeney et al. (2007) confirms Kyle's sensitivity to abandonment. This commonplace fear can often be found in adult adoptees but is not always apparent to their peers. For the audience, hearing the impassioned message from Kyle might be out of place in other circumstances, but it fits well here and forces the audience to consider the plight of adopted children from a new perspective, without addressing the audience directly.

In another scene, Suk-ho and Kyle are sitting outside a café. Suk-ho looks at Kyle a bit sheepishly, perhaps from embarrassment, and says, "I'm hurt, you should have told me. What's wrong with being adopted?" Suk-ho's question, "What's wrong with being adopted?" may be the most important question posed to any adoptee character in the Korean dramas discussed here. Not only is he making it clear that it is fine for Kyle to have been adopted, he is also throwing off the stigma so often pinned on adoptees and is making a bold statement for the audience to hear: there is nothing wrong with being adopted, so you don't have to hide it. Kyle's response, though, is important. He says, "I didn't care much about it when I was in the States. It seems different in Korea. I thought I would get looked down on" (46:15–23). Kyle's distinction between the two countries is not lost on anyone. The Korean audience is aware that adoptees are treated poorly at home; they know tens of thousands of Korean children were adopted internationally and raised abroad, they know adoption is viewed more kindly in other countries. In this scene and the one discussed above, *Entertainer* makes the case for treating adoptees well. They are upstanding citizens and have a lot to contribute to society, as modeled by Kyle's character. He is a strong person who is talented and wants to be successful at home and abroad. Although he is wistful about his biological family, his adoption did not hinder him in any noticeable way.

The comments on adoption in the drama reflect positivity. Not only is Kyle comfortable with his status, so are the people around him. The happiness with which he was raised in his family reflects, also, what Ahn and Choi (2020) found in their study of happiness among Korean domestic adoptees:

> the happiness score of adopted children was generally higher than that of the general population of children in South Korea. The comparison between the two groups based on the factors of gender, age, and household income showed similar results: adopted children reported a similar or significantly higher happiness score than non-adopted children.

The prevalence of happiness among adopted children is reflected in the depictions in *Pinocchio* and *Entertainer* which reinforce the notion that the dramas portray positivity toward adoption in Korean society generally. Of course, not all adopted children are happy and there is still plenty of stigma and negativity about adoption that those children have to face, but as more positive attitudes show up in K-dramas and those dramas do well in ratings, there is hope for a great shift away from the negativity. *Entertainer*'s ratings were not nearly as high as *Pinocchio*'s, but they were consistent for most of its run, suggesting it had a solid base of fans. Episode 18, the finale, saw a slight uptick in nationwide ratings, which suggests the adoption focus in episode 17 was more than acceptable to its audience.

Mother

Mother is a Korean remake of the Japanese drama *Mazâ* (2010). In this version, it is about a woman ornithologist, Soo-jin, who "kidnaps" a little girl, Hye-na, who is being abused by her mother, Ja-young, and her mother's boyfriend. The woman and the girl bond so well that Hye-na changes her name and comes to recognize Soo-jin as her mother and sees her birth mother as someone who she can acknowledge but not as someone who deserves to be her mother. Secondary plots involve Soo-jin's birth and adoptive mothers, her foster mother, and her adoptive siblings. Within these tangled relationships we see different kinds of mothers and mothering while the overall message of the drama is that family is not dependent on blood relationships and adoption can result in a beautiful life.

Sung Hee Yook and Hosu Kim (2018) write about Korean birth mothers whose children were given up for transnational adoption. In talking about the absence of documentation from these birth mothers, they note that

> the figure of the birth mother is firmly constructed as uneducated, a helpless victim of poverty, sexual and domestic violence, and the further social stigma of single motherhood, all trapped in a Third World (and disproportionately Asian) problem.

Appearances of birth mothers in Korean dramas often fit this description; however, *Mother* breaks from this stereotype. It presents two birth mothers who are polar opposites. Ja-young is a lonely woman in her 20s who was obviously not ready to have a child. The birth father is absent and her current boyfriend is a narcissistic abuser and a possible pedophile. Ja-young clings to him because she fears being alone and she doesn't understand that her sweet, precious daughter, Hye-na, would be a better companion even though she is only eight years old. Ja-young suffers from what may be a mild form of PTSD and is unable to care for her child properly. Sadly, she allows herself to be so manipulated that she abandons her daughter in a horrific manner and is eventually arrested and jailed. The second birth mother is Nam Hong-hee, a hairdresser in her 50s whose identity and story are revealed slowly throughout the first half of the series. At first, her character meets the stereotype identified by Yook and Kim. She is middle-aged, uneducated, and seemingly helpless. Later on, we discover that she is in fact selfless, brave, and devoted to the daughter she gave up.

The contrast between these two women is important because of the perceptions in Korean media culture that birth mothers are often portrayed as women who just abandoned their children, as in the dramas *Legend of the Blue Sea* (mother is forced to leave her son with his father after a divorce because the father is wealthy and powerful) and *Pinocchio*, for example. Sometimes birth mothers are redeemed, especially if they were thrown out by strong, wealthy husbands (*Legend of the Blue Sea*). In *Mother*, Ja-young could have been redeemed had she not been so scheming and calculative. After she has been arrested for the abuse Hye-na suffered, she opts for a jury trial; she wants the public to know that she stayed with her man because she was afraid of being alone in the world: "Oppa was the only one who stayed by my side then. If you were in my shoes, what would you have done? Do you think you could have done any better?" (episode 14) She asks these questions with a straight face with nothing soft, emotional, or regretful in her gaze. The audience cannot feel sympathy for her, having been witness to Hye-na's suffering and the better life she has away from her birth mother. Ja-young sees Hye-na as something she owns, something that belongs to her. She wants to have Hye-na back, to retrieve her possession. She does not consider what Hye-na might want or what is best for her. Ja-young lost the right to be Hye-na's mother through her selfishness and narcissism.

Hong-hee was a young woman who gave birth to Soo-jin out of wedlock, but she adored her daughter. Hong-hee lived with her boyfriend who became abusive to her. After he cut off one of Hong-hee's fingers, she feared for the safety of her daughter and killed him. Terrified and ashamed by what she had done, Hong-hee took five-year-old Soo-jin to an orphanage where she knew the foster mother was loving and kind. She tethered Soo-jin to the fence of the orphanage and promised she would return. Soo-jin did not see her mother again for 30 years. In the meantime, she spent two years at the orphanage and was then adopted by Young-shin, a famous actress. Soo-jin was raised with two sisters, Yi-jin and Hyun-jin. At the moment the drama begins, Soo-jin is estranged from her family; she returns home to hide Hye-na from the police, only to find that Young-shin is dying from cancer.

Hong-hee's abandonment of Soo-jin has caused deep psychological wounds. Soo-jin has vague memories of her mother and believes her mother hated her. Soo-jin is a quiet, stoic adult who does not express emotion; the trauma of her childhood is very apparent in her demeanor. As the drama develops, the audience sees Hong-hee as a hardworking, kind woman, in sharp contrast to Ja-young who wants to be taken care of and shirks responsibility for her child. Hong-hee lives and works in Soo-jin's neighborhood and eventually the audience, and Soo-jin, learn that she is her birth mother. They are thrown together in an odd relationship triangle with Hye-na, which gives the audience more evidence that Hong-hee is a good person and they feel sympathy for her when Soo-jin rejects her birth mother's attempts to reclaim her position as "mother." In the end, of course, Soo-jin learns that after she was tied to the fencepost, Hong-hee went to the police and confessed to the murder she committed. She thought it would be better for Soo-jin to believe her mother abandoned her rather than to know her mother was a murderer. She tells her, "I didn't abandon you. I sent you away because I was so ashamed of myself." Years later, she found out where Soo-jin was living and moved into the neighborhood to watch her. Once they reunite, Hong-hee doesn't want to replace Young-shin in Soo-jin's life, but she does want to reconnect.

The characters of these two birth mothers demonstrate women at opposite ends of the abandonment trope. Ja-young has no redemptive qualities while Hong-hee thought she was doing the right thing for her daughter. Both of these women gave birth to daughters, and both seek some kind of connection with their children, although one wants possession and the other wants love. These relationships are complex and become even more complicated when seen alongside the adoptive mothers in the drama.

When Soo-jin and Hye-na run off together, Soo-jin has never intended to be "mother" to anyone. Her life has been dedicated to studying birds and that is where her passion lies. She does not even have a boyfriend or any close friends. She sees herself in Hye-na when she learns about the abuse because the hurt of being abandoned feels like being abused to her. Hye-na could have been her and she wants to save her from the agonizing pain that comes with feeling abandoned and not knowing why. It does not take long for Hye-na to accept Soo-jin as "Eomma" and for Soo-jin to love Hye-na and to feel maternal. She is protective and fierce in her devotion to the little girl. She is conflicted by the crime she has committed and doing what she feels is best for the child. Being "mother" comes to feel so natural to her that she is temporarily stunned when she loses Hye-na and is charged with kidnapping. It means nothing to her that she did not give birth to Hye-na; what matters is that Hye-na is a child deserving of love and protection and Soo-jin can give that to her.

The strong relationship formed between Soo-jin and Hye-na happens quickly; Hye-na recognizes that Soo-jin is going to protect her, even though she (Hye-na) is at first protective of her birth mother. Santos-Nunes et al. (2017) note that "being adopted by a responsive and warm family may serve to relieve [negative] effects, enabling relationship representations and attachment bonds to be (re)constructed." So, the security that Soo-jin provides from the start causes Hye-na to shift her filial attachment from Ja-young and to place her trust in Soo-jin. Even though Soo-jin has not become Hye-na's mother legally, the audience sees her selfless behavior that saves Hye-na from a likely death. It is not difficult to accept Soo-jin as an adoptive mother because she behaves as a mother should. Subconsciously, Soo-jin reflects the same kind of love and protection she received from her own adoptive mother.

The audience is shown from the start that Young-shin adores Soo-jin and is as proud of her and her sisters as she can be. She is proud of being an adoptive mother and makes it clear several times that she is as much a mother as if she had given birth to Soo-jin. And when Hye-na is brought into the family, Young-shin becomes "Halmonie" without question and makes sure Hye-na knows that she is loved and accepted. The writer, Jung Seo-Kyoung, drew these characters so that the audience sees the intricacies and immediacy of their connections. Soo-jin is not aware that her attitude toward Hye-na comes from Young-shin's attitude toward herself—the notion of acceptance and love for a child simply because the child deserves that love and attention is unquestioned and unconditional. Albert and Grotevant (2020) demonstrate that when adoptive parents are open with their children and recognize that being an adoptive family is different from being a blood-related family, those children are much more likely to have strong bonds with their parents during adolescence. When parents acknowledge and understand how coming into a family instead of being born into it can have challenges and issues, it is easier to develop trust between the parents and child and helps the child attach to the parents. Young-jin discussed adoption with Soo-jin all her life and Soo-jin and Hye-na discuss openly how they are forming their own family. Both Soo-jin and Hye-na attach easily to their adoptive mothers and families as children because of the open and positive attitudes that embrace them.

Hye-na is embraced by the family and all the caregivers become responsible for her at different times once she is away from her birth mother. She thrives within the family and even though she misses Soo-jin while she is away from her, she does well in foster care, too. Lawler et al. (2018) posit that the collectivist nature of Korean society, particularly rural society, has a strong influence on the well-being of adopted children. They suggest that "a reliance on an interdependent microsystems structure of *family-parents-school-neighborhood* [*sic*] for their subjective well-being" supports these children and thus they can grow up well as adoptees in Korean society. *Mother* shows clearly that a strong family bond and a strong support system of adults result in adopted children growing up to be independent, strong adults who are primed for success. As Hye-na shifts from an unsupportive to supportive structure, the audience knows that she will be a strong adult, also.

The bonds of family become more complex toward the end of the drama. Soo-jin's second sister, Yi-jin, has two children by birth, a boy and a girl. She is in a stable marriage and is a good daughter and mother. Yi-jin is a strong character whose happy, lively children are a bright spot in Young-shin's life. Soo-jin's *maknae* (youngest) sister, Hyun-jin, finds a tin of mementos and video tapes that reveal that Yi-jin was brought into the family as an infant adoptee after her mother abandoned her, but at the time, Soo-jin begged Young-shin to keep it secret so that Yi-jin would never feel the stigma and pain that she had felt. Yi-jin was raised always believing she was Young-shin's natural daughter; she walks in on Hyun-jin watching the tape and is shocked and horrified to find that she has been lied to all her life. Overnight she accepts the situation after she watches all the tapes and realizes that family is not about blood; it is love and protection that create those bonds. How she came into the family is less important than her place within it. The final plot twist comes later when Yi-jin discovers that her father is Young-shin's close advisor, Jae-beom; Young-shin offered to raise his daughter when Jae-beom had trouble functioning well as a single father. They kept his identity as Yi-jin's father secret, so as not to confuse the children. Jae-beom worked as Young-shin's assistant while the girls grew up, so he was a de facto father to them all. When Yi-jin finds out that she, too, is not Young-shin's daughter, she wonders if her older sisters resented her coming into the family as she did. Soo-jin tells Yi-jin: "We loved you not as someone's daughter, but as yourself" (episode 15). Regardless of the complication of the family relationships, the underlying, consistent message is that families are made through love and loyalty; blood connections do not make a family.

Mother is significant as a stereotype breaker. Through this drama, audiences can believe that adoption is a secure and nurturing option when the child is wanted by the adoptive family. Single motherhood is a difficult and complicated situation at times, but it can also be rewarding and fulfilling. Although the drama's ratings averaged only about 3.8%, they were consistent with the final episode earning the highest rating of 5.8%, indicating it had a solid fan base during its run. That consistency indicates that it found an audience that both welcomed and accepted the plot and content of the drama. Ratings for the original Japanese drama, reported only for the great Tokyo region, were somewhat higher than the Korean version's ratings in the Seoul region, but were similarly unswerving (Asianwiki.com).

CONCLUSION

Korean dramas are sources of entertainment first and foremost. They have been important elements of Korean media for over 40 years and reach all age groups and segments of Korean society, to say nothing of their international appeal. Their popularity and longevity depend heavily on the actors, writers, and PDs (program directors) who make the dramas. Without strong content that audiences are willing to embrace and accept, K-dramas (and their creators) fail. Dramas that contain social messages and make palatable controversial issues give viewers the chance to consider perspectives they might not want to confront in their daily lives. When a favorite actor gives voice to the benefits of domestic adoption, his audience might be willing to listen.

Machada et al. (2019) write about the importance of "the myth of origin" in the lives of adopted children. All adopted children become curious about "where they came from," and for them, since the person who chose to give birth to them is not the person who is parenting them, they need to have their own kind of "creation story" that helps to situate them in their adoptive families: "For adoptive children to constitute his identity [*sic*], they needs [*sic*] their adoptive family to legitimize their place in the generational chain and, for such, it is necessary to legitimize their own history." The children in *Pinocchio, Entertainer*, and *Mother* are each aware of how they came to be adopted and how their adoptive families embraced them. Korean dramas are mythologic in their fantasies of adoption, often ending with the adoptee discovering his or her wealthy birth parents or marrying into a wealthy family, which sometimes seems to be an apology from the universe for the hard life the adoptee has had. In these three dramas, the mythologies of the stories end with the adoptive families and their friends figuratively embracing the adoptees; "all's well that ends well" and the audience is satisfied after having a peaceful and fitting end, perhaps unaware that they are also left with the message that being an adoptee can be a good thing and being an adoptive parent can be joyful.

Dramas are sending messages to audiences in South Korea and beyond that women have the right to make decisions for themselves and their children that are in their own best interests; dramas are also reflecting changes in how Korean society views adoptees and adoption. Whether the choice is adoption or single motherhood, the decision is not one that is the fault of the child and they should not be stigmatized for what their mother has done. At the same time, society should not be censuring women for the choices they make nor should it be putting women in situations that cause them to make decisions they are forced into because they will lose their jobs or be subjected to abject poverty. By the same token, the adoptee should not be held responsible for his/her status and should be treated properly. As adoption is normalized in dramas, Korean audiences will be more accepting of the practice and the stigma placed on adoptees will lessen.

Lee (2014) discovered that

> despite the support pledged in the Single Parent Family Support Act in 2007, financial aid from the government continues to be minimal. The act claims to provide expenses for education and childcare, as well as legal and counseling services. At present, however, unwed mothers with children under 12 years old and who earn less than roughly 1.2 million won a month are provided 70,000 won a month by the government, while parents who adopt receive almost three times as much.

Jamie Kemp (2000), a Korean adoptee raised in Minnesota, returned to her homeland to understand more about her adoption. She visited a home for unwed mothers and was stunned to learn that many of them wanted their children to be adopted internationally. "In Korea, if children are adopted domestically, the chances that the birth mothers will meet their child again are very slim since the Korean family will more than likely never tell them they are adopted. They said they would wonder constantly as they walked past children on the streets whether that was their child." Kemp's observations are startling but understandable. In the decade following her visit, the Korean government took steps to make domestic adoption more comfortable for families but only in the past six years or so has it begun to address the needs of single, unwed mothers.

According to *The Economist* (SCS, 2015), 85% of children who end up at orphanages are raised there until adulthood, despite the financial support for adoptive parents cited by Lee above. Even though the government has touted adoption as a good option for couples (it is still difficult for single people to adopt), potential parents need to be convinced that raising a child who is not their own bloodline is a fine way to create a family. Given the consistent viewership of Korean dramas domestically, the dramas are a convenient and easy way to reach those potential parents, their relatives, and their friends. Discussions about drama content could lead to action.

Kim (1998) asserts a strong connection between audiences and the content of Korean dramas. If this is true, then we can assume that the production companies are purposefully signaling to their audiences that adoption is okay and that the audiences are responding well. When the K-drama audience hears characters stating that adoptees are unconditional members of the families; when characters proclaim that it is not a big deal to be adopted; when plots follow women who are fine adopting instead of having children, then that audience is fine with it, too. Viewers cheer on these adoptee characters and agree they are good people who deserve to have good lives. Noguti and Russell (2015) insist that "fictional television programs both reflect and create social norms: They emulate and modify current social values, lifestyles, and behaviors." If it is true that fictional programs emulate and modify social values, then it must be true that Korean dramas have an impact on Korean society. Emulating society means, for the purpose of this study, that attitudes toward domestic adoption must be changing somewhat; modifying society then means that the dramas can and will influence the audience who will change because of what they have seen. Future studies will prove the extent of that impact.

NOTES

1. Translated dialogue from the dramas cited in this paper come from the subtitles produced by Dramafever.com and Viki.com. Dramafever.com no longer exists.
2. Comments in brackets by me.
3. The conversation continues:

> DP *[also looking pained]:* I'm sorry.
> GP: Living with us all this time, was it that hard for you?
> DP *[on the verge of tears]:* Yes . . . [begins to cry] It was hard.
> *[then internally]:* No, I was happy. I was happy to the point that I'm sorry to my brother.
> GP: It must have been. That kind of cruel fate, since you lived swallowing it by yourself, how could it not have been hard? All right, all right.
> DP: I want to go by my real name.
> GP *[looking stunned]:* What?
> DP: Do that for me, Father. You have to dissolve my adoption.
> [Both now crying]

GP: What? How could you say that so easily? How could . . . something like that? [sobbing] How?
DP [internally]: I'm sorry, Father. I don't think I should be happy any longer.

BIBLIOGRAPHY

Ahn, J. (2020). Domestic Adoption. *Email to author*, 25 October.
Ahn, J., and Choi, W. (2020). What Affects the Happiness of Adopted Children in South Korea? Does the Adoption Matter to Their Happiness? *Child and Adolescent Social Work Journal* 1. https://doi.org/10.1007/s10560-020-00718-9
Arirang Issue. (2015). 4 Angles—Decline in Domestic Adoptions '국내 입양이 줄어들고 있다'. *Video* 5: 36, May 17, 2015, https://www.youtube.com/watch?v =If6NXttQza8
Burwell, Stacey. (2018). Child Abandonment and Adoption in South Korea: A Post-KoreanWar and Present-Day Analysis. *New Visions for Public Affairs* 10 (Spring): 11–18. https://cpb-us-w2.wpmucdn.com/sites.udel.edu/dist/4/10696/files /2018/12/Child-Abandonment-and-Adoption-in-South-Korea-A-Post-Korean-War -and-Present-Day-Analysis-2eblcrw.pdf
Cheang, A. (2015). K-Dramas as a Window into the Realities of Korean Society. *Kultscene*, May 15, http://kultscene.com/k-dramas-as-a-window-into-the-realities -of-korean-society/
Chira, S. (1988). Seoul Journal: And Now the Painful Questions. *The New York Times*, April 21, http://www.nytimes.com/1988/04/21/world/seoul-journal-babies -for-export-and-now-the-painful-questions.html
Choe, S. (2009). Group Resists Korean Stigma for Unwed Mothers. *The New York Times*, October 7, http://www.nytimes.com/2009/10/08/world/asia/08mothers.html
Evans, S. (2015). Taking on South Korea's Adoption Taboo. *BBC News*, January 6, 2015, http://www.bbc.com/news/world-asia-30692127
Feeney, J., Passmore, H., and Peterson, C. (2007). Adoption, Attachment and Relationship Concerns: A Study of Adult Adoptees. *Personal Relationships* 14 (1): 129–147.
Hankyoreh. (2020). S. Korea's Fertility Rate Drops to Historic Low during 2nd Quarter of 2020. *Hankyoreh*, August 27, http://english.hani.co.kr/arti/english_edi-tion/e_national/959616.html
H'ng, Y., and Yazdanifard, R. (2018). How Does Sponsorship Marketing in Korean Dramas Bring in Lucrative Business?" *International Business Research* 8 (1).
Hong, M. (2015). The question of child abandonment in South Korea: Misplacing blame on personhood. Master's thesis [unpub.], Scripps College.
Hübinette, T. (2005). Representations of International Adoption and Overseas Adoptees in Korean Media and Popular Culture. Presented at the Sixth Conference of the Global Overseas Adoptees' Link, Konkuk University, Seoul, South Korea, August 2005.
Jones, M. (2015). Why a Generation of Adoptees is Returning to South Korea. *New York Times*, January 14, https://www.nytimes.com/2015/01/18/magazine/why-a -generation-of-adoptees-is-returning-to-south-korea.html.

Jung, S. (writer) and Kim, C. (director). (2018). 마더/*Mother* [*Mother*]. South Korea: TvN. Via Dramafever.com [no longer active].

Kemp, J. (2000). Voices of Adoption: Korean Adoptee Perspectives. Learning to Trust. *PBS: First Person Plural*. http://www.pbs.org/pov/firstpersonplural/korean -adoptee-perspectives/2/

Kim, D-G. (1998). TV, Culture, and Audience in Korea: A Reception Study of Korean Drama. Master's thesis [unpub.], Texas Technical University.

Kim, S. (2015). Abandoned Babies: The Backlash of South Korea's Special Adoption Act. *Washington International Law Journal* 24 (3): 709–725.

Kim, T. (2008). Korea Urged to Write New Chapter for Adoption. *The Korea Times*, August 27, http://www.koreatimes.co.kr/www/news/nation/2008/08/117_30098 .html

Korean Adoption Service (KAS). (n.d.). History of Adoption in Korea. http://www .kadoption.or.kr/en/info/info_history.jsp

Korean Unwed Mothers' Families Association (KUMFA). (2017). http://kumfa.or.kr/

Lawler, M. J., Choi, C., Yoo, J., Lee, J., Roh, S., Newland, L., et al. (2018). Children's Subjective Well-being in Rural Communities of South Korea and the United States. *Children and Youth Services Review* 85: 158–164.

Lee, B. (2006). Adoption in Korea: Current Status and Future Prospects. *International Journal of Social Welfare* 16 (1): 75–83.

Lee, D. (2014). A Silent Sacrifice for Korea's Single Moms; A Human Cost for All. *Web blog post*, October 18, https://theculturemuncher.com/2014/10/18/a-silent -sacrifice-for-koreas-single-moms-a-human-cost-for-all/

Lewin, T. (1990). South Korea Slows Export of Babies for Adoption. *New York Times*, February 12, 1990, http://www.nytimes.com/1990/02/12/us/south-korea -slows-export-of-babies-for-adoption.html

Lo, A., and Grotevant, H. (2020). Adoptive Parenting Cognitions: Acknowledgement of Differences as a Predictor of Adolescents' Attachment to Parents. *Parenting* 20 (2): 83–107.

Loeb, V. (1991). South Korea Slowly Shifting on Adoptions There's a Strong Cultural Emphasis on Blood Ties. Families Who Adopt Do it in Secret. *Philadelphia Inquirer*, October 14, 1991.

Machado, R., Terezinha Féres-Carneiro, A., and Mello, R. (2019). The Myth of Origin in Adopted Families. [O mito de origem em famílias adotivas]. *Psicologia USP* 30, e160102.

Mazâ. [*Mother*] (2010). Ep. 11. Directed by Nobuo Mizuta. Aired April 23, 2010 on Nippon Television, https://www.youtube.com/watch?v=Rw438x44cPk

McGinnis, H. A. (2017). Mental Health and Academic Outcomes Among Adolescents in South Korean Orphanages. PhD diss., Washington University, St. Louis.

McKee, K. D. (2016). Monetary Flows and the Movements of Children: The Transnational Adoption Industrial Complex. *Journal of Korean Studies* 21 (1): 137–178.

Mother. [Japanese drama]. (n.d.). Asianwiki.com. https://asianwiki.com/ Mother_(NTV-2010 Japanese_Drama)

Mother. [Korean drama]. (n.d.). Asianwiki.com. https://asianwiki.com/Mother_ (Korean_Drama)

Noguti, V., and Russell, C. (2015). The Moderating Role of Social Norms on the Effects of Product Placement in Television Fiction: A Field Study in Brazil. *Journal of Current Issues & Research in Advertising* 36 (1): 20–34.

Park, C. (2005). Adoptee Life Portrayed as Tragic by Pop Culture. *Han Cinema*, August 21, 2005. http://www.hancinema.net/adoptee-life-portrayed-as-tragic-by-pop-culture-3739.html

Park, H.R. (Writer), and Won, J.S. (Director). (2014). 피노키오/*Pinocchio*. South Korea: SBS Korea. Via viki.com.

Qizi, Sun. (2014). TV Drama is Driving a South Korean-Chinese Trade Boom. *Worldcrunch*, September 8, http://www.worldcrunch.com/business-finance/tv-drama-is-driving-a-south-korean-chinese-trade-boom

S. C. S (2015). Why Adoptions Are so Rare in South Korea. *The Economist*, May 27. https://www.economist.com/the-economist-explains/2015/05/27/why-adoptions-are-so-rare-in-south-korea

Santos-Nunes, M., Narciso, I. et al. (2018). Adoptive Parents' Evaluation of Expectations and Children's Behavior Problems: The Mediational Role of Parenting Stress and Parental Satisfaction. *Children and Youth Services Review* 88: 11–17.

Schoenmaker, C., Jufer, F., Van IJzendoorn, M., and Bakermans-Kranenburg, M. (2014). Does Family Matter? The Well-being of Children Growing Up in Institutions, Foster Care, and Adoption. In *Handbook of Child Well-being*, edited by A. Ben-Arieh, F. Casas, I. Frønes, and J. E. Korbin, 2197–2228. Dordrecht: Springer.

Shoos, D. (2020). Birth Mothers and Adoptive Mothers Onscreen: Visibility, Iconography, and Ideology in Rodrigo García's Mother and Child. *Adoption & Culture* 8 (1): 33–54.

Statista. (2020). Number of Children Born in South Korea Who Were Adopted Domestically and Internationally from 2009 to 2019. https://www.statista.com/statistics/647918/south-korea-children-adoption-number-region/#:~:text=In%202019%2C%20the%20number%20of,317%20children%20were%20adopted%20abroad

Tu, W. (1996). *Confucian Traditions in East Asian Modernity*. Cambridge, MA: Harvard University Press.

Valley, A. (2020). Here's Why These International Hit K-Dramas Got Such Low Ratings in Korea. *Koreaboo*, August 4, 2020, https://www.koreaboo.com/stories/heres-international-hit-k-dramas-got-low-ratings-in-korea/

Yeo, K., Wildman, J., and Choi, S. (2017). The Effects of Confucian Values on Interpersonal Trust, Justice, and Information Sharing of Korean Workers: A Multilevel Analysis. *Journal of Pacific Rim Psychology* 11: E11.

Yoo, Y.A. (Writer), and Hong, S. C. (Director). (2016). 딴따라/*Ddandara* [*Entertainer*]. South Korea: SBS Korea. Via viki.com.

Yook, S., and Kim, H. (2018). Decolonizing Adoption Narratives for Transnational Reproductive Justice. *CLCWeb: Comparative Literature and Culture* 20 (6). https://doi.org/10.7771/1481-4374.3323

Chapter 7

Crying Men Watching Webtoons

Misaeng *and Korean Male Audiences*

Jahyon Park

INTRODUCTION

Author, I am very grateful for your hard work! It's really touching. However, as work and life does not end, I can wipe my tears away. I realized I was silently shedding tears in my heart, when it seemed that you wiped them away. Thank you. (Jin, 2013)

A man sheds tears and expresses his complex feelings in a cathartic manner. The image of a silently crying man in this short comment provokes us to ask what evoked his tears and why he felt as if the author had wiped them away. This type of response, associated with the tears of a man, is often encountered in online comments posted about the webtoon *Misaeng* (*Incomplete Life*),[1] which appeared on the Korean website Daum from January 2012 through June 2018. Male audiences of this series found themselves shedding tears online and were willing to share that experience with fellow readers. Something in the webtoon resonates with Korean men such that they are willing to reveal their emotions online, even admitting to tears as an emotional response to what they read.

The main plot centers on a young man who, after spending his entire childhood and adolescent years aspiring to become a professional *baduk* (also known as *go*) player, ends up entering a large trading company as an intern. Without a college degree, or the impressive educational background that most of the other new employees have, and with the responsibility of supporting his aged mother, Jang Geu-rae has to learn to survive in a corporate world. While the title of this series, *Misaeng*, implies an "incomplete" life, its characters, including Geu-rae, seem destined to work and live, aiming ceaselessly for both survival and a sense of completeness. The title of the series is thus symbolic of the unstable lives of members of contemporary Korean society, where unemployment has become a critical social problem. Many corporate employees and members of the younger generations describe themselves as "misaeng," identifying with Geu-rae and other characters. Within the drama and in response to it, both the characters of, and the audiences for, *Misaeng* shed sympathetic tears as they strive to become completely alive. At the same time, they wipe away each other's tears because the fact that both their lives and the narrative will go on in any event offers some comfort.

Misaeng gained an enormous following when it was serialized as a webtoon (the term "webtoon" was coined in Korea to name comics published online).[2] A webtoon is generally created on a computer platform and distributed via the Internet and mobile devices. The webtoon has been reputed as a major cultural commodity of the Korean Wave in recent academic debates,[3] as the popularity of webtoons has quickly spread to other Asian countries and even to the United States because they are easily accessible. With the traditional comic book, and even the largest e-book format, readers are required to continuously flip a page to see the content that comes next. In contrast, the vertical layout of this webtoon is an optimal medium for small screen circulation, allowing readers to read and view content simply by continuing to scroll down the smartphone or computer screen. Its distinctive and easy accessibility has attracted many media productions, and *Misaeng* was renowned as one of the most popular webtoons to be recreated in various types of media productions, including a television drama and an online film (Seo, 2015). *Misaeng* set a record for accumulated views reaching almost a billion when the television drama adaptation aired;[4] as a cable television drama, it posted a high rating of 10.3% during the peak real-time airing on TV, compared to the usual ratings of 1 or 2% for cable TV dramas.

This webtoon series was popular among office workers and attracted particularly the interest of male audiences. According to AGB Nielsen Korea's research in 2014, while the TV drama series won higher ratings among female viewers during its run, other ratings on the cross-platform report show that male audiences actively consumed (watched) *Misaeng* by using VOD (video on demand) and mobile devices. Many fans who post comments online appear to be comfortable revealing their gender identities, writing openly as men, freely discussing their emotional reactions, including tears. The average number of comments for each episode of the first season of *Misaeng* in 2021 has been approximately 1,000. The number of comments for the last episode reached around 5,824.[5] In these comments for the last episode, "tears" were mentioned 410 times. Male-related vocabulary, such as "man," "men," "father," "dad," "patriarch," "male employees," and "military service" appeared approximately 1,434 times. In contrast, words related to female identity, such as "woman," "women," "female employee," "mother," and "mom" showed up only 56 times. The phrase of "as a father (or dad)" appeared 78 times while the phrase of "as a mother (or mom)" was found 22 times. More than 10 male fans used the language of "man" in their account names, while fewer than five users revealed their gender identity as a "woman" in their account names. Considering the amount of male-associated terminology in the comments section for just the last episode, this data suggests greater popularity of *Misaeng* among male viewers. Furthermore, "tears" appeared together with words indicating male identity 210 times. Although many online users do not tend to clarify their gender identities, this empirical approach can be effective in terms of showing the frequency of gender associated language in the comments section and helps identify male audiences in the reception of webtoons.

This kind of intimate engagement among male audiences can be said to go beyond the mere process of viewing/reading media content to constitute a field of discourse on changing cultural aspects of masculinity. A user whose account name is "KeonBae," in recording his reading experience of *Misaeng* in the online comment section,[6] describes the webtoon series as a mandatory textbook for office workers and complains about how long he will need to wait for the next season.[7] He ends his comment with a question, "Why does it make me cry . . . I wondered if my wife could understand a patriarch's mind if I bought the books for her to read."[8]

This phenomenon of admitting men's tears raises the question of what might be changing, specifically in evolving cultural forms in contemporary Korean media consumption, which encourages men to express their emotional response to media content, such as *Misaeng*, through the virtual space of the comments section. The *Misaeng* fever among men, who are the principal driving force behind its popularity, has been missing from Korean media. The *Misaeng* narrative itself deals with affectionate male bonding and men's tears, spurring audiences to sympathize with male characters. These male characters are engaging in homosocial bonding by creating more affectionate and emotional relationships with other male characters. Audiences pay attention to these relationships and use the term "bromance" to distinguish them from those of typical masculine characters in heterosexual relationships (DeAngelis, 2014). The concept and mode of masculinity is changing and requires to be reformulated according to new cultural values. Considering this observation about the emergence of affective male audiences in the reception of webtoons and related media forms, the new reception practices, occurring in response to advanced technology in media productions and circulations, enable men's tears; and, moreover, this social phenomenon leads to the reformulation of masculinity, which can be examined as indicative of transformations in society and culture.

Webtoon *Daetgeul*

A significant number of individual readers appear to have established a close rapport with the narrative and its characters while reading and watching *Misaeng*. Audience comments reveal that they sympathize with Geu-rae and other characters. They also share their own stories of struggles for survival and self-growth in the virtual space of the comments section, which is called *Daetgeul* in Korean. *Daetgeul* is available at the end of each episode of the webtoon and provides a new affective form of communication where webtoon audiences describe their emotionally touching moments. Particularly in the *daetgeul* section of the last episode of *Misaeng*'s first season, many commenters confess that they shed tears because they feel as if they are consoled and encouraged by other *daetgeul*. One of the commenters writes:

> Again, thank you Author Yun Tae-ho for making such a thrilling work. Also, thank you to those who have given me strength to work again through *Daetgeul*, who moved me to tears with their comments. Although our professions, educations, and backgrounds are different, I won't forget the precious experience of sharing these feelings in *Misaeng*. (Kim Gwang-taek, 2013)[9]

It could be said that webtoons became popular because of the active participation of media users through *daetgeul*. Online audience engagement through comments is slowly gathering the attention of scholars in the field,[10] who are analyzing how these forms of audience participation are creating an emerging cyberspace expressed through liveness, reaction videos, or Viki timed comments. In particular, Woori Han, Claire Shinhea Lee, and Ji Hoon Park (2017) investigated the Korean reality TV show *Real Men* and its "online-bulletin-board" comments to argue that this show serves as a vehicle for men to attempt a recovery of their hegemonic masculinity through female viewers' understanding and appreciation of the difficulty that men experience in their compulsory military service. In order to reveal and discuss damaged masculinity and reverse discrimination under changing gender roles in post-IMF South Korea, the authors analyze online reviews and comments to identify some keywords, such as "female viewers," "military service," and "reverse discrimination," in relation to audience perception (Han et al., 2020). The *daetgeul* space, mediating relationships between the media and audiences, then may be addressed as a new space of communication based on affectionate bonds that encourage men to articulate and develop their emotional responses as active agents in reception.

Daetgeul can be translated as "replies," but it should be regarded as a neologism that combines the words for "following (*daet*)" and "writing (*geul*)." Indeed, the *daetgeul* space invigorates online communication since it opens for anyone who has an account name on Internet portal sites. Compared to the highly one-sided line of communication usually found in traditional media sectors such as newspapers, magazines, radio, and television, *daetgeul* has reconfigured the relationship between the media and their audiences by letting the audiences become more visible and voiced. The audiences directly communicate with other members through the dual acts of "following" and "writing." They can express when/what they like or agree with each other's comments by clicking on fellow audience members' comments, a process known as "following." Besides "following," the audiences post their writings as an active form of engagement. This behavior reflects a form of reception that creates a discourse on media content by encouraging engagement in the Internet forum.

Deleuze's (1992) concept of "social apparatus" and his term "line of force" can be helpful in explaining audiences' active online engagement in the *daetgeul* space. Deleuze uses the expressions in relation to Foucault's writings on knowledge and power, but I will borrow his terms to conceptualize the affective and fluid space of *daetgeul*. The *daetgeul* space can be considered "social apparatuses" that allow people to exchange their knowledge and emotions and thereby form mutual connectivity. Audiences create connections by clicking, following, and responding to other comments, and secure subjectivity by expressing their ideas and feelings. For example, by operating computers and other social devices, they enter a virtual space in which they can simultaneously enter the space of everyday practice (social space) and the place of perception (individual imagined space). The self-organizing mechanism in the virtual space of *daetgeul* shows audience members expressing themselves in fluid and constantly changing ways: the identity of an individual or groups in the *daetgeul* space is a temporary community. In a variety of ways, they express and identify themselves in the connections formed with others through networking lines that are fluid and evolving.

ACTIVE AUDIENCES IN DIGITAL MEDIA CULTURE

The role of the audience has become increasingly important in the new and evolving environment of media reception. In Korea, reception studies emerged in the 1990s by introducing earlier Western theories to explore television viewership. Yi Gang-su compiled theoretical backgrounds in terms of reception studies in Britain, Canada, and the United States by mapping out the trajectory of active audiences in 1989. Along with Yi's theoretical introduction about audience reception in mass media communication studies, Yi Eun-mi, Kim Jeong-gi, Park Dong-suk, and Ju Chang-yun started to examine domestic audiences through the framework of active audiences.[11] As Kim

Su-jeong (2010) argues, an influx of scholars from overseas contributed to the emergence of audience reception as a component of Korean media studies. The idea of audience autonomy started from Stuart Hall's criticism of theories of social reproduction. According to Hall's Marxist culturalist approach, major media forms, such as newspapers, films, and television, are used to reinforce the view of the ruling class in the political and economic domains and thus constitute media texts in a way that reproduces and strengthens mainstream ideologies; however, audiences read/view the text and autonomously interpret their own ideologies. His suggestion of polysemy in decoding texts implies the possibility of resistance to the existent power structure embedded in media messages. Applying Hall's approach to their own work in the wake of South Korea's transition in 1993 from decades of military dictatorship to civil government, Korean media studies scholars have attempted to contextualize audience reception and brought about an increased focus on social issues, including democratization and resistance to ideologies.

The spontaneity of online activities generated by using cutting-edge digital technologies transcends the temporal and spatial boundaries that used to be significant factors in the dominant theorization of audience reception in television studies. Unlike audiences of other media forms, webtoon audiences no longer need to be at home or in a theater in order to read and watch their favorite webtoons at a given time. Within a conservative functionalist approach, mass communication research often tended to examine how much viewers watch television or what types of programs they watch; examining accumulated comments in the *daetgeul* sections of webtoons serves as a useful method of reception studies. While some functions and management policies still need improvement to promote the *daetgeul* culture, this new type of communication in webtoons enables individuals to engage directly with each other in the media and urges an innovative approach to the question of audience reception.

The *daetgeul* sections of webtoons document the participation of audiences in reception practices through "following" and "writing" and further elicit their emotional reactions, such as sympathy and rapport. This approach helps develop discourses on audience agency rather than the transmission and interpretation of ideological messages. Audience agency will be discussed in terms of the cultural and communal sense aroused through *daetgeul* by expanding John Fiske's (1987) reformulation of his theory of active audiences, specifically in terms of the individual versus the subject. Fiske proposes, "the individual is produced by nature, the subject by culture" (Fiske, 1987). He differentiates the subject from the individual, an actual person. The subject reflects a consciousness that is constructed by dominant social, cultural, and historical elements, such as social class, gender, race, ethnicity, age, and religion. Thus, audiences who actively engage in the reception of webtoons and related media forms should be considered as subjects, which exist in relation to changing cultural, social, political, and technological factors.

Webtoons and their audiences, and even multiple transmedia productions, demand a close examination in different cultural contexts and situations. The complex process of contemporary media consumption involves multi-dimensional acts of production, distribution, reception, and re-production. Nonetheless, academics in cultural and media studies opt to stick to the term "active audience" due to the conventional approach of a binary structure of passive versus active frames. The term "active audience" apparently helps conceptualize affective male audiences' active engagement with webtoons and their transmedia productions. However, this tendency excludes in-depth consideration of drastic changes in the media environment. Awareness of this tendency draws attention to inadequacies with the existing approach, such as in its failure until now to contextualize the intertwined relationships among media users. The lineal relationship between media contents and their audiences prioritizes an act of interpretation: audiences can be producers and reproducers to other audiences through the simultaneous acts of following and writing.

THE EMERGENCE OF AFFECTIVE MALE AUDIENCES

The participation of audiences is playing a significant role in the growth of the Korean webtoon industry. Considering the online medium and the measurable involvement of Internet users, it is possible to assess male users' active participation in reading, watching, and consuming webtoons. A commenter named "Slowly but Together" notes that men are unable to talk to their family members about what happens at their corporate jobs because the family members, once apprised of everyday occurrences at company offices, would be concerned about their husbands/fathers. In the *daetgeul*, he shares a question his wife asked him about male behavior when drinking: "Why do men become garrulous at drinking sessions?" Right after this question, he writes his answer in short but clear words: "Because of loneliness." He also emphasizes that the content of *Misaeng* and other people's *daetgeul* entries help temper his loneliness. Kim Won-seok, the director of the K-drama version, perceives the loneliness of male audiences as a sociocultural phenomenon. Kim, according to dramasROK's review of *Misaeng*, has indeed pointed out that he "wanted to broadcast the television drama *Misaeng* [to] let house-wives understand why their office worker husbands drink so much."[12] Kim stated that he had received many comments about the emotional reactions of South Korean wives to the male characters in *Misaeng*, whose situations reflect the working experiences of such women's husbands in the real world; he also mentioned that these wives had spoken in tears to their husbands after watching the *Misaeng* drama.

Male audiences in *daetgeul* shed tears over their lives as men, husbands, fathers, and patriarchs. Not only is a crying man disapproved of in accordance with social constructs, but a weeping man is also considered inappropriate in cultural context. For example, because of a double standard for men in contemporary Korean society, the conventional wisdom is that a crying man is unsuitable for public view in a culture where patriarchy still pertains. With regard to this paradoxical situation of Korean men, An Kyeong-hwan (2016) argues that as the influence of the patriarchal system decreases throughout society and at home, men must cede their privilege to other family members. Nevertheless, men are forced to perform masculinity by taking family responsibility more than ever. Men are now on the edge of patriarchy and feel compelled to bear this contentious situation. As An continues to state, men's primary responsibility to support family members creates the paradox that men cannot weep in front of others, particularly women, while social changes revoke the traditional notion of masculine power and authority. Once men show their tears to others, the commonly accepted idea emerges that they are weak, and thus other people cannot depend on them. An's conclusion regarding the behavior of a man shedding tears would thus confirm his abnormality or deviation from the category of what is generally perceived to be a *normal* man who fulfills his mission of taking responsibility while concealing his emotional reactions.

Considering the blurred and intertwined boundary between active participation and unconscious movement in audience theory, Shanti Kumar (2020) suggests the term "affective audiences" to move the debate on television and its audiences away from conventional categories, such as the active and passive division. Affective male audiences appear in the virtual space of *daetgeul*; when a man feels intense emotion while reading *Misaeng* and is moved to tears, these tears can be described as a bodily action that occurs without consciousness. However, the action of writing about tears and sharing the experience of tears in the *daetgeul* space involve active engagement. For Foucault, this space can be a "marginal space" that constitutes a form of localized resistance to the normative ideology of hegemonic masculinity, which produces and reproduces structured, hierarchical relationships.[13] Along with the intimate male bond depicted between Geu-rae and his superior, Manager Oh Sang-sik, the *daetgeul* space enables the creation of new types of relationships between people of different classes and cultures, and thus generates alternative cultures and ethics by devising new lifestyles through the celebratory depiction of diversity.

MANLY EMOTION AND NEW MASCULINE IDEALS

As argued previously, masculinity can provide a lens to understand socio-cultural transformations. This means that masculinity is constructed as a collection of discourses rather than a description of physiological states. The concept and form of masculinity is in the reciprocal relationship with social phenomena and thus can be analyzed in relation to its social constructionism. My focus on male corporate employees in the webtoon *Misaeng* and its cross-media platform adaptations may address reciprocal masculinities emerging in the cultural context of changing social moments for contemporary Korean media consumers.

In response to the emergence of new and diverse types of masculinity represented in the media, Kim Mira (2014) and Chung Young-Hee and Jang Eun-mi (2015) posit that the changing mode of masculinity functions to break down traditional gender-emotion stereotypes (Kim, 2014; Chung and Jang, 2015). Pervasive and popular beliefs about gender-emotion stereotypes have been documented across many studies including An Kyeong-hwan's (2016) and Woori Han, Claire Shinhea Lee, and Ji Hoon Park's (2017) analyses of the paradoxical situation of contemporary South Korean men; a man's crying is regarded as abnormal or deviant behavior because of the social norm that still requires men to show their mental "toughness" by performing the role of patriarch to take family responsibility, even though an increase in women's social activities has forced men to renounce the authority of traditional patriarchy. Earning capacity, along with emotional control, has been described as one of the most significant values of "maleness." However, Kim's analysis of recent popular television programs, including *Appa eodiga?* (Dad, Where Are We Going? 2013–2015) and *Syupeomaeni dorawatda* (Superman Returns, 2013–present), demonstrates that these programs created a new type of masculinity by centering the narrative on fathers who perform the traditionally recognized female roles of child care and housekeeping. According to Kim's findings, the male figures' engagement in emotional intimacy with their children ruptures the stereotypes of divided gender roles by proposing "non-authoritative" and "emotionally expressive" fathers as newly emerging masculine ideals (Kim, 2014).

Chung and Jang explore changing gender roles as an indicator of socio-cultural transformations. They analyze *Misaeng* by focusing on Manager Oh's leadership and An Yeong-i's (Geu-rae's female co-worker) survival strategies. Men's emotional expression and pursuit of communal values are highly evaluated as a new, gender-hybrid form of leadership in a company, while women's confidence and high performance are degraded as a threat to a society that values neoliberal competition. As Chung and Jang point to the problematically unequal application of blurred gender roles for men and women in the public space, An Yeong-i's struggles to survive invoke a question about a rupture of the nominal ideology of gender and its inconsistency in the current waves of social transition.

In analyzing An Yeong-i, Chung and Jang argue that the *Misaeng* narrative liberates women from the stereotype of their emotional entanglements by abandoning heterosexual romance. In citing An Yeong-i as a representative female figure who challenges gender norms, they point to her emotional inexpressiveness (Chung and Jang, 2015). When Geu-rae is appointed as an intern, An Yeong-i also joins the company as a new employee. She received the highest score when she entered, and thus her cohort and even her department seniors closely watch her performance and behavior. One of the senior members reviews a document and praises her excellent "boldness, logic, and expression";[14] nevertheless, she barely shows emotional variation in response to the compliment and also refrains from stating anything personal. When she finds out that her manager has stolen her ideas for projects and taken credit for them, she never reacts emotionally, instead, she tries to solve her problem rationally. Her remarkable work performance and consistency in a highly competitive (male-centered) working environment can be viewed as her struggle to escape from the existing gender order and class conditions.

In spite of An Yeong-i's portrayal as a character who is "shaking up" the existing gender norms, Chung and Jang (2015) point out the limitations of her challenge because she eventually chooses to compromise with the norms. Demoralized by the fact that the more she attempts to behave "just like men" in a masculine organizational structure, the more her team rejects her, she begins to consider "adjusting to" the expressions of her male team members. During a drinking session with some male seniors who confess that they consider her a selfish woman who ignores her male seniors and only cares about her own success, An Yeong-i admits that she is also uncomfortable and unhappy when her seniors feel discomfort around her.[15] By masquerading as an "unproblematic woman," her team requires, even though her male colleagues still view her apprehensively, she participates in maintaining the tranquillity of the community. The narrative flow of conflict, resistance, and compromise in the case of An Yeong-i follows a conventional narrative, revealing the paradox that the patriarchal system is still influential.

In contrast, Manager Oh is often portrayed as a figure who deviates from the commonly associated imagery of performance-driven masculinity. In contrast to other managers who pressure team members to perform to stringent standards and form political alliances to ensure career promotions through compromise and conspiracy, he refuses to participate in political manipulations and instead actively helps his team members survive and grow by prioritizing intimate bonds, recognition, and consideration. Due to these values, Manager Oh has conflicts with other department managers, but his emotional closeness with his team members and community-oriented thinking are considered as an alternative new style of leadership that helps humanity retain its essence in a rapidly changing labor environment centered on survival and competition.

In the unstable working environment of neoliberalism, in which individuals themselves have to step on others in an endless cycle of competition, Manager Oh's leadership of looking after subordinates as if they were family has brought about extraordinary popular among viewers, even though this type of leadership is uncertain to thrive in reality. For Chung and Jang (2015), Manager Oh's leadership is described as "hybrid" by infusing a "femininity-associated" quality into his management style. Chung and Jang's analysis is notable in terms of delineating challenges to masculine authority, more specifically hegemonic masculinity. However, this type of new, hybrid leadership has also drawn criticism regarding the fantasy of a "compassionate patriarch," which seems impossible in an insecure, neoliberal labor environment.

DREAMING OF A COMPLETE LIFE

Considering the increase in unemployment and ongoing uncertainty in South Korea, the male *Misaeng* fans who identify and sympathize with Geu-rae understand that they can be categorized as a loser or part of a "precariat" that is demarcated as marginalized in the social normalization of global neoliberal competition.[16] Nevertheless, they cannot stop pursuing their dream for a stable job and secure life. People who have full-time jobs and live comparatively stable lives are not free from the pressure to maintain these life conditions and values. To sustain their lives, they make every effort to uphold the hegemonic system, even if it means they are participating in privileging a hierarchical social structure.

The term *misaeng* (incomplete life) derives from the game *baduk* and, in the context of *baduk*, denotes the in-between state in which it is unclear whether a stone is alive or not. Each episode of the *Misaeng* webtoon starts with a stone-by-stone broadcast of the fifth and final match between Cho Hun-hyun and Nie Weiping at the first Ing Cup.[17] Even though this historical match ended with Cho Hun-hyun's victory in 1989, the webtoon viewers try to figure out the meaning behind each move and wonder if Geu-rae's choice leads to a way to a state of being *completely alive*, as the stones are interlaced scenes depicting Geu-rae's survival in the corporate world. Furthermore, one *Misaeng* fan, named "hehehehe," has written a commentary in the *daetgeul* section of every single episode since episode 18, analyzing that fifth and final match between Cho Hun-hyun and Nie Weiping in connection with the main narrative of Geu-rae's growth. hehehehe's *daetgeul* have always appeared as the first *be-daet* (best comment) and contributed to other readers' active engagement by encouraging them to write *daetgeul* on the relationship between *baduk* and the lessons Geu-rae learns.

Without the formal educational background that most new employees have, Geu-rae has to achieve outstanding performance levels to survive in a hyper-competitive corporate culture, entangled with academic elitism and social corruption. Geu-rae's narrative of struggle and suffering demonstrates his feelings of inferiority and self-denigration. These feelings embody the experience of frustration that most company workers and employee candidates develop in the course of pursuing job security in reality. The vicissitudes that Geu-rae experiences in the beginning episodes of the webtoon reflect the severity of unemployment in contemporary South Korea. His lack of a college degree, language skills, and job experience disappoints his superiors and his incompetence exposes him to the mockery of his cohorts. Assistant Manager Kim Dong-sik, on the same sales team asks, "What have you been doing for the past 26 years that you have no skills?" Geu-rae inwardly admits that he did not work hard in the past and blames himself by repeating the same question. In a flashback scene on his way home, Geu-rae monologizes:

> Their opinions that my talents were lacking, or that bad luck caused me to lose the game by 0.5 points, I reject.
> It wasn't because I held a part-time job at the same time that I played *baduk*.
> It wasn't because my parents couldn't give me an allowance.
> It wasn't because my mother had to take my father's role after he died.
> Because that would be too painful.
> So, that's why it had to be that I was just a person who didn't work hard.
> It's not really that I didn't work hard . . .
> But I'll just think of it that way.
> I came out into the world because I didn't work hard.
> Since I didn't work hard, that's the only reason why I was abandoned.[18]

Geu-rae's self-blame and endless endeavor for survival relate to the problematic fantasy of meritocracy in neoliberal society. Infinite competition in neoliberalism forces younger generations to engage in this system despite uneven economic opportunities. The younger generations are uncertain if they will secure jobs and be able to maintain them. However, they cannot simply abandon this hopeful vision and thus they work hard to achieve a "complete life." The more viewers and readers hope for Geu-rae's survival in the text, the more desirous they become of survival in their own journeys.

Lauren Berlant (2011), in her book *Cruel Optimism*, analyzes this phenomenon by tracing the historical sensorium of optimistic attachment to the "good-life" fantasy represented in mass media, literature, film, and television between 1990 and the present. Berlant addresses how the prevalence of contemporary attachment to the fantasy of obtaining desired objects or intimate relationships can be linked to political ideas that have shaped a dominant, but problematic, feeling in liberal-capitalist society. This attachment sustains an individual's pursuit of fantasy within the social system in spite of the "crisis ordinariness." For example, the social problem of unemployment labels joblessness as undesirable and non-normative. Geu-rae cannot give up this opportunity to work at a company and will make every endeavor to be normative in society by hardly attaching to the wish to become "completely alive," even if his attachment to this desire demands more effort and at the same time cruelly frustrates his dream.

Borrowing Berlant's term "impasse" allows me to conceptualize the contradictory situation in which Geu-rae desires to survive, despite uncertainty and cruelty in his trials, in terms of the context of neoliberal capitalism. According to Berlant, an impasse is a time of dithering or hesitancy in which someone cannot directly move forward. People move around with "a sense that the world is at once intensely present and enigmatic." Thus, the impasse requires a "hypervigilance" to find "composure" amid unpredictable crises and threats (Berlant, 2011). In South Korea, many fathers and husbands as breadwinners have experienced an impasse since the so-called IMF financial crisis in 1997. The IMF and other international financial supports organizations rescued South Korea from the financial crisis, which caused unprecedented business bankruptcy and massive dismissals. This traumatic experience continued when the overseas relief loans allowed limitless competition and job insecurity, caused by an influx of neoliberal globalization. Neoliberal capitalism has extended the impasse, in which fathers and husbands have floundered in the transition of economic values from development to hyper-achievement. Thus, the men who read and watch *Misaeng* shed tears and hope that Geu-rae survives against the impasse of neoliberal capitalism.

Subordination and Marginalization

The trading company where Geu-rae and Manager Oh work is a conventional example of male-dominated corporate culture. This culture requires an intensively hierarchical structure, which legitimizes obedience to the orders of one's superior. During Geu-rae's first conversation with his direct superior Assistant Manager Kim, he tells Geu-rae to step down because Geu-rae is literally standing on higher ground unintentionally and thus looks down at him. The assistant manager's first order indicates his attempt to clarify their hierarchical relationship. This scene is symbolic to show that Geu-rae is subordinated in the company. Indeed, his social position is a clear instance of "marginalization." Even before Geu-rae enters this company, he already failed as a *baduk* player in his previous career. Then, he tries to get a new job but always faces the cruel truth that no one offers him a job. When his *baduk* sponsor happens to know that he suffers financially but needs a job to support his mother, the sponsor gives him the opportunity of an internship through the connection. Thus, this job is his only and last chance. His failure and desperation exacerbate and more likely perpetuate his place as subordinate in the social structure.

In addition, the scene of Geu-rae asking for help from An Yeong-i can be interpreted as revealing his social position as a marginalized figure. But, at the same time, his subordinated and marginalized position complicates the power dynamics of masculinities in relation to gender relations. Geu-rae is only one male employee who persistently asks for her help. An Yeong-i is the person who gives him advice, but she feels comfortable talking about her own work-related issues when she helps Geu-rae. She is always an excellent worker, but she shows her potential as a team mate or equal more fully in the moments when she talks and works with Geu-rae, while his association with An Yeong-i is perceived as even more subordinate in the minds of his male co-workers. Thus, Geu-rae's companionship with An Yeong-i complicates his subordination and marginalization in corporate culture.

An Yeong-i's outstanding performance and her complex relationships with male employees can be discussed as another layer of gender relations: no other men, except Geu-rae, ask her for help even though every male employee knows that she is very capable and competent. Asking for help would mean admitting that she is superior; thus, they choose instead to exclude her. The exclusion brings about her isolation, which explicitly shows her marginalization in a male-dominated company, regardless of her capability. She puts in more effort to prove her abilities, but her male team members simultaneously avoid and exclude her. In the end (episode 43), she relents, saying "We are a team" and decides to adjust to their culture which may empower her male co-workers to obtain hegemony. Her decision to adjust to the male-centered corporate culture suggests rethinking masculine ideals in the media representation of male-oriented corporate culture.

Communal Values and Fraternity

Geu-rae was described as embodying subordinated and marginalized masculinities, yet his relationship with An Yeong-i and Manager Oh's recognition increase the degree of relationships that Geu-rae has with other employees in the company. The more Manager Oh recognizes and involves Geu-rae in teamwork, the more he emerges as an agent able to transcend the demarcations of subordination and marginalization.

Through his relationship with Manager Oh, Geu-rae learns about camaraderie and how to develop relationships. In the connotative reading of *Misaeng*
in terms of *baduk*, whether the stone will survive or not does not depend
on where the stone is placed. Instead, its survival depends on how the surrounding stones are placed. If there are a lot of allied stones placed around,
the probability of survival is high. After experiencing a failure as a *baduk*
apprentice, Geu-rae decided to give up the game entirely. After joining One
International, however, he has played *baduk* again in his mind to reflect on
his lessons from work with other people at the company. In each episode, the
baduk game is compared to the situation that his team, his colleague, or Geu-
rae himself faces. In the past, Geu-rae struggled alone with the game, but now
recognizing his position as a member of Sales Team 3, he takes a step forward
by looking at the stones all together on the board and more closely ponders
them in relation to the communal sense that he has acquired through his relationship with his co-workers. Geu-rae learns that he cannot work alone but
should aim to work together as a team member.

Geu-rae was isolated from the start when he entered the company as an
intern. Due to his unusual educational background, no one expected that
he would complete the full period of his internship even though he strived
hard to show his capacity. As shown in an elevator scene in the television
adaptation, Geu-rae is ostracized by his co-workers because he joined the
trading company through a "parachute (connection)" appointment. Manager
Oh denounces nepotism and criticizes Geu-rae's lack of skills that most new
employees have. Sales Team 3 needs an ordinary employee who can produce
results immediately. Manager Oh assumes that Geu-rae cannot contribute
to the team, and thus he (Geu-rae) feels pressured to work harder than his
teammates.

When an executive finds a confidential sales document in the company
lobby, he brings it to Manager Oh's team and interrogates people about who
lost it; Geu-rae is forced to claim that the accidental loss of the document was
his fault. Later, Manager Oh finds out the truth: it was lost due to negligence
by a staff member on another team. He begins to change his attitude toward
Geu-rae and even defends him by calling him "my kid" when he encounters
the team manager of the staff who made the mistake at a get-together. This
scene serves as a turning point in the relationship between Geu-rae and
Manager Oh. Manager Oh's unexpected emotional reaction results in tears in
the television series.[19] His crying encourages Geu-rae to open up and move
beyond his isolated state, leading Geu-rae to develop a sense of belonging as
he builds up his relationships with Manager Oh and other co-workers. Geu-
rae's newfound sense of belonging enables him to attain a sense of composure. He becomes more open to his team members and begins to understand
their feelings. After this point, Geu-rae internalizes other employees' stories

on conflict, struggle, and resolution when he reflects on the events of the day and narrates them while playing his own *baduk* in his mind.

The weeping scene is absent in the webtoon series; however, the panels in which Geu-rae and Manager Oh stare at each other suggest the emergence of an emotional bond between them. When Assistant Manager Kim asks who did it then, Manager Oh watches Geu-rae and then says in a low voice, "Secret" (episode 14). Both Manager Oh and Geu-rae know that the person who made the mistake is a new father. A new intern's mistake may be acceptable, but a full-time employee's fault may have a negative impact on his career. They share a secret and, at the same time, begin to appreciate each other. In male–male social relationships, the construction of manhood relies on other man's gaze and male recognition. Geu-rae feels Manager Oh's acceptance through his emotion-enacted gaze. Manager Oh's recognition enables Geu-rae's awareness of fraternity.

BROMANCE

Misaeng fans' *daetgeul* writing highlights the aspect of a character's masculinity as a separate subject from the character's personality and actions. While analysis of the form taken by masculinity still dominantly focuses on the texts involving heterosexual relationships, the popularity of *Misaeng* draws their attention to other features, such as sympathy and intimate male bond, in leading them to analyze new, diverse forms of masculinity.[20] In particular, the *Misaeng* narrative brought about sensational reactions from audiences by portraying the close relationship between Geu-rae and his manager Oh Sang-sik. Unlike conventional narratives centered on a heterosexual romantic relationship in a private space, the male friendship between the manager and the employee in the office, excluding any hint of a man-woman love story, emerges as the center of the narrative.

This emotionally intimate form of closeness between men, emerging as significant in *Misaeng*, is described as a "bromance" among audiences in the *daetgeul* space. The term "bromance" can be considered as reflecting a sociocultural phenomenon that urges audiences to develop a new perspective that shifts away from a focus on the critical domain of hegemonic masculinity, centered on men's privilege through their gender and social status. This term is often used to depict a deeply emotional male friendship that is different from the romantic closeness that men share with their girlfriends or wives. As a non-sexual but emotionally charged, and sometimes physical relationship, bromance can be addressed as a form of reflecting the changing social value of accepting and appreciating diverse masculinities. Close male bonds among friends are usual in Korean society, but the concept of bromance suggests boundaries that go beyond the norm; within bromance, physical closeness can happen through hugging, wiping tears, and other non-sexual touch. Because this kind of closeness is sometimes mistaken for homosexual relationships and it is accepted by *Misaeng*'s male audience, we may be seeing a shift in how Korean society views homosexuality.

Stefan Robinson, Eric Anderson, and Adam White have noted a rapid change in their recent research on male friendships and homosocial boundaries. Their scintillating 2014 research on bromance is useful in contextualizing the relationship between bromance and same-sex intimacy, even though varying forms of masculinity diverge in accordance with the examination of a particular social group at a certain place and time. From interviews with 30 undergraduate men in the United Kingdom about their friendship experiences, Robinson and his colleagues found that all 30 participants, who identified themselves as heterosexual or mostly heterosexual, had at least one bromantic friend whether in the past or the present. According to the research team's analysis of the interviews, the participants describe "shared interest," "emotional intimacy," and "physical intimacy" as the distinctive characteristics of the bromance. In their study, a shared interest is a prerequisite in building a bromance (Anderson et al., 2009). For example, Manager Oh and Geu-rae are always concerned about their team's performance and evaluations; Geu-rae is unable to become a full-time employee at the company and against the odds, Manager Oh keeps trying to find a way to secure Geu-rae's job. When he quits One International and eventually runs a new company, he hires Geu-rae, bringing them back together.

The next characteristic, intimacy, is significant in identifying bromance. Intimacy involves a sense of deep or profound relationship, such as trust and love, but one cannot be an intimate friend without reciprocity of intimacy from another. It means that intimacy can be reached through mutual understanding and engagement. A deep and intense mutual interaction entails emotional intimacy and sometimes physical intimacy as well. According to the Anderson team's research, physical intimacy is considered non-essential among the male participants. However, physical intimacy is integral in forming a bromance because it implies that the person has a genuine "bro" who does not have any boundary with his friend. Anderson, Robinson, and White also admit that physical intimacy can be valued as a significant element in defining bromance while emotional intimacy emerges as vital to their experiment (Anderson et al., 2009). In *Misaeng*, Manager Oh often shows his physical intimacy by putting his arms around Geu-rae's shoulders after he recognizes Geu-rae as his "kid." Manager Oh sometimes pats Geu-rae's back to encourage him. When Manager Oh staggers after a drink, Geu-rae takes Manager Oh to his home. The full shot of Geu-rae helping Manager Oh shows a very intimate level of physical closeness.[21] Geu-rae falls asleep in front of Manager Oh's house; the close-up of his face shows him looking happier than he has for most of the series so far. Another scene showing Geurae's tearful face with him saying mentally, "I am sorry that I cannot do anything" in his mind, reveals his intimacy with Manager Oh, at a moment when Manager Oh gets scolded by an executive. Their physical contacts show their affective closeness and also affirm their bromance, which is distinguished from the commonly accepted friendship between a manager and staff.

The emotional intimacy and physical closeness remind the *Misaeng* fans of the feeling of romance. In both the webtoon series and television adaptation, there are many shots in which these two men appear together in one frame. Some fans edited clips centering on the bromance-related shots and circulated them on YouTube to share their fever toward *Ogwajanggeurae mello* [Manager Oh, Jang Geu-rae melodrama].[22] This phenomenon shows that the viewers are even more enthusiastic about their bromance-associated relationship. Furthermore, some viewers directly complained to the broadcasting station when there was a scene implying romantic tensions between Geu-rae and An Yeong-i.[23] Might these *Misaeng* fans' reactions be seen as an indicator of change in the perception of homosexuality? When asked, "Should Society Accept Homosexuality?" in 2013 by the Pew Research Center, 39% of South Korean respondents answered "Yes."[24] The survey shows that homophobia is still entrenched in Korea, compared with the affirmative responses in Canada, Spain, and Germany exceeding 80%; considering that in a 2008 survey only 18% of South Koreans answered positively, this difference suggests a change in the social perception of homosexuality. According to a survey conducted in 2019 by Gallup Korea, 53% of the respondents answered "Yes" to the question, "Is homosexuality a form of love?" indicating that a change in social perception is still happening.[25] In particular, 75% of males in their teens and 20s gave affirmative answers. This result implies changes in cultures and generations, which also applies to the diversity of masculinities in contemporary Korean society.

Homosociality

The concept of inclusive masculinity is valid in addressing a change in perceptions toward not only male intimacy but also gay men among younger generations in contemporary Korean society. In this respect, the emergence of the term "bromance" reifies a social change reflecting a movement from a dominant perception of heterosexual normalization to a pursuit of equally accepting and valuing diverse, non-heterosexual intimate relationships. However, it is still questionable whether this phenomenon can be refined as a change to overcome the historically constructed homophobic culture. In Anderson's research with his colleagues, we should note that they enunciated the gender and sexual category of these male participants as heterosexual. Their premise of the bromance is that two heterosexual men emotionally and physically engage in a profoundly intimate relationship by sharing their own common interests. Their characterization of the bromance can be seen as their attempts to distinguish the emotional and physical bonds between straight men from homosexual associations. Although the experiment is about male friendship experiences, the hidden existence of women functions as an essential prerequisite for defining the male relationship.

In this regard, the bromance can be viewed as another cultural form of the male "homosociality" that Eve Kosofsky Sedgwick (1992) articulated in her famous triangular model, whereby a female presence is necessary to act as the foil to intimacy and bonding between men. According to Sedgwick, the word "homosocial" can be understood by analogy with "homosexual," but it is at the same time used as a distinguished form of the emotional tie between same-sex peers or friends. Thus, this term involves a paradoxical situation in which the emotional openness softens gender demarcation while colluding with the connotative sense of fear of homosexuality. Journalist Choi Na-yeong's (2014) interpretation of the code of "bromance" between Manager Oh and Geu-rae explicitly substantiates Sedgwick's triangular model that desire or erotic sense between men is mediated through women. Choi analyzes the neologism, *Ogwajanggeurae mello*, indicating the melodramatic relationship between Manager Oh Sang-sik (Manager Oh/*Ogwajang*) and (Jang) Geu-rae, by focusing on the scene in which the presence of An Yeong-i, reminds Geu-rae of Manager Oh, is absent in the scene.[26] When An Yeong-i feels chilly, Geu-rae takes off his jacket and covers her. This scene seems to follow the conventional narrative of the heterosexual romance, however the next scene clarifies that the intimacy between An Yeong-i and Geu-rae is a type of fellowship rather than a heterosexual romantic closeness. In her analysis of that scene, Choi argues:

> However, it was not An Yeong-i, but Manager Oh, who was not there. When An Yeong-i said "we" during the conversation, Geu-rae immediately blushed, but not because of her. It was because he remembered the moment when Manager Oh said "we" for the first time in the early phase of his internship.

Choi's interpretation of *Ogwajanggeurae mello* explicitly substantiates Sedgwick's triangular model. According to Sedgwick, the word "homosocial" can be understood by analogy with "homosexual," but it is at the same time used as a distinguished form of the emotional tie between same-sex peers or friends. Thus, this term involves a paradoxical situation in which the emotional openness softens gender demarcation while colluding with the connotative sense of fear of homosexuality.

By employing Sedgwick's perspective, Geu-rae's blushed face can be understood as a form of "homosocial desire." The male-male bond, despite the presence of a woman, strengthens their own male territory, which is often described as male privilege over women. By relating the male-male bond to the social structure of men and women or privileged and non-privileged, Sedgwick chose the word "desire" to develop the discourse on the complexity of homosociality. Desire in *Misaeng* encompasses a social system in which Geu-rae aims to be recognized as a "member of society." Geu-rae's ultimate goal is recognized as a responsible adult man of society. Manager Oh's recognition is indispensable and can prove his growth. In this sense, Geu-rae's homosocial bond with Manager Oh is multilayered and complex.

Homosociality is considered crucial in boys' growth and often exerts powerful influences on their adult lives in homosocial contexts, such as male-dominated institutions and workplaces. Considering Geu-rae's social environments, a homosocial bond is critical in his growth as a responsible adult member of society. For example, he primarily spoke with his uncle when he aspired to become a professional *baduk* player.[27] His interactions with other men continue when he enters the trading company, one of the most male-centered working places. The company slogan, "becoming a trading company man," champions the androcentric culture of trading companies.[28] According to Michael Flood's (2008) research on male-male relations in the lives of adults, the homosocial relationship extends through heterosexual men's participation in highly homosocial collective activities of men, such as sporting groups, gangs, and male-oriented subcultures. Flood (2008) argues that adult male involvement in homosocial bonds consolidates the cultural construction of masculinity by keeping men at a distance from the feminizing and same-sex influences of exclusive heterosociality. Men prove their manhood in front of other men by showing their qualities as men, including their sexual relations with women. Flood's perspective explains how the sexual coercion of women continues unabated because male-male social relationships encourage men to use their sexual relationships with women as a medium to enhance their status among men. Flood's finding explains why men need other men to become men. The homosocial enactment is thus vital to building masculinity.

Significantly, Flood links men's narratives of their sexual relations with women to a storytelling culture in which men establish their status through recognition and authority from other men. The gender-relation narrative gathers male audiences and simultaneously strengthens their male bonds. He does not address the emotional entanglement of male audiences in other men's stories, but his approach to homosociality in relation to men's narratives involves the potential of extending men's bodily experiences into existence through discourse. In this way, homosociality can be viewed as a catalyst to evoke dynamic social relations among men whose bodies are intersected with emotions. Not only does their emotional expression and recognition contribute to male homosocial bonds, but it also constitutes a changing mode of masculinity.

CONCLUSION

The emotional understanding and intimacy that Geu-rae and Manager Oh share encourages audiences to engage in perceiving and developing their emotional bonds with the *Misaeng* world by writing about their own emotional response in the space of the *daetgeul* comment section. Male audiences shed tears in that space and comfort each other by reacting to their tears. The homosocial bond between Manager Oh and Geu-rae, and the emotional bond between male viewers in the *daetgeul* space as well, has played a decisive role in the popularity of *Misaeng*, the narrative of which is intertwined with social, cultural, economic, and political changes, and which furthermore promotes a new way of perceiving and building relationships in the social setting of the workplace.

The bromance shown in the relationship between Manager Oh and Geu-rae brings up the issue of male emotions that has been excluded from the public space, such as corporate offices, due to the traditional social norm, "a grown boy doesn't cry." Emotional control has been considered an important condition of *manly emotions* in this context. In *Misaeng*, instead of obsessing over male emotional control and independence, these two male characters reveal their emotional vulnerability, and even depend on each other. In this sense, masculinity is reformulated as being relational, reciprocal, and emotionally bonded.

NOTES

1. *Misaeng* (Incomplete Life) was originally created as a webtoon (online comics) by Yun Tae-ho and published on the Daum portal site from January 2012 through July 2013. Webtoon readers and fans have shared their thoughts and reactions through the comments section at the end of each episode. Jin is a Daum account name. This comment was left in the comments section of episode 145, the last episode of *Misaeng*: Season 1, on July 20, 2013.

2. Webtoon is one of the representative genres of Korean popular culture as an increase in Internet users and digital cultural consumption has fostered platforms for webtoons and their production.

3. See Cho, "The Webtoon"; Jang and Song, "Webtoon as a New Korean Wave in the Process of Glocalization"; Jin, "Digital Convergence of Korea's Webtoons"; Seo, "Potentials and Limitations of *Misaeng* as Transmedia Storytelling"; Seo and Ham, "A Study on the Expansion of Spatial Expression in Webtoon"; Song, "Considerations on the Functionality and Promotion of Webtoon-marketing"; Song et al., "The Impact of Spread of Webtoon on the Development of Hallyu"; Yecies et al., "Global Transcreators and the Extension of the Korean Webtoon IP-engine"; Yi, "Redrawing the Division Lines?"

4. The *Misaeng* drama (soap opera) was released on tvN from October 17, 2014, through December 20, 2014.

5. The number of comments was last confirmed in February 2021.

6. See the comments section in episode 145.

7. The first season was published from January 20, 2012, through July 19, 2013, and the second season (*Misaeng*: Part II) was published from November 10, 2015, through June 5, 2018.

8. Refer to the comment *daetgeul* in episode 145 of *Misaeng*. The webtoon series *Misaeng* was also published as a print book in 2014 and ranked as the bestselling book for men in their 30s in that year, according to a list from *Korean Publication Yearbook* in 2014, provided by *Yes24* and *Kyobo Books*, and *Online Yonhap News*.

9. Kim Gwang-taek is the user's Daum account name. This comment was left in the comments section of episode 145 on July 25, 2013. The user name "Gwang-taek" indicates that his gender is likely male.

10. See Cho, "Three Ways that BTS and Its Fans are Redefining Liveness"; Choi, "Hallyu versus Hallyu–hwa"; Han, Lee, and Park, "Gendering the Authenticity of the Military Experience."

11. Kim et al. published a volume called *Maeseu Midieo wa Suyongja* (Mass Media and Audiences) in 1999.

12. DramasROK, "tvN 2014 office drama 'Misaeng' An Incomplete Life Review."

13. Refer to Foucault, "Friendship as a Way of Life,"137–138. And to the citation in Mark Kingston, "Subversive Friendship," 7–17.

14. Refer to *Misaeng*, Episode 42.

15. Refer to *Misaeng*, Episode 43.

16. In sociology and economics, the "precariat" is a neologism for a social class formed by people suffering from precarity, which is a condition of existence embracing risks and insecurity due to the increase of labor market flexibility under the maximized competition of the "neoliberal" system since the 1970s. Guy Standing analyzed the creation of a global "precariat" to urge a political action in his book, *The Precariat: The New Dangerous Class* (London, New Delhi, New York, Sydney: Bloomsbury, 2014).

17. The first round was held on August 21, 1988, and the tournament concluded with the fifth and final match of the finals on September 5, 1989. Cho Hun-hyun won the tournament, defeating three Nihon Ki-in players along the way.

18. Refer to tvN *Misaeng* (2014), Episode 1.

19. The *Misaeng* drama (soap opera) was released on tvN from October 17, 2014, through December 20, 2014.

20. Sympathy implies *konggam* in Korean in this context. Refer to Seo, "Potentials and Limitations of *Misaeng* as Transmedia Storytelling," 283–284. And to Choi, "'Misaeng' Ogwajanggurae ui Mello ("The Melo between Manager Oh and Geu-rae in *Misaeng*)."

21. Refer to tvN (2014), episode 7.

22. Eundun Eundun, "Manager Oh Kwajang Geu-rae (Manager Oh and Jang Geu-rae)."

23. Choi, "'Misaeng' Ogwajanggurae ŭi Mello (The Melo between Manager Oh and Geu-rae in *Misaeng*)."

24. Refer to Pew Research Center's survey, "The Global Divide on Homosexuality."

25. Refer to Korean Gallup's survey, "Korea Gallup Daily Opinion."

26. Choi, "'Misaeng' Ogwajanggurae ui Mello, Reobeurain boda Ganghada (The Melo between Manager Oh and Geu-rae in *Misaeng*, Stronger than a [heterosexual] love relationship)." The term "Ogwajanggeurae" is a combination of two male characters' names: Manager Oh and Geu-rae.

27. When Geu-rae was a child, he started playing *baduk* at the recommendation of his uncle. However, Geu-rae stopped playing *baduk* when his father died and he began looking for a job to take responsibility as the head of the family.

28. *Sangsa maen* (商社man) originated from Japanese 商社マン, meaning a hardworking office man at a commercial association organized for trade or commercial activities.

BIBLIOGRAPHY

An, K. (2016). 남자란 무엇인가 – 남자는 왜 행복해지기 어려운가? (*What Is a Man: Why Can't Men Be Happy?*) Seoul: 홍익 출판사.

Anderson, E. (2009). *Inclusive Masculinity: The Changing Nature of Masculinities.* New York: Routledge.

Anderson, E, Robinson, S., and White, A. (2018). The Bromance: Undergraduate Male Friendships and the Expansion of Contemporary Homosocial Boundaries" *Sex Roles* 78: 94–106.

Berlant, L. (2011). *Cruel Optimism.* Durham, NC: Duke University Press.

Cho, H. (2016). The Webtoon: A New Form for Graphic Narrative. *The Comics Journal.* http://www.tcj.com/the-webtoon-a-new-form-for-graphic-narrative/.

Cho, M. (2018). Three Ways that BTS and Its Fans are Redefining Liveness. *Flow. TV.* https://www.flowjournal.org/2018/05/bts-and-its-fans/.

Choi, J. (2015). Hallyu versus Hallyu-hwa: Cultural Phenomenon versus Institutional Campaign. In *Hallyu 2.0: The Korean Wave in the Age of Social Media*, edited by Lee, S. and Nornes, A., 31–52. Ann Arbor, MI: University of Michigan Press.

Choi, N. (2014). '미생' 오과장그래의 멜로, 러브라인보다 강하다 (The Melo between Manager Oh and Geu-rae in *Misaeng* Stronger than [Heterosexual] Love Relationship). *Huffpost.* https://www.huffingtonpost.kr/2014/11/21/story_n _6202840.html.

Chŏng, Y., Kim, W., Yim, S., Yi, S., Kang, S., and Kang, H. (2015). *Misaeng*: = *Wei Sheng*. DVD. Kuala Lumpur, Malaysia: PMP Entertainment (M) SDN. BHD.

Chung, Y., and Jang, E. (2015) Shaky Gender, the Changing World: Focusing on Drama *Misaeng*. *Korean Women's Association for Communication Studies* 30 (3): 153–184.

DeAngelis, M. (2014). *Reading the Bromance: Homosocial Relationship in Film and Television*. Detroit, MI: Wayne State University Press.

Deleuze, G. (1992). What is a Dispositif? In *Michel Foucault Philosopher*, edited by T.J. Armstrong, 159–168. Hemel Hempstead: Harvester Wheatsheaf.

DramasROK. (2021). tvN 2014 Office Drama 'Misaeng' An Incomplete Life Review. https://www.dramasrok.com/2015/03/tvn-2014-office-drama-misaeng-review/.

Fiske, J. (1987). *Television Culture*. London: Methuen.

Flood, M. (2008). Men, Sex, and Homosociality: How Bonds between Men Shape their Sexual Relations with Women. *Men and Masculinities* 10 (3): 339–359.

Foucault, M. (1997). Friendship as a Way of Life. In Edited by P. Rabinow, Ed. *Ethics: Subjectivity and Truth*, 137–138. New York: New Press.

Han, W., Lee, C., and Park, J. (2020). Gendering the Authenticity of the Military Experience: Male Audience Responses to the Korean Reality Show Real Men. *Media, Culture and Society* 39 (1): 62–76.

Jang, W., and Song, J. (2017). Webtoon as a New Korean Wave in the Process of Glocalization. *Kritika Kultura* 29: 168–187.

Jin, D. (2015). Digital Convergence of Korea's Webtoons: Transmedia Storytelling. *Communication Research and Practice* 1 (3): 193–209.

Kim, C., et al., eds. (1999). 매스미디어와 수용자. *(Mass Media and Audiences)*. Seoul: 커뮤니케이션 북스.

Kim, M. (2014). New Types of Masculinity Represented in TV and Its Limitations: Focusing on Weekend Variety Programs. *Journal of the Korea Contents Association* 14 (1): 88–96.

Kim, S. (2010). Audience Studies' Decoding Model and a Reappraisal of John Fiske: Towards a Critical Reflection on Korean Audience Studies and Open Debates. *Media & Society* 18 (1): 2–46.

Kingston, M. (2009). Subversive Friendship: Foucault on Homosexuality and Social Experimentation. *Foucault Studies* 7: 7–17.

Korea Gallup Daily Opinion. *Korea Gallup* 356, May 2019, https://www.gallup.co.kr/gallupdb/report.asp.

Kumar, S. (2020). The Affective Audience: Beyond the Active vs. Passive Audience Theory Debate in Television Studies. In *The Routledge Companion to Global Television*, edited by Shawn Shimpach, 99–110. New York: Routledge.

Pew Research Center. (2013). The Global Divide on Homosexuality: Greater Acceptance in More Secular and Affluent Countries. *Pew Research Center*. https://www.pewresearch.org/global/2013/06/04/the-global-divide-on-homosexuality/.

Sedgwick, E. (1992). *Between Men: English Literature and Male Homosocial Desire*. New York: Columbia University Press.

Seo, C., and Ham, J. (2010). A Study on the Expansion of Spatial Expression in Webtoon. *Cartoon and Animation Studies* 20: 63–74.

Seo, S. (2015). Potentials and Limitations of *Misaeng* as Transmedia Storytelling. *The Korean Language and Literature* 128: 283–284.

Song, J. (2014). Considerations on the Functionality and Promotion of Webtoon-marketing. *Journal of Cultural Contents Research* 4: 33–61.

Song, J., Nahm, K., and Jang, W. (2014). The Impact of the Spread of Webtoons on the Development of Hallyu: The Case Study of Indonesia. *Korea Entertainment Industry Association Journal* 8: 357–367.

Standing, G. (2011). *The Precariat: The New Dangerous Class.* London: Bloomsbury Publishing.

Ŭndun ŭndun. (2014). "Manager O kwa Jang Geu-rae," *YouTube.* https://www.youtube.com/watch?v=R96CDZrUCRQ.

Yecies, B. et al. (2019). Global Transcreators and the Extension of the Korean Webtoon IP-engine. *Media, Culture & Society.* 42 (1): 40–57.

Yi, K. (1989). 미디어 수용자론의 이론적 전개. (Theoretical Development of Audience Studies). *Sogang University Journalism & Culture Institute* 5: 9–23.

Yi, K. (2001). 수용자론. (*Audience Studies*). Seoul: Hanul Academy.

Yi, W. (2020). Redrawing the Division Lines?: Surplus, Connectivity, and Remediation in the South Korean Webtoon *Secretly, Greatly. Positions* 28 (4): 701–727.

Yun, T. (2012–2020). *Misaeng* (Incomplete Life). 20 January 2012–5 June 2018, http://cartoon.media.daum.net/webtoon/view/miseng.

Chapter 8

"LISTEN TO K-POP, BURN THE POLICE!"

Swastikas, Feminism, and LGBTQ+ Rights in the 2019–2020 Chilean Protests

Moisés Park

INTRODUCTION

In late 2019, graffiti on a Chilean public school wall facing the streets says "LISTEN TO K-POP, BURN THE POLICE" (*"ESCUCHA K-POP, QUEMA A LA YUTA,"* see figure 8.1). "Yuta" is a derogatory term in Chile to refer to the police. Earlier that week, Chilean newspaper *La Tercera* revealed that a "big data report" conducted by the Ministry of the Interior asserted that "foreign influences" caused country's largest protests in its history that had been happening since October 2019. One of the foreign influences was *fanáticos del K-pop*. A follow-up march was organized, *La marcha K-pop* ("The K-pop March") on December 27, as a response to those findings, although the march was not entirely organized and attended by K-pop fans, it was clear that protesters were mocking the big data findings. The alleged militant influence of South Korean pop music supposedly exacerbated demonstrations. The culmination of the national discontent resulted in continuous protests through the pandemic and on October 25, 2020, an overwhelming majority of voters (78.28%) approved to rewrite a new constitution addressing several of the demands.

This chapter will problematize the relations between fandom and protest for two reasons: (1) *Correlation:* K-pop fandom and protesting are a result of demographic association (fans are progressive) and the less favored conclusion that in fact (2) fans *caused* more social agitation; that is, K-pop music and/or K-pop fans exacerbated protests, though the direct influence in the manifestations is difficult or impossible to measure.

Figure 8.1   In December 2019, Graffiti in Santiago, Chile Says, "LISTEN TO K-POP, BURN THE POLICE."

Limited but available data suggests that working-class adolescents, mostly girls and *disidentes* (sexual minorities), make up a majority of the fandom, with an increasing fandom among male adolescents and young adults (Min, 2019, 2021). Although K-pop artists and the industry were not directly involved in or vocal about the protests, fans of second- and third-generation K-pop engaged or at least "amplified" the cause of social unrest in 2019 and 2020 through social media. Demographic data reveals fans' affinity to left-leaning politics, and to their favoring gender equity and LGBTQ+ activism. At the same time, K-pop fans around the globe have had political influence in the United States during the 2019–2020 #metoo and #blacklivesmatter protests that ultimately have become global social movements (Bruner, 2020; Hong, 2020; Johnson, 2020). Generally speaking, K-pop consumers (beyond Chile and Latin America) support gender equity, LGBTQ+ rights, and progressive politics (Min, 2021). These political protests blended support for racial justice, intersectional progressivism, and what originally might have sparked the initial protests in Chile: economic disparity and the lingering impact of neoliberal authoritarianism.

THE "ESTALLIDO SOCIAL" OF 2019
#WEARENOTATWAR #CHILEWOKEUP

In October 6, 2019, the Santiago Metro's fare was raised by a few *pesos* much to the discontent of some citizens who vented their frustrations on social media. Online platforms intensified with additional complains that revealed a much deeper dissatisfaction that had resulted in previous demonstrations.

Most notably, high school and college student-led protests demanded equity in education, feminist marches demanded gender equity, opposed aggressive privatization of health care, and demanded more political autonomy from indigenous groups (Vivero et al., 2020). Previous Chilean student protests included these efforts in social movements, most notably in the 2006 student protest (aka. *Movilización estudiantil*), which consolidated a growing political bloc and reformulated a political force that demanded progressive policies. Chilean K-pop fans were inevitably included in these dialogues via social media because of their demographic affinity, but also because culture wars were often manifested in all social media platforms, where K-pop fans often engage. The country had become part of the OECD (Organization for Economic Co-operation and Development) in 2010, an indication that Chile was no longer a third world country, but these protests defied neoliberal triumphalisms.

On December 21, 2019, according to the 112-page report, part of the foreign influence on the protests was K-pop fans (Ayala, 2019). Every Chilean mainstream media outlet reported the findings and talk shows addressed this as a scandal, and quickly reformulated the findings to mock them, but paying attention to the K-pop reference among the foreign influencers. According to *La Tercera*, The Ministry of the Interior hired a third party (Alto Analytics) to text-mine and examine social media data that revealed K-pop fandom tendencies among those who posted and distributed information regarding the protest (Ayala, 2019). The late 2019 and early 2020 demonstrations happened daily and in waves of violent escalations, so data could expose possible influences that tangibly affected the number of protestors, locations for protests, the tone of the demand, and the many failed attempts from police force to covering up violent clashes that were scorned by human rights organizations. It was reported that several Chilean policemen were targeting youth's eyes: the *New York Times*, The BBC, *El País*, and other international news outlets would report on an "epidemic" of "ocular violence" by Chilean police, who were targeting protestors' eyes to cause severe damage, in spite of the use of pressured water and rubber bullets as alleged ways to avoid protester casualties. More than 300 victims have claimed their eyes were wounded due to police violence, and many were documenting the violence and horror and sharing it on social media (Albornoz, 2020). The gravity of the political situation and the seemingly apolitical escapism of K-pop music increased the ridicule among the public that K-pop should be blamed for these clashes.

Two months prior to the report, tension had already been aggravated when right-wing President Piñera publicly echoed authoritarian bellicose language by declaring that "Chile is at war against a powerful enemy" (*Chile está en guerra contra un enemigo poderoso*) on October 21, 2019, meaning it was at war with itself, in an ideological civil war. News that the government announced an internal war was catastrophic. Chile was a nation that lived through a military dictatorship from 1973 to 1990, and more than 3,000 Chileans were either killed or had disappeared. There are close to 30,000 cases of torture claims and/or violations of human rights. Immediately, social media reacted to the president's language, insisting that Chile was not at war with #noestamosenguerra (#wearenotatwar), as a way to insist that protests were peaceful and that the majority supported non-violent resolutions. The unrest united against the president's remarks and eventually the #Chiledesperto (#Chilewokeup) became part of a larger sentiment. Coincidentally, that social activism equated with what in the United States is referred to as "being woke," at times pejoratively; that is, being aware and critical of social disparities that ostracize gender, sexual, and ethnic minorities. Netizens defied the presidential hyperbolic escalation, and emphasized social issues rather than spectacle that evolved into physical and violent confrontations such as altercations, destruction of property, looting, and so on. Days after the report, Chilean social media was saturated with memes that equated the "powerful enemy" and "war" with K-pop groups and fans, particularly boy bands that projected soft masculinities and girl bands that projected teenage naïveté, contradicting the stereotype that K-pop was indifferent to political causes.

In March, after more than four months of protests, COVID-19 interrupted the frequency of demonstrations, which squashed the demonstrations in the streets. Yet, activism grew through social media, combining the discontent from 2019, and adding the frustrations of 2020 and 2021 regarding the handling of the virus by the incumbent and outgoing right-wing government. At this point, as a method of pushback, K-pop hashtags were adopted by Chilean fans and non-fans alike to connect on social media, strengthening the link between fandom and protest.

The news of the report caused such a sensation that the phrase "big data" circulated and trended in Chile's Twitter-dome and became well known in media and among average citizens. "Big data" became synonymous with the government's frustrated attempts to pivot from the more evident reasons for the social unrest. This phrase eerily echoes *1984*'s "Big Brother is watching you," reminding us of Orwellian authoritarian scenarios and Edward Snowden's well-documented concern that the U.S. government had the ability to spy on millions of citizens and had been covertly monitoring non-threatening activities for years. This digital text mining also alluded to technocratic attempts to use "science" and "technology" to uncover ideological fanatism and alleged domestic acts of terrorism. President Piñera referred to the cause of violence as a "powerful enemy," in order to discipline the nation that social demands were part of communist propaganda from nearby Venezuela and/ or military superpower Russia. The five most read newspapers in Chile and major national broadcasting news channels (Televisión Nacional de Chile,

Mega, Chilevisión, Canal 13, La red) and cable news channels like CNN Chile reported on the government's statistical conclusions with skepticism.

Across the Pacific, Korean mainstream media did not elaborate on all the demands by protestors and reported on the subway fare rise and the absurdity that K-pop was part of communist propaganda in Chile. *Joong Ang Ilbo*, for instance, did report that Chile's government analyzed the context of the massive protests that had been happening for more than two months, and highlighted the report mentioning K-pop fans as an influence. The Korean newspaper remarked on the lack of scientific and pragmatic rigor in the conclusions according to local experts. The report synthesized social media posts for about a month from October 18 to November 21, when protests intensified. *Joong Ang Ilbo* reiterates that big data analyzed 60 million posts written by 5 million users "related" to the protests. Some "unusual factors" were linked between these posts and online actors, "including Russian broadcaster RT, Venezuelan broadcaster Telesur, Argentine leftist celebrities, and users both inside and outside Chile" (Oh, 2019). The *Joong Ang Ilbo* article also mentions that the Ministry's report contends that 19.3% of the analyzed posts were produced abroad, suggesting that "external forces had influenced Chilean protests." Supposedly, "young internet users [who listen to K-pop] led the intensification of protests by pouring out more than 4 million retweets on Twitter during the first eight days of the protests [questioning] the government's data, frequently cited human rights violations, and criticized media silence or blocking social media" (Oh, 2019). *Yonhap* reported almost identical details in a report entitled "K-pop behind Chile protests? Report sparks controversy" (Ko, 2019). *Yonhap* added that the Chilean government was blaming external forces while ignoring the root cause of the protests (Ko, 2019).

K-pop music, in general, is considered an escapist form of entertainment with no politically explicit agenda, but rather, ambiguous messages of love, self-love, and confidence. Attempts to read K-pop lyrics and their visual narratives as subliminal and subversive are not rare (Kim, 2021; Chun, 2017). Currently, hundreds of social media platforms, blogs, and even scholarly publications have already examined songs, music videos, and live performances; some academic publications even use "close reading" methodology that resemble hermeneutics of K-pop lyrics to recognize that perhaps some lyrics have evolved to address serious social and political issues (Kim, 2021). These interpretations might suggest formulaic establishment of neoliberal conservatism, while others affirm the contrary, that some of these groups are becoming assertive in breaking stereotypes and glass ceilings, deconstructing images and institutions, and even demanding changes in policies, and not just attitude. But the majority simply dismiss the idea that listeners pay too much attention to the lyrics even if they might understand the meaning in Korean or can read them in translation. Perhaps, this reminds us of Bob Dylan's

"Blowin' in the Wind" (1963) and "The Times They Are a-Changin'" (1964), which have ambiguous lyrics and have become iconic protest songs with firm interpretations about literal protest and civic unrest due to racial discrimination and systematic issues.

BTS famously promoted self-love in a speech to the UN on September 24, 2020, and later in September, 20, 2021. Their fashion and androgyny might seem countercultural and invite queer friendliness, but few would take their content as anything but predictable in the realm of pop music production and careful marketing perfection. Even if third-generation K-pop artists have become more explicit in addressing taboos (sexuality, sexual promiscuity, gender identity, political views, etc.), projecting "safe" countercultural images is part of the formula within youth culture (Kim, 2018, 2021).

In Marxist terms, the pop music industry sells a commodity, which is not necessarily the music itself. Take into consideration the limited but viral reactions to K-pepsi, a Chilean quintet boy K-pop group in 2020. The name is not ironic or coincidental; PepsiCo, the American multinational beverage corporation, financed the formation of the group, singing in Korean, English, and Spanish, with prospects of creating singles and perhaps joining the K-pop industry by becoming one of many corporations exploiting K-pop aesthetics and formulas to promote a product, from Chile with American monetary investment. In other words, it is paradoxical to think that K-pop music itself would engage in dismantling capitalism, á la Rage Against the Machine.

Reactions toward the possibility that this escapist, neoliberal, consumerist music would motivate Chilean youth to revolt along with left-leaning masses that waived Che Guevara and multicolored rainbow flags (which symbolize support for LGBTQ+ but also Chilean indigenous groups) were bizarre. The most trending hashtag was #piñerarenuncia or #renunciapiñera (President Piñera, resign!), which massively circulated after the report. K-pop fans were not supportive of the incumbent leader as the big data report was conducted under his leadership, and he represented the status quo, conservatism, fundamentalist Catholicism, patriarchy, and market-driven neoliberalism. The most shared meme following the big data report consisted of a BTS group picture with a digitally added banner demanding the president's resignation, "PIÑERA RENUNCIA." Netizens recognized the irony that boy bands would somehow be demanding political changes in Chile.

CORRELATION, NOT CAUSATION: WHO LISTENS TO K-POP IN CHILE?

Although some suggest that youth are apolitical, naïve, and indifferent to political processes and movements, the protests that culminate in the new

Chilean constitution prove the opposite. In fact, data is not necessary to deduce that youth were featured in demonstrations. The link between K-pop fans (who are mostly younger Chileans) and activism is largely a correlation rather than a causation in Chile; thus, data does not merely reflect ineptitude by the Ministry of Interior by pivoting the blame to K-pop and other celebrities. Likely, protestors who were connected to K-pop cyber networks indirectly influenced political activism by association. The government findings simply confirmed that many protesters also happen to listen to K-pop (and other non-Korean singers). Analyzing social media was a predictable strategy to avoid the more obvious explanation that the majority of the country was dissatisfied with the conservative status quo, and the militarized remnants of the dictatorship.

Additionally, in Chile, just like in other countries where *Hallyu* is rapidly growing, K-pop is not just listened to privately. The visual aspect of K-pop (music videos and local street dance groups) is central to the genre and its fandom. K-pop is perhaps synonymous with choreographed high-energy performances and colorful fashion. Most K-pop dance groups gather in public spaces such as parks and open areas in downtown Santiago Centro rather than the uptown Vitacura and Las Condes neighborhoods (similar to the Peruvian fans discussed in chapter 10 of this book). A study suggests that an overwhelming majority of Latin American K-pop listeners in 2019 were female teenagers and adolescents (college age) from working-class families (Min et al., 2019). Although Korean media and government marketing ploys portray the Korean Wave as a phenomenon that is on par with European and American hegemonic dominance—but cleaner and more positive—scholars have been less triumphalist and favor more critical verdicts (Kim, 2021; Min, 2017, 2020, Min et al., 2019). For instance, Wonjung Min challenges the perception that *Hallyu* is massively and transversally consumed in all Latin American countries and by everybody regardless of any demographic differentiation.[1] She recognizes that consumption of Korean cultural production in Latin America is increasing but not as widely as reported. She concludes after examining several ethnographic publications that the "largest countries in Latin America in terms of population and geography," and "relatively stronger economically" tend to have larger populations that consume South Korean cultural products (Min, 2017). In other words, financial and technological access to streaming services and online platforms is proportional to K-pop fandom. South Korean media exaggerates reception and massive consumption of the nation's cultural exports. In Chile, at least, there are "prevailing class prejudices" with regard to K-pop, which "helps to understand why K-pop is well-known, [but] ignored or unaccepted by the upper-middle and upper-class in general—as if to say 'If it is beneath my class, it cannot be accepted'" (Min, 2017). More recent works by Min and others have determined that currently fandom is not limited to teenagers, but extends to the age group between 30 and 40 years and their knowledge of the Korean language and culture has allowed them to become active participants in translating, interpreting, and explaining lyrics and images. These "translation practices enable cultural understanding and reinscribe transcultural identity politics, inverting, and unsettling 'traditional' center-periphery dynamics" (García Cruz et al., 2019). Many fans are voting professional adults that have followed K-pop since their teenage years and 20s (Borges de Castilho, 2015). Nonetheless, more quantitative research is required to further and more accurately quantify the changing demographics of the consumption of Korean cultural products, particularly K-pop and its impact on fashion, cosmetics, and tourism, among others. Data collected in Latin American K-pop fandom is incomplete, but enough to determine that there is a growing number of adolescents listening to K-pop as young adults.

Understanding the demographics of Chilean fandom could explain the political affinities of those fans who also joined the protests in the streets beyond social media activism. Progressive activists and netizens were quick to mention the real causes of the protest: education, health, pensions, gender gap, discrimination against sexual and racial minorities, and so on (Jiménez-Yañez, 2020; Vivero et al., 2020). The incumbent office used a scientific approach to involve foreign actors as the agitators, neglecting the nature of social media networking that was not bound to solely come from local national IP addresses. In other words, the local demands were not mere issues that concerned Chileans living in Chile. First of all, fellow Chileans abroad (more than 600,000 or 3.2%) were not the only ones interacting with social media, which could have been enough to explain the high number of social media engagement from abroad. Many of them have lived abroad since the 1970s due to the dictatorship, which would explain their apathy toward a president who defended Pinochet in the past and was insinuating that the country was at war again. Second, the already established network of progressive users who voiced their opinions by sharing the discontent were actively involved in addressing Chile's protests (Diaz Pino, 2019). Those who were part of that progressive network were not necessarily Chilean, but Spanish-speaking netizens who were connected through K-pop fandom and/or progressive leanings. Even non-Spanish speakers who are aware or are mildly educated in international affairs might have followed this story. Conflagrating K-pop as part of extreme-left voices, against market-friendly government, would mean that they are part of a concerted multinational force, a "powerful enemy" in Piñera's words, championing a violent communist and/or anarchist agenda, as if the Chilean intelligence forgot that K-pop is a phenomenon produced from modern neoliberal South Korea, not communist North Korea.

The intersection of feminist and LGBTQ+ activism among K-pop fandom that has been studied as scholarship regarding *Hallyu* 2.0 abandoned the stereotype of fans as entirely consisting of teenage bobbysoxers (Oh, 2015; Kwon, 2019; Hall et al., 2021). Some scholars conclude that Korean female fans are ardent supporters of gay representation and homoerotic representation in the media (Kwon, 2019). The feminist and sexual minority causes were central in the marches in 2019. In other words, identity politics are seminal to understanding the correlation of fans, identity, and politics (Kwon, 2019). Supporters who were younger teenagers and young adults formed part of the correlated demographic that mostly consumed and supported K-pop. Moreover, social media networks already have algorithms that fast-tracked the communication of topics, including social causes that can result in action beyond the clicks. Along with the rise of several young women global activists (Chile's own Camila Vallejo, Greta Thunberg, Emma Gonzalez, Malala Yousafzai, etc.), the *Ni una menos* (Not one [woman] less) movement recognized in social media under #NiUnaMenos also became part of the ongoing marches that demanded equity beyond class warfare. The #NiUnaMenos was a literary movement against gender-based violence, coordinating massive demonstrations on June 3, 2015, in Argentina, at the height of second-generation fandom growing in Latin America as several tours in sold out stadiums consolidated K-pop's global popularity. Generational, gender-specific, and class-specific demographics reveal that involvement in social movements already networked in left-wing politics and Korean popular music since at least 2015 if not earlier (Wells and Li, 2020; Lorenz et al., 2020).

The connection between working-class young listeners and K-pop fandom is a correlation that was effectively maneuvered by K-pop concert organizers in Latin America. Often, K-pop groups would do covers of well-known popular songs that were connected to local and historical social movements and artists. The most exemplary cases are those of *Gracias a la vida* by Chile's most celebrated political folk songwriter, artist, and women's empowerment icon Violeta Parra (1917–1961). The song was covered in 2012 in Chile by Korean R&B ballad duo Davichi. In that same event, all participating K-pop groups (Afterschool, CN Blue, Davichi, MBLAQ, and RaNia) covered the Chilean folk fusion rock Los Jaiva's 1972 song *Todos juntos*, an anthem that calls for unity, but it is also considered part of a repertoire of tunes by artists that supported Chile's turn to left-wing politics in the 1960s and early 1970s before the coup. It is still often heard during marches that support progressive movements (Park, 2019).

Gracias a la vida is a song about heartbreak and moving on. It manifests gratefulness for the senses, reason, and freedom to right to live and love. In a way, it is a melancholic proposition of carpe diem. Yet, rather than just emphasizing enjoyment of the present by celebrating the blessings in life, or cherishing memories and feeling nostalgia as coping mechanisms for heartbreak, the poetic voice insists on expressing longing for her departed (or unrequited) love, while ultimately striving to express ambivalent freedom by calling for underlying Marxist notions of solidarity, "the fundamental ethic of the workers' movement, obliging workers to support the struggles of all other oppressed people" (MIA: Encyclopedia of Marxism). The duality of love for a man and love for *ustedes* (you all) and *todos* (all of us) is conclusively resolved by opting for hope in unity toward political solidarity with the people. But Violeta Parra's writings often included personal and social dilemmas she wrestled with, opting to evoke emotions from different aspects of life: romantic love but also, love for revolutionary Marxism. The listener is the implicit proletariat who is invited to join her "singing" as an act of revolution. Inviting "you all" to a collective cause over personal romantic feelings recalls a political solidarity that fits the ideological expectations of the Marxist revolution (Park, 2019). In other words, the K-pop industry is aware of the political activism by most musicians in Chile, such as Violeta Parra, Víctor Jara, Inti-Illimani, Los Jaivas, and Quilapayún, but their covers would lean toward the more universalist interpretations.

THE ZAMUDIO LAW AND A CASE FOR CAUSATION

The case for K-pop fandom as a cause or influence for protest and additional demands for gender equity and LGBTQ+ rights is not taken seriously by the Chilean media, but more direct links between them do exist. Daniel Zamudio was violently murdered in 2012 (same year that Music Bank had their first visit to Chile) at the age of 24. Mainstream media and several organizations reported that the murder was linked to a neo-Nazi gang who targeted Zamudio for being gay, as they found his body with swastikas carved with a broken bottle on his body (Steidl, 2016; Morales, 2013). Although the four attackers who battered and tortured Zamudio for several hours were convicted, the social uproar expedited Chile's law on hate crimes to pass, banning discrimination based on "race, ethnicity, religion, sexual orientation, gender, appearance, or handicap" (Pérez, 2017). His murder resulted in political mobilizations that insisted in policies that legally banned discrimination and hate crimes. An important detail that was not ignored by some sectors of social media among *K-poperos* was Zamudio's admiration and participation in K-pop dancing groups. According to interviews conducted by Kyoung H. Park (1982), a Korean-Chilean-American playwright, some youth in the K-pop scene rumored that Zamudio had an affinity for South Korean pop music and dance (Park, 2016). This incident might seem insignificant in relation to the 2019 protest, but since 2012, the "geography of K-pop" in the city changed, and it explains some causation of K-pop fans becoming politicized and more conscious of the marginalization of sexual minorities. Before the murder of Zamudio, K-pop dance fans would gather at Parque San Borja in downtown Santiago and practice dance routines. This relocation might also seem unrelated to the politicization of K-pop, but the new space, the Centro Cultural Gabriela Mistral (aka. La GAM), is a more public space, near very busy bus and subway stations (Olave de la Barrera, 2012). In other words, K-pop dancing and fandom became more public and visible, as their support for social causes became more evident. Zamudio was not just an iconic person who became the *cause célèbre* for the ban of discrimination and hate crimes against LGBTQ+ members. He became a martyr who mirrored the resilience of fans who publicly supported South Korean popular bands and choreographies, even if it meant being bullied or risking their lives.

TVN's (Chile's Television Nacional) *Zamudio: Perdidos en la noche* (2015) is a documentary based on journalist Rodrigo Fluxá's *Solos en la noche: Zamudio y sus asesinos* (2014) where the journalist debunks links between the aggressors and neo-Nazis, while he also profiles Zamudio as a young adult who was gay but no mentions of his passion for K-pop dance. The four-episode series by TVN recreated the profile of all four convicted men and Zamudio with none of them linked to K-pop (though one of the aggressors was known to be an avid dancer and imitator of Michael Jackson). Nonetheless, in Fernando Guzzoni's feature film *Jesús* (2016), inspired by Zamudio's death, the four aggressors themselves are K-pop dancers in a group, and at least two of them are either bisexual or gay. In the real-life case, the aggressors were not *K-poperos*, and one of them was rumored to be bisexual (Pérez, 2017; Morales, 2016). The 2016 film, thus, problematically reverts the representation of *K-poperos* as transgressors and as queer. Additionally, Pablo Sheng's novel *Charapo* (2016) has a moment when South Korean business-owning immigrants torture a Peruvian immigrant while singing a K-pop song. These and other representations in Chilean cultural products contain *K-poperos* as violent, perhaps linking those in lower-class youth as criminal youth and Orientalized Korean immigrants as aggressive. Nevertheless, there is no study that links K-pop consumption in Chile and crime. In fact, *K-poperos* are more often victims of bullying, and South Korean immigrants are not necessarily fans of the genre.

The exact musical taste of the aggressors and Zamudio is secondary to the outcome of the case and the repercussions in social media. The tragedy united a progressive community K-pop fans and sympathizers that were appalled at the horrific murder. Ideologically, solidarity for Zamudio's murder and K-pop fandom is not surprising, given that K-pop fandom values unity among fans, rejecting bullying and being more inclusive.

K-pop fans are not bothered by the genre's androgyny of male singers, gender fluid performances, and alternate masculinities that supposedly reject "Occidental patriarchal mentality" (Koetzsch, 2019). There is abundant scholarship that "much attention has been paid to female fandom for homo-erotic cultural texts in English language sources," but transnational Korean Wave fandom has reshaped Korean genderscapes supporting queer issues and identities (Kwon, 2019). This support for homoerotic normativity and androgyny in K-pop is recognized globally. For instance, in a 2017 and 2018 survey in Jujuy, Argentina, 81% recognized androgyny in K-pop artists, while 88% considered it positive or did not care. Some suggest that "Koreans consider positively a soft image of men [and] there is no connotation as in Western cultures" and "more boys use makeup in their daily life, though not as conspicuously as in dance performances, due to the fact that male cosmet-ics carry a strong gay connotation in general Argentina society" (Koetzsch, 2019). In Chile, data is similar, as South American popular notions of K-pop maintain Asian masculinity as soft, compared to the hegemonic patriarchy from Western representations, where soft masculinity is considered androgy-nous (Jung, 2010). Nevertheless, more recent studies suggest K-pop and K-Dramas noticeably influence Asian (largely Korean) remasculinization, per some interviewees describing Korean men as "perfect" (Min, 2021), although it is not necessary to assume that by "perfect" they mean hypermasculine, or merely fantasy, rather than a realistic affinity to pursue relationships and social commitments.

Among second-generation boy bands, Big Bang might have become the most daring ensemble featuring reformulations of masculinities that chal-lenged heteronormative iterations of the heteronormative archetypes in Anglo boy bands. During the transition from second- to third-generation K-pop bands, some artists garnered a highly inclusive fandom, no longer shying away from the alleged emasculation of the artists, and openly establishing themselves as pioneers in diversifying representations of masculinity and femininity, be it heteronormative or androgynous (Hall et al., 2021). For instance, BTS is recognized as promoting self-love, a more modest take on anti-bullying in support of body positivity, although some argue that for a Korean pop band, it was radical and out of the norm. There are some indications that the group was supportive of same-sex relationships, mental health awareness, and acceptance. For instance, RM's tweet from March 6, 2013 praised Macklemore and Ryan Lewis's "Same Love" (2012) as "great without knowing the lyrics, but better if understood [. . .] highly recom-mended" and recently, the leader of the group recommended Troye Sivan's "Strawberries and Cigarettes" which was featured in the gay coming-of-age film *Love, Simon* (2018) although the lyrics have no content that can be attrib-uted to same-sex relation (Kim, 2018).

WHAT WERE CHILEAN PROTESTORS SINGING?

A few videos do show some K-pop dancing and fans among the 1,300,000 protestors in Chile, but they are miniscule and negligible compared to the global virality of acts such as Las Tesis, a Chilean feminist performance collective, whose "A Rapist in Your Path" ("Un violador en tu camino") (2019) which became a powerful performance protesting violence against women.[2] It might not have the same kind of commercial and feel-good fanaticism that K-pop has but the explicit demands in their words are unmatched by any lyrics by Korean (or any non-Korean) musical artists with regard to violence against women. Their act was replicated and translated in at least 40 countries and well-over a 100 cities. In addition, the few K-pop dances were eclipsed in those marches by other acts: classical orchestral pieces, flash mobs for education by teachers, and most notably, local Chilean popular social anthems that had been part of the protest repertoire that consolidated through years of protest since and before the military coup in 1973.

The grassroots movement mostly adopted Latin American protest music, which is already rooted in social movements. Violeta Parra and Víctor Jara were still the staple protest songwriters, the obvious soundtrack of the protests in 2019. Folk rock bands such as Los jaivas, Inti-Illimani, and Quilapayún were also already vocal supporters of left-leaning and progressive politics since the 1960s and 1970s. During Pinochet's dictatorship, several were exiled or self-exiled, but influenced younger generations of musicians. Among them, the highly successful pioneering Chilean rock pop band Los prisioneros has become the iconic countercultural voice. Songs such as *La voz de los 80* ("The voice of the 80s") or "South American Rockers" demanded change and for the youth to freely voice their discontent toward the authoritarian government. In 2019, once again, it was the local artists that united the marches that included at least two million protesters (more than 10% of the population). Among the more memorable moments of the marches was the communal singing of the 1986 song *El Baile de los que Sobran* ("The Dance of the Leftovers"), a rock ballad anthem that was particularly relevant to the disgruntled youth during the dictatorship with the famous "join the dance of the leftovers / nobody will miss us / nobody really wanted to help us" line that summarized the apathy from youth who viewed obvious class differences in Chile's education (González, 1986; Albornoz, 2020). In 2019 and 2020, those voices were not forgotten, and several chants resurrected those anthems. K-Pop fans might have joined, or maybe they already knew the lyrics as they were part of their commonly known repertoire.

From Chile, Mon Laferte (1983) has become the most globally successful and popular Chilean musician since Violeta Parra and Víctor Jara. She was iconic in leading and demanding transparency and justice during the

2019 protests. Her direct denunciation of Piñera's right-wing politics and police brutality was impossible to ignore in social media. In November 2019, at the height of the protests, the Chilean artist exposed her breasts at the Latin Grammys with a message painted on her chest and torso: *EN CHILE TORTURAN VIOLAN Y MATAN* ("IN CHILE THEY TORTURE, RAPE, AND KILL") accusing police force and ultimately the highest leadership for perpetuating excessive violence that echoed Pinochet's dictatorial rhetoric and tactics. Throughout the entire 2019–2020 protests, there have been no interventions by K-Pop artists, its industry, or the Korean government with regard to the *estallido*. On the other hand, BTS became highly featured headlines by publicly supporting the Black Lives Matter Movement after the George Floyd murder. BTS donated $1 million to the organization, which was matched by ARMY (Hong, 2020; Johnson, 2020). Other K-pop fans were also explicitly in support of #blm in the aftermath of George Floyd's death (Liu, 2020). If K-pop industry and their fans were ever directly involved in political causes, it was more obviously felt in the United States, not in Chile.

PRELIMINARY ETHNOGRAPHIC FINDINGS: TOWARD FURTHER STUDIES OF CORRELATION AND CAUSATION

Interviews conducted in the summers of 2016–2019 attempted to survey the public's perception of these urban tribes, social class, political affinities, and K-pop fandom. A total of 100 surveys were conducted in Patronato, Santiago's "Korea Town." I paid special attention in detecting a possible pattern that *K-poperos* were often referred to as *flaites*, a pejorative term to refer to low-class youth, or belonging to the subgroup of *otakus*, a Japanese word that is used to refer to those who followed *manga* and *anime*. While some self-identified middle-class and privileged participants suggested that K-pop fandom was more noticeable among working-class Chileans, K-pop fans from undisclosed social statuses insisted that the fandom traversed all social classes. My conclusions are not definite, and can only consider a small sample ($N=60$) of K-pop fans under the age of 30; yet, the survey confirmed what previous scholars have pointed out about the tendency for K-pop fans to belong to lower and lower-middle working class in Latin America, particularly in Chile. Other papers have explored other spaces were K-pop was more commonly popular among lower-middle-class youth, and hidden by those who would identify as upper middle or privileged youth (Min, 2021). In another survey ($N=40$), focusing on Korean diaspora in Santiago, most Korean Chileans or Chilean residents with Korean ancestry under 40 (Gen X and millennials) (*N*=20) who historically and currently have belonged to and self-identify as middle and upper-middle class due to relative success in small businesses, consistently (90%, *N*=18) suggested that in Chile, K-pop fans belonged to the lower-middle and working class or were *flaites*. One interviewee confidently affirms that "the ghetto [*"la pobla"*] listens to K-pop [. . .] they spend all their money in their music, posters, food, and accessories." The two that suspect that K-pop is also consumed by upper-middle class pointed out that it is exclusively generational and that perhaps, social media democratizes fandom, and according to one interviewee, "K-pop is becoming respectable. At least less ghetto [*"menos flaite"*] than *reggaetón* and *trap*." In contrast, interviews with Korean immigrants over 40 (*N*=20) contradicted the younger generation's perception of class and fandom suggesting that K-pop was beloved by all social classes in Chile (and globally), triumphally equating K-drama, cars, and home appliance success and consumption, and K-pop consumption, almost unanimously suggesting "all young Chileans love K-pop" or that "'Made in Korea,' 'Made in Japan,' 'Made in Germany,' it's all the same. Korea caught up." When asked about political inclinations, most of the diaspora interviewed (*N*=34) suspects that younger generation favors the progressive agenda, and thus, would support a new Chilean constitution. This clear generational divide confirms that correlation and causation of fandom and protest can be studied quantitatively; nevertheless, more data needs to be collected with much larger and diverse samples, in order to categorically claim this social phenomenon. The rise in popularity is increasing so rapidly and transversally that the demographics and perceptions are likely to have shifted, evolved, and diversified, particularly, with the massive success of other Korean cultural products, such as *Parasite* (2019) and *Squid Game* (2021).

BEYOND CHILE: TULSA, TIKTOK, K-POP

K-pop fans impacting the U.S. presidential campaign rally in Tulsa, Oklahoma on June 20, 2020, highlights the likelihood that social media activism is not just theoretical and relegated to digital realm. Allegedly, there was a concerted effort from K-pop fans on TikTok who reserved seats for the rally with no plans to attend, enacting what is called a "cultural jamming" (Bandy and Diakopoulos, 2020). The pandemic amassed a far larger number of high school and college "zoomers" (post-millennials) at home and online for longer hours. Zoomers are tech-savvy, coordinated, and impactful, engaged for longer hours than before the pandemic. Bandy and Diakopoulos suggest in "#TulsaFlop: A Case Study of Algorithmically-Influenced Collective Action on TikTok" that the heightened activism might have been a consequence of the algorithmic nature of the medium. They synthesize other scholars' findings and their own data, and suggest that TikTok's algorithm might have exacerbated the attendance in the rally. Perhaps, the "power of the algorithm" was a better explanation of the impact on that rally than the "power of the people." That is, the relation between fandom and political activism could leave the correlation and causation debate at rest, as the algorithm accelerated and magnified something that was already causing political engagement. In other words, while fans actively intervened, the algorithm heightened and accelerated the effect. K-pop fans (who disliked the then U.S. president) used #EmptySeats to reserve seats and not attend. The reaction to the rumors, however, was not mockery; on the contrary, K-pop fans were recognized as a force that did not just influence music charts and fleeting trends, but perhaps, rally attendance, democratic participation, and election outcomes. In addition, political activists and apolitical social media content creators often used and use K-pop trending hashtags (e.g., #bts #kpop #army #blackpink) to reach the well-established K-pop social media fandom, in order to rapidly spread information, whether their content was political or unrelated, which confirms Bandy and Diakopoulos theories that the reductionist link between the use of hashtags and serious committed political activism is not as simple as news media and big data studies assert.

Blaming "foreign influences" for anti-establishment sentiments is common. Lyndon B. Johnson demanded proof from the CIA that "global communism" was behind the anti-Vietnam war demonstrations in October 1967 near The Pentagon. Recently, after the U.S. January 6 riot, an attorney and several politicians attempted to link the 2020 U.S. elections, as a corrupted process, influenced by Hugo Chávez and other communists. In March 2020, in between impeachments, the then U.S. President Donald Trump affirmed that the fight against COVID-19 was "a war" against "an invisible enemy" (referring to the virus) resembling Piñera's attitude during the Chilean protests. In both cases, "powerful force" in Chile or "invisible enemy" in White House rhetoric, the said enemy was "Asian," renewed forms of "yellow peril" fearmongering. Although the former U.S. president was not referring to other Asian and Asian Americans as responsible for the pandemic, and the Chilean Ministry of the Interior included other actors in the alleged influence, both discourses blamed social unrest to orientalized "forces" connected to Asia: China and South Korea, respectively. Whether the references were toward China or South Korea, a communist or a neoliberal country, the fear that foreign adversaries are attempting to destroy a nation are predictable tactics to reformulate soft power and/or "Oriental" culture as dangerous ideology. Ultimately, protests in Chile and demands against Asian hate are "the right to live in peace." This phrase is uniquely familiar to Chileans, as it refers to arguably the country's most prominent singer songwriter Víctor Jara, whose most famous song "El Derecho de Vivir en Paz" ("The right to live in peace") (1971) was inspired and dedicated to Vietnamese communist leader Ho Chi Minh and the struggle as a nation under war for two decades (1955–1975) to demand the right to live in peace. Perhaps, political ideological influence from Asia is indeed palpable in Chile, but since the 1950s, rather than since *Hallyu* 2.0. Víctor Jara was tortured and murdered five days after the 1973 coup, on September 16. Soldiers and guards smashed his fingers and his body was riddled with more than 40 bullets. Along with "El Baile de los que Sobran" by Los prisioneros, "El Derecho de Vivir en Paz" was the most sung and shared song during the 2019–2020 Chilean marches, though some would argue that big data suggests it could have been Big Bang's "Fantastic Baby" because their music video has some scenes of youth protesting against militarized police.

NOTES

1. See Wonjung Min's bibliography as she is the most important scholar who has studied and published the Chilean case and K-pop fandom. Also see, Choi, J. (2014). Loyalty Transmission and Cultural Enlisting of K-pop in Latin America, in *K-pop: The International Rise of the Korean Music Industry*, edited by Choi, J. and Maliangkay, R.

2. "Patriarchy is our judge That imprisons us at birth / And our punishment Is the violence you DON'T see. Patriarchy is our judge That imprisons us at birth / And our punishment is the violence you CAN see. It's femicide. / Impunity for my killer. / It's our disappearances. / It's rape! / And it's not my fault, not where I was, not how I dressed. And it's not my fault, not where I was, not how I dressed. And it's not my fault, not where I was, not how I dressed. And it's not my fault, not where I was, not how I dressed. And the rapist WAS you / And the rapist IS you / It's the cops, / It's The judges, / It's The system, / It's The president. / This oppressive state is a macho rapist. / This oppressive state is a macho rapist." (Translation from original Spanish from https://womensmarch.com/2020-dance)

BIBLIOGRAPHY

Albornoz, C. (2000). Dele Cotelé: El Baile de los que Sobran. *Boletín Música* 54: 111–12

Ayala, L. (2019). El Big Data del Gobierno: Los Detalles del Informe por El Estallido Social que Entregó a La Fiscalía. *La Tercera,* December 21, https://www.latercera.com/la-tercera-domingo/noticia/big-data-del-gobierno-los-detalles-del-informe-estallido-social-entrego-la-fiscalia/947967/

Bandy, J., and Diakopoulos, N. (2020). #TulsaFlop: A Case Study of Algorithmically Influenced Collective Action on TikTok. In 3rd FAccTRec Workshop: Responsible Recommendation (at RecSys 2020). https://www.jackbandy.com/publications/

Borges de Castilho, V. (2015). South Korean Pop Style: The Main Aspects of Manifestation of Hallyu in South America. *Romanian Journal of Sociological Studies* 2: 149–176.

Bruner, R. (2020). How K-pop Fans Actually Work as a Force for Political activism in 2020. *Time*, July 25, https://time.com/5866955/K-pop-political/

Choi, J. (2014). Loyalty Transmission and Cultural Enlisting of K-pop in Latin America. In *K-pop: The International Rise of the Korean Music Industry*, edited by Choi, J. and Maliangkay, R., 98–115. New York: Routledge.

Diaz Pino, C. (2019). Weaponizing Collective Energy: Dragon Ball Z in the Anti-neolibera. l Chilean Protest Movement. *Popular Communication* 17 (3): 202–218.

Fluxá, Rodrigo. (2014). *Solos en la noche: Zamudio y sus asesinos*. Santiago: Catalonia.

González Ríos, J. (Los Prisioneros). (1986). El Baile de los que Sobran. *Pateando Piedras*. EMI Records Ltd.

Guzzoni, F. (Director). (2016). *Jesús*. Santiago: Burning Blue, Graal Films.

Hall, K., Borba, R., and Hiramoto, M. (2021). Relocating Power: The Feminist Potency of Language, Gender and Sexuality Research. *Gender and Language* 15 (1): 1–10.

Han, B. (2017). K-pop in Latin America: Transcultural Fandom and Digital Mediation. *International Journal of Communication* 11: 2250–2269.

Hong, J. (2020). BTS on the Decision to Donate to Black Lives Matter: Prejudice Should not be Tolerated. *Variety*, October 2, https://variety.com/2020/music/news/bts-black-lives-matter-donation-1234789434/

Jiménez-Yañez, C. (2020). #Chiledespertó: Causas del Estallido Social en Chile. *Revista Mexicana de Sociología* 82 (4): 949–957.

Johnson, L. (2020). K-pop Band f Explains Why They Decided to Give $1 Million to Black Lives Matter. *CNN*, October 3, https://www.cnn.com/2020/10/03/entertainment/bts-trnd/index.html

Jung, S. (2010). *Korean Masculinities and Transcultural Consumption: Yonsama, Rain, Oldboy, K-pop Idols*. Hong Kong: Hong Kong University Press.

Kim, J. (2018). How BTS are Breaking K-pop's Biggest Taboos: The Chart-topping Korean Group Has Spoken Out on LGBTQ Rights, Mental Health and More. *Rolling Stone*, May 29, https://www.rollingstone.com/music/music-news/how-bts-are-breaking-K-pops-biggest-taboos-628141/

Kim, J. (2021). BTS as Method: A Counter-hegemonic Culture in the Network Society. *Media, Culture and Society* 43 (6): 1061–1077.

Ko, M. (2019). Chile's Protests Caused by K-pop? Mockeries of Government. *YonHap*, December 24, https://www.yna.co.kr/view/AKR20191224002500087

Kwak, Y. (2019). 89,000,000 'Hallyu' Fans Worldwide. *Korea Times*, January, https://www.koreatimes.co.kr/www/art/2019/01/732_261877.html

Kwon, Jungmin. (2019). *Straight Korean Female Fans and Their Gay Fantasies*. Iowa City: University of Iowa Press.

Las Tesis. (2019). Un violador en tu camino. ("A Rapist in Your Path"). https://womensmarch.com/2020-dance

Liu, Marian. (2020). When Race, Fandom and Pop-music Dollars Collide. *Washington Post*, September 23, https://www.washingtonpost.com/business/2020/09/23/blm-kpop-bts-blackpink/

Lorenz, T., Frenkel, S., and Browning, K. (2020). "These Kids are Smart, They Thought of Everything": TikTok Users Claim Some Responsibility for Low Turnout to Trump's Tulsa Rally. *Independent*, June 21, https://www.independent.co.uk/news/world/americas/tulsa-rally-trump-us-tiktok-K-pop-ticket-sales-a9577741.html

Min, W. (2017). Korean Wave Reception and the Participatory Fan Culture in Latin America: What Lies Beyond the Media Reports. In *The Korean Wave*, edited by Yoon, T. and Jin, D. Lanham, MD: Lexington Books.

Min, W. (2020). Mis Chinos, Tus Chinos: The Orientalism of Chilean K-pop Fans. *International Communication Gazette* 83 (8): 799–817.

Min, W. (2021). The Perfect Man: The Ideal Imaginary Beauty of K-pop Idols for Chilean Fans. *The Journal of Korean Studies* 34 (1): 159–194.

Min, W., Jin, D., and Han, B. (2019). Transcultural Fandom of the Korean Wave in Latin America: Through the Lens of Cultural Intimacy and Affinity Space. *Media, Culture & Society* 41 (5): 604–619.

Morales, I. (2013). Daniel Zamudio: Hacia la Construcción de una Noción de Ciudadanía Pluralista Radical. *ISEES: Inclusión Social y Equidad en la Educación Superior* 12: 143–160.

Oh, Chuyun. (2015). Queering spectatorship in K-pop: The androgynous male dancing body and western female fandom. *The Journal of Fandom Studies* 3 (1): 59–78.

Oh, W. (2019). Chilean Government: 'K-pop Fans Instigate Protests Report Controversy: Mockery and Criticism'. *JoonAng IlBo*, December 14, https://news.joins.com/article/23664478

Olave de la Barrera, M. (2012). Viaje al Centro del K-pop Chileno. *Paniko*, October, https://paniko.cl/viaje-al-centro-del-K-pop-chileno/

Park, K. H. (2016). Kyoung Update: Chile. February, https://www.kyounghpark.com/2016/02/kyoung-update-chile/

Park, M. (2019). Gracias a la Vida: Violeta Went to Heaven and Came Back Wearing a K-pop Miniskirt. *Studies in Latin American Popular Culture* 37 (1): 25–50.

Pérez, J. (2017). Virtual Hagiography and Sexual Rights: The Case of Daniel Zamudio. In *Diversidad Sexual y Sistemas Religiosos: Diálogos Transnacionales en el Mundo Contemporáneo*. Lima, Perú: CMP Flora Tristán/UNMSM.

Sheng, P. (2016). *Charapo*. Santiago: Cuneta.

Steidl, J. (2016). Politicized Devotion to a Popular Saint: Daniel Zamudio and LGBT Rights in Chile. *Spiritu* 16 (2): 189–214.

Vivero, L., Molina, W., and Huenulao, M. (2020). Acceso Inclusivo a la Educación Superior en Chile: Un Análisis desde el Capital Social de Estudiantes Vulnerables. *Intercambios. Dilemas y Transiciones de la Educación Superior* 7 (1): 30–42.

Wells, G. and Li, S. (2020). How TikTok Users Targeted Trump Rally. *The Wall Street Journal*, June 21, https://www.wsj.com/articles/how-tiktok-users-targeted-trump-rally-11592795368

Zamudio: Perdidos en la noche. (2015). Directed by Sabatini, J., and Sallato, J. P. Aired March 29, 2015, on Televisión Nacional de Chile.

Chapter 9

Queering the Wave

Drag Queens and Drag Kings in the K-pop Industry

Tiago Canário

The series of transformations South Korean cultural industries have gone through since the 1990s turned K-pop music into a transnational and powerful phenomenon, which now shapes tastes, sets trends, and influences audiences across the world. In a postindustrial context of fluid capital mobility, this particular industry became a massive phenomenon composed of multinational enterprises and a platform for multiple (and often conflicting) voices coming from society and its radical changes. Particularly considering how the country's youth has grown active in questioning and reshaping dominant discourses on popular imaginaries, gender, and sexuality became the main issue on some groups' agendas. From the foundation of queer organizations in the 1990s, sexual minorities have grown to fight for their own desires, concerns, and visibility. Despite centuries of Confucian hierarchy and more recent Christian fundamentalism since the early twentieth century, South Korea's strict and heteronormative gender binary has been publicly challenged—producing new discourses that slowly pervade society on different levels.

Drag cultures have been part of those transformations. An element of the country's underground queer scene for decades, they recently made their way into the mainstream. From the previous dark and hidden nightclubs, this gender-questioning artistry was brought to fashion magazines, social media, museum exhibitions, festivals, and music videos. Step by step, drag artists are slowly becoming part of Korean postindustrial capitalism. They are still underrepresented, but they are making themselves present, and the number of artists keeps growing. This chapter focuses on the dialogue between *Hallyu* and gender and sexuality studies to investigate how the mainstream connects with, gets influenced by, and transforms drag (and queer) cultures in South

Korea. Looking at the representation of deviant gender expressions in contemporary Korean music videos, the thriving relationship between the mainstream idol industry and drag culture helps to explain how non-normative gender expressions have been portrayed by K-pop music videos in the last decade.

The current dialogue between drag cultures and the mainstream idol industry creates a narrative that gives priority to some voices over others, directly affecting marginal cultures. This chapter argues that the confluence of queer culture and the Korean wave might have a similar effect, building a standardized narrative of Korean queer culture and its agents. Although, even if built as a strategy to please audiences and expand some groups' popularity, drag art brought to the mainstream might bring attention to marginalized individuals, increasing their recognition.

PERFORMING GENDER IN K-POP, QUEERING THE IDOL SYSTEM

South Korea is a society in which heteronormativity and patriarchy have strongly shaped discourses on gender, particularly the 20th-century developmental state and its "patrilineal community with hyper masculine men and hyperfeminized women" (Cho, 2020). Since the abrupt end of Japanese colonialism and division of the peninsula, the country went through consecutive disruptions, with instabilities with regard to governance, economy, and culture, turning gender into a discursive domain. Gendered expectations and roles became a medium for the reinforcement of the tradition; of what was thought of as appropriate against aspirations of independence and individualism (Nelson and Cho, 2016).

During the country's compressed project of modernization from the 1970s to the early 1990s, individuals were urged to subscribe to the heteronormative patriarchy and sacrifice for the collective, abiding to the model of a heterosexual nuclear family that could regulate the population and increase the economy through a gender-based labor system. In result, only a few hidden physical spaces allowed dissident individuals to reveal themselves to others and have non-normative experiences, as coming out to their families or society, in general, was not seen as an option. During the 1960s, 1970s, and 1980s encounters happened mostly in bars and small theaters (Kang, 2020), with a prevalent crowd of married middle- and upper-middle-class individuals (Cho, 2020), whose queer experiences were often directed toward sexual intercourses.

It was only after the end of the almost three decades of a military dictatorship that the atmosphere of free censorship and patriarchal authoritarianism made it possible for previously silenced groups to establish their communities and organize themselves, redefining their relationship and value system (Bong, 2009; Cho, 2020). The democratic movements had a fundamental influence on the formation of non-normative communities, which allowed individuals to explore different cultures and lifestyles. But as the general society was rapidly changing at that moment, other fields were also affected, such as mainstream popular cultures and the country's idol system in particular.

Embraced by the government and society, the K-pop idol industry is expected to provide transnational experiences that engage audiences from different cultures, increasing economic growth and symbolizing the national power (Cho and Stark, 2017; Fuhr, 2017). Artists have their whole aura meticulously designed for that. Through strict control over their bodies, clinical assistance, and fashion/makeup/hair management, the image-production system creates perfect visuals and behaviors that can translate into a profitable experience and forge close ties with fandoms. Also, to assure them some chances at a "multi-layered lottery where there are few winners" (Cho and Stark, 2017), gender performances have become an important part of it.

To resonate with global discourses and appeal to other cultures, agencies manage idols to play specific personality types and portray distinctive visuals,[1] designing their images individually and (often) as part of a group. Among the usual portrayal of male-identified idols in South Korean popular media, for instance, scholars have observed how the traditional notions of Korean masculinity that marked the first-generation boy groups and idols engage with audiences through a masculinity conceptualized as a "manufactured versatile masculinity" (Jung, 2011), "liminal masculinity" (Oh, 2015), or "overlapping masculinity" (Anderson, 2014).

The images projected by male idols have evolved to present a mix of the Western standardized muscular and well-toned bodies with Confucian ideals of *seonbi* masculinity (Jung, 2010), which represents intellectually and culturally nuanced men, who are self-restraining, and obedient to authority. These visuals range from a soft-colored fashion and cuteness that overemphasize their youthful innocence to hip-hop aesthetics, with muscular shirtless bodies and ripped jeans. Performances of femininity, on the other hand, have been crafted in the first-generation female idols and groups to mostly engage heterosexual men's sexual fantasies (Oh, 2014) through lovely yet sexually enticing images. Those girls are expected to build thin and slender bodies, with doll-like faces, v-shaped chins, and big eyes. Behavior-wise, they heavily played with *aegyo* (Fuhr, 2017), an act of exaggerated charming/childish poses and expressions thought to arouse desire.

Gender and beauty ideals have been in constant transformation, but these main norms and expectations have been orienting the industry for over two decades, as those who are able to prosper in such a highly competitive market inevitably set a path of triumph that others would carefully follow. However, in a market where new artists are constantly debuting and only a few prosper, diversity became almost compulsory to reach new audiences, those with different tastes and preferences in particular (Oh, 2018). Carefully expanding the borders of K-pop gender norms, some have tried (and succeeded) in offering alternative expressions, creating some "space liminality that allow[s] for the transgression of social boundaries of gender and sexuality" (Oleszczuk and Waszkiewicz, 2020)—and their success also opened new (smaller) paths for others to follow.

Some of the widely noticeable deviations in gender expressions in the idol system came through performers such as Amber, G-Dragon, Ren, and Lee Hong-gi (Laforgia and Howard, 2017; Laurie, 2016; Oh, 2018). Yet not publicly identifying themselves as queer individuals, their particular gender-blurring visuals often stretched industries' hegemonic norms. Amber became known for her short hairstyle and sporty, tomboy looks; G-Dragon for androgynous and fashion-forward outfits, followed by an always-changing hairstyle; Ren for modeling in skirts and having long hair; and Lee Hong-gi for his open passion for nail art. Even in some subtle ways, they were changing the strict gender stereotypes carefully created by the industry.

As most of the idols who debut in groups are put together in a combination of members according to the agency's decisions, creating a strong and appealing collective is key to surviving in South Korean market. The more diverse a group is, the bigger the chance to sell a multifaceted dream that can maximize its consumption potential. In this way, dissident styles are permitted and promoted as they become alternative business possibilities—and a multimedia introduction of their personality has been particularly important for that. Built through a curious interplay between the iconic status of their visuals and the intimacy created with their audiences, idols are "produced and marketed as attractive people" (Oh, 2018). To do so, their daily lives are heavily publicized through reality shows, social media accounts, fan meetings, and transmedia circulation. Amber, for example, had her initially controversial image extensively promoted on TV reality variety shows during the early 2010s (Laforgia and Howard, 2017).

At the same time, the investment in gender-bending images grew influenced by the popularity of foreign artists, like Lady Gaga, whose rise in the early 2010s brought club-kid culture and avant-garde fashion—together with drag references[2]—to the center of mainstream culture, reshaping the aesthetics of the pop music industry worldwide (Daw, 2020). By referring to artists like her, domestic agencies could provide audiences with trendy flavors and place their artists as part of global narratives. For instance, in 2012, when Lady Gaga had the second biggest audience[3] for a foreign artist in South Korea, and one year after being placed as the most streamed and downloaded foreign artist with the release of Born This Way (Korea Music Content Association, 2011), Jo Kwon performed "Animal" at MBC's Show! Music Core and at SBS's Inkigayo. Dressed in tight outfits, with leather, chains, feathers, 19.5cm high heels, accessories, and strong and dark makeup, the singer built a gender-bending image that directly confronted the gender expectations put on male idols. Local media automatically described Jo Kwon as "the Korean Lady Gaga" (Hankyung News Team, 2012).

Jo Kwon and dancers' iconic visuals were influenced by other queer experiences also through dance, as the performance was built on sharp moves coming from vogue, waacking, and heels dance, adding new layers of non-binary gender representations. After that, with the public attention given to the act and Jo Know's alternative performance of masculinity, the aesthetic was also seen in other boy groups like N.O.M (Nature of Man). In their 2013 debut single "The Beginning," the three performers of N.O.M were shirtless and wore black leather harnesses, metal accessories, skinny pants, hats, and gloves in a sexy and provocative concept. They danced to waacking and heels dance moves, wearing heavy eyeliner and high heels. Interestingly named N.O.M as an acronym of Nature of Man, the group debuted under Danal Entertainment with a short press release that introduced the trio as "The 3rd Sexuality: Beyond" (Danal Entertainment, 2013). Although, the members have not yet publicly discussed their sexuality, rather reinforcing their gender identity as men who create a new performance of masculinity based on heels to add an "extra charm" and "sex appeal" to masculinities[4] in the K-pop industry (Lee, 2020).

Together with gender-bending performances by idols such as Amber, Miya (Gwsn), G-Dragon, and Jo Kwon, N.O.M slowly stretched the boundaries of the gender binary in the Korean music industry. And those become not only "tolerated" but sometimes particularly desired, as in the case of Global Icon. Inspired by the popularity of the tomboy idol style, transformations in women's fashions and fashion trends in TV dramas (Kwon and Lee, 2014), Simtong Entertainment announced their new groups as: "We're going to be different from the cute and sexy girl groups that come out almost once every week with our music and style. You can look forward to them" (Allkpop, 2013).

Global Icon (also known as GI) debuted in April 2013 as a tomboy group, with all five girls in a typical tomboy aesthetics, performing an alternative femininity already legitimized. Their debut song, "Beatles," included lines such as "I'm different so I won't do anything fake" and "Take out everything that you've been hiding / In your heart," as if they were both reasserting their truth and encouraging (queer) fans to do the same. However, after a turbulent beginning and personal issues that lead to a few members' replacements, the group went on a hiatus and returned two years later with a conventional feminine and sexy concept that re-branded the group. The case is particularly relevant for exemplifying how expressions of dissidence have entered the mainstream as marketing strategies more than political activism. After all, if a group's *design concept* (the unique qualities that sell a group against competition) does not resonated well with audiences, it should be either refreshed or recreated from scratches to assure the group's wide popular appeal (Oh, 2018).

Regardless of each group's acceptance and profitability, the existence of dissidences does seem to affect the limits of hegemonic masculinity and femininity in Korean society. These mediatized experimentations, coupled with general sociocultural transformations, made room for other queer gender expressions to also grow and try their way into the industry. And once idols had already proven the viable success of gender-bending practices among national and foreign audiences, the gender subversion of drag performances also made its way into the mainstream.

QUEER COMMUNITIES ENTER THE STARDOM

As discussed in the previous section, some idols have been extending the boundaries of femininity and masculinity from inside the music industry, but this section starts to look at those who publicly create a gender performance that radically opposes the expectations put on their bodies. And many have not been accepted. Differently than non-queer-identifying idols who project a gender-bending or even queer-inspired visual without publicly addressing their gender identity or sexuality, those who are open about it are still likely to be seen as threats, as deviant gender performances are better accepted than deviant gender identities and sexualities. Lady and Hong Seok-cheon are clear examples of how strongly society can refuse those.

Lady was a four-member K-pop girl group composed only of transgender women. Created in 2005 by Logi Entertainment, who selected the trainees from a pool of 400 applicants (Arirang News, 2005), the group had fully female-presenting image, subscribing to the same beauty standards female idols are oppressed by, but lasted for less than two years.[5] Hong Seok-cheon became known as the first gay-identifying male celebrity in the country. After coming out during an interview in 2000, the actor, comedian, and reporter for TV variety shows saw all requests for on-camera appearances vanished (Cho, 2009), in a strong backlash that banned him on children's TV shows and advertisements.

Both cases refer to the early 2000s, a period when a generalized fear about the collapse of the nation followed the IMF economic crisis (Shin, 2020), making society condemn queer experiences that could not fit the model of the normative, heterosexual nuclear family. Together with the lack of legal protection, and the cultural and economic meaning of a family-based culture, non-conformity became a possible threat[6] (Bong, 2009; Outright Action International, 2003). That reflected even on queer individuals who had to retreat from their communities to focus on developing their careers, as a way to increase their chances of survival.[7] In that context, only a very few were able to succeed, like Harisu, South Korea's first transgender idol.[8] She was able to enter a transnational and transmedia stardom (Ahn, 2009), but queer-identifying entertainers are uncommon in the country's mediascape.

In a heteronormative and patriarchal society that expects idols to be admired as "sparkling symbols of economic wealth and national pride" (Fuhr, 2017), how can queer individuals be worthy of it? To increase economic potentials and connect with worldwide trends, queer cultures are often absorbed into the mainstream, but without being necessarily accepted. And even following others' steps is not a guarantee, as Lady did, inspired by Harisu. In the groups' farewell statement, they directly addressed their termination due to the prejudice they experienced during the span of their activities, which included transphobic and depreciative comments from the audiences, even during live performances.

As a highly competitive industry in which only a few create a profitable and long-lasting career, those who cannot sustain their profitability and/or publicly support are dismissed, while being also exposed to violence and prejudice. In consequence, cis-hetero-identifying artists (or those who avoid coming out in terms of gender identity and sexuality) have been creating a far more acceptable dialogue with queer-aesthetics, as discussed in the previous section. Drag art entered the Korean mainstream media like that, as an unthreatening and mocking theatrical act, mostly through male-identifying idols who became peculiarly recognized for occasional performances of (K-pop) femininity, avoiding any commentary on sexuality.

Drag art is here understood as a temporary performance of gender, a provocative and confrontational act that builds on cross-gender attire and mannerisms to play with gender concepts (Miller, 2016) and subvert expectations, often for entertaining reasons. This type of performance ranges from representing hypermasculinity to hyperfemininity, and everything in between. Each artist freely adds or subtracts elements that are culturally associated to the hegemonic notions of femininity or masculinity when creating their character (Rupp et al., 2010). Performances can greatly vary on creating effects closer to parody, impersonation, or social criticism (Halberstam, 1998), which can result in undermining or reinforcing gender stereotypes, as the following cases reveal.

During main stage concerts or music competition TV shows between the late-2000s and mid-2010s, groups such as Super Junior, TVXQ!, B1A4,

BtoB, 2AM, Vixx, and NU'EST often appeared in drag queen acts. In those, they dressed up to perform famous songs by female idols and groups, based on exaggerated fictional role-playing. As satirical theatrical numbers, male idols frequently performed as innocent and sexually enticing girls to amuse their audiences, heavily referring to the stereotypes that marked the first-generation girl groups. Chuyun Oh and David C. Oh (2017) describe[9] the Wonder Girls' song "So Hot" performed by the boy group VIXX at SBS's Chuseok Star Face Off:

> Some members of the group wear skinny leopard-print leggings with tight black tops, and others have on miniskirts with sheer black stockings and showy costume jewelry, including necklaces and bracelets. They wear women's wigs and high heels [. . .] The camera zooms onto female fans and then a female judge who erupts in laughter and claps loudly with excitement. [. . .] The performers sing in a high pitch falsetto, while dancing together in a chorus girl formation. They stand in a line and put one hand on the shoulder of the person in front and sway their hips. While swinging their hips, they close their eyes slightly and open their mouths as they seductively stare at the amused audience.

As in drag, they cosplayed female idols to entertain their audiences, yet avoided any confrontational act or radical political claim. They performed an intentionally failed version of normative K-pop femininity. Through careless fashion and mannerisms, their acts stood in contrast to their perfectly tailored performances of masculinity, which the audiences understood as their "true" identity; that discrepancy on the efforts put into both could then avoid a queering effect over their public image. Audiences could see those drag acts as temporary, makeshift, and lighthearted performances that existed as an almost improvisational joke that, by lacking power, had no strong chance to subvert idols' public image. In an "alienation effect" (Oh and Oh, 2017), audiences were constantly remembered of the differences between the "real" idol and the role being played. However, more confrontational acts found their way into the mainstream from the 2010s, mainly through the drag art that grew connected with marginal queer entertainment businesses.

THE RISE OF QUEENS: DRAG FEMININITY IN THE K-POP INDUSTRY

The first queer-affirming drag performances in Korean music videos, which oppose to the previously discussed comic drag cosplay conducted by male idols, were short and part of independent small projects, meaning not all are easily found or well known. Also, as drag performances can be more or less produced, follow different trends, and appeal to gender stereotypes in multiples ways, those are hard to fully map and investigate. Therefore, although understanding that there are more videos to be found and added to the list, this section builds on a set of music videos[10] that were identified as picturing conventional ideas of drag art. From the early 2010s, these music videos have established a new approach. Starting with Park Jung-min's solo debut "Not Alone" (2011), drag art comes as visual support to a song about tolerance and inclusion. When released, the lyrics ("So I can believe that I'm not alone / Not alone now, I'm able to return again / I can feel it, I'm not alone / Definitely not alone, never be exhausted again") particularly resonated among minorities, but the video added new layers to that.

Starting with a dark and shadowy atmosphere, the video introduces one by one a series of outcasts who wander lost until they find each other. These soon-to-be "not alone" anymore are a punk-like guitarist, a disabled man, a young student, and a drag queen, among others. As each of them need to surpass their limitations until they can get together and celebrate, the drag queen is depicted as in need to break free of the limitations of her "closet," as she gains the courage to perform beyond the limits of her room, where she only had a mirror as an audience. No more as a purposely failed parody of femininity, Park Jung-min's video set a new approach to drag art and drag performers that is rather related to acceptance and inclusion.

A similar discourse can be found in two music videos released in 2013 by Girls' Generation and Lee Hyo-ri. First, the cheerful song "Love & Girls," part of Girls' Generation's third Japanese studio album, became a music video composed of very colorful and summer-like Carnival scenes, with people happily dancing in the streets. The crowd is composed of only female-presenting individuals, including a few drag queens. They dance and cheer together, wearing similar outfits in bright colors, with the *queens* portrayed as part of it. Accepted by and blending with the crowd, their presence stands as equally valid performance of femininity. They exist in this bright and outdoor scenery of "love and girls" as much as the others.

Under that more accepting approach, and also resembling Park Jung-min's social discourse in "Not Alone," Lee Hyo-ri's "Miss Korea" brings out the oppression of beauty standards put on women who are all expected to be as perfect as Miss Korea, a symbol of the country's femininity. In the video, Lee Hyo-ri is a diva going through different beauty pageants, but accompanied by Korean drag queens who are her backup dancers and backup singers. Placed side by side with Lee Hyo-ri, the queens are not othered. As said in the video description on YouTube, "The song conveys a positive message to women, especially Korean, in the current generation that everything is alright and each of us is MISS KOREA" (Stone Music Entertainment, 2013). In that way, the drag artists are shown side by side with the idol, all of them embodying the pageant figure. In a shared visual identity, Lee Hyo-ri and the drag queens all wear big wigs, sparkling dresses, jewelry, and strong makeups, referring to the old pinup-diva beauty.

These three music videos offered a drag performance of femininity that went beyond the caricature offered by male idols cosplaying female idols. They are not limiting the success of their gender performance to reinforce how deviations should naturally fail; they are not shy on stage to represent their lack of interest and preparation; and they are not being introduced as a surprise element intended to amuse, shock, or disgust others.[11] On the opposite, those new images are commendable experiences. They still refer to a normalized gender binary, following codes of expected femininity, but they are confident about it. They are not an entertaining tool for male-identifying idols to joke about female stereotypes while reinforcing their masculinity, but a convincing transformation of non-AFAB individuals who are there to co-exist with idols and turn their bodies into a medium.

Also, South Korea's mediascape was equally transformed by a stronger exposition to Western musicals and TV shows that relied on non-normative gender performances. That might also explain how traditional diva-like images of drag queen have grown in the country's mainstream media, including movies, TV dramas, and social media although, domestic productions of international musicals seem to have been particularly influential. The first success was *Hedwig* (2005), which became an instant and still ongoing fever, with new seasons produced every year since then. *Priscilla, Queen of the Desert* (2014), *Kinky Boots* (2014, 2016, 2018), and *Everybody's Talking About Jamie* (2020) have also been produced in the country.

Telling the story of a gender-queer punk-rock singer, *Hedwig* had the highest audience share in the history of small and medium-sized theater performances in Korea in 2015 (Choi, 2015). After 10 years of a cumulative audience, the South Korean production was the one with the highest numbers of performances and audiences in the world (Guri City Hall Press Release, 2015). Also showing a similar success, *Kinky Boots* had around 300,000 cumulative audiences throughout its three runs (Jo, 2020)—and was the number one most watched theater play for 20 consecutive weeks in 2016. The appeal of these domestic productions of Broadway spectacles seems to have grown also out of the fascination audiences have with watching their favorite idols fully dressed as drag queens.

To attract wider audiences, all musicals starred famous actors or K-pop artists in leading roles, including Astro's MJ (*Everybody's Talking About Jamie*), Jo Kwon (*Priscilla, Queen of the Desert* and *Everybody's Talking About Jamie*), Infinite's Sunggyu (*Kinky Boots*), and H.O.T's Kangta (*Hedwig*). As result, the art of drag was under double pressure, as they had to match both the quality of high-grossing Broadway original productions and the quality of idols' agencies and their international careers. Performers were painted with professional makeup, had neatly designed wigs and high-quality outfits, and projected themselves through perfectly trained and put-together moves. They built an image as flawless as their K-pop stage personas, and that might have been translated into an idea of mainstream drag queens as idol-like artists built for media appearances.

Reshaped by cultural industries, the image got detached from marginal queer spaces and influenced the social perception of who were those worthy of attention. The art form grew its appeal by avoiding references to underground aesthetics and pleasing the desires of cis-gendered straight audiences, as corporate-sponsored drag (Muñoz, 1999). They create a palatable image that resonates with normative categories of sex and gender, avoiding allusions to sexuality deemed as promiscuous or gender expressions that look excessively androgynous and "unstable." They try not to produce a disruptive noise, but an accessible referent. And that seems to have become a strong influence on the contemporary depiction of drag artists in K-pop music videos. If the early and mid-2010s music videos portrayed female-looking drag queens that subscribed to a gender binary model, the late-2010s works pushed those boundaries further.

DRAGS AS IDOLS

Following the music video "Love & Girls" (2013), Girls' Generation's released another production with drag queens four years later. But in "All Night" (2017) the drag queens are partying *together with* Girls' Generation members, as close friends. They are not lost in the crowd. Even in a few short scenes, the girl group members and the three drag queens are shown happily enjoying the moment—and most likely as a real celebration, as the music video was the first single of Girls' Generation 10th anniversary album. In this celebratory moment and while sharing scenes with one of the prominent K-pop groups in the country's history, the drag queens have long, weaved, and blond hair, skinny bodies, and a young-looking appearance. Their makeup is professionally done and their outfits follow a dress code similar to the one the idols were following.

This association between drag queens and idols in terms of both shared spaces and shared beauty standards can be found in Brown Eyed Girls' "Wonder Woman" (2019) and MAMAMOO's "Hip" (2019) music videos, which operate similarly to Girls' Generation "All Night" but with more screen time to drag queens. Different from the 2017 music video, these two 2019 productions gave a bigger platform to drag queens, revealing a growing trust in their appeal and confidence in their performances. Both music videos include *queens* who are portrayed as young, sexy, and attractive performers, with a strong and confident attitude. They often have close-up shots of their faces, runway-like moments, and choreographies, besides some additional roles. In MAMAMOO's "Hip," they are the musicians playing instruments for the idols to sing along, as a powerful and edgy girl band, while in Brown Eyed Girls' "Wonder Woman" they are the brides for the Brown Eyed Girls' members, who dress in suits that resemble grooms' outfits.

Brown Eyed Girls' "Wonder Woman" is to date (2021) the music video in which drag queens appear the most, sharing the screen with the K-pop group throughout the whole video. The drag queens have scenes dancing, acting, partying, pole dancing, and interacting with idols, among others. The idols portray a more masculine image, with short or tight hairstyles, dressed in dark-colored suits with walking canes, as opposed to the normative female idols' images, while all other individuals in the music video are wearing white dresses, most of them similar to wedding ones. They also wear white headpieces and wedding veils, together with strong makeup, jewelry, and high heels. The majority of these brides are AMAB individuals with short black hair, who create an androgynous image, but there are also drag queens who resemble the fully feminine-like transformation, including soft gestures and long wigs in soft colors. They are also often placed close to the idols, as a link in between Brown Eyed Girls' "masculinized" image and the other AMAB individuals' "feminized" images.

These more contemporary images of drag queen directly relate to k-pop *ssen-unni* (Lee and Yi, 2020), or *strong sister*, image. The *ssen-unni* figure has grown in resistance to gender hierarchies and patriarchal structures, and opposing to the first female idol images as naive, cute, and submissive girls ready to please the older men (*oppa*) part of their audiences. The image of "the *ssen-unni* replaces the position of the oppa [as a subject of desire], and in so doing, she becomes the object of admiration as the epitome of female strength and stability for younger sisters" (Lee and Yi, 2020). Building on Laura Mulvey and the concept of a gendered gaze, Jieun Lee and Hyangsoon Yi (2020, 23) propose that those female figures operate to subvert power dynamics in gender.

On the one hand, it distances the male gaze by performing outside of the cherished patriarchal feminine norms. On the other, it highlights a sexualized connotation to re-invite the male gaze. This duality generates a schizophrenic view on what it means to be an independent, strong, and empowered woman. The complexity of gaze hijacking unveils ssen-unni's inherent contradiction that the image of the strong sister embodies women artists' fear of losing male fans while simultaneously attracting female fans to the message of women's empowerment.

As rebellious figures, they project themselves as fearless, independent, and unapologetic women. Following a way paved by artists such as BoA, Lee Hyo-ri, CL, and Jessi, BLACKPINK is identified by Jieun Lee and Hyangsoon Yi (2020) as the embodiment of the *ssen-unni* figure. The emergence of this "masculinized" type of femininity reveals how the idol system can simultaneously embrace opposing discourses once they resonate among audiences. This way, they assume a personality with traits socially seen as masculine, yet conserving a sexualized image socially seen as feminine. This sexualized yet empowered femininity performed by some idols was one of the main references for Korean drag queens in K-pop music videos. They are no longer the joke, but personalities with agency. Just like the female-identifying idols, they place themselves in a position of powerful admiration. But foreign influences also came into play.

Together with the changing concepts of female idols' femininity, media appearances of drag queens seem to be also related to the global success of *Rupaul's Drag Race* TV show. The show has not been officially released on Korean TV channels, being only available on Netflix Korea, but when Kim Chi (the first-ever Korean contestant on the show) was featured for the first time in Seoul in 2016, the appearance was reported by new and traditional media, particularly by those related to fashion and young culture. Following this, other events were produced with former *Rupaul's Drag Race* contestants,[12] attracting new audiences and attention from mainstream media. Building on this expanding popularity of drag art, the first Seoul Drag Parade was held on May 26, 2018, when around 1,000 performers and supporters marched the streets of Itaewon, accompanied by journalists, photographers, and videographers (Park, 2018). With events like these, which attracted hundreds of participants and received intense media coverage (unlike the underground and hidden drag events that were being organized before), drag art gained more recognition and reached newer audiences.

Since then, articles on drag culture have been published on *Vogue Korea*, *Elle Korea*, Yonhap News, *JoongAng Ilbo*, *Busan Ilbo*, MBC, *Hankyoreh*, and *Vice Korea*, among other, besides artists' appearances on TV shows and social media channels. Also, as former-*Rupaul's Drag Race* contestants were brought to perform in Korea, events guest-starred local performers, who gained visibility and publicity. That allowed local drag queens to invest in their performing career and create well-articulated LGBTQ+ collectives like Neon Milk, which have been present in most of the contemporary music videos with drag artists.[13] In this way, drag performances of femininity grew in South Korean mediascape through the transformations of queer communities, the popularization of musicals, the presence of foreign performers, and the professionalization of local performers and communities. But no other type of drag artistry has gained as much attention as drag queens have.

BEYOND FEMININITY: WHAT THE INDUSTRY
HASN'T BEEN TALKING ABOUT

Different from the drag performances of femininity in K-pop, which seems to be the only type of drag art getting attention in the expansion of drag art in the Korean mediascape, masculinities portrayed through drag king performances are hardly found. While drag queens increase their presence in contemporary music videos, drag king art can be only found in very occasional performances, which are all limited to acts performed by female-identifying idols, as Brown Eyed Girls members did in "Wonder Woman" (2019). But before Brown Eyed Girls' video, Lee Hyo-ri and MAMAMOO had already been in dialogue with drag king art.

One month after releasing "Miss Korea" (2013), Lee Hyo-ri was again referring to *king* aesthetics in the music video "Going Crazy." While singing about bad love experiences and the frustration related to them, Lee Hyo-ri stars in the video dressing and acting like a stereotypical womanizer playboy. Dressed in a suit, with short hair, beard, and a mustache, Lee Hyo-ri's character flirts with dozens of pinup women in a Broadway-inspired setting. Acting as a misbehaved playboy, the character seduces all women around him, as an archetypical Don Juan. If drag queens were previously portraying beauty pageant contests, *kings* are here present to portray a typical womanizer bon vivant. They perform genders that oppose society's alignment of biological sex, sexuality, and gender, but still conforming to expectations on gender roles, presenting (to the heteronormative gaze) a comforting, acceptable, and identifiable idea of masculinity. And similar to Super Junior, B1A4, or Vixx cosplaying girl groups in drag queen acts, these drag king moments are not intended to promote a queer reading of idols' public image. They rather exist as a parody.

Audiences are asked to read that masculinity as a temporary and funny extra layer placed over the idol's well-known femininity. Instead of nurturing a queer imaginary or an alternative to the Korean normative binary, those roles can be read as a way for female idols to conquer masculine spaces and act in a more dominant way, which could directly refer to the transformations in idol's femininity through the *ssen-unni* figure. They are comic, theatrical moments organized to be seen as a joke. Unsurprisingly, Lee Hyo-ri appears at the end of the music video in her public feminine image, as a reminder of her "fixed" gender identity. As a brief theatrical hiatus in her image, that archetypical Don Juan masculinity exists for no more than a few minutes. That differs from the "anonymous" drag queens who are part of the music videos discussed before. As those have no different public image that audiences would rather refer to, their bodies exist in the mediascape only through that queer experience.

A similar use of drag king art can be found in MAMAMOO's "Um Oh Ah Yeh" (2015). Here, Moonbyul, Whee-in, and Hwasa perform typical stereotypes of masculinity: the flower boy, the nerd, and the greaser. The plot mostly covers the comic interactions between the three of them and Solar, the only MAMAMOO member who performs a female character, flirting with the others to reproduce cis-heterosexual romantic clichés. This drag king role is not to be played by an anonymous AFAB individual who would interact with them and be probably perceived as queer, but rather a comic way for those idols to prove they can be more masculine (yet preserving their heteronormative identity). Similar to Lee Hyo-ri's video, MAMAMOO's drag king is used here as a comic relief based on the misbehaviors of straight men. That seems to summarize the presence of drag king art in contemporary K-pop music videos. *Kings* are restricted to archetypes of masculinity played by famous female-identifying figures who can easily dissociate themselves from any queer readings.

A significant presence of drag kings with alternate masculinities, and played by queer-readable individuals, is still lacking in the mainstream. Referring to Muñoz (1999), kings only exist as corporate-sponsored figures that cause no disruptions or uneasiness in desire—and apart from these parodies played by idols, no significant presence of drag kings can be noticed. That radically differs from the marginal Korean queer scene drag king art, which is active and in expansion. Similar to a scene observed by Audrey Yue in Australia, in the local underground scene, "Masculinity as a political, social, and cultural expression of maleness, patriarchy, and power is a discourse constructed not only in relation to an orthodox femininity but also to alternative masculinities" (Yue, 2008). Hence, out of mainstream spaces, Korean drag king artists have been organizing important queer/feminist events, such as the All Hail Drag King Contest 2018 and 2019 (Jang, 2019).

Contemporary Korean drag scenes tend to cover a vast spectrum of masculinities, freely transiting between male stereotypes, non-binary male expressions, posthuman masculinities, and male butches to question binaries and the patriarchal order (Seong, 2019), to destabilize the intelligibility of Korea heteronormative masculinity. By doing so, they make room for the vast possibilities of masculinities ignored by cultural industries to artistically investigate how normative masculinities are produced (and played) as gender identities and roles in society.

The South Korean drag king scene has also connected with traditional arts like *pansori* in marginal events as DRAG Yeoseong Gukgeuk (2019). In dialogue with the female-performers-only traditional art of Yeoseong Gukgeuk, the event used drag performances to dismantle gender-oriented narratives and question gender hierarchies in the culture, replacing the male figures who are traditionally the center of the narrative (Kim, 2020). That radically differs from the few experiences present in the K-pop industry as queer subjects and practices are always inevitably compromised when in exchange for visibility. For the radical politics of a contemporary Korean drag king, they have been reduced to tomboy styles and female idols playing male stereotypes. For drag queens, yet better accepted and celebrated, they have been confined to gender binary expectations. Turned into visual references, they can be accepted when conforming to Korean dominant expectations. Therefore, only a few artists have portrayed non-binary gender performances in their music videos.

Apart from already socially accepted gender-bending fashion trends, non-binary drag has been part of the K-pop industry mostly when idols' performances rely on choreographies influenced by vogue, waacking, and heels dance, as in AOA's live performance of "Egotistic" (at *Queendom*, 2019) and Chung Ha's "Stay Tonight" (2020), when AMAB performers display an alternative masculinity built on high heels, fashion, and dance movements culturally associated to women. J Black & J Pink's "Move, Groove, Smooth" (2020) music video exemplifies this non-normative masculinity. In a song about self-empowerment and living as free and proud as one can be, "Move, Groove, Smooth" shows non-binary-presenting AMAB performers and female-presenting performers who follow J Black/J Pink as backup dancers. The video is divided into two types of scenes. One shows performers dancing with J Black as male-presenting individuals (considering both outfits and moves) and the other shows non-binary-presenting dancers when they are together with J Pink, a female-presenting version of J Black, a fully dressed drag queen.

LAST WORDS

Queer-originated practices create space for a reverse influence once cultural industries cannot engage with those without getting exposed. As they become topical material for everyday talks and interactions, they allow queer individuals to catch a glimpse of alternative ways of living and expressing themselves, and make explicit what broad heteronormative audiences "do not even know exist or that they have repudiated" (Halberstam 2005, 158). In that way, as some K-pop idols succeeded with gender-bending visuals, some groups theatrically played with drag performances, and audiences became in general more familiar with queering individuals and their experiences.

The influence dominant practices have on queer narratives always implies a price, as discussed in this chapter. In exchange for visibility and acceptance, queer subjects and practices are inevitably compromised. Queer existences are accepted when kept under control, representing no threat. For instance, K-pop music videos with depictions of same-sex couples transgress norms concerning sexuality but usually conform to expectations on gender identities, while videos depicting gender-non-conforming individuals mostly do not refer to non-normative sexualities. Queer audiences cannot have both at the same time.

Historically misunderstood, condemned, and abused by the oppressive norms of the dominant culture, queer communities still exist in (and through) a constant struggle. Therefore, if those who fail (or actively avoid) to enter the mainstream are often sentenced to exclusion, and erased from society's main narratives, investigations from within the perspectives of queer communities are needed to understand how queer individuals have been affected by those. The history of queer communities is often composed as "disorderly narratives" (Halberstam, 2005) full of silences, gaps, and ruptures, but many of those missing pieces can still be found, particularly with deeper investigations of how drag communities have been created and transformed in South Korea—or even how less mainstream genres out of the idol system have proposed a different dialogue to drag art, as in small indie music videos,[14] art projects,[15] and indie-folk collectives like Ssing Ssing.

New inquiries are necessary to understand not only the possibilities of drag performances out of gender binaries, but also to investigate how gender is performed in multiple ways in the South Korean industry when idols perform K-pop ideals of masculinity and femininity. In that way, a drag frame may help to understand how AFAB drag queen (or hyper queens) and AMAB drag king (or hyper kings) influence the industry through heteronormative, yet theatrically extravagant, gender performances.

NOTES

1. Oh (2018) argues that each idol does have a detailed crafted image but those are in constant update. As new music releases are often supported by new visuals through marketing survival strategies, frequent updates of idols' concepts are used to keep audiences interested in the artists' developments and create new engagement. In this way, agencies provide idols with strong and distinctive (yet always changing) images.

2. To name a few, Lady Gaga's alter-ego Joe Calderone, a drag king character she played in 2011, in magazines (*Vogue Japan*), music videos ("You and I"), and live performances (VMA), and Ronnie, a male character she played in 2017, when she was a guest judge on *Rupaul's Drag Race*—while Ronnie was a fictional extra contestant in the competition. Later in the film *A Star is Born* (2019), Gaga would appear once again closely tied to drag queens, sharing the screen with some drag performers.

3. To better understand Gaga's local popularity, after her first performance in August 2009, with a pocket show at a club for about 700 people (Lim, 2009), Gaga returned in April 2012 for a stadium concert that launched her Born This Way Ball

Global Tour. The show attracted more than 45,000 people, despite being confronted with protests organized by Christian groups, which accused the singer of promoting pornography and homosexuality, and also threatening youth's integrity with obscene stage performances. That was the second biggest audience for a foreign artist in South Korea at that time, after the two-day Michael Jackson's concert that was held in the late 1990s (Kim, 2012). The singer returned again in 2014 as the headliner at a two-day project organized by Live Nation and YG Entertainment, the AIA Real Life: NOW Festival 2014. The event also presented BIGBANG, 2NE1, PSY, Epik High, Lee Hi, Akdong Musician, WINNER, Crayon Pop, and Glen Check.

4. In interview (Lee, 2020) the group admitted they are constantly asked about their sexual orientation. But instead of addressing the issue, they prefer to define themselves as a "powerful and unique" performance of masculinity, through wearing high heels and moving inspired by dances that often get underrated in South Korea for their origins in queer sub-cultures.

5. The disbanding was motivated by mainstream media attention been given only to the group members' gender identity (with little interest on the group's releases and artistic achievements), the strong criticism their official photo-book *Women, Reflect!* received for portraying members in sexy poses, and controversies surrounding their military duties, as part of the audience accused them of identifying as transgender women to avoid serving the country through military training.

6. The Youth Protection Act created in 1997 to protect society and young citizens classified homosexuality as a "harmful" and "socially unacceptable" practice. The discriminatory act equated homosexuality to sexual assaults, by putting it together with incest and sexual intercourse with animals, and it was also used to justify the banning of any queer-related content on websites accessed from South Korea. It was only after a trenchant appeal made by sexual minority groups that the Korean National Human Rights Protection Committee decided for amending the Youth Protection Law, in 2003—which happened not without the protest of conservative Christian groups, as the Christian Council of Korea issued a press release entitled "Does the Korean government promote homosexuality to youth?"

7. The freedom and growth queer communities experienced in the 1990s were affected as young people's attitudes began to shift toward a more conservative life-style in the 2000s. Living among the insecurities of the country's economy and the daily pressure for self-development meant that time for recreation or self-discovery was a luxury only a few could afford. Queer communities were particularly affected because of the almost non-existent ways for them to translate those activities into working experiences, certifications, or new skills (Cho, 2020; Shin, 2020).

8. Harisu became nationally famous in 2001 for starring in a commercial campaign for Dodo Cosmetics. In the same period, she also debuted in the music industry, with the techno-pop album *Temptation* (Seoul Records, 2001), and started her acting career. She has been in films such as *Emergency Act 19* (Kim Tae-gyu, South Korea, 2002), *Colour Blossoms* (Yonfan, Hong Kong, 2004), and *Possessed* (Bjarne Wong, Malaysia, 2006). She was also part of the TV series *Hi! Honey* (CTV, Taiwan, 2004).

9. Yet the authors choose to name the practice as "cross-dressing," the term "drag" seems to be more appropriate, as the former is commonly used to describe regular practices through which one expresses one's *identity*.

10. Park Jung-min's "Not Alone" (2011), Girls' Generation's "Love & Girls" (2013), Lee Hyo-ri's "Going Crazy" (2013), Lee Hyo-ri's "Miss Korea" (2013), Cheetah's "My Number" (2015), MAMAMOO's "Um Oh Ah Yeh" (2015), Hyukoh's "Love ya!" (2018), Holland's "I'm Not Afraid" (2018), Brown Eyed Girls' "Wonder Woman" (2019), Brown Eyed Girls' "Wonder Woman" Special Clip (2019), Changstarr (feat. Jeremy Quest, Kinnshaa Wish, Eggu's "Diamonds Eternal)'s (2019), Endless Zanhyang We Are's "Hero" (2019), MAMAMOO's "Hip" (2019), SUMIMN's "OO DA DA" (2019), Wetter's "Ggondae" (2019), Jenyer's "Illusion" (2019), CL's "Hwa" (2020), J Black & J Pink's "Move, Groove, Smooth" (2020), and Vanner's "Form" (2020).

11. See, for instance, BTOB's performance at SBS's *The Boss Is Watching* (SBS Entertainment, 2016). The TV show segment starts with a heavily blurred image of a group getting on stage after "Dumb Dumb" starts playing. The take is followed by scenes of audience members bursting out laughing and close-up scenes of Noh Hyun-Tae (identified on screen as vice-president of Cube Entertainment) looking down, visibly uncomfortable and in disapproval. Following the reactions, the editing goes back to the previously blurred group on stage to suspend the filter and reveal their identity. Those are BTOB members who came to perform Red Velvet's song wearing doll-like dresses and long wigs. Out of the four boys in drag, only one enters the stage smiling and with his head up. The others are serious, looking down, or visibly shy. They all start to sing and dance the choreography, but always keeping overdramatized facial expressions that emphasize their awkwardness, as if reminding audiences that they do not belong (and do not want to belong) there.

12. Kim Chi's first show in South Korea in 2016 was later followed by others in 2017 and 2018. Others events have also been organized with Naomi Smalls (2017, 2018), Violet Chachki (2017), Detox (2017), Pearl (2018), and Soju (2019), all of them former contestants from *Rupaul's Drag Race*. Those were all shows organized by local producers, but in 2020 the *Werk the World* tour, an official event organized in collaboration with *Rupaul's Drag Race* producers, included Korea in its world official schedule. The event happened in February 25, 2020, starring Aquaria, Detox, Kim Chi, Monet X Change, Plastique Tiara, and Violet Chachki.

13. After co-producing, hosting, and co-performing in events with former-*Rupaul's Drag Race* contestants in Korea, a group of local artists created Neon Milk, a drag culture collective. They have built a strong social media presence with over 100,000 followers on YouTube and Instagram, which allows them to work in partnership with makeup brands, fashion designers, and other businesses. Artists who are part of the collective, or are close to it, have been part of multiple K-pop music videos, including Holland's "I'm Not Afraid" (2018), Brown Eyed Girls' "Wonder Woman" (2019), Brown Eyed Girls' "Wonder Woman" Special Clip (2019), MAMAMOO's "Hip" (2019), SUMIMN's "OO DA DA" (2019), Changstarr (feat. Jeremy Quest, Kinnshaa Wish, Eggu's "Diamonds Eternal)'s (2019), Wetter's "Ggondae" (2019), Jenyer's "Illusion" (2019), and Vanner's "Form" (2020).

14. For instance, The Endless Zanhyang We Are's "Hero" (2019), in which an older drag performer that contrasts to the young, idol-like bodies portrayed in mainstream videos. The same drag performer participated in CL's "Hwa" (2020). Mainstream artist but currently under her own indie label, CL re-started her career

singing about her artistic trajectory and impact in the music industry. "Hwa" presents a drag artist who diverges from the contemporary drag beauty standard, with no dramatic makeup, visible bare chest, and no young, idol-like image, in a music video strongly based on avant-garde art and fashion.

15. See HornyHoneydew's "Kiss of Chaos" (2020), a project Commissioned by the National Museum of Modern and Contemporary Art, Korea, which brings a monstrous type of drag performer (with an aesthetics closer to the Tranimal movement) to discuss on shamanic practices, rituals, the concepts of "queerness" and "gender."

BIBLIOGRAPHY

Ahn, P. (2009). Harisu: South Korean Cosmetic Media and the Paradox of Transgendered Neoliberal Embodiment. *Discourse* 31 (3): 248–272.

Allkpop. (2013). New tomboy girl group GI (Global Icon) releases their 1st teaser for "Beatles"! March 26, https://www.allkpop.com/article/2013/03/new-tomboy-girl -group-gi-global-icon-releases-their-1st-teaser-for-beatles.

Anderson, C. (2014). That's My Man! Overlapping Masculinities in Korean Popular Music. In *The Korean Wave: Korean Popular Culture in Global Context*, edited by Kuwahara, Y., 117–131. New York: Palgrave Macmillan.

Arirang News. (2005). Manufactured Transgender Pop Group 'Lady' Set to Debut in Korea. March 26, http://www.arirang.co.kr/News/News_Print.asp?type=news &nseq=32359

Baker, R., Burton, P., and Smith, R. (1994). *Drag: A History of Female Impersonation in the Performing Arts*. London: Cassell.

Bong, Youngshik D. (2009). The Gay Rights Movement in Democratizing Korea. *Korean Studies* 32: 86–103.

Butler, J. (1990). *Gender Trouble and the Subversion of Identity*. New York: Routledge.

Cho, H, and Stark, J. (2017). South Korean Youth Across Three Decades. In *The Routledge Handbook of Korean Culture and Society*, edited by Kim, Y. London: Routledge.

Cho, J. (2009). Breaking the Gay Taboo in South Korea: In Korea, Talking About Sex, Let Alone Gay Sex, Is a Strong Social Taboo. *ABC News*, April 16, https:// abcnews.go.com/International/story?id=7351116&page=1

Cho, J. (2020). The Three Faces of South Korea's Male Homosexuality: Pogal, Iban, and Neoliberal Gay. In *Queer Korea*, edited by Henry, T. Durham, NC: Duke University Press, 263–294.

Choi, M. (2015). Musical Hedwig. The Most Stylish Rock of the Century. *Uijeongbu News*, June 2, http://www.ujbnews.kr/news/articleView.html?idxno=2670

Danal Entertainment. (2013). The Beginning N.O.M _MV. *YouTube Video*, 3:24, October 7, 2013, https://www.youtube.com/watch?v=zWJAzCI5L-4

Daw, S. (2020) How Lady Gaga's 'The Fame' Made Her a New Industry Standard For Pop Superstardom". *Billboard*, August 19, https://www.billboard.com/articles /columns/pop/8470910/lady-gaga-the-fame-pop-stardom

Freeman, E. (2010). *Time Binds: Queer Temporalities, Queer Histories*. Durham, NC: Duke University Press.

Fuhr, M. (2017). K-Pop Music and Transnationalism. In *The Routledge Handbook of Korean Culture and Society*, edited by Kim, Y. London: Routledge.

Guri City Hall Press Release. (2015). Guri Art Hall, Musical 'Hedwick' Performance. Yonhap News, May 14, https://www.yna.co.kr/view/RPR20150514004700353

Halberstam, J. (1998). *Female Masculinity*. Durham, NC: Duke University Press.

Halberstam, J. (2005). *In a Queer Time and Place*. New York University Press.

Hankyung News Team. (2012). Jo Kwon, 'Korean Lady Gaga' or 'Too Much'... Show Off an Unprecedented Performance. *Hankyung*, July 2, https://www.hankyung.com/life/article/2012070250347

Jang, E. (2019). Why do I wear 'manly' clothes and do drag? *Kyunghyang Shinmun*, June 1, http://news.khan.co.kr/kh_news/khan_art_view.html?art_id=201906010600055

Jo, Y. (2020). All of us are Kinky!"... 'Kinky Boots' Park Eun-tae, Kang Hong-seok, Synergy Explosion. *dongA*, July 15, 2020, https://sports.donga.com/ent/article/all/20200715/101977070/2

Jung, S. (2010). Chogukjeok Pan-East Asian Soft Masculinity: Reading Boys Over Flowers, DBSK, Coffee Prince, and Shinhwa Fan Fictions". In *Complicated Currents: Media Flows, Soft Power and East Asia*, edited by Black, D., Epstein, S. and Tokita, S., 8.1–8.16. Melbourne: Monash University.

Jung, S. (2011). *Korean Masculinities and Transnational Consumption: Yonsama, Rain, Old Boy, K-pop Idols*. Hong Kong: Hong Kong University Press.

Kang, O. (2020). 'LGBT, We are Living Here Now': Sexual Minorities and Space in Contemporary South Korea. *Korean Anthropology Review* 4: 1–37.

Kim, T. (2020). The Things that Female Gukgeuk Left to Us: Concentrating on DRAG x Female Gukgeuk. *Journal of Korean Theatre Studies Association* 73 (1): 269–283.

Kim, W. (2012). Lady Gaga's Unexpected Concert, "No Surprises. *dongA*, April 29, https://www.donga.com/news/Entertainment/article/all/20120429/45883306/1

Korea Music Content Association. (2011). Week 12 Streaming Chart (Foreign Songs). *Gaon Music Chart*, http://gaonchart.co.kr/main/section/chart/online.gaon?serviceGbn=S1040&termGbn=week&hitYear=2011&targetTime=12&nationGbn=E&year_time=

Kwon, S., and Lee, I. (2014). Development of a Tomboy Look Design Based on Styles in Trendy TV Drama Series. *Journal of The Korean Society of Fashion Design* 14 (1): 211–223.

Laforgia, P., and Howard, K. (2017). Amber Liu, K-Pop Tomboy: Reshaping Femininity in Mainstream K-Pop. *Kitrina Kultura* 29: 214–231.

Laurie, T. (2016). Toward a Gendered Aesthetics of K-Pop. In *Global Glam and Popular Music: Style and Spectacle from the 1970s to the 2000s*, edited by Johnson H., and Chapman, I. New York: Routledge.

Lee, B. (2020). The Concept of High Heels Is Our Personality... Expect Males Dancing On Stage. *Segye Ilbo*, July 13, https://www.segye.com/newsView/20200713517606

Lee, J., and Yi, H. (2020). Ssen-Unni in K-Pop: The Makings of "Strong Sisters" in South Korea. *Korea Journal* 60 (1): 17–39.

Lim, E. (2009). Decadent Beauty' Lady Gaga's stage in Korea. *Yonhap News*, June 17, https://www.yna.co.kr/view/AKR20090617219100005

Litwiller, F. (2020). Normative Drag Culture and the Making of Precarity. *Leisure Studies* 39 (4): 600–612.

Miller, S. (2016). Drag. In *The Wiley Blackwell Encyclopedia of Gender and Sexuality Studies*, edited by Naples, N. Hoboken, NJ: Wiley.

Muñoz, J. (1999). *Disidentifications: Queers of Color and the Performance of Politics*. Minneapolis, MN: University of Minnesota Press.

Nelson, L., and Cho, H. (2016). Women, gender, and social change in South Korea since 1945. In *Routledge Handbook of Modern Korean History*, edited by Seth, M. London: Routledge.

Oh, C. (2014). The Politics of the Dancing Body: Racialized and Gendered Femininity in Korean Pop. In *The Korean Wave*, edited by Kuwahara, Y. New York: Palgrave Macmillan.

Oh, C. (2015). Queering spectatorship in K-Pop: The Androgynous Male Dancing Body and Western Female Fandom. *Journal of Fandom Studies* 3: 59–78.

Oh, C., and Oh, D. (2017). Unmasking Queerness: Blurring and Solidifying Queer Lines Through K-Pop Cross-Dressing. *The Journal of Popular Culture* 50 (1): 9–29.

Oh, I., and Lee, H. (2014). K-pop in Korea: How the Pop Music Industry Is Changing a Post-Developmental Society. *Cross-Currents: East Asian History and Culture Review* 3 (1): 72–93.

Oh, Y. (2018). *Pop City: Korean Popular Culture and the Selling of Places*. London: Cornell University Press.

Oleszczuk, A., and Waszkiewicz, A. (2020). Queerness of Hallyu 2.0: Negotiating Non-Normative Identities in K-pop Music Videos," *Res Rethorica* 2 (2): 117–131.

Outright Action International. (2003). South Korea: Homosexuality Removed from Classification of 'Harmful and Obscene' in Youth Protection Law, April 22, https://outrightinternational.org/content/south-korea-homosexuality-removed-clas-sification-harmful-and-obscene-youth-protection-law

Park, J. (2020). What is the relationship between K-pop and queer? *Ildaro*, June 28, http://www.ildaro.com/8770

Park, S. (2018). Do you Know the First "Drag Parade" Held in Korea?" *Hankyoreh*. June 1, http://www.hani.co.kr/arti/culture/culture_general/847305.html

Park-Kim, S, Lee-Kim, S., and Kwon-Lee E. (2007). The Lesbian Rights Movement and Feminism in South Korea. *Journal of Lesbian Studies* 10 (3-4): 161–190.

Rupp, L., Taylor, V., and Shapiro, E. (2010). Drag Queens and Drag Kings: The Difference Gender Makes. *Sexualities* 13 (3): 275–94.

SBS Entertainment. I love BTOB's Toki. Red Velvet's 'Dumb Dumb' sung by B2B; My strength | The Boss Is Watching | SBS ENTER. *YouTube Video*, 1: 56, February 6, 2016, https://www.youtube.com/watch?v=OWAQhpN4IwA

Seong, J. (2019). The thickness of image and the thickness of reality: 2019 Korean women-sexual minority image theory. *Seminar*, http://www.zineseminar.com/wp/issue02/이미지의-두께와-실재의-두께-2019년-한국-성소수자-이/

Seoul Queer Culture Festival Organizing Committee, SQCFORG. (2020). https://sqcf .org/sqcforg

Shin, L. (2018). Queer Eye for K-Pop Fandom, Popular Culture, Cross-gender Performance, and Queer Desire in South Korean Cosplay of K-pop Stars. *Korea Journal* 58 (4): 87–113.

Shin, L. (2020). Avoiding T'ibu (Obvious Butchness): Invisibility as a Survival Strategy Among Young Queer Women in South Korea. In *Queer Korea*, edited by Henry, T., 295–323. Durham, NC: Duke University Press.

Song, S. (2020). The Evolution of the Korean Wave: How is the Third Generation Different from Previous Ones? *Korea Observer* 51 (1): 125–150.

Stone Music Entertainment. (2013). Lee Hyori - Miss Korea MV. *YouTube Video*, 4: 17, https://www.youtube.com/watch?v=Huu3H5ei_-8

Yue, A. (2008). King Victoria: Asian Drag Kings, Postcolonial Female Masculinity, and Hybrid Sexuality in Australia. In *AsiaPacifiQueer: Rethinking Genders and Sexualities*, edited by Audrey, Y., Fran, M., Jackson, P., and Mark, M. Champaign, IL: University of Illinois Press.

Chapter 10

K-pop Performance, Transcultural Negotiation of Gender Identity, and Belonging

A Case Study of a Peruvian Drag Queen Dancing to K-pop

Min Suk Kim

I met Kriss at the MegaPlaza, the meeting place for our interview on August 16, 2018. I was nervous on my way to this enormous open-air style shopping center located at the northern part of Lima because it was far from the central Liman areas where I conducted my ethnographic research. The streets from the bus stop to the mall looked unfamiliar and unorganized, but once I entered through the MegaPlaza entrance, the view changed completely. Its luxurious interiors struck me with its gigantic square with modernly tiled floors and a large, round shaped water fountain at the center. Perhaps, the drastic contrast of the exterior and interior views showcases the nation's wide gap in economic inequality and people's unbalanced lifestyles driven by neoliberal capitalism.

When I arrived, I called Kriss for his[1] whereabouts, as we had been in contact via Facebook Messenger on the way to the mall. He did not answer at first, but instead, he immediately messaged back and said that he did not answer the call on the street due to a robbery nearby. A few minutes later, he walked in, and my first impression was that he is a fun, buoyant, fashionable young man. Kriss was tall, light-skinned, with pale ash pink dyed hair, lightly gelled in a slick-back hairstyle with shaved sides. He was donned in ripped black jeans, a black polo T-shirt, and a ripped vintage-style pale denim jacket, oversized thin gold metal frame glasses, and black round stud earrings. Excluding the polo, all his fashion was very unusual for a Peruvian male. In addition, Kriss was wearing Korean-style everyday natural makeup like a K-pop idol star, which comprises BB cream, faintly penciled-in eyebrows, and light glitter eyeshadow complete with eyeliner. He seemed comfortable and confident wearing makeup as he walked through the crowd of people.

Thus, it was surprising to learn about his childhood full of emotional wounds and traumas just because he was "feminine." I asked him how he could look so self-confident today. He responded:

> I swear to you that I see myself from here in a few years ago, ten years mini-mum, [. . .] I am not the person that I was before. Now, like all these things [of K-pop] helped me to become, like to know, to dance, and everything, have helped me a lot to raise my self-esteem. Knowing that there are people who like what I do [drag] and I know that there are people who support me for who I am.

Kriss was indeed a person who had changed dramatically because of K-pop. It was striking to know that a foreign culture like K-pop music could meaning-fully impact someone's life and identity on the opposite side of the earth. Of course, his drastic change had not been acquired only by passively listening to or "consuming" K-pop, but more actively by "re-producing" or "perform-ing" his own K-pop stages for the local K-pop fan communities. Kriss's story evolved into an outset of this empirical study to examine a concrete case that evidences K-pop's actual living influence on its global fans' gender identity (re)construction and transcultural negotiation since his experience and voice offer understudied insights into the relationships between K-pop and its queer fan community, which can often be neglected in data.

While research on K-pop and its transgressive characteristics on the tradi-tional gender dynamics has increased in recent years (e.g., Anderson, 2014; Garza, 2018; Jung, 2010; Laurie, 2016; Manietta, 2015; Oh, 2015; Oh and Oh, 2017), only a few studies focus on the receiving ends of its queer fanbase, more specifically, on queer K-pop cover dancers, or K-pop fan dance practitio-ners (Echenique, 2018; Guevarra, 2014; Käng, 2014). Echenique, for example, investigates how Liman tomboy female fans appropriate K-pop masculinities through dancing male idol groups' powerful dance moves and stylizing like their favorite stars in resistance to local gender codes regardless of their sexual orientations. In a similar fashion, Guevarra and Käng examine, respectively, Filipino queer teens and Thai "sissies" (young feminine gay men) who dance or "cover" K-pop choreographies as a form of performed sexuality and/or gender presentation. What remains unstudied, however, are drag performers in the K-pop cover dance culture. Thus, we have limited understanding of how the theories of gender identity and performativity can be applied to the varying relationships between K-pop's gender esthetics and its queer fan population in Latin America, and how some queer fans perform *their* particular gender on stage through the lens and influence of this musical genre.

Figure 10.1 Kriss Chae Rin Covering the Front Page of a Local Fashion Institute's Advertisement Magazine. *Photo courtesy of Kriss Chae Rin.*

K-pop cover dancing has become a global cultural phenomenon. Many K-pop fans around the world are involved in the disciplined and competitive practice of reproducing the choreographies and extravagant stage customs of K-pop artists. Today, one can readily witness local K-pop dance groups practicing their moves in public spaces, such as streets, parks, and/or public libraries' rest areas. Many of these groups present their talents at local, national, regional, and global K-pop cover dance competitions and on television shows, and upload an abundance of dance cover videos to social media, highlighting choreographies, recordings, and video editing abilities, that range in quality from amateur to highly professional. Objectives and motivations, however, vary greatly by demographic (gender, class, race, sexual orientation, education, etc.) and locality (social expectations and criteria of inclusion and exclusion). To present an example of the importance of K-pop cover dancing, this chapter 'examines the influence of K-pop on the life and gender presentations or assertation of a gay fan from Peru, following the process of how he began to express himself while dancing to K-pop choreographies to finding freedom through performing K-pop as a drag queen for a public audience. I further delve into the relationships between public performativity of gender and its inevitable effects on the performer's identities—fluid yet sometimes fluctuating gender identities—based on the close relationships between gender identity and performance (Butler, 1990, 1993; Schrock, Reid, and Boyd, 2005; Taylor and Rupp, 2004; Valocchi, 2005).

METHODS

This chapter is based on a case study first undertaken in August 2018, as part of larger research concerning the consumption of Korean popular culture in Latin America and its impacts on fans' self-fashioning and gendering. While conducting qualitative interviews and participant observations in Lima during summer 2018, I employed the snowball sampling method that relies on the existing subjects' referrals to recruit future subjects, and that was how I was introduced to Kriss Chae Rin, a well-known drag queen within the local K-pop communities. I asked open-ended questions to invite him to talk freely about his thoughts on Korean popular culture and his life experiences related to K-pop, and later on, asked more in-depth follow-up questions. Communications via Facebook Messenger continue to further shape current qualitative studies.

The on-site interview was conducted at one of the largest and most-visited shopping centers, MegaPlaza, located in an underdeveloped industrial zone of Northern Lima, an area known for attracting newly emerging middle and lower-middle classes with growing purchasing power. The interview at MegaPlaza lasted three hours, and was recorded and transcribed to be analyzed, along with subsequent text and audio conversations via Facebook. Moreover, photographs and observations of Kriss's on stage performance videos and his two Facebook accounts, one personal and the other of his performing persona, lent depth to the analysis. When I interviewed him in person, Kriss was a 23-year-old first-generation college student with a fully funded fellowship at a local theater/art school. He self-identified as socioeconomically middle class and ethnically a "proud 'cholo Serrano'" Peruvian, a term for mixed-blood people of Spanish and indigenous heritage. Kriss elevated his heritage as "proudly *cholo Serrano*" because the term in Peru is often linked with derogatory implications to people with Amerindian contributions, characterized as a tanned brown skin peasant *serranos*, a group who migrated to the capital from the *sierra* ("mountains" in Spanish).

I will refer to Kriss using the designated names and corresponding gender pronouns as Kriss wanted to be addressed, including how I would refer to him in this chapter: feminine as "Kriss Chae Rin," his artistic drag persona, and masculine as Kriss, out of drag.[2]

To paint a descriptive picture of the empirical impact of K-pop on a queer subject and his evolutionary process of gendering through K-pop, I use the "thick description" method. This method "builds up a clear picture of the individuals [. . .] in the context of their culture and the setting in which they live" (Holloway, 1997). This type of description in detailed or "thick" information is imperative to make sense of Kriss's lived experiences, subsequent emotions, and progression of thoughts. It helps readers experience what life might be as a feminine gay male in a patriarchal Catholic society with compulsory heterosexuality, institutionalized societal prescriptions for women and men (Rich, 2003), and therefore, better comprehend "the circumstances, meanings, intentions, strategies, motivations, and so on that characterize a particular episode" (Schwandt, 2001). By providing a thick description of societal circumstances, along with an autobiographical account voiced by Kriss himself, I seek to understand what K-pop means to him, what motivated him to be drawn to and dance to female K-pop groups in public, and what he intends to accomplish via performing K-pop in drag. Moreover, drawing on a grounded theory approach, I will further provide a close reading of my fieldnotes, interview transcripts, and Kriss's performance video footage so that I can allow themes to emerge from the reading based on the inductive thematic analysis.

Kriss Chae Rin's Gender Performativity

In August 2019, Kriss Chae Rin reproduced a performance by K-pop singer/rapper CL for Asiamania TV, a local cable channel airing on weekends with themes of Asian cultures and its local fans of the cultures in Peru. She opened the show lip-synching CL's rap lines: "This is for all my bad girls around the world, [a moment of silence, sound of audience cheering out] Not bad, meaning bad, but bad, meaning good, you know. Let's light it up and let it burn like we don't care, Let 'em know how it feels *damn* good to be bad" (original sonic emphasis).[3] The camera pans a small studio. On the left, a television screen is playing the K-pop megahit girl group Blackpink's music video, "Kill This Love" (2019), and Kriss Chae Rin stands still in the center alongside two other female dancers, with their backs facing the audience. They are wearing matching tight black shorts and fishnet tights, contrasting Kriss's wardrobe of a shiny silver jacket, complete with a high and long ponytail with white and grey hair extensions (figure 10.1). The music begins with a whistle sound and male voices shouting low, and the aforementioned rap narration begins in English. Lip-synching, Kriss Chae Rin turns her head firmly to the side showing her left profile decorated with heavy makeup: a smokey eye look in thick cat winged eyeliner, lashes, silver glitters in the eye centers, and hot-pink lips. With a confident diva attitude, she holds her gold, diamond-laden mic up high as she makes a 180-degree turn to fully face the front and starts delivering a commanding performance in a "glam-swaggy-chill" vibe. She smiles from time to time staring at the camera directly and intensely while performing and rapping the line "Set them on fire."

After the "The Baddest Female" intro, the music quickly switches to the song, "I Am the Best" (2011) by 2NE1 (2009–2016), consisting of three other female artists, for which CL was the lead singer, rapper, and performer.

Next, other dancers turn to the front and join the performance, powerfully synchronized. Like Kriss, they are also wearing smoky eye makeup, but with dark, blue-colored lips. The performance lasted about four minutes and was followed by an exclusive interview with Kriss; afterward, the program continued with activities typical of Korean variety shows like "2X speed dance" that plays a K-pop song at two times the regular speed to challenge guests to dance the exact choreography quickly and includes a quiz game between hosts and guests with funny punishments for wrong answers (e.g., drinking a cup of lime juice). Kriss Chae Rin and her K-pop cover group, 4Diamonds, consisting of her and three non-drag female members, have been (re)presenting or covering girl group 2NE1's stage performances since 2016; also, Kriss Chae Rin has been performing CL in drag since that time.

Kriss founded 4Diamonds, which has become a well-recognized K-pop cover group in the local fandom communities in Lima. They are commonly invited on stage at K-pop events held in Lima and provinces nearby, and have won numerous K-pop dance cover competitions including the 10th Friki Festival in Peru in January 2020, where thousands of people attended to celebrate Asian cultures such as anime, comics, videogames, and Asian music such as K-pop and J-rock. The festival was transmitted by Willax TV, a small local broadcaster particularly oriented to Asian culture.[4]

Kriss Chae Rin's current descriptions sound glamorous as a unique and recognized drag dancer in the local K-pop community; however, this biography is quite the opposite of Kriss's real-life story as a young gay man in his mid-20s. To understand what motivated Kriss to begin and continue to drag CL, it is important to examine his K-pop covering trajectory. CL was not the first or the only K-pop artist that Kriss has interpreted on stage over his decade-long covering experience. He has tested diverse gendered presentations and naturally went through gradual (trans)formations of his own by impersonating different K-pop artists and their treatment of gender. Around early 2007, he was a mere fan listening to K-pop and then started covering a boy group. When he came across a tomboy girl group member, he would opt this figure to dance female choreography and "perform" a femininity—masculine femininity, specifically—for the public. Somewhere between his love of K-pop as a fan and his coming out as a drag queen figure in the Liman K-pop scene, the music and artistry of the genre affected Kriss deeply. His involvement with the K-pop world provides insight into how K-pop exists as more than a pleasurable listening experience. His story opens questions that could be asked of many dancers and drag queens like him: What happens when an individual continues to perform intentionally opposite gender and/or diverse versions of gender embodiments as a performer? Why did Kriss chose to focus on CL and 2NE1 for her identarian performativity and formation? What are the implications and semiotics of performing CL's empowered "fearless diva" personality in drag and what has this brought to his gender identity? Especially, what type of effects can these gendered on stage performances have on an individual like Kriss, a once-repressed homosexual adolescent/young adult living in a homophobic society?

BEFORE K-POP: KRISS'S CHILDHOOD; AND HIS FIRST K-POP GENDERING/DANCING

Kriss knew sexual orientation "since I had use of reason;" he found himself attracted to a male classmate around the age of six at elementary school. Although he was little, he *knew* something was "wrong" with him, so he consequently felt unexplainable shame and feared that his classmates would become aware of his orientation. "So, I didn't have friends," he explains; however, as he got older, classmates recognized something different in his behaviors and began to bully him at age 11. He was beaten up and constantly threatened. He thought he would be killed by the violence. When the school day ended, he tried to run out of the school building as fast as he could because other kids chased after him: "I hid under cars, parked cars, I hid myself beneath, terrified!" He described his childhood using words like "horrible," "panicking," "constant harassment," "fear," and "terror." When Kriss entered junior high, the situation worsened so he quit school in the second year. "I didn't have friends or anything." He repetitively talked about the deprivation of childhood friendship and emphasized the importance of the friendships he later made from K-pop dancing through the entirety of our interview. Eventually, Kriss finished his high school education by attending an alternative night school with older classmates who were indifferent to his gender expressions because, according to Kriss, they had other priorities such as work and family matters.

Kriss's first encounter with Korean culture began circa 2007, from Korean television dramas broadcasted via local television channels. Kriss found himself captivated by the dramas' storylines and mise-en-scène, and by their soundtracks. He used to go to the local Internet cafes to watch missed episodes and search for the dramas' music. Around 2010, according to Kriss, people in Peru began to talk about "Korean Fever," what now is known as *Hallyu*. By chance, he watched a local TV show featuring TVXQ, a Korean boy group, and was amazed by their *look*. He searched for more information and ultimately discovered more K-pop groups, "but still, I did not have friends. I was still very shy. I used to be at home watching my K-dramas, listening to K-pop, TVXQ and Girls' Generation [a girl group], nothing else."

Kriss described his younger, 16-year-old self, as a young, isolated adolescent who did not like to socialize with people. He listened to K-pop and

wanted to learn the groups' choreographies. Then *Zona Joven*, a youth magazine, began featuring the latest K-pop news in a small section, besides its
traditional stories on American artists such as Lady Gaga and Katy Perry. By
this time, he acknowledged that he liked boys, but never admitted it "*a viva
voz* [literally "out loud" or publicly]." One day, he read a post in the magazine
about a local event held by the TVXQ fan club, so he bought a ticket and went
by himself. There, he saw his first K-pop cover stage delivered by local amateur dancers and commenced to meet people who shared "something in common" with him: a love for K-pop. It was his first time experiencing a feeling
of commonality, sharing something with others. He eventually joined their
predominately female Facebook fan club and slowly expanded his friendship
for the first time with girls, what he always wanted. Kriss says, "I was still not
openly gay though. They asked me, and I told them 'I am not gay.'"

Kriss had desires to dance to K-pop but could not dare do so in public, so
he practiced at home. When he saw the K-pop girl group, F(x) and its "tomboy" member, Amber, he persuaded himself, "Okay, this can work, imitating
her in a female group *but dancing as a boy*" (emphasis added). His desire to
dance K-pop girl group choreographies could be "substantiated" only through
enacting a tomboy femininity on stage as a performance. To him, it was the
only possibility or "in-between" space where he could safely play with gender boundaries and explore a type of femininity without revealing his gender
identity. He learned the choreography of their electropop-based song "Nu
ABO" (2010) alone at home and stepped upon the stage of a local K-pop
cover dance contest and flash mob event that took place in a downtown park
in 2010:

> The feeling of the first time to dance in public and a girl song was like, oh, how
> nervous I was! I mean, now people are going to think that I am gay; everyone is
> going to say. I plucked up my courage and went on the stage, and they put on the
> music and I danced. My first-time dancing. I did it bad, but I danced! [. . .] My
> friends said, "You did great, you did beautiful." I felt *very* good. [. . .] Because
> people see a boy dancing to a women's song that they hadn't seen in that time
> because I was like the first boy, and people cheered. I felt good.

The public's applause and friends' support were the first validation of his
non-binary gender expression. It was the unexpected reward of having overcome his worst fear and the first step toward coming out of the closet. At
the event, he met more female K-pop fans and another fan club of the group
SS501. This boy group became famous in Latin America due to the K-drama,
Boys Over Flowers (2009), in which a SS501 member, Kim Hyun-joong,
played a role. The drama is one of the first and biggest Korean cultural hits
that swept across Latin American countries and consequently drew many

young audiences into this cultural phenomenon (KOCIS, 2011). Kriss joined the SS501 fan club becoming part of a second community that embraced him.

GENDER POLITICS IN PERU

Peru is largely a conservative de facto Catholic society with a predictable attitude that expects heterosexuality among its citizens. The country has reported a high number of crimes against queer youth (Rivera and Ruiz, 2018; Suarez et al., 2020). The only official data that has been collected on Peruvian LGBTQ+ populations is the First Virtual Survey for LGBTI People, conducted by Peru's National Institute of Statistics and Informatics (INEI) in 2017. This survey included 12,026 adult LGBTI people and 63% of the participants answered that they had been the victim of discrimination or violence (Gámez and Bello, 2020; Hernández et al., 2015). Although the global perception of gender issues in recent years, particularly after the 2015 legalization of same-sex marriage in the United States, suggests a positive improvement of queer human rights, the editors of *The Unfinished Queer Agenda After Marriage Equality* (2018) claim that it is a false perception when viewing the increase of statistical records of violence against queer people around the world. They assert that "it is crucial that any discussions of a queer agenda are contextual and take into account the varying needs and experiences of individuals around the world based on their geographical location." It is therefore essential to understand what K-pop really brought to Kriss's life and gender presentations at his locality. When I conducted my field research in 2018, I encountered many dance groups practicing choreographies of the opposite sex, such as men dancing to K-pop girl groups and tomboy-looking women dancing to boy groups. I asked Kriss about this "seemingly progressive" queer phenomenon and he opened up, talking about the nation's "closed-mindset" that makes it difficult to even discuss the term "gender" or any queer attempt to step out of the hegemonic masculinity framework.

Conversely, Peruvian television programs are likely to display pervading images of the hyper-sexualization of women and macho masculinity. TV shows where muscular male guests openly comment and touch women's curvy bodies with no consent or crawl under women's wide-opened bare legs in miniskirts during a matchmaking show are abundant; yet, they do not allow a drag show like *RuPaul's Drag Race* or crossplay (cross-dressing cosplay) on television. Cross-dressing has been limitedly displayed and almost exclusively performed by fully grown men imitating certain populations, such as the *chola* look that characterizes indigenous women's traditional dresses and hairstyles from the mountainous provinces, as a form of comedy. It is, therefore, a social problem when cross-dressing becomes a serious performative practice or lifestyle, without the purpose of mockery or ridiculing others. For instance, *Trapito al aire* (2017–2018) was a TV show that regularly invited local K-pop and J-pop (Japanese pop music) cover dance groups and cosplayers to compete. On August 10, 2018, a conservative Christian organization, *Con mis hijos no te metas* [Do Not Mess with My Children] (established in Lima in 2016, in opposition to the implementation of the gender education in its school system), posted on their Facebook account a screen capture of *Trapito al aire* that featured a male crossplayer in a *Sailor Moon* costume, modeled after the famous Japanese anime female character. The post criticized this show for broadcasting "transvestite children as something normal and to even be rewarded" especially "at a [supposed] regulated time block for protecting minor audiences (*en horario de protección al menor*)" and ended its tirade with the statement, "Respect the identity of our children [*hijos*] #GenderNeverAgain (*#GéneroNuncaMás*)." Willax TV apologized for the content and shortly after, the program was discontinued.

The major concern from *Con mis hijos no te metas* was that their children would be exposed to other minors[5] wearing outfits of the opposite sex "as something normal," and that they may wish to imitate it, resulting in the collapse of traditional social norms, especially those related to the gender/sex-based norms. These heteronormative impositions showcase the paradoxical duality of Peruvian society with conservative groups that tolerate sexual objectification of women on television yet reject anything that defies normativity dictated by traditional gender norms in the name of "educational" concerns for children. Furthermore, the nation's gender rigidity is reflected in people's fashion and clothing. Everyday dressings in urban areas are standardized and "fairly conformist" (Dunnell, 2018), but when it comes to women's clothing, many caution against wearing shorts or other revealing clothing to avoid potential unwanted street harassment (Dunnell, 2018). It is also rare to see men with longer or dyed hair and fashion items, or adult women wearing something cute and loose, baggy clothes.

K-pop's Cross-gendering Culture and the Rise of Local Queer Fandom

It is an inevitable consequence that contemporary digital-literate youth consuming global cultures are drawn toward the overtly visual-intensive and new esthetics of gender-fluid K-pop artists over many of their national and regional counterparts. K-pop offers high-budget music videos in which good-looking idol members continuously challenge esthetic boundaries to stand out. Fans can easily watch male artists wearing makeup, pastel-colored hair, or even a crop top for their stage performance, and then see them meticulously groomed and stylized as "metrosexual" in other settings. The Korean mediascape introduces the culture of cross-dressing or cross-behavior performed regularly by both celebrities and ordinary people. For instance, male idol groups dance to girl groups' choreographies dressed as women on variety shows, and women artists sometimes perform dressed as men. This type of cross-dressing show is frequently performed by students as a recreational activity during school trips or for festivals in Korea.

Kriss highlighted that this cross-dancing culture is indeed widely practiced in the global K-pop dance cover fandoms. In response to the global popularity of K-pop cover dancing, the South Korean government (e.g., Ministry of Foreign Affairs) and entertainment industry have cultivated K-pop dance cover culture by inaugurating global-scaled competitions like *K-Pop World Festival*, an annual K-pop cover competition sponsored by various Korean government sectors. This TV show contest invites the finalists from around the world to compete in the last round in Korea and offers the opportunity to experience the K-pop idol training system at no cost, along with other prizes. Such offerings nurture diverse local K-pop cover competitions and YouTube culture where amateur dance teams around the world upload their cover performances in search of fame. This online global engagement with other fans became a cultural space where young Peruvian K-pop fans are exposed to new gender practices watching other talented fan-dancers who perform characteristics and attributes of the opposite sex. As Kriss pointed out, this global K-pop fan culture motivated many local fans, including some who have not yet made their gender identity and/or sexuality public, to transgress the gender rigid traditions and gave rise to queer K-pop dance groups in Lima.

At the K-pop dance cover event where Kriss "debuted" as SS501, he encountered his first queer local group. The male group, Missx Peru, covered Girls' Generation (hereafter SNSD), an originally nine-membered girl group that earned their global stardom based on their signature styles of bubblegum pop, a musical subgenre primarily marketed for pre-teens with positive upbeat sounds. It astonished him and he said, "this is what I want to do." Witnessing a group of male compatriots dancing in public to a female group that is particularly famous for a "girly-cute-feminine" appeal offered a space for "imaginative possibility" of gender (Shapiro, 2007). This "opened up a previously unavailable space to question gender" (Ibid.) to Kriss, where he could dare explore and imagine "the possible ways of being gendered" (Shapiro, 2007). It was a life-changing experience for him because this new possibility before his very eyes inspired him to question the traditional molds of gender and raised awareness of gender fluidity.

Kriss quit the SS501 cover group and spent a month preparing the SNSD song "Geni" (2009), which had been well-received for its lyrics granting the wishes of boys, and its more mature-concepted choreography that uses a synchronized seductive leg movement. With hard work and education, Kriss passed the casting audition and became a member of Missx Peru. It was his first experience belonging to a gay community. He began his social relationships and friendships with queer people who were more comfortable with their gender identities and performing queerness in public through K-pop covers.

EXPLORING WAYS OF BEING GENDERED, OBSTACLES, AND THE INCEPTION OF KRISS CHAE RIN

The first "feminine" stage performance that Kriss debuted was the remix of K-pop girl group Rania's songs entitled "Style" (2012) and "Dr. Feel Good" (2011) (in the order of their performance remix), upbeat dance tracks with sexy-powerful-femme-fatale concepts. The crews, consisting of five men and two women, stepped on the stage of a local K-pop dance competition that took place in the Park of the Exposition in 2013. All members wore natural black hair and all-black outfits while they performed strong, sensual, and provocative choreographies in sync. In Peru, dying hair used to be an uncommon practice even in the K-pop fan communities in the early 2010s; today, however, it is easier to find diversely colored hair and hairstyles both in female and male fans. Kriss stood out in black jeans and a black vest sans undershirt. Despite the fact that there was no overt cross-dressing, the performance delivered a provocative gender-distorting act as the audience watched male bodies expressing and embodying feminine sensualities with confidence. In an enthusiastic ovation, the audience raised their voices the most when two male dancers simulated a kiss. The group won first place.

This incident left a tremendous effect on Kriss's gender presentations. It was his first show in which he executed a feminine sensuality on stage for a public audience. The previous performance of the K-pop tomboy artist, Amber, was an improvised and one-time occurrence that a male fan could attempt at a local K-pop festival stage for fun to win a prize, but the performance of Missx was not, it was an act of announcement. The opportunity of performing an empowered female character served "as an identity incubator" (Shapiro, 2007) for Kriss, in which he was encouraged to explore a diverse array of femininities. He said that this experience was different and personally challenging "because I used to do more soft, cuter [covers]" before, but this time he had to perform a "very strong, very sensual" femininity on stage. The shift from "cute" toward the "strong" feminine impersonation also influenced the development and creation of his later and ultimate drag persona that is Kriss Chae Rin. Becoming a part of Missx Peru gave him much-needed comfort for an isolated adolescent who had suffered cruel bullying and harassment due to his sexual orientation and feminine behaviors.

> I already felt super alleviated, I had friends, it was like I felt a little more popular, so sweet [experience/feeling], which I had never had. It was like finally realizing at that moment that going out on stage, having friends, dancing to girls' song on stage. . . I thought about it and said, "I would never have done this if I hadn't known K-pop!" I mean, I set myself to think, and said, "I would have never done it out of fear."

Belonging to a gay group with whom he could share his fan activities, produce stage performances, and talk about queerness functioned as a healing. He emphasized the importance of having male friends for the first time in his life by using the masculine gendered noun *amigos*, that includes both male and female friends. To a man late in adolescence who used to have a great deal of fear and trauma, the entire course of actions from collecting courage to finally carrying out sexy and strong womanhood with fellow queer members was a chance to broaden his thoughts about gender and gender expressions. It is equally important to note the influential role of the inclusive local K-pop fan community that attends those events and sends its support with an enthusiastic ovation for this type of gender-bending performance because it provides a validation to queer performers and their subjectivities.

Kriss felt some barriers still; he needed to protect himself: "And just at that time of Missx, I said, 'I prefer to dance like girl [groups], but dressed as a boy [in men's clothing]. They cannot make me dress as a girl, I mean, I will never wear a wig, I will never wear makeup." Although he encouraged himself to stage femininities, he simultaneously had a compulsive counter-urge to be more reserved: "Even though I had friends and danced well, I felt like, outside of an event and the friends [K-pop communities], [when] I came back home, I had to reserve." He decided to leave the group when members aimed to pursue a clearer identity as a feminine gay group with "smaller [more revealing] outfits" and makeup looks. "I couldn't dare yet," he said. He left not only the group, but the entire K-pop covering scene. Dancing to K-pop was already inextricably bound to manifesting and expressing him and his gender. He did not want to perform male K-pop choreographies anymore, but could not completely come out of the closet either. Moreover, Kriss worried about his mother and people who knew him and what they might think of him. He stayed out of the K-pop cover scene for a year, almost until the end of 2014.

During that year, he felt something was missing. He missed the ovation of the public. After a year of hiatus, "I decided to go back; I will confront anything people may say," he told me. The cover group that he joined this time, Sweet Secret, was preparing a cover stage of the girl band, EXID, in heels. Taking this as an opportunity, he finally came out to his sister about his sexual orientation and together they went out to buy him some heels. This partial coming out occurred at the end of 2014, almost five years after he began dancing to K-pop. In January 2015, Sweet Secret's first EXID stage was delivered at a local K-pop cover event as five members, just like the band EXID, but with two male dancers in heels, performing to the remix of the songs, "Every Night" (2012) and "Up & Down" (2014). The first song began with a vocalized prelude melody accompanied by phone ringing sounds, and all five members stood in their own confident sexy poses. Replicating the main colors of the music video of "Every Night," all the members wore loose-fitting red silky blouses while the rest of their ensemble (hair, pants, inner tops, and boots/heels) was black. They swayed their hips simply yet firmly; when the rap line "I know this is a booty call" hit, the audience cried out with approval. "Up & Down" made EXID rise in global popularity; the song received a lot of criticism upon its release because of the music video's sexual implications with images of cut-in-half fruits, narrow long balloons inflating upward, and its signature hip thrusting and back twerking dance moves at the repeated chorus. Kriss, adorned in a black inner top, opened red short-sleeve shirt, narrow tie scarf, black jeans, and kitten heel booties, did not seem comfortable at first, walking and dancing in the heels as he displayed sensual, provocative, and occasional cute female moves. However, his performances changed gradually showing more fierce and confident movements and effortless feminine attitudes in his later EXID covers when Sweet Secret performed in 2018, three years after his first EXID show.

The transition of Kriss's gender presentation required careful steps. Through K-pop he had to go through several stages of (self-)adaptations and declarations. He chose to put on heels but still refused to wear makeup. He hid himself within the sanctuary that K-pop offers with its cross-gendered and gender-neutral esthetics and cultures: "I could not say in a loud voice that I was gay. [. . .] I didn't come out of the closet yet. I told my family that 'it is something revolutionary, K-pop, we just dance,' trying to manipulate the topic." When the cover group Sweet Secret disbanded, a woman approached him to make a 2NE1 cover group, but Kriss did not know much about the group initially. It was not his type of music. "Because I used to like more cute songs like from Girls' Generation," he said. However, he accepted the offer and began practicing the song "I Am the Best" (2011). He describes, "I had to make stronger steps, like I stopped dancing to girls." 2NE1's choreographies were strong and powerful, to Kriss, almost like boy groups and did not fall into the typical femininity of cute or sexy, but *turra*. According to Kriss, *turra* is a locally used adjective for a woman who is "more manly, powerful, [and] more rapper." As he is a tall man of a bigger stature and could make stronger steps, he was designated to interpret 2NE1's rapper persona, CL. Time after time, he admitted, "it [his CL impersonation] came out like the *cute* things, the *kawaii* [Japanese term for cute][6] thing." He had to force himself to better interpret CL's bossy femininity, an attitude which is still not very common in Latin American cultures.

Kriss practiced with this CL character for two years at the Campo de Marte, a large local public park in the urban center of Lima, where hundreds of K-pop cover dancers practice their choreographies during the weekends. One day, an event organizer invited his cover group to a "YG Family Party" event held in a local night club. YG is one of the top K-pop entertainment companies that have trained and debuted many artists of global stardom, such as Big Bang, Blackpink, and 2NE1. Today, this type of "casting" is a common practice that showcases the growth and localization of K-pop as an established local subculture. This paid event was distinctive in terms of the high-demand stage performances that included DJing and audiovisual effects. The organizer not only recruited the best cover groups of YG artists in Lima and other cities, but also specifically ordered the exact same look to recreate the verisimilar experience for local audiences attending a real YG concert. Aptly, she ordered Kriss and his group to wear the iconic 2NE1 wardrobe, which included mini shorts, sparkling military jackets in blue, dyed hair in the same colors as of the original performers, and even gave makeup specifications. Kriss dyed his hair for the first time ever in his life in platinum ash grey and wore a mini short and heavy makeup with eyelash and thick eyeliners. It was on this day, June 26, 2016, that the drag queen Kriss Chae Rin was born.[7]

COMING-OUT, GENDERING ON
K-POP, AND WHY DRAG

"I realized that K-pop helped me quite a lot! [. . .] To come out of bullying, have friends, be more social, open myself up": On February 1, 2016, Kriss used Facebook as the platform to publicly come out and reveal his sexual orientation. The post was directed to his friends, Facebook contacts, but most importantly, his mother, who was tagged on the post. Talking about the post, he elaborated on his thoughts and feelings, from the decisions that led him to form his own 2NE1 cover group, to wearing makeup in public, and the feelings of support and encouragement in succeeding in the local K-pop scene, all of which gave him the courage to disclose his sexuality. The Facebook post expresses that "[smile emoji] [heart emoji] 'I AM GAY' [heart emoji] [smile emoji]. I know that after this [post] many will stop being my friend or maybe many family members will turn their back on me but I believe saying this will nothing change in me. I will be the same person you know, and I believe if you love me as I do you may want my happiness [. . .] I HOPE YOUR SUPPORT." Unlike his concern, the post received more than 200 supportive messages. Kriss admitted that he also owed a debt to K-pop for sparking his interest in pursuing his acting and theatre makeup career at a local art school as a scholarship recipient, in addition to his continued passion in dancing and transforming, all of which have evolved through performing K-pop.

During the interview, I asked how different he might have been today if he had not discovered Korean culture or K-pop. With no hesitation, Kriss quickly replied: "I think I would have remained suppressed in the closet." To him, K-pop was the first cultural form in which he actively "prosumered" (both consumed and produced) gendered presentations for the public and could become gender constructive by experimenting with distinctive gender expressions through this platform. Moreover, consuming and experiencing the communal fandom of this Asian cultural product had a direct influence on his self-development and gender identity negotiation and (re)construction. I still wondered whether the influence could have been provided by any other different culture such as American pop music or Japanese pop culture. Kriss said no, as he did not see something remarkably distinctive in terms of a wider spectrum of gender knowledge productions linked to other cultural products. To him, they were similar to Peruvian or Latin cultures, both of which lean more toward the heteronormative conceptions based on hegemonic masculinity. In contrast, gender esthetics in K-pop were distinct and suggestive to him: "the [Korean] guys are super. . . I mean. . . how can I say? They take good care of themselves, [and] they are very *metrosexual*! They like to dress well, and they don't care if their clothes are pink or yellow. They wear it to look cool and cute (emphasis added)." With great excitement, Kriss continued explaining how metrosexual and non-binary men's fashion is present in Korea. "[In Korean men's fashion], They have wallets, and I saw men wearing handbags! It's beautiful. I've seen a purse here in a store, and I said, wow, I'd buy it. But here in Peru, it's like seeing a boy with a purse, uh, people are gonna bother you."

Besides K-pop's gender-fluid esthetics, Kriss talked about Ren, a member of the quintet boy band NU'EST, and emphasized the incorporation of sexually ambiguous figures in the K-pop industry. When the group debuted, Ren gained people's attention with his androgynous, even effeminate, look and style. It is true that many K-pop male groups that have been perceived "manly" in Korea are often considered "effeminate" to Western eyes, due to the different gender codes and preferences that Koreans have for the contemporary ideal of manhood (Morin, 2020; Pham, 2019; Song and Velding, 2020). Korean audiences tend to dislike voluptuous male bodies with big muscles or facial hair (Monocello and Dressler, 2019), so it became more common to see male idols dancing with sophisticatedly developed muscles in tall and slim bodies, refined facial features enhanced with makeup, extravagantly dyed hairstyles, wardrobes, and accessories in vibrant colors to amplify stage presence, all of which are not considered effeminate, but rather, stylistic choices[8]. Even so, Ren and his entertainment company tried to push the envelope by breaking more boundaries. In the school concept music video of NU'EST's debut song "Face" (2012), Ren walks in the opposite direction of everyone else passing by and sings the cynical line "Get out of the way or you're gonna get hurt. Being too brave is a problem." Dressed in a dark school uniform, bright red/pink sneakers, long blond hair with bangs above his eye-lined porcelain skin, and slender face and body silhouette, Ren deliberately illustrates, even celebrates, a feminine masculinity in a cynical criticism of gender codes.

Whether or not it was a marketing gimmick, the conventional male-idol image had been shifted once again thanks to those male idols' androgynous, genderless, or gender-refusing visual statements, which had gone much farther than the former popular "flower boy" esthetics tradition. This normalizing culture of gender-bending, regardless of whether or not it was a marketing call, is one of the reasons why K-pop is well-received by global LGBTQ+ communities. One could surmise that fans in more gender-flexible societies celebrate K-pop's pioneering or groundbreaking gender esthetics as a fashion trendsetter because gender-fluid images are not particularly unique, yet LGBTQ+ fans in more homophobic societies use K-pop as a site to unveil their gender identities in a safer way. As cross-dressing, androgynous esthetics favored in "flower boys" value, and cute and metrosexual stylization and demeanors (impeccably groomed men) are widely practiced and normalized in the K-pop sphere, queer fans can easily replicate this culture and wear cultural differences without necessarily revealing their gender identities.

The queer-friendly and inclusive atmosphere of the K-pop community in Lima certainly eased the transition of Kriss's gender performances, from simply covering choreographies and femininities of girl groups to performing them as a drag queen. To Kriss, drag is a form of art and stage performance, and, as he said, being a drag queen is "being a transformist." By putting on makeup and bold stage attire, Kriss not only transforms his appearance but also "their" (Kriss's and Kriss Chae Rin's) gendered self and expressions. The feelings of empowerment could have only been achieved by becoming a Kriss Chae Rin, a drag queen, a diva. "I feel totally different when I'm Kriss Chae Rin. I totally feel like the *diva*" (original emphasis). I then asked how he feels when he simply dances to girl groups as a male subject, as opposed to drag performing. Kriss replied with the notion of "divaness":

When I did Missx, no [diva feeling]. Now that I am doing [drag], [it feels] as revolutionizing, as one could say. As a drag queen, in the version of any

character, any girl [other K-pop strong female artists]⁹, I feel like I'm more of
a diva because I have one more production of magical-makeup (*maquillágico*).
And the attitude that I have to display at that moment when entering the stage
for people, I mean, hearing nothing more than the cries of the people. . . I feel
like wow, [I'm] the diva, and it's great.

Kriss's term *maquillágico*, the combination of *maquillaje* (makeup) and
mágico (magical), accurately illustrates the irreplaceable feeling of empowerment that the makeup and drag acts render in him. Kriss further explained that
whenever he finds himself vulnerable or in a hostile situation, "I feel good
opting a bit like Chae Rin. . . .I don't care what people say to me, [and] if I
want to paint my lips, I paint them."

In a January 2, 2021, conversation, Kriss spoke out about the harsh treatment against gay drag queens, even within local gay communities. Despite
their somewhat shared negative experiences of discrimination owing to their
sexual minority, they are also social subjects that have been enculturated
in a rigid, non-gender-flexible society. Performing drag has raised Kriss's
gender consciousness and self-confidence, but ironically, it became the
reason for many terminated relationships. Kriss explained that it is because
"here in Peru, even gays themselves discriminate against gays who are more
effeminate," and doing drag, or "dressing as a woman," is not well-accepted
although it is a stage performance. This is based on Kriss's personal and
limited scopes of experiences and can change anytime in the near future, but
one thing is clear: Kriss perceives that drag and dressing as a woman makes
it difficult for him to be in a relationship.

Over a decade, K-pop and Korean culture have served as a source of
knowledge for Kriss. They created the first cultural form and community in
which he felt "okay" to be queer and was applauded by performing gender-
transgressive presentations as a drag queen. It was the first platform in which
he could establish friendships. By dancing to K-pop and doing drag within a
K-pop performance, he launched his own cover group, learned how to take
a leadership role, experienced winning a competition, and being the center
of people's ovations. Performing K-pop in drag was a form of declaration of
who he is, out of the many layers of his identity. Performing one of the most
intricate layers of his (gender) identity in probably the boldest way in public
made him feel liberated and empowered, and the responsive ovations from
the audience functioned as a form of validation of his true self. K-pop and
drag queen performance are inextricably linked to who Kriss is today.

It is hard to deny that Kriss's and Kriss Chae Rin's intentional performance
of gender has potential to create a significant ripple effect to the audience by
challenging their traditional notions of gender and inviting a debate about the
nature of sex and gender.¹⁰ However, the ultimate recipient and beneficiary of

those gendered performances is Kriss himself: "Korean culture gives me. . . like. . . a lot of joy, the desire to move forward, [and] to know that you are going to do many things if . . . I mean, with my effort, and if I leave my fears behind. I know that I can do many things because I didn't know that I could go out on stage dressed as a woman and make people cry for me. But I know it now."

CONCLUSION

Drag is an art form of performing gender. It is a counterculture that allows performers to embody different gender identities and expressions that are otherwise rejected by the hegemonic gender order. K-pop, on the other hand, is a quasi-mainstream culture that is heavily consumed by digital-literate global youth and thus, being perceived as a new rising source of global soft power. What is interesting about K-pop is that it is known for its stunning visuals that frequently bend and distort gender norms and esthetics. With this, international fans are multiplying rapidly because they are attracted and drawn to the ideas or images that K-pop shapes and presents; the gender-bending is not a premediated selling point, but it is an unintended effect. The K-pop industry has always been eager to renew and alter the standard practices to propose something different and unique so that it can continue to satisfy a wide range of customers or fans. As K-pop often blends a variety of musical genres in one song to offer unexpected sonic experiences, the creators of this cultural form continue to make an effort to leave their fans in awe with fresh and cutting-edge visualizations. Dynamic choreographies play an important role,[11] but the most prominent visual strengths of K-pop are its gender-hybrid or gender-breaking fashion and esthetics. These two visual components of K-pop provide a foundation of K-pop dance cover culture practiced by local fans on its receiving ends and, indeed, becomes a reason why many queer-coding cisgender and LGBTQ+ youth around the world get involved in this practice. Overall, this fanbase has a space to perform, no matter the gender identities they want to explore, exhibit, and play with.

The process of performing gender, and more importantly, performing unconventional representations and narrations of gender repeatedly, must influence performers in some ways. In Lima, performing in drag through K-pop cannot be understood the same as, for instance, performing drag in Hollywood or on *RuPaul's Drag Race* television show. Peru is a country with rigidly binary and patriarchal gender norms based on the conservative Christianity and hegemonic masculinity order. In this context, K-pop became the only open door for Kriss to overcome the childhood trauma caused by school bullying and violent harassment. K-pop is predominantly androgynous and gender-fluid, yet it became a validated and celebrated global culture: its gender-crossing esthetics are "followed" and its choreographies, regardless of sex, are "covered." This covering culture in the K-pop fandom offered Kriss a way to explore, (re)construct, and express his gender identity. As he presented and cultivated different forms of gender based on the likeness of K-pop artists, his consciousness about his own gender and identity evolved through K-pop. Additionally, the queer-inclusivity of the local K-pop fan community that attends those events and shows their support with an enthusiastic ovation for these types of gender-bending performances played an influential role for Kriss to feel sure and confident about his queer subjectivity.

K-pop is certainly not the sole reason Kriss has come to accept himself, but as Kriss declares, *doing* what they like and having a support system greatly help people build self-confidence, especially for those who are extremely passive, introverted, and afraid of judgment or criticism. It is true that the gender-crossing esthetics and different gender manifestations and expressions in K-pop performing arts provide an empowering space and a platform for queer people who live in a society with extreme oppression and expected heterosexuality. Kriss says, "I always realize, thanks to K-pop or Korean culture, and dance, [that] I have developed a lot in myself. . . in the aspect of self-esteem, [and] in every personal aspect. And of course, I could come out of the closet, too."

NOTES

1. Throughout the article, I refer to Kriss in the masculine pronoun and his drag persona "Kriss Chae Rin" as the feminine pronoun out of respect and consideration of Kriss's preferred way of being addressed.

2. I acknowledge, however, that identities, including gender identities, are never fixed, but fluid. Since "gender [. . .] is a doing rather than a being" and there is no essential or enduring quality on queerness (Horowitz, 2020), it might be not appropriate to use masculine and feminine pronouns to refer to Kriss and Kriss Chae Rin, respectively. I also admit that I have recognized this fluidity or changes in the ways Kriss has expressed his gender throughout the years since I initially interviewed him in 2018, and to the present. Or it is better to say, that if there is an essential quality when we talk about identity, it is ever-changing, fluctuating, self-doubting, confusing, substantially complicating, and also continuously negotiating and hiding.

3. This is a performance opening that Kriss Chae Rin derived from CL's song "The Baddest Female" (2013), originally performed at the 2018 Winter Olympics' closing ceremony in PyeongChang, South Korea.

4. Willax TV regularly transmits two or three Korean dramas and one or two Japanese anime television series, all dubbed in Spanish, per week, plus other

occasional Asian-themed programs like the aforementioned *Trapito al aire* or the highlights of *Music Bank,* a South Korean weekly based music program.

5. The crossplayer in a *Sailor Moon* costume looked young, but he was not a minor as the organization claimed, but a young adult.

6. It is often used by Latin American K-pop fans to express something "cute" because (1) a large fanbase of K-pop has migrated from the fanbase of Japanese popular culture like anime, comics, or J-pop, and/or (2) it is because there is no corresponding word to translate "cute" in Latin American Spanish. The Spanish word *lindo* is the closest alternative for cute, but it does not represent the whole meaning and nuance of the word, and thus, Latin American fans of Asian culture use the alternatives in English, Japanese, and now in Korean.

7. Kriss explains that, to him, Kriss Chae Rin as the artistic name was christened much later in May 2019 when she covered the front page of a local magazine, which was a friend's school project (seefigure 10.1). However, Kriss Chae Rin as the drag queen character first performed on stage and was born in June 2016. Furthermore, when I interviewed him in 2018, he already used the name, Kriss Chae Rin, to distinguish himself with his drag character.

8. Note that Korea a few decades ago used to also be a very heteronormative and patriarchal society. Contemporary Korean gender-bending esthetics are the recent product of modern Korean popular culture, mostly by K-pop.

9. The other female K-pop artists that Kriss mentioned were HyunA of 4Minute, Hyolyn of Sistar, or Chungha, beside CL. They are all iconic artists in the K-pop sphere for their female-empowerment and versatile image makings across strong, independent, successful, sassy, but also sometimes cute and vulnerable in their personal lives.

10. There is a burning question about drag queens that whether or not they challenge or reinforce traditional construction of gender systems and both stereotypical and binary imageries of femininity and masculinity. Some scholars analyze the aspects of drag performances that destabilize gender and sexuality hierarchies by making visible the imitative and performative nature of gender construction and social basis of heteronormativity (Butler, 1990; 1993; Garber, 1992; Halberstam, 1998; Lorber, 1994; 1999; Newton, 1972; Taylor and Rupp, 2004). In contrast, others view drag as more of a gender-conservative that reinscribes heteronormative gender norms or exercises male authority because they inevitably appropriate traditional gender displays, or due to the theatrical nature of hyperbolic femininity (Dolan, 1985; Schacht, 1998; 2000; 2002; Tewksbury, 1993; 1994). However, I argue that the drag performances of Kriss do not fit into the latter discourse. For one, neither Kriss nor Kriss Chae Rin performs or hyperbolizes traditional femininity, as they interpret CL, an independent, empowered, and relatively asexual, female character. Also, Kriss's drag has its boundaries within the K-pop dance cover scene covering CL's stage performances, unlike other amplified drag shows that include talk show segments and stand-up comedy.

11. It is eye-catching to see multiple members, most commonly from four to thirteen, delivering powerful dance moves in perfect sync and creatively changing their formations.

BIBLIOGRAPHY

Anderson, C. (2014) That's My Man! Overlapping Masculinities in Korean Popular Music. In *The Korean Wave: Korean Popular Culture in Global Context*, edited by Kuwahara, Y., 117–31. New York: Palgrave Macmillan.

Butler, J. (1990). *Gender Trouble: Feminism and the Subversion of Identity*. New York: Routledge.

Butler, J. (1993). *Bodies that Matter: On the Discursive Limits of Sex*. New York: Routledge.

Dolan, J. (1985). "Gender Impersonation Onstage: Destroying or Maintaining the Mirror of Gender Roles?" *Women and Performance: A Journal of Feminist Theory* 2: 5–11.

Dunnell, T. (2018). The Dress Code in Peru: From Day-to-Day Clothing to Formal Events. *New Peruvian*. http://www.newperuvian.com/dress-code-in-peru/.

Echenique, C. (2018). *"Es mejor si eres* tomboy*" construcción de identidad de género en la performance de las practicantes de* covers *del k-pop limenño* (Master Thesis), Pontificia Universidad Católica del Perú.

Gámez, S. and Bello, G. (2000). The Rights and Inclusion of LGBTI People in Peru in Times of Coronavirus. World Bank, June 30, https://blogs.worldbank.org/latina-merica/rights-and-inclusion-lgbti-people-peru-times-coronavirus.

Garber, M. (1992). *Vested Interests: Cross-Dressing and Cultural Anxiety*. New York: Routledge.

Garza, J. (2018). *"This is For All My Bad Girls Around the World": Globalization and the Linguistic Construction of Gender and Sexuality in K-Pop* (Dissertation), University of California.

Guevarra, A. (2014). Creating a Safe Space for Queer Teens? Some Initial Findings on Queer Teens in K-Pop Cover Groups and Fan Community. *Ateneo Korean Studies Conference Proceedings* 1: 102–19.

Halberstam, J. (1998). *Female Masculinity*. Durham, NC: Duke University Press.

Hernández, A., Miller, K., and Schneeweis, I. (2015). *Peru LGBTI: Landscape Analysis of Political, Economic and Social Conditions*. Astraea Lesbian Foundation for Justice, New York.

Holloway, I. (1997). *Basic Concepts for Qualitative Research*. London: Blackwell Science.

Horowitz, K. (2020). *Drag, Interperformance, and the Trouble with Queerness*. London: Routledge.

Jones, A., DeFilippis, J., and Yarbrough, M. (2018). *The Unfinished Queer Agenda After Marriage Equality*. London: Routledge.

Jung, S. (2010). *Korean Masculinity and Transcultural Consumption: Yonsama, Rain, Oldboy, K-Pop Idols*. Hong Kong: Hong Kong University Press.

Käng, D. (2014). Idols of Development: Transnational Transgender Performance in Thai K-Pop Cover Dance. *Transgender Studies Quarterly* 1 (4): 559–71.

KOCIS (Korean Culture and Information Service). (2011). *K-Drama: A New TV Genre with Global Appeal*. Republic of Korea: KOCIS and Ministry of Culture, Sports and Tourism.

Laurie, T. (2016). Toward a Gendered Aesthetics of K-Pop. *Global Glam and Popular Music,* edited by Chapman, I., and Johnson, H., 214–31. New York: Routledge.

Lorber, J. (1994). *Paradoxes of Gender.* New Haven, CT: Yale University Press.

Lorber, J. (1999). Crossing Borders and Erasing Boundaries: Paradoxes of Identity Politics. *Sociological Focus* 32: 355–70.

Manietta, J. (2015). *Transnational Masculinities: The Distributive Performativity of Gender in Korean Boy Bands* (Master Thesis), University of Colorado Boulder.

Monocelo, L and Dressler, L. (2019). Flower Boys and Muscled Men: Comparing South Korean and American Male Body Ideals Using Cultural Domain Analysis. *Anthropology & Medicine* 27 (2): 176–91.

Morin, N. (2020). What K-Pop's Beautiful Men Can Teach Us About Masculinity. *Refinery29,* https://www.refinery29.com/en-us/2020/05/9674149/kpop-male-singers-masculinity.

Newton, E. (1972). *Mother Camp: Female Impersonators in America.* Chicago, IL: University of Chicago Press.

Oh, C. (2015). *K-Popscape: Gender Fluidity and Racial Hybridity in Transnational Korean Pop Dance* (Dissertation). Austin, TX: University of Texas.

Oh, C. and Oh, D. (2017). Unmasking Queerness: Blurring and Solidifying Queer Lines Through K-Pop Cross-Dressing. *The Journal of Popular Culture* 50 (1): 9–29.

Pham, J. (2019). BTS Is Redefining What It Means to Be Masculine & Attractive in America. *Stylecaster,* November 08, https://stylecaster.com/bts-masculinity-america/.

Rich, A. (2003). Compulsory Heterosexuality and Lesbian Existence (1980). *Journal of Women's History* 15 (3): 11–48.

Rivera, C. and Sanchez Ruiz, L. (2018). Queer Latinx American Bodies in Transnational Contexts: Case Studies from Brazil, Chile, and Perú. In *The Unfinished Queer Agenda After Marriage Equality,* edited by Jones, A., DeFilippis, J., and Yarbrough, M., 145–61. London: Routledge.

Schacht. S. (1998). The Multiple Genders of the Court: Issues of Identity and Performance in a Drag Setting. In *Feminism and Men: Reconstructing Gender Relations,* edited by Schacht, S. and Ewing, D., 202–24. New York: New York University Press.

Schacht. S. (2000). Gay Masculinities in a Drag Community: Female Impersonators and the Social Construction of 'other'. In *Gay Masculinities,* edited by Nardi, P., 247–68. Newbury Park, CA: Sage.

Schacht. S. (2002). Four Renditions of Doing Female Drag: Feminine Appearing Conceptual Variations of a Masculine Theme. *Gendered Sexualities* 6: 157–80.

Schrock, D., Reid, L., and Boyd, E. (2005). Transexuals' Embodiment of Womanhood. *Gender & Society* 19: 317–35.

Schwandt, T. (2001). *Dictionary of Qualitative Inquiry.* Thousand Oaks, CA: Sage.

Shapiro, E. (2007). Drag Kinging and the Transformation of Gender Identities. *Gender & Society* 21 (2): 250–71.

Shin, Layoung. (2018). Queer Eye for K-Pop Fandom: Popular Culture, Cross-Gender Performance, and Queer Desire in South Korean Cosplay of K-Pop Stars. *Korean Journal* 58 (4): 87–113.

Song, K. and Velding, V. (2020). Transnational Masculinity in the Eyes of Local Beholders? Young Americans' Perception of K-Pop Masculinities. *Journal of Men's Studies* 28 (1): 3–21.

Suarez, E., Logie, C., Arocha, J., Sanchez, H., and Shokirova, T. (2020). Contesting Everyday Violence: Resilience Pathways of Gay and Transgender Youth in Peru. *Global Public Health* 16 (5): 1–23.

Taylor, V and Rupp, L. (2004). Chicks with Dicks, Men in Dresses: What It Means to Be a Drag Queen. *Journal of Homosexuality* 46 (3–4): 113–33.

Tewksbury, R. (1993). Men Performing as Women: Explorations in the World of Female Impersonators. *Sociological Spectrum* 13: 465–86.

Tewksbury, R. (1994). Gender Construction and the Female Impersonator: The Process of Transforming 'He' to 'She'. *Deviant Behavior: An Interdisciplinary Journal* 15: 27–43.

Valocchi, S. (2005). Not Yet Queer Enough: The Lessons of Queer Theory for the Sociology of Gender and Sexuality. *Gender & Society* 19: 750–70.

Index

#NiUnaMenos, 193

2019–2020 Chilean protests: protest, 8, 11, 185–90, 192, 197, 198, 200, 222

2NE1, 222, 233, 234, 242, 243

AAPI hate, 10

Academy of Korean Studies, 5

adoption, 11, 104, 137–48, 150–55, 188, 197

Akdong Musician, 222

androgyny, 190, 196

Appa eodiga?, 167

Arirang (song), 42

Asian American, 10, 71–74, 200

Asian Canadian, 63, 67, 73, 78, 79, 82

ASMR, 98

audience theory, 166

Baby V.O.X., 41

baduk, 159, 169, 170, 172–74, 178, 181

Baekbeum Ilji, 4

Baekje, 122, 124, 125, 134

Beijing, 46, 47, 51

BIGBANG, 196, 201, 222, 243

birth rate, 138

Black Lives Matter, 6, 8, 71, 198

BLACKPINK, 7, 22, 84, 217, 233, 243

Boal, Augusto, 18

Bong, Joon Ho, 9

boy band, 2, 7, 10, 146, 188, 190, 196, 244

Boys Over Flowers (2009), 236

Britain, 90, 123, 163

bromance, 161, 174–77, 179

Brown Eyed Girls, 215, 216, 218, 223

BTS, 6–8, 21, 180, 190, 196, 198

Buddhism, 122, 123

Butler, Judith, 7, 8, 231, 249

Canada, 57, 64, 65, 67–70, 76, 78, 79, 82–84, 163, 176

Candlelight Demonstrations, 8

capitalism, 96, 171, 190, 205, 229

catharsis, 106

CBC (Canadian Broadcasting Corporation), 63–65, 68, 81, 82

Chile, 185–201

Chilean protests (2019–2020), 8, 11, 186–91, 193, 198, 199, 201, 223

China, 4, 5, 25, 38, 40, 41, 46, 48, 50–52, 55, 58, 103, 105, 125, 126, 200

Choi, Ins, 64, 65, 70, 82

Chongbong Band, 45, 46, 48, 57

Chongryon, 52, 54

CJ Group, 5

CL (2NE1), 22, 223, 233, 234, 243, 248, 249

communism, 188, 189, 192, 200, 201

258

Index

TVXQ, 211, 235, 236
Twitter, 52–54, 188, 189

unification, 41, 56, 126, 135

Viet Cong, 32, 33
Vietnam, 2, 10, 15, 17, 18, 20, 25, 28–35, 107–9, 201

Wangjaesan Light Music Band, 38, 46, 56
webtoons, 11, 64, 159–62, 164, 165, 167, 171, 173, 175, 177, 179–81

When the Camellia Blooms, 96
Winter Sonata, 4, 5
Wintour, Anna, 16

Xi Jingping, 46

Yến, 28
Yonsei University, 15
YouTube, 4, 21, 68, 176, 213, 223, 239

Zainichi, 52, 54
Zamudio, Daniel, 194, 195

About the Contributors

Tiago Canário is a Brazilian journalist with a master's degree in Contemporary Communication and Culture Studies (Universidade Federal da Bahia, Brazil) and a PhD in Visual Culture Studies (Korea University, South Korea). Currently based in Seoul as an independent scholar, Tiago has been studying the intersections of media, popular culture, queer expressions, and everyday life, with works published in South Korea, Brazil, Canada, Mexico, and the United Kingdom.

Snigdha Gupta is a researcher, literary translator, and editor currently based in Seoul. Previously, she was a fellow at the KLTI Academy, under the Ministry of Culture, translating fiction, films, poetry, and plays from Korean to English. A former Korean Government Scholarship recipient, she holds a master's degree in International Affairs (Korean Studies) from Seoul National University, where her research focused on women's agricultural movements in the Asian context. She earned her BA in English Literature from LSR College, University of Delhi. She recently translated for the Korean Film Archive and is currently working on a translation of Kim Sowol's poetry due to be published in *Azalea*, Harvard University's journal of Korean literature and culture.

Seunghee Ha is a research professor at Dongguk University and is affiliated with the university's Institute of North Korean Studies. Her main research interests include North Korean society and culture, particularly music and media. Her recent publications include "An analysis of the 2018 Inter-Korean Music Exchange" (2021), "North Korea's Use of Propaganda Media on YouTube" (2020), and "The Utilization of Electronic Music Bands in North Korea-Japan Relations" (2020). She is currently conducting research on the framing of North Korea in the new media with a grant from the Republic of Korea's Ministry of Education and the National Research Foundation of Korea.

Michael W. Hurt is a photographer and professor living in Seoul. He majored in History and American Civilization at Brown University and received his doctorate from UC Berkeley's Department of Comparative Ethnic Studies. He also started Korea's first street fashion blog in 2006 and published the first English language book about Korean Fashion in 2009. He researches youth, street fashion, and digital subcultures in Seoul while lecturing on cultural theory and art history at the Korea National University of the Arts. His present research focuses on using the camera to access and document emergent digital subcultures in Korea, including the political economy of the "pay model" on Korean Instagram. He can be reached on Instagram @ kuraeji and via email at kuraeji@gmail.com.

Min Suk Kim is an Assistant Professor of Instruction at the University of Texas, Austin. She received her PhD from the Department of Spanish and Portuguese at the University of Texas, Austin. Her dissertation "Hallyu Fandom in Latin America: New Media Self-Fashioning of Transcultural Metropolitan Youth Beyond the Nation-State" analyzes the consumption and reception of Korean popular culture by contemporary, digital-literate youth in Latin America. Her research focuses on the ways in which young adults (mostly first-generation female college students and/or sexual minorities) utilize Korean popular culture into their local contexts in order to (re)imagine and fashion their identities beyond social constraints of the nation-state.

Peter Moody is a researcher of modern Korean history and politics. He is particularly interested in music as a means through which to detect and anticipate broader cultural, ideological, and social changes. He is a PhD candidate at Columbia University and has been awarded fellowships from the U.S. Fulbright Program, the Foreign Language and Area Studies grant, the Northeast Asian Studies Council, and the Academic Exchange Support Program for North Korean and Unification Studies. His most recent research has been on North Korea's cultural relations in the East Asian region and its internal processes of indigenization.

Michael Ormsbee is a PhD candidate in the Department of English at the University of Rochester. He is writing a dissertation on recognition and literary form in the Victorian realist novel, and has written previously about the Bildungsroman. Before beginning graduate study, he taught in Singapore and South Korea.

Jahyon Park received her PhD from the Department of Asian Studies at Cornell University. Her research focuses on the representation and reception of gender images and minorities in contemporary Korean media, particularly focusing on the reception of new media webtoons and their transmedia content to complicate genre logic and reception theory. She published a book chapter, "Webtoon and Intimacy: Reception of North Korean Defectors' Survival Narratives," in *South Korean Popular Culture and North Korea* in 2019. She joined the Mario Einaudi Center for International Studies as a visiting scholar with global racial justice research priorities in Spring 2021 and currently teaches modern and contemporary Korean media, cinema, and online literature at Cornell University.

Moisés Park is an Assistant Professor of Spanish at Baylor University. He earned his PhD at UC Davis. His research interests are Latin American literature and film, masculinity, otherness, Orientalism, and popular culture. He is author of 20 articles and book chapters, as well as the 2014 book *Desire and Generational Conflict in Chilean Postdictatorial Literature and Cinema*. His first poetry book, *El verso cae al aula*, was published in 2017. His second poetry book, *Poemas marciales*, was published in Spanish and English in 2019.

Marcy L. Tanter is an active teacher-scholar. She earned her PhD at the University of Massachusetts, Amherst, with a dissertation on Emily Dickinson. After many years teaching American literature, she shifted her focus to Korean popular culture, and the Gwangju Uprising (1980). She is an international education advisor for the May 18 Memorial Foundation in Gwangju, South Korea, and is a Fulbright Senior Scholar (Seoul, 2018). She is currently researching American involvement in the Gwangju Uprising.

Kyong Yoon is Professor of Cultural Studies at the University of British Columbia, Okanagan. He is the author of *Digital Mediascapes of Transnational Korean Youth Culture* (Routledge, 2020) and a coauthor of *Transnational Hallyu: The Globalization of Korean Digital and Popular Culture* (Rowman & Littlefield, 2021). His forthcoming book *The Korean Wave in Korean Canadian Youth Culture* (Palgrave, 2022) examines how diasporic Korean youth engage with transnational cultural flows of *Hallyu*.